The Senior Year Experience

The Senior Year Experience

Facilitating Integration, Reflection, Closure, and Transition

John N. Gardner
Gretchen Van der Veer
and Associates

Jossey-Bass Publishers
San Francisco

Substantial discounts on bulk quantities of Jossey-Bass books are available to corporations, professional associations, and other organizations. For details and discount information, contact the special sales department at Jossey-Bass Inc., Publishers (415) 433–1740; Fax (800) 605–2665.

For sales outside the United States, please contact your local Simon & Schuster International Office.

Jossey-Bass Web address: http://www.josseybass.com

 Manufactured in the United States of America on Lyons Falls Turin Book. This paper is acid-free and 100 percent totally chlorine-free.

Library of Congress Cataloging-in-Publication Data

Gardner, John N.
The senior year experience: facilitating integration, reflection, closure, and transition / John N. Gardner, Gretchen Van der Veer, and associates — 1st ed.
p. cm. — (The Jossey-Bass higher and adult education series)
Includes bibliographical references and index.
ISBN 0-7879-0927-0 (alk.)
1. College seniors—United States—Social conditions. 2. College seniors—Services for—United States. I. Van der Veer, Gretchen. II. Title. III. Series.
LA229.G27   1997
378.1'98—dc21   97–18833

FIRST EDITION
HB Printing   10 9 8 7 6 5 4 3 2 1

The Jossey-Bass Higher and Adult Education Series

John Gardner dedicates this work to all of the Marietta College faculty who taught, encouraged, and inspired him during his senior year experience in 1964–65; to all his colleagues three decades later who support him in his senior experience initiatives at the University of South Carolina: the Office of the Provost, the College of Liberal Arts, the Department of Psychology, the College of Education's Department of Educational Leadership and Policies, and the National Resource Center for The Freshman Year Experience and Students in Transition; and to Betty Siegel, President of Kennesaw State University, for inspiring him to develop a senior capstone transition course at the University of South Carolina by emulating her outstanding leadership example in developing and teaching such a course for Kennesaw seniors.

Gretchen Van der Veer dedicates this work to all those at the University of Maryland at College Park who participated in the creation of a vision for the senior experience and to those who continue to endeavor to see the vision realized.

CONTENTS

PREFACE

This book is about the final period of the undergraduate experience, a year or series of final terms that we define as *the senior year experience*. Every college student faces at least two critical transitions. The first concerns the transition into higher education; much attention has been directed toward the assimilation of new students into the academy. Until recently (about 1990), however, there was little similar discussion regarding the transition from college to situations of work or graduate or professional school, new social relationships, community and national service, and leadership in society. Now in an era of institutional accountability, declining legislative support, and public dissatisfaction with high tuition costs, a growing number of educators and prospective employers are suggesting that colleges need to do more for seniors than simply hand them a diploma.

Just what this "more" should be is the question at the core of a national movement to rethink how we teach and provide holistic curricula and support services for seniors as they prepare to leave their undergraduate experience. Although still in its infancy, a review and synthesis of the proceedings from four

The Senior Year Experience national conferences (1990, 1991, 1993, and 1994) and two Students in Transition conferences (1995 and 1996) suggests that there are a number of major themes and practices embraced by the movement and that this is an issue for all institutions, regardless of type. The purpose of this book is to provide a general understanding of the issues related to the senior year transition: why it is imperative for institutions to take a more strategic and intentional approach to the senior experience; how various institutions are already responding; and to advocate for more attention to this critical final period of the undergraduate experience. In the following chapters, many imaginative interventions and resourceful methods to better assist students through the senior transition are presented and the institutional benefits described.

This book does not propose to focus on the senior experience to the exception (or expense) of the rest of the undergraduate experience. Possible deficiencies that precede the senior experience cannot be eradicated by specific programs implemented in the senior year. Fortunately, through efforts such as The Freshman Year Experience and numerous undergraduate education reform efforts over the past decade, campus consciousness about the importance of the freshman year and the need for more support for the undergraduate experience as a whole has been elevated. These efforts are to be applauded, for they have indeed contributed to increased student retention and satisfaction while students are on campus. Similarly, this book highlights policy and programmatic initiatives suggesting that increased attention to the specific needs of seniors can improve their expectations and probable future success, as well as encourage lifelong commitment as alumni.

A discussion is in order about the terminology for the central concepts on which this book is based: *the senior experience* or *the senior year experience.* Readers will note that these terms are used interchangeably by our chapter authors, and we have not attempted to standardize to make their use consistent throughout. This is because we have intentionally decided to use these terms interchangeably. We realize that the senior year, typically, represents a calendar period that corresponds to one-quarter of the baccalaureate degree completion process. But we further recognize that many seniors do not complete the final quarter of the curriculum in one calendar year, let alone in two semesters or three quarters.

Many seniors have work schedules and family responsibilities that preclude them from enrolling for what would correspond to a full-time academic load. In addition, many other students may have accumulated enough hours to be technically classified as seniors, but in order to complete the major they have finally chosen, they will not be able to complete their degree requirements in the equivalent of an academic year. We further recognize that many seniors are part-time students for whom the senior "year" stretches out much longer than that. We further wish to acknowledge that some of the programmatic initiatives discussed in this book in all probability could be more readily and conveniently accessed by the full-time enrolled senior who is less than full-time employed. But we believe that most of the attributes of the senior experience must and can be applied to seniors of any status.

Thus, the senior experience is by no means solely or primarily a set of academic initiatives and experiences. The term refers to the total experience of seniors inside and outside the classroom, as provided by the faculty, student affairs officers, academic administrators, and seniors themselves. The Senior Year Experience focuses on efforts to help seniors make meaning of their final undergraduate work, bringing closure, connectedness, integration, and reflection to the diverse set of activities they have experienced as undergraduates. The senior experience also involves a concluding effort on the part of the institution to help students graduate with the kinds of skills they need to be successful in the workforce or in graduate school in the immediate or long-term future.

It is said, correctly, that the senior year experience is a very flexible concept. Indeed, the term can be made to mean whatever its advocates, proponents, and developers want it to mean. It can be used to describe a solely academic initiative, as in a senior capstone transition course such as the one John Gardner developed at the University of South Carolina. Or it can be used to describe myriad other appropriate programmatic initiatives to strengthen the final period of undergraduate education, such as a career planning initiative, a senior service project or internship requirement, or an achievement or recognition ceremony. We believe that just as we have seen in the development of the freshman year experience movement, the readers of this book—who are the present and future practitioners in The Senior Year Experience—will help give meaning, shape, and definition to this still very embryonic and evolving concept. Thus we resist further attempts to give this an all-precise, closed definition, as much as editors, reviewers, and readers might prefer one. After all, the mark of a well and liberally educated baccalaureate degree recipient is tolerance for ambiguity!

Readers encounter much discussion in these chapters about the need and desirability to prepare students for transition to the world of work. We wish to acknowledge to our readers that we are well aware that the vast majority of our students, especially seniors, are already in the workforce. It is not as if an improved senior year initiative is needed to prepare them for initial entry into the workforce. Rather, it is more a matter of preparing students for different kinds of work postcollege, with greater degrees of autonomy, flexibility, responsibility, and leadership and much higher demands for accountability, productivity, initiative, and excellence. We also realize that many seniors do not enter the civilian workforce full-time after receiving their baccalaureate degree, but instead enter the armed forces, other forms of national or private service work, or graduate school. Nevertheless, the majority of American seniors is seeking improved, better remunerating, and full-time employment status after graduation and before beginning graduate study. Our book and its contributors do focus intensively on this latter cohort, but not exclusively.

A further note of explanation is in order. One type of senior year initiative that is frequently referred to in this book but not treated comprehensively, definitively, or perhaps sufficiently, is very much still a work in progress: the senior capstone course. Although these courses have a long history in American higher education, there is very little literature about this genre. Gardner has made it a principle of his own professional service, research, and teaching not to advocate at any great length on a reform topic or innovation before a sufficient literature base has been accumulated. We wish we could say that the literature base exists to support an extensive treatment of senior capstone courses in this book. Unfortunately, it does not. Therefore, Gardner and the National Resource Center for The Freshman Year Experience and Students in Transition, for which he is responsible at the University of South Carolina, are currently in the process of attempting to develop that literature base to study and serve educators who are at work developing and teaching senior capstone courses. Gardner has also demonstrated, in his own national advocacy work, a preference to test out certain ideas and practices for enhancing undergraduate education, such as the freshman seminar, by first teaching or developing and engaging in such reform practices on the level of his own campus. With respect to The Senior Year Experience, he has been actively working there to develop and teach a pilot capstone senior year transition course, an analog to the freshman seminar University 101. The senior course, taught since 1994, is Psychology 589, Psychology and the Transition to the World of Work (see Resource B for a sample syllabus). Gardner also worked with three faculty colleagues at his alma mater, Marietta College, to produce a textbook for seniors in transition (Hartel, Schwartz, Blume, and Gardner, 1994).

This topic of senior capstone courses, then, will be the subject of a future and more definitive work. In this book, however, a number of chapter authors do describe their experience with senior capstone courses (see in particular Chapter Two by Joseph Cuseo, Chapter Four by Arthur Levine, Chapter Six by Barbara Leigh Smith, Chapter Ten by George Kuh, Chapter Twelve by Denise Dwight Smith and Linda Gast, and Chapter Fifteen by Karl and Karen Schilling). In addition to a sample syllabus of the capstone senior transition course that Gardner has developed at the University of South Carolina, we have also included for readers, in Resource A, a list of characteristics of capstone courses and experiences Gardner has identified in his own research and practice. We look forward to doing a second edition of this book, in which we will, happily, be able to provide much more substantive treatment of this critical academic component of a senior year experience. We invite readers who have experience, literature, assessment outcomes, and other types of research and insights on this unique course genre that they are willing to share to get in touch with us and express their willingness to contribute to such an ongoing work, whether in the second edition or a separate, freestanding work on the topic of senior capstone courses.

Finally, as a review of the biographies of the chapter contributors shows, we saw that we alone and unassisted do not know enough about the senior experience as it unfolds as a dimension of campus undergraduate reform. We recognize the primacy of the academic experience of departing seniors, but we believe that in order to give readers a comprehensive and true overview of the great variety of initiatives underway to improve the attention paid to departing students, we needed to go beyond the students' classroom experience. Thus, we assembled a partnership of contributors who are faculty; academic, alumni, and student personnel administrators; researchers; and practitioners to yield a much more comprehensive and holistic perspective. We believe this approach will prove most beneficial to our readers.

AUDIENCE

The Senior Year Experience: Facilitating Integration, Reflection, Closure, and Transition is written for multiple audiences: faculty; academic administrators; student personnel professionals; development officers; chief executive officers; policymakers such as trustees, legislators, accreditors, and staff and members of state coordinating and governing bodies; and educational researchers. Institutional attention to this issue not only benefits graduating seniors but has the potential for realizing larger organizational goals as well: (1) promoting faculty development, (2) enhancing institutional research and student outcomes assessment, (3) improving college-community and college-corporate relations, (4) forging alliances between academic and student affairs, and (5) improving alumni relations. Therefore, this book will be beneficial to faculty who teach advanced courses; institutional researchers; and career development, student affairs, and institutional advancement professionals.

OVERVIEW OF THE CONTENT

Part One, "Understanding the Unique Needs of Today's Seniors," examines the characteristics and needs of seniors in light of the impending transition from classroom to the world of work and roles other than "student." In this part, we also look at some of the broad themes associated with the senior experience and explore the rationale for and benefits to institutions that choose to embrace this new movement. The introductory chapter provides a definition of the senior year experience and discusses its importance to the future of American higher education. In Chapter Two, Joseph Cuseo identifies the objectives of the senior experience movement, looks at exemplary programs initiated by various colleges and universities, and describes the benefits for both students and the institution in addressing these issues. Arthur Chickering and Nancy Schlossberg elaborate on the transition needs of seniors in Chapter Three and suggest that the process of helping students to "move on" from an institution is a tremendously satisfying experience for seniors and educators alike, but it is more successful for both if colleges have also helped their seniors to "move in" and "move through" the undergraduate experience. In Chapter Four, Arthur Levine contrasts his own senior experience with those of students today and discusses the history of how the need for closure has been addressed in the curriculum through senior projects, seminars, and capstone courses. The first part concludes with the question posed in Chapter Five, "Are College Seniors Prepared to Work?" and Philip Gardner's assertion that many graduating seniors lack competencies in the areas of interpersonal communication, initiative, teamwork, applied problem solving, and self-management of time and priorities.

Part Two, "Enhancing the Senior Year Experience," provides more information on the theme areas associated with the senior experience and implications for academic, administrative, and student affairs practices. In Chapter Six, Barbara Leigh Smith examines curricular issues and presents a variety of ways in which curricular structures and faculty and student roles and practices are being rethought to enhance cumulative learning in the senior year. In Chapter Seven, Elwood Holton III questions the extent to which college is a realistic preparation experience for professional and organizational worklife after college and promotes a new role for higher education in enhancing seniors' preparation for professional success beyond the classroom. In Chapter Eight, Stephen Schwartz and Nance Lucas question the effectiveness of colleges and universities in equipping graduates for future leadership roles; they advocate a new definition of leadership development as preparation for social responsibility. On the same theme, in Chapter Nine, Linda Sax and Alexander Astin show civic virtue to be affected by a variety of college environments and student experiences and recommend several specific ways for institutions to enhance the citizenship development of seniors. In Chapter Ten, George Kuh examines cultural (and ritual) events common to the senior year and discusses the importance of institutionally sponsored and student-initiated rituals and traditions to the conclusion of college and the transition to the next phase of life. Richard Lawhon concludes the second part with a chapter in which he reflects, from his role as director of admissions of a research university graduate school, on the process of preparing seniors to become successful graduate students, now or later.

Part Three, "Developing Special Support Services for Seniors," looks at the roles that certain specific offices or campus units can play in organizing to address issues related to the senior experience. Denise Dwight Smith and Linda Gast examine the role of and argue for the comprehensive career center in Chapter Twelve and maintain that traditional campus career counseling and job placement efforts are no longer sufficient. Linda Bates Parker, Katrina Jordan, and Ann

Keeling continue the discussion of career services in Chapter Thirteen, but they examine more specifically the college-to-career transition issues facing multiethnic college students, especially those of African Americans as an illustration; the authors believe the need continues for targeted programs to prepare and address the unique transition issues of these students. In Chapter Fourteen, Jeffery Johnson and Peter Eckel promote an enhanced role for the alumni affairs office based upon their belief that institutions can no longer afford to take future alumni support for granted and must cultivate students while they are still on campus.

Part Four is entitled "Implications for Campus Services and Practices." Its authors address converging issues such as assessment, policymaking, and program development, which provide suggestions for organizing campus efforts in these areas. Chapter Fifteen, by Karl Schilling and Karen Maitland Schilling, examines the status of the assessment movement in higher education, identifies the benefits of assessment for both the institution and the student, and provides some assessment models that they believe are appropriate particularly during the senior year. William Thomas, Jr., focuses on institutionalizing campus support for seniors in Chapter Sixteen and provides concrete suggestions for how faculty, staff, and administrators new to the senior experience movement might organize colleagues to examine and address these issues. Part Four and the book conclude with final thoughts, reflections, and—most important— recommendations from the editors for those seeking to advocate and institute specific senior year initiatives based upon the editors' own campus experiences and a synthesis of the content of the entire book.

ACKNOWLEDGMENTS

We wish to acknowledge special individuals who made this book possible. At the University of Maryland, Vice President for Student Affairs Bud Thomas had the vision to take a concept (The Senior Year Experience) presented by John Gardner at a regional meeting and turn it into a major campus reform initiative. Thomas's involvement with the senior experience movement and professional support has been invaluable.

We acknowledge the contributions of the many senior students at the University of South Carolina and the University of Maryland whom we have advised, counseled, and celebrated with upon their graduation from our institutions.

We acknowledge the wise counsel and the enormous amount of editorial assistance we have received for this project from Betsy O. Barefoot, codirector for research and publications, National Resource Center for The Freshman Year Experience and Students in Transition, University of South Carolina.

We acknowledge the enormous amount of time, patience, care, and diligence exercised by Vicky P. Howell of the National Resource Center for The Freshman

Year Experience and Students in Transition for preparation of the manuscript, in more drafts than she wants to remember.

We acknowledge our editors at Jossey-Bass, Gale Erlandson, Michele Hubinger, and Rachel Livsey, for their support of and vision and hope for this project, and for their subsequent advice and patience.

We acknowledge our respect and appreciation for the extremely helpful advice we received on the manuscript from reviewers commissioned by Jossey-Bass, especially M. Lee Upcraft of Pennsylvania State University. John Gardner also wishes to cite Upcraft's powerful mentoring influence on him for showing how advocacy for higher education reform can be accomplished through good scholarship published by Jossey-Bass.

We acknowledge the many higher educators: faculty, academic administrators, and student affairs professionals who have presented their knowledge, research, and recommendations for the improvement of The Senior Year Experience at The Senior Year Experience conferences organized by the University of South Carolina.

In a similar vein, we acknowledge with special appreciation the University of South Carolina's providing the framework and support, through its National Resource Center for The Freshman Year Experience and Students in Transition, for the Students in Transition conferences convened by that center to bring together educators who wish to enhance the success of departing students. That framework enabled the editors of this book to collect much of their information, which is now made available to readers such as yourself.

We especially thank our chapter authors for their special talents, knowledge, and commitment to improving the senior year experience and their willingness to join us in this project, which we hope will raise a new level of national consciousness and conversation on campuses about the importance of the experience of our departing students.

Finally, we acknowledge you, the reader, for your openness to consider our thoughts on the senior year experience, and especially for whatever actions you may take subsequently to improve the learning and support of your departing students.

August 1997

John N. Gardner
Columbia, South Carolina

Gretchen Van der Veer
Washington, D.C.

THE AUTHORS

John N. Gardner is the executive director of the National Resource Center for The Freshman Year Experience and Students in Transition and professor of library and information science at the University of South Carolina at Columbia. He earned his B.A. degree (1965) in social sciences at Marietta College in Ohio and his M.A. degree (1967) in American studies at Purdue University. He is also the recipient of three honorary doctoral degrees in recognition for his work on behalf of America's first-year students. Gardner also provides leadership for University 101, the nationally acclaimed and widely replicated freshman seminar course. The center, founded by Gardner in 1986, organizes the popular and influential The Freshman Year Experience and Students in Transition conferences. The center also collects and disseminates information through an extensive series of scholarly publications, workshops, and seminars.

Gardner is the recipient of his university's highest award for teaching excellence, the AMOCO Award for Outstanding Teaching (1975), and the Division of Student Affairs Faculty Award "for outstanding contributions" (1976). In 1986, he was selected by the American Association for Higher Education (AAHE) as one of twenty faculty in the United States who have "made outstanding leadership contributions to their institutions and/or American higher education." He has served on the board of directors for AAHE and currently serves on the board of trustees for his alma mater, Marietta College, and the International Partnership for Service Learning.

Gardner is best known as the initiator of an international reform movement in higher education to call attention to and improve what he coined The Freshman Year Experience. He also developed and now champions what he calls the second critical transition for college students, The Senior Year Experience.

Some of his most recent published works are *College Is Only the Beginning* (2nd ed., 1989), *Step by Step to College Success* (1987), *Your College Experience* (with A. Jerome Jewler, 3rd ed., 1997), *The Freshman Year Experience* (with M. Lee Upcraft, 1989), and *Ready for the Real World* (with William Hartel and Associates, 1994).

Gretchen Van der Veer is the executive director of the Presidio Leadership Center and director of staff training for the Corporation for National Service, an independent federal agency created by the National and Community Service Trust Act of 1993 to engage Americans of all ages in service to their communities. Van der Veer joined the Corporation for National Service after fourteen years in higher education because of an opportunity to help establish the AmeriCorps*National Civilian Community Corps (A*NCCC), a ten–month residential service experience for young people aged eighteen to twenty-four, with facilities located on closed military bases. After helping to launch the first A*NCCC campus and establish the educational, training, and service learning component, she was appointed to her present position at the Corporation for National Service's headquarters to develop and manage the leadership development program for staff and leaders of nonprofit organizations across the country.

Van der Veer served in various roles in student services at the University of South Carolina and the University of Maryland. During her tenure as assistant to the vice president for student affairs at Maryland, she chaired a major campus initiative to evaluate the needs of graduating students. The effort became known as The Senior Experience Task Force and resulted in the introduction of a variety of new programs and services for students preparing to leave the campus.

Van der Veer received a B.A. degree in psychology from the University of Cincinnati (1980), an M.Ed. degree in college student personnel services in higher education from the University of Vermont (1982), and a Ph.D. degree in education policy, planning, and administration with a focus on higher education leadership from the University of Maryland (1991). She also is an affiliate faculty member in the Graduate School of Management and Technology at the University of Maryland University College and volunteers time in the Washington, D.C., community by serving on the board of the Greater Southeast Community Hospital System and the Capitol Hill Neighborhood Learning Center.

Alexander W. Astin is Allan M. Carter Professor of Higher Education at the University of California-Los Angeles, and director of the Higher Education Research

Institute at UCLA. He is the author of eighteen books and more than two hundred other publications in the field of higher education. For this work, he has received numerous awards from national associations and ten honorary degrees. A 1990 study in the *Journal of Higher Education* identified Astin as the most frequently cited author in the field of higher education.

Linda Bates Parker is director of career development and placement at the University of Cincinnati, where she is responsible for managing staff, budget, programs, and services and has instituted numerous innovative programs. She has worked consistently throughout her professional life on diversity issues on and off campus. Outside the university, Bates Parker has held leadership roles in a variety of community organizations, receiving numerous awards recognizing her contributions. She is president and founder of Black Career Women, a national professional development organization, and is campus adviser for *The Black Collegian*. She has a B.S. degree in English from the University of Dayton (1965) and an M.A. degree in English from the University of Cincinnati (1971). She is a 1991 graduate of Harvard University's Management Development Program.

Arthur W. Chickering is distinguished visiting professor at the Vermont College Campus of Norwich University and professor at George Mason University. He received his B.A. degree in comparative literature from Wesleyan University, an M.A. degree in teaching from the Harvard Graduate School of Education, and a Ph.D. degree in school psychology from Columbia University. He is an internationally recognized scholar concerned with college impacts on human development, educationally powerful institutions, experiential education, and adult learning. He has been a member of and has chaired the boards of the American Association for Higher Education, the Association for the Study of Higher Education, the Council for Adult and Experiential Learning, and the National Society for Experiential Education.

Joseph B. Cuseo is an associate professor of psychology at Marymount College (California), where he serves as director of the freshman seminar and coordinator of faculty development. He received his B.A. degree (1971) in psychology from St. Francis College and his M.A. degree (1974) and Ph.D. degree (1978) from the University of Iowa. His research interests center on student retention, student transitions, student advancement, the freshman seminar, and the senior year experience.

Peter D. Eckel is the project consultant on the American Council on Education's Project on Leadership and Institutional Transformation. He earned his B.A. degree in journalism from Michigan State University (1989) and M.A. degree in counseling and personnel services from the University of Maryland (1991), for which he wrote his thesis on the senior year transition. He is currently ABD at the University of Maryland in higher education policy, planning, and administration. Prior to working at the American Council on Education, he worked at the University of Maryland with its senior experience efforts, coadvising the senior council and authoring sections of the report from the Senior Experience Task Force.

Philip D. Gardner is research director of the Collegiate Employment Research Institute at Michigan State University. He received his B.A. degree (1969) in chemistry from Whitman College and his M.S. (1975) and Ph.D. (1979) degrees in resource development and public policy from Michigan State University. Gardner's main research activities have focused on transition from school to work, early career experiences of college graduates, starting-salary modeling, and workplace skill assessments. He has published numerous articles on the career development of the college-educated workforce. His concurrent session presentations have contributed significantly to the success of The Senior Year Experience and Students in Transition national conferences.

Linda K. Gast has been director of the career center at the University of Maryland since 1985, where she is also an assistant professor in the counseling and personnel services department. She has more than seventeen years' experience in the field of career development and employment. Gast received her B.A. degree cum laude from Indiana University, and M.S. and Ph.D. degrees in counseling and personnel services from Purdue University. She has served as a consultant and trainer to business, government, and education organizations in the areas of college relations and recruitment, human resource planning, training, and organization development.

Elwood F. Holton III is an associate professor of human resource development (HRD) at Louisiana State University, where he also coordinates the degree programs in HRD. His research focuses on analysis and evaluation of organizational performance systems. His work has been published in such journals as *Human Resource Development Quarterly, Performance Improvement Quarterly, Human Resource Management Review, Journal of Organizational and Occupational Psychology, Training and Development,* and the *Journal of Business and Psychology.* In addition, he is coeditor of the *HRD Research Handbook* (with Swanson, 1997), coauthor of the forthcoming *The Adult Learner: A Neglected Species* (with Knowles, 5th ed., in press), editor of the forthcoming case book *Leading Change in Organizations,* and coeditor of *Conducting Needs Assessment* (with Phillips, 1995). He received his B.S. degree in business and his M.B.A. and Ed.D. degrees in human resource development from Virginia Tech.

Jeffery W. Johnson is director of alumni affairs at the University of Illinois at Urbana-Champaign. He earned his M.A. degree (1995) in higher education administration at the University of Kansas, Lawrence, his B.S. degree (1986) in computer science with a minor in business administration at the University of Southern Mississippi, Hattiesburg, and his A.T. degree (1983) in data processing at Jones County Junior (now Community) College, Ellisville. Before joining the staff at Illinois in 1996, he was senior vice president for external affairs and membership development for the Kansas University Alumni Association, Lawrence, and assistant to the director and student alumni association adviser for the University of Southern Mississippi Alumni Association. Johnson's research and much of his work is spent looking at how the student affairs experience assists the university and the association in developing loyal alumni.

Katrina S. Jordan is an associate director of career development and placement at the University of Cincinnati. She earned her B.S. degree (1974) in office administration and her M.A. degree (1975) in public affairs from Kentucky State University's school of business and public affairs. Jordan is responsible for overseeing the internal campus recruiting operations, coordinates an annual ethnic student career fair, and has taught professional development courses to both engineering and business undergraduate students. She has presented regionally and nationally on career services and diversity and was a member of the research team that conducted a study resulting in the coauthored article "Black College Graduates in Transition: A Longitudinal Study" in the *Journal of Career Planning and Employment* (1994). She is an active member of the Midwest Association of Colleges and Employers, where she has served as a committee member and has chaired the diversity advance committee.

Ann E. Keeling is associate director and professor in the Division of Professional Practice at the University of Cincinnati. She received her B.S. degree (1967) in elementary education with certification in special education-MR from Norfolk State University; her M.S. degree (1971) in special education-MR from Ferkauf Graduate School, Yeshiva University; and dual specialist certificates (1972) in learning disabilities and mental retardation from Ferkauf Graduate School, Yeshiva University. Keeling is very active in a number of professional organizations and has held three vice president positions in the National Cooperative Education Association. She also serves on the executive board of Black Career Women, a career development organization in Cincinnati.

George D. Kuh is professor of higher education in the Center for Postsecondary Research and Planning in the School of Education at Indiana University Bloomington, where he directs the College Student Experiences Questionnaire research and distribution program. He has also served as president of the Association for the Study of Higher Education. His research and scholarly activities focus on campus cultures, out-of-class experiences of undergraduates, and the institutional conditions that foster student learning.

Richard B. Lawhon is director of admissions at the graduate school of the University of South Carolina at Columbia. He is also the director of the Instructional Development Project in the Graduate School, a program to prepare graduate teaching assistants to teach college freshmen. In this project, he uses teaching strategies that he learned in the University 101 freshman seminar program, in which he has helped train instructors to teach the course since 1977. He has taught the freshman seminar since 1974 and has taught English at both the high school and college levels. His career at the University of South Carolina also included directing the USC TRIO program's Talent Search initiative to recruit disadvantaged young people and academically gifted high school students in South Carolina. His Ph.D. degree is in English (American literature) from the University of South Carolina, and he has a B.A. degree in journalism, also from the University of South Carolina.

Arthur Levine is president and professor of education at Teachers College, Columbia University. He received his B.A. degree (1970) from Brandeis University and his Ph.D. degree (1976) in sociology and higher education from the State University of New York at Buffalo. Prior to working at Teachers College, he served as chair of the higher education program and chair of the Institute for Educational Management at the Harvard Graduate School of Education. Levine is the author of dozens of articles, reviews, and books. A 1982 Guggenheim Fellowship winner, his other awards include the 1996 Council of Independent College's Academic Leadership Award, the American Council on Education's Book of the Year award in 1974 (for *Reform of Undergraduate Education*), three annual awards for writing from the Educational Press Association, and thirteen honorary degrees. He is executive editor of *Change* magazine and has served as consultant to more than 250 colleges and universities. Levine was also president of Bradford College (1982–1989) and senior fellow at the Carnegie Foundation and Carnegie Council for Policy Studies in Higher Education (1975–1982).

Nance Lucas is associate director of the Academy of Leadership and faculty director of the College Park Scholars Public Leadership Program at the University of Maryland. She was the first director of the National Clearinghouse for Leadership Programs at the University of Maryland. She received a B.A. degree in industrial psychology and an M.A. degree in college student personnel administration, both from Pennsylvania State University, and is completing a doctoral degree in college student personnel at the University of Maryland. Her research and scholarship interests focus on moral and ethical leadership. She teaches leadership courses, has published on topics of leadership, and was a contributor to Roberts and Ullom's *Student Leadership Program Model* and Astin and Astin's *Social Change Model of Leadership Development*. She is also associate editor of the *Journal of Leadership Studies*. Lucas is a faculty member at the National LeaderShape Institute in Illinois and served as cofounder of the National Leadership Symposium and as a past chair of the National InterAssociation Leadership Project.

Linda J. Sax is a visiting assistant professor of higher education at the University of California-Los Angeles, and director of the Cooperative Institutional Research Program (CIRP) at UCLA. She is responsible for CIRP's annual survey of incoming freshmen, an annual survey of college students, and a triennial survey of college faculty. She teaches graduate courses in research methodology, evaluation of higher education, and gender issues in higher education, and currently serves on the editorial boards for *The Review of Higher Education* and *Research in Higher Education*. Sax received her B.A. degree (1990) in political economy from the University of California, Berkeley, and her M.A. (1991) and Ph.D. (1994) degrees in higher education from UCLA.

Karen Maitland Schilling is professor of psychology at Miami University in Ohio. From 1990 to 1995, she served as Miami's first university director of liberal education, overseeing implementation of a major reform of the undergraduate curriculum at the institution. In this role, she developed a comprehensive portfolio-based approach to assessment of curricular impact. She received her B.S. degree (1971) in psychology from Jackson College of Tufts University and her M.A. degree (1972) in psychology and Ph.D. degree (1975) in clinical psychology from the University of Florida.

Karl L. Schilling is associate dean and associate professor of the School of Interdisciplinary Studies (Western College Program) at Miami University in Ohio. He received his B.A. degree (1971) in English and psychology from Adrian College and his M.A. (1972) and Ph.D. (1975) degrees in clinical psychology from the University of Florida. Prior to coming to the Western College Program, he was assistant professor and college counselor at Earlham College. He has served as director of the American Association for Higher Education's Assessment Forum (1992–1994) and president of the Association for General and Liberal Studies (1996).

Nancy K. Schlossberg's major interests and expertise are in adult development, adult transitions, career development, adults as learners, and intergenerational relationships. Schlossberg is a professor emerita in the Department of Counseling and Personnel Services, College of Education, and director of the Center of

Human Services Development, both at the University of Maryland. She was the first woman executive at the American Council on Education (ACE). Later she established the Office of Women in Higher Education (1973) and served as a senior fellow at ACE's Center on Adult Learning. Her most recent publications are a trade book, *Going to Plan B: How You Can Cope, Regroup, and Start Your Life on a New Path* (with Susan P. Robinson, 1996), *Getting the Most Out of College* (with Arthur Chickering, 1995), and *Counseling Adults in Transition* (with Elinor Waters and Jane Goodman, 2nd ed., 1995). Schlossberg received her Ed.D. degree (1961) in guidance and student personnel administration from Teachers College, Columbia University and a B.A. degree (1951) in sociology from Barnard College.

Stephen W. Schwartz is currently dean of the McDonough Center for Leadership and Business at Marietta College. Founded in 1986, the center serves Marietta's students with two major leadership programs. Before becoming dean, Schwartz served as associate dean of the college and has supervised the collegewide advising program, the freshman seminar program, and the college honors program. Schwartz has been at Marietta College since 1964. He is also professor of English and a specialist in Medieval and Renaissance English literature. His B.A. degree in English is from Wilkes College, his A.M. degree from University of Pennsylvania, and his Ph.D. degree from New York University. Schwartz has written two texts, one on the teaching of freshman seminars, *Teaching Strategies for Success* (1993), and *Ready for the Real World* (1994), on the student transition from college to the workplace.

Barbara Leigh Smith is provost and vice president for academic affairs at Evergreen State College. She previously served as dean from 1978 to 1994. Before coming to Evergreen, Smith taught at Lawrence University and the University of Nebraska. Smith is the founding director of the Washington Center for Improving the Quality of Undergraduate Education, located at Evergreen, a state-supported consortium of forty-four colleges and universities in Washington. Smith has also served as chair of the board of directors of the American Association for Higher Education. She is author or coauthor of many books and articles on educational reform, collaborative learning, and learning communities, including the chapters "What Is Collaborative Learning?" (with J. MacGregor, in the *Collaborative Learning Sourcebook,* 1990) and "Team Teaching Methods" (in *Handbook of College Teaching,* 1994); the articles "Taking Structure Seriously" (*Liberal Education,* 1991) and "Creating Learning Communities" (*Liberal Education,* 1993); the monograph *Learning Communities: Creating Connections Among Students, Faculty, and Disciplines* (with J. MacGregor, R. Matthews, and F. Gabelnick, 1990), and the book *Against the Current: Reform and Experimentation in Higher Education* (with R. Jones, 1984).

Denise Dwight Smith is director of the University Career Center at the University of North Carolina at Charlotte and adjunct lecturer in human services and counseling. She is also president elect of the National Association of Colleges and Employers. In the field of career planning and college relations, she has served as director and manager at Bucknell University, the Ohio State University College of Business, and ICI Americas, Inc. She has publications in the *Journal of Career Planning and Employment, Success* magazine, and newspapers. She holds an M.S. degree in college counseling from Shippensburg University (1980) and a B.A. degree in psychology from Millersville University of Pennsylvania (1978).

William L. Thomas, Jr., is vice president for student affairs at the University of Maryland, a position he has held since 1973. He holds B.S. and M.S. degrees from the University of Tennessee and a Ph.D. degree from Michigan State University. In recognition of the exceptional quality of student affairs services and programs at the University of Maryland, his leadership on campus, and his extensive professional work in the field of student affairs, Thomas was awarded the prestigious Scott Goodnight Award for Outstanding Performance as a Dean by the National Association of Student Personnel Administrators (NASPA) in 1986. His leadership and success at Maryland, his range of experiences, and his active involvement in important professional issues and concerns have identified him as a significant colleague among student affairs educators. In the 1990s, his work at Maryland has also been characterized by special leadership and advocacy efforts to enhance The Senior Year Experience.

The Senior Year Experience

PART ONE

UNDERSTANDING THE UNIQUE NEEDS OF TODAY'S SENIORS

What are some of the hopes, fears, concerns, beliefs, and characteristics of today's graduating students? Are they prepared to face the future beyond the hallowed halls of alma mater? Part One examines the characteristics and needs of seniors in light of the impending transition from classroom to multiple societal roles other than "undergraduate student." This section provides a rationale for a focus on seniors as a special population on our campuses and a definition of *the senior year experience,* and discusses the relevance of this growing movement to current higher education reform efforts.

The thesis presented and explored in this section is that the senior year is an important but neglected period of transition on most college campuses. This problem is examined from a variety of perspectives including the transition needs of seniors, a historical look at how colleges and universities have traditionally approached closure of the undergraduate experience, and the question of whether or not college graduates are adequately prepared.

Given the diversity of issues associated with the senior year, the following chapters attempt to identify the broad themes associated with the senior year and the potential objectives of and benefits to institutions which choose to embrace this new movement.

In summary, this first section attempts to lay a foundation for the following sections, which go on to explore the various themes and implications for practice in greater detail.

CHAPTER ONE

The Emerging Movement to Strengthen the Senior Experience

John N. Gardner
Gretchen Van der Veer

At the end of this academic year, approximately 1.2 million college seniors will officially complete the academic requirements necessary to receive a baccalaureate degree, and another five hundred thousand–plus students will receive associate degrees (Young, 1996). As they leave their undergraduate careers behind, these new alumni will face the complex demands of a new economy; a demanding, fluctuating, and highly competitive job market; ever-changing technology; and an increasingly diverse America. Given these realities, are today's college graduates adequately prepared to address the challenges of the future? Are they prepared to enter or reenter the world of work or the world of graduate/ professional school? Are they prepared for leadership roles in their organizations and communities? Are they prepared for the inevitable decisions involving family obligations and personal finance? Based on their undergraduate experiences, will today's graduates embody a sense of responsibility and obligation to support the future development of our institutions in their role as alumni?

Several decades ago, as high school enrollments were declining, college educators became interested in improving student recruitment and retention. As a part of that effort, they began to define and champion *the freshman experience* by studying the transition needs of entering students and identifying factors that contributed to success in college. Now, as institutions of higher education face increasing scrutiny from the general public—legislative bodies, governing boards, accrediting associations, and students and their families—in regard to the real and perceived value of postsecondary education, there is a growing circle of educators and prospective employers who say colleges need to do more for seniors than simply confer upon them a diploma. Some believe that *the senior experience* must also be better defined and improved; they advocate that higher education has a moral obligation to pay more attention to the preparation of students for practical success beyond graduation (Magner, 1990).

As explained in the Preface, in this book *senior* is defined as a college student in the process of completing the final quarter of the baccalaureate degree. For one student, this may be equivalent to an academic year, and for another, the process could take several years if the student is not full-time or has switched majors during the undergraduate career. At first glance then, seniors on our campuses appear more different than alike. Some are of traditional college-going age while others are older or returning students. Some lack work experience while others have been or are still full-time employees. Some are part-time commuters while others are full-time campus residents. Senior students also differ in terms of family obligations, age, gender, major, ethnicity, socioeconomic background, life experiences, and many other personal characteristics. Yet in spite of these differences, we believe that seniors share important characteristics that have long been neglected in planning campus policies and services.

This book is a comprehensive examination of strategies to improve the senior year experience. In this chapter, we provide a rationale for a focus on the senior year by reviewing the literature and identifying institutional and societal factors supporting the need to pay more attention and give a higher priority to this particular population on our campuses. We then define what we mean by *the senior year experience* and describe the growing movement to address the needs and issues of graduating students. Finally, although we believe the senior experience to be a fluid and evolving concept, a number of specific themes and benefits associated with this movement are identified, most of which are then discussed in greater detail in subsequent chapters.

A RATIONALE FOR A FOCUS ON SENIORS

Research on the senior year experience is limited because the topic has only recently received attention in the higher education community. More has been written about related concepts such as the purposes of higher education, desired outcomes of the undergraduate experience, and student development and transition issues during the college years. However, after reviewing the available literature and the contributions of the authors in this volume, we propose that the following characteristics are common to seniors.

Seniors are a captive audience. Because they are the most likely to graduate and have already invested the most time and money on our campuses, they may be our most captive audience. Certainly they are not as "at risk" as the beginning cohort of students in the freshman year. Consequently, seniors are an extremely important and potentially influential group. They are the ones most likely to graduate and become supportive alumni, and to be evaluated by employers and graduate schools as a reflection of our institutional quality. As a group, they provide us with a host of research and assessment possibilities, including senior satisfaction surveys, alumni perceptions of success and preparation, and employers' feedback on the performance of graduates.

Seniors have high expectations. Because they have invested so much time, energy, and resources, they and their families have the highest expectations. Seniors expect that finishing their degree will be a big deal: an exciting, satisfactory, rewarding, and proud accomplishment; a celebratory experience; the ticket to a high-paying job and an immediate improvement in living standards coupled with the immediate means to repay the student loans they have accumulated (Sullivan, 1993; Ellin, 1993). The implication is very clear that we need to deliver on these expectations.

Seniors have special needs unique to them as students in transition. During students' final months as undergraduates, they finish required coursework, apply for graduation, and prepare for an unknown future. Whether they are aware of it or not, these students are moving in and through a time of personal transition. The transition issues for some graduates may be larger or more complex than for others, given personal characteristics such as age and experiential background, but several of our authors suggest that the senior year is particularly critical to student development because of the need for all students to reflect on and make meaning of the undergraduate experience (Feitler-Karchin and Wallace-Schutzman, 1982; Holton, 1993).

According to the literature, the undergraduate experience should involve a series of changes and transitions that influence student growth beginning in the freshman year and continuing through to graduation (Astin, 1993b; Chickering, 1969; Karr and Mahrer, 1972). Schlossberg defines transition as a change in one's behaviors or relationships in response to the occurrence of an event or nonevent that affects one's beliefs about oneself or the world (1981). When students first arrive at college and again when they leave, changes occur in their lives. On both occasions, students must contend with major frustrations as they end one phase of life and begin another (Vickio, 1990). Chickering and Sanford identify the senior year as including clusters of upsetting problems (Chickering, 1969), with a particularly high level of instability during the semester prior to graduation (Sanford, 1967).

The transition from student to postcollege life can often be difficult because of the expectations and pressures of different settings in the workplace or graduate and professional school. Most research conducted with college graduates focuses on the transition to the world of work. This process often involves stress and disorientation due to differences between the campus and workplace cultures and the behaviors that are required to succeed in each (Holton, 1993). The inability of many graduates to cope successfully with the new expectations of the workplace may be responsible for the high number of turnovers within the first eighteen months of employment (Holton, 1992; Louis, 1980). As a result, students need to be provided with specific support and opportunities to learn new skills and survival strategies in order to cope during this critical period (Brammer and Abrego, 1981).

The college environment promotes student growth by providing the appropriate challenges and supports necessary to learn and create knowledge and acquire new skills, behaviors, and attitudes (Astin, 1993b; Ewell, 1993; Owens, 1989; Sanford, 1967). In the senior year, special emphasis needs to be placed on helping students cope with impending change, become aware of how all aspects of their lives have contributed to their development as learners, and find connections between their academic experience and future plans. Although there appears to be a general acceptance of the need for specific interventions to help students successfully transition *into* the college environment, the problems and needs associated with the transition *out of* the college setting (Weinberg, 1988) have received little similar attention from college and university personnel, let alone researchers.

Seniors are our last chance. There is a mounting body of evidence, as presented in Chapters Five (by Philip Gardner) and Seven (by Elwood Holton) that even though colleges are doing a very competent job of producing students with requisite cognitive skills, this is not the case for many other behavioral and attitudinal skills and competencies needed by graduates and demanded by employers. The senior year is the last window of opportunity to address this potential deficit before students leave our custodianship.

Seniors will soon be our alumni. Alumni participation in the life of our campuses is important for a variety of reasons. However, we need the support of these soon-to-be alumni more than ever because of increasing costs and reduced state and federal support. Economists estimate that between now and the year 2040 more than $10 trillion in assets will have been handed down by parents to their children (Nicklin, 1995). These inherited assets may then be available for potential distribution to the offsprings' favorite charities, such as their alma maters.

We need to impress upon our students while they are still on our campuses that alumni generosity has supported their own education, and that they have the same responsibility to invest in the education of future students. Yet development staff are significantly hampered in using this argument with seniors if the students perceive that the institution does not have an investment in what happens to them (Baade and Sundberg, 1993). The senior year may be our last chance to cultivate students for future roles as involved alumni.

Diverse in age, ethnicity, experience, and individual interests, graduating students nevertheless share common characteristics. The present review of the literature suggests that as a group seniors are a neglected, captive, anxious audience who need to be better cultivated and supported to enhance long-term goodwill, student satisfaction, and more effective learning. According to various authors (Astmann, 1969; Baade and Sundberg, 1993; Ellin, 1993; Holton, 1992; Sullivan, 1993), the senior year can be isolated as a particular point of transition involving the culmination of all the knowledge and skills learned through experiences with peers, faculty, and staff. What is most striking to us as the editors of this book is the consensus developed among the various chapter contributors—with no intentional plan to direct and achieve such consensus—that the most basic needs of seniors are for (1) opportunities for reflection on the meaning of the college experience, (2) integration and closure, and (3) holistic facilitation and support of graduating students' transition to postcollege life. The senior year experience provides a vehicle for raising campus consciousness in order to address these long-neglected issues.

THE INSTITUTIONAL AND SOCIETAL CONTEXT

Since the 1980s, several emerging institutional and societal trends have prompted calls for new structures and policies to address perceived deficiencies in higher education. These trends include repeated calls to reform the undergraduate experience and examine the purposes of higher education, promotion of student learning through introducing a "seamless curriculum," employer criticism of the quality of graduates and growing public dissatisfaction with the high cost of higher education, the assessment movement, the frustrations of new alumni in the job market, and economic realities and a growing dependence on alumni support (Cuseo, 1993; Magner, 1990; Feitler-Karchin and Wallace-Schutzman, 1982). We believe there is a relationship between these trends and the growing national discussion about the senior year experience.

Repeated calls to reform the undergraduate experience and examine the purposes of higher education. Two questions are continually being asked: What should the purposes of higher education be? What do we get from this enormous investment of our national treasure? Much has been written about this issue and the outcomes that should be associated with a baccalaureate degree. A review of the literature reveals myriad goals: development of students' love for learning, awareness of contemporary issues, ethical and moral development, values transmission, technical competencies, citizenship preparation, ability to engage in self-assessment, development of intellectual skills, and career preparation ("The College Park Experience: Quality Education Right from the Start," 1987).

In the 1980s, many U.S. colleges and universities reformed their undergraduate curricula in response to numerous calls to transform American undergraduate education. One fairly recent report calling for change is that of the Wingspread Group on Higher Education, entitled "An American Imperative: Higher Expectations for Higher Education" (1993). The report claims that there is a "disturbing and dangerous mismatch between what American society needs of higher education and what it is receiving" (p. 1). Wingspread maintains that the ability of the United States to compete in a global economy is threatened and that the American people's hope for a civil, humane society rides on the outcome. According to the Wingspread Group on Higher Education, what the United States needs from higher education "is stronger, more vital forms of community and graduates who will perform as informed and involved citizens ready to assume leadership roles in American life" (p. 2).

Increasingly, the expectation is that campuses should pay more attention to preparing citizens and public servants, college graduates who serve their communities as leaders in every sense of the word. Why else would a society enroll 14.5 million of its citizens in thirty-six hundred institutions if it were not expected that the higher education culture should be the primary conduit for educating and preparing its future leaders? Yet the business of higher education is often organized in discrete units with fixed boundaries, making delivery and assessment of interdisciplinary concepts such as leadership development, values transmission, and citizenship preparation very difficult to measure (Cronin, 1983; Marchese, 1993; Rost, 1993). Cronin says that although "the mission of the college may be to educate the 'educated person' and society's future leaders, in fact the incentive system is geared to training specialists" (p. 9). The result is that these stated goals of higher education are approached serendipitously rather than intentionally (Magner, 1999). According to the Wingspread Group on Higher Education (1993), higher education is also organized more around the convenience and preferences of educators and the institution's procedures than around students' needs. These same issues have also been raised by advocates of the continuous improvement and total quality movements, who maintain that higher education is in desperate need of reorienting itself to the customer (Marchese, 1993).

Promotion of student learning through implementation of a seamless curriculum. Another goal of higher education is to promote student learning. Research suggests that several critical factors can influence student learning—among them involving students actively in the educational process and providing opportunities for applying material learned and meaningfully interacting with faculty, staff, and peers (Pascarella and Terenzini, 1991). We also know from research on cognition that students who have opportunities to reflect upon their learning are better learners than those who do not (Weinstein and Meyer,

1991) and that student experiences outside the classroom often serve as vehicles for practice and application of course material.

Review of various higher education publications reveals numerous references to the concept of the seamless curriculum as a vehicle for enhancing undergraduate education and student learning (American Association of Higher Education, 1993; American College Personnel Association, 1994; Kuh, 1996). The argument for this approach maintains that student learning is not restricted to sixty- or ninety-minute class periods. Therefore, if we want to enhance student learning, we should mobilize the entire campus to develop and incorporate more comprehensive and integrated curricular and cocurricular structures that actually reflect how students learn (Terenzini and Pascarella, 1994). This means that institutions should be more intentional about linking in-class and out-of-class experiences, thereby encouraging higher levels of student learning (Kuh, 1996).

As an example of the kinds of institutional structures or policies that could be created to enhance student learning, students could be required to do volunteer community service while enrolled in a course on social change theory that incorporates opportunities for reflection on the service experience, and simultaneously to conduct social policy research as part of an undergraduate research internship. In Chapter Nine, Linda Sax and Alexander Astin report the results of their research examining the issue of student involvement in service and the benefits to learning, leadership, and citizenship. They report a positive relationship between student participation in community service activities and development of civic virtue. According to Astin, "it seems clear that service learning can provide a powerful vehicle for colleges and universities to make good on their commitment to prepare students for responsible citizenship" (1996, p. 19).

Many barriers exist on campus to achieving a seamless curriculum, but the senior year experience provides faculty, administrators, and student personnel professionals with a context for discussion of this new paradigm for teaching and learning. The senior year experience requires the campus community to rethink basic assumptions about how education has been delivered in the past and encourages new approaches such as student reflection and assimilation of all different learning experiences—both inside and outside the classroom—prior to graduation.

The assessment movement. The senior year is a critical focal point for assessment. In 1984, the National Institute of Education's report *Involvement in Learning* was released, calling for greater accountability on the part of higher education. The charge was subsequently accepted by state legislators across the country. Over the years, more and more institutions have responded by recognizing the need and institutionalizing assessment methods into the daily functioning of campus life. The movement for accountability in higher education is not going to go away. It is not a flash in the pan. The pressures are only going to increase. More important, assessment is a desirable end in itself to facilitate improvement of student learning. According to Karl Schilling and Karen Maitland Schilling in Chapter Fifteen, on assessment, "by virtue of their transitional status, seniors' perspectives on their experiences within an institution and on the institution itself offer the potential for bringing new dimensionality to our understandings—providing a more complex picture than can be gained from students at other points during their college or postcollege years." Senior year assessment initiatives also provide opportunities for more connections to baseline assessment data accumulated in the freshman year. Therefore, the senior year presents an unparalleled opportunity to collect meaningful outcomes data for purposes of accountability and to provide meaningful insight regarding the full spectrum of the undergraduate experience.

Growing employer criticism and public dissatisfaction with higher education. The world of work and the rest of society have changed dramatically since the end of the Cold War and with the globalization of the world economy. It is absolutely essential that the curriculum continue to be strengthened and adjusted to meet the changing needs of graduating students. Peter Drucker (1994) describes a societal transformation in progress that is affecting almost every type of organization. He believes that the workplace of the future will be smaller because of continued corporate downsizing, ever-changing in response to market trends, and more autonomous as frontline employees replace management as decision makers. Burdick and Mitchell report that, according to their sources, employers in these transformed workplaces also have particular expectations of skills for the college graduates they hire: (1) computer literacy, (2) the ability to function as part of a team, (3) effective interpersonal and communication skills, (4) the ability to change and adapt, (5) ambition and drive, and (6) good personal characteristics (1993).

Yet evidence suggests that today's graduates are unprepared for these requirements (Wingspread Group on Higher Education, 1993; Holton, 1992, 1993; McWilliams, 1993) and that far too many have inadequate skills in the face of the demands of contemporary life. In Chapter Five, "Are College Seniors Prepared to Work?" Philip Gardner argues that college graduates do not acquire these skills as a result of the current approach to undergraduate education. This reality has resulted in growing public dissatisfaction with higher education. As the Wingspread Group says: "The withdrawal of public support for higher education can only accelerate as students, parents, and taxpayers come to understand that they paid for an expensive education without receiving fair value in return" (1993, p. 2).

In addition, a number of other trends and issues have had a negative impact on the public's perception of higher education. Legislative criticism and misunderstanding of faculty workloads, athletic scandals, abuse of faculty overhead grant moneys, and extravagant spending by some campus CEOs angers a public already concerned about annual tuition increases outstripping the rise in the cost of living. On-campus controversies such as political correctness and increasing incidents of bigotry, intolerance, violence, and crime further fuel public dissatisfaction with the use of personal, federal, and state tax dollars. In addition, the length of time to degree completion and the public perception of the lack of connectedness between college and "the real world" further exacerbates the perception that what students and parents get for their investment is less than what was expected.

By acknowledging the need to prepare students for success beyond the classroom and by examining the structures, partnerships, policies, and processes necessary to facilitate student success, the senior experience provides a context for addressing these concerns of employers and the public.

The frustrations of new alumni. What do students expect for their investment in higher education? According to several authors, most students and parents expect a college degree to be an immediate ticket to a high-paying job (Sullivan, 1993; Ellin, 1993). However, given the realities of a changing workplace with smaller, downsized organizations (Drucker, 1994), many graduates are having difficulty securing employment. The result is further emotional upheaval and conflict between the students' own expectations and reality (Ellin, 1993). This mismatch between expectations and reality can lead to frustration and bitterness, often directed back at the supplier of the degree for failing to produce the expected results (Holton, 1993). The plight has become true for so many graduates that one journalist actually defined and named it "post-parchment depression" (Ellin, 1993).

Economic realities and growing dependence on alumni support. Particularly since the recession of the early 1990s, many campuses, both public and private, have seen growing dependence on long-term alumni support as opposed to immediate tuition-driven or state-supported revenues. As a result, there is a growing desire to begin cultivating alumni early, before they leave campus. This is strongly linked to student transition issues. Although alumni and development officers can reach out to alumni after graduation, ultimately it is the academic ties that bind. If faculty fail to demonstrate concern for students' careers and the institution fails to communicate a desire to stay connected, alumni fundraising efforts inevitably suffer.

The common needs and expectations of seniors, regardless of age or experience, and the institutional and societal pressures of the last decade and a half present a dilemma for educators. Given the high cost of a college education, the measure of institutional worth is becoming more closely related to the post-college success of graduates. These realities have prompted a growing number of educators to identify the senior experience as an opportunity to institute interventions to intentionally address their own stated goals as well as the expectations of students, parents, employers, and the general public (Magner, 1990).

DEFINING THE SENIOR EXPERIENCE

What exactly do we mean by the senior experience? Obviously, we believe it should be something more than a student's finally completing degree requirements and obtaining the necessary credits to graduate. Concisely, we mean a variety of initiatives in the academic and cocurricular domain that serve to promote and enhance greater learning and satisfaction and a more successful transition for college students during the final quarter of the baccalaureate educational experience. The term describes a set of relatively new initiatives to provide more attention and support for this important population of present students, future alums, and future American leaders. We believe that most fundamentally, these initiatives must support, enhance, and promote the academic objectives of the institution. We also believe they must and do address a number of the more holistic objectives the institution has for the total educational experience of its students (as cited in the catalogue mission statements of most campuses). We believe the senior year experience (if it takes place within a year), or the senior experience (over a much more extended period), is the set of newly defined initiatives to increase the probability that our institutions will successfully fulfill their mission statements during their students' final phase of education and academic residency.

At their core, these initiatives must be dependent on, emergent from, and related and connected to the curriculum of the institution and the goals, objectives, and teachings of its faculty. However, the senior experience also acknowledges that learning occurs both inside and outside the classroom, and that along with faculty many other individuals on campus play a role in facilitating and supporting student learning. Metaphorically, the senior year experience serves as an architectural blueprint for a student's final quarter of the baccalaureate degree. A blueprint illustrates how different systems, separately designed, can be integrated into the total construction of a clearly defined and carefully drawn building; so, too, the senior year experience serves to integrate the different aspects of campus life to achieve a better-defined outcome for graduating seniors.

The senior experience is therefore an effort to address the needs of graduating students through marshaling institutional resources and attention. And we emphasize once again that examination of the contributions of our various authors reveals agreement that at the very minimum, the senior experience— still an evolving concept—involves providing opportunities for reflection on personal growth and development, integration and closure to the undergraduate experience, and efforts to facilitate and support holistically the graduating students' transition to postcollege life.

THE GROWING SENIOR EXPERIENCE MOVEMENT

Until recently, the primary institutional acknowledgment of the senior transition was the advent of career planning and placement centers. As a result of the institutional and societal pressures previously discussed, a growing group of educators are now advocating that institutions should do more for seniors than offer them a career planning service, arrange for employers to interview them on campus, and ceremonially award them a diploma. In 1990, the University of South Carolina's Division of Continuing Education hosted the first national conference entitled The Senior Year Experience. The conference was cohosted by Kennesaw State University, the University of Maryland, and Marietta College. A statement of the conference purpose and background, as published in the "Call for Papers," said that "conferences on the Freshman Year Experience, attended by some [twenty-five thousand, as of 1997] educators from approximately two dozen countries, have been widely recognized as literally changing the face of freshman education. Having addressed successfully the critical transition process into higher education, we now take a look at another vital transition of equal concern to the nation's interest: the transition from college to the post-college situations of work, family obligations, community and national service, and leadership" (Division of Continuing Education, University of South Carolina, 1989, p. 2).

Approximately 180 educators met at the conference to discuss issues surrounding the senior transition and share different institutional interventions, almost exactly the same number as attended The Freshman Year Experience first national conference in 1982. Since the 1990 conference, there have been three more devoted exclusively to the senior year experience; additionally, the inaugural Students in Transition conference in 1995 included seniors as a focus, and it was followed by a second Students in Transition conference in 1996 (a third will be held in 1997).

The decision by the University of South Carolina to organize a new series of continuing education meetings for higher educators to call attention to another student transition topic was the result of many, many factors that seemed to coalesce in the late 1980s. As that decade progressed, and faculty and staff of the National Resource Center for The Freshman Year Experience and Students in Transition worked with hundreds of colleges and universities to improve the experience of first-year students, much was learned about how institutions could sponsor more successful transitions. A number of generic themes and components of transition emerged. For example, the same educators on campus who were highly involved with helping students make a successful transition into college were also frequently the same educators helping them transition out successfully (for example, academic advisors, career planning center staff, and many individual faculty and academic administrators). It was apparent that both the freshman year experience and the senior experience were two critical and stressful transitions during the college era, the successful completion of which could determine upward social mobility for American college students. Both transitions seemed to beg for more attention to student development and transition issues. Both called for and were dependent upon improved working partnerships between officers in academic affairs and student affairs.

Increasingly, the transitions were understood to be more successful when intentional support groups were created for students experiencing a common life transition, and when the group was led by successful survivors of the same transition. It came to be realized that just as in the freshman experience, successful transitions for students leaving the institution involved a holistic approach, one that emphasized the interconnection and combination of the academic, social, emotional, physical, and spiritual dimensions of learning. It became apparent that both the freshman transition and the senior transition needed to link more intentionally the curricula and cocurricula. The argument also began to develop that these transitions could be supported and facilitated more successfully by creating special credit-bearing courses involving both faculty and student affairs officers, as in freshman seminars or senior capstone seminars.

Those attending the national conferences exploring the nature of an improved senior year experience brought with them a number of common questions and areas of interest:

- How do you lay the foundation for the desired senior year experience outcomes in the freshman year experience?

- How can we more intentionally connect the two ends of this continuum of the undergraduate experience?

- Is it possible to apply some of the same tenets of the philosophy that enhances the freshman year to create a more successful departure process for students?

- Can we encourage a longer-range view of institutional cultivation of student loyalty and long-term support for providing a more satisfying and fulfilling departure process?

- Is it possible to achieve serious institutional examination of the senior transition on the same scale as the reexamination of the freshman transition, even though the potential for immediate financial rewards through increased student retention does not exist in improving the senior experience?

- What is the connection between the senior year and the growing national interest in connecting leadership education to the curriculum and the liberal arts, that is, moving leadership education beyond primarily the purview of noncredit student affairs leadership programming?

- How can we link the growing interest in assessment with greater specificity to senior capstone experiences?

The initial discussions of the nature of the senior year experience and the desirability of improving it were also related to a number of societal issues influencing the thinking of higher education practitioners and reformers in the late 1980s and early 1990s (described earlier in this chapter). Thus coincidentally and intentionally, these factors all seemed to coalesce in the thinking of the staff of the National Resource Center for The Freshman Year Experience and Students in Transition and the University of South Carolina's Division of Continuing Education, leading to plans in 1989 for the first national conference in 1990.

THEMES ASSOCIATED WITH THE SENIOR YEAR EXPERIENCE

Through the offering of the first conference, followed by three more, a number of programmatic themes of the senior year experience have become very apparent, themes that permeate the contributed chapters of this book. They are the basis for the most characteristic, programmatic illustrations of senior year experience programs, interventions, and efforts.

Capstone experiences. These are defined as summative curricular approaches such as courses synthesizing all of the content to date within a particular major (and often attempting to connect that concept back to the institution's basic theme of general education and the liberal arts). They include final projects, theses, recitals, and internships.

Attempts to link the liberal arts with a major and make the academic experience coherent. In Chapter Six, Barbara Leigh Smith suggests that for many seniors "the undergraduate experience feels like fragments, a series of unrelated courses and relationships." Senior experience initiatives try to address this deficiency through courses or interdisciplinary classes and projects attempting to link the general curriculum to the major.

Leadership education. In Chapter Eight, Stephen Schwartz and Nance Lucas remind us that a democracy cannot be sustained without a constant infusion of younger leaders. This theme includes intentional efforts on the part of an institution to provide students with curricular and cocurricular opportunities to learn about and experience leadership and to gain an understanding of their responsibility to society as graduates of institutions of higher education.

Career planning. Several chapter authors in this book argue for career development to be better integrated as a component of the undergraduate experience. Included in this theme are a broad range of initiatives to support the needs of seniors to explore and decide upon options after graduation, including the special needs of minority students who still face greater barriers to successful employment after college.

Job search and transition planning. In addition, career planning activities should be accompanied by development of job and career skills specific to current workplace requirements. Many colleges and universities are implementing creative programs to prepare seniors for searching, interviewing, and entering new professional employment situations. Special programs are also being developed to support and assist older, multiethnic, and disabled student populations with what many believe to be more difficult job search and transition issues.

Alumni development. In Chapter Fourteen, Jeffery Johnson and Peter Eckel suggest that cultivation of active alumni begins prior to graduation and should be an important element of a senior year experience. As dependence on alumni has become more critical to colleges and universities, intentional efforts to build senior loyalty and encourage a lifelong relationship with the institution are being introduced across the country.

Preparation for life after college and practical life skills (for example, financial planning, finding a place to live). According to an American Express study, an alarming number of college graduates do not know even basic information about credit and personal finance (Young, 1993). Studies of this kind support the need for colleges and universities to develop and introduce seminars, workshops, and residence hall discussion groups around practical life issues and skills.

Preparation for graduate school. For many seniors, the job search is supplanted by the graduate or professional school application process. Many colleges and universities are finally recognizing that assisting students in thoughtful and purposeful decision making about their futures should include providing resources about graduate programs and better information about what to expect. This can come from opportunities to interact with faculty through such activities as undergraduate research internships.

Preparation for adult life as spouses; partners; parents; and community, civic, and political leaders. In Chapter Nine, Sax and Astin suggest that "citizenship development is particularly important during the senior year, as it marks a period of transition into adulthood—a time when many students are deciding what to do with their lives as well as how to live their lives." Several recent education reform reports have suggested that higher education can no longer afford to ignore the development of the "whole" person. As a result, colleges and universities are looking at ways to engage students in discussions and exploration of character and lifestyle issues and what it means to be a citizen contributing to a local, national, and global community.

In Chapter Two, Joseph Cuseo provides a review and synthesis of the proceedings from The Senior Year Experience and Students in Transition conferences. Through his analysis, he identifies a total of ten themes or objectives of the senior year experience movement (similar to those discussed above):

1. To promote the coherence and relevance of general education
2. To promote integration and connections between general education and the academic major
3. To foster integration and synthesis within the academic major
4. To promote meaningful connections between general education and the academic major and work (career) experiences
5. To explicitly and intentionally develop important student skills, competencies, and perspectives that are tacitly or incidentally developed in the college curriculum
6. To enhance awareness of and support for the key personal adjustments encountered by seniors during their transition from college to postcollege life
7. To improve seniors' career preparation and preprofessional development
8. To enhance seniors' preparation and prospects for postgraduate education
9. To promote effective life planning and decision making with respect to practical issues likely to be encountered in adult life after college
10. To encourage a sense of unity and community among the senior class, which can serve as a foundation for later alumni networking and future alumni support of the college

These objectives are developed and elaborated in both Cuseo's chapter and throughout this work.

Some of the initiatives proposed to address these objectives are curricular while others are cocurricular. Many involve introduction of specific courses; implementation of new workshops, internships, and career or mentorship programs; incorporation of leadership, values, and character development activities; direct involvement of faculty in partnership with student affairs personnel, alumni, and employers; and introduction of teaching methods incorporating small-group work, final student research projects, and oral and written communication exercises. Regardless of specific initiatives, an important aspect of the movement is the need to integrate the whole college experience and help students understand the relevance of their undergraduate education.

INSTITUTIONAL BENEFITS OF THE SENIOR YEAR EXPERIENCE

Although the movement is still too new to have acquired vocal critics, one can anticipate various points of opposition. From some faculty members in an electronic network exchange regarding issues connected to the senior experience, we have heard concern about vocationalism versus the education of the individual for life. Although the senior experience does indeed embrace and acknowledge the need for both, the call to involve employers and faculty in discussing career education, along with the desire to respond to students as customers, challenges faculty autonomy and authority for curriculum and course content. In addition, external constituencies are calling for higher education to be more deliberate in its preparation of society's future leaders (Wingspread Group on Higher Education, 1993).

In response to skeptics, proponents of the senior experience are quick to point out the institutional benefits to addressing the senior transition. According to Cuseo's summary of the perspectives of those attending The Senior Year Experience conferences, embracing the movement and its objectives could have the following institutional impacts: (1) improving college-business and college-state relations, 2) improving alumni relations, (3) promoting faculty development, (4) forging alliances between academic and student affairs, and (5) enhancing institutional research and student outcomes assessment. "The Senior Year Experience can stimulate increased dialogue between the college and corporate employers with respect to the issue of how to better prepare graduates for work-related roles," Cuseo concludes (1994, p. 11). By-products of such dialogue can include more collaborative relationships between the campus and corporate neighbors as well as the possibility of corporate funding for various projects.

Levitz and Noel (1989) suggest that "fostering student success in the freshman year is the most significant intervention an institution can make in the name of student persistence" (p. 65). This argument has been used repeatedly by educators to justify additional institutional attention and resources directed toward entering students. Similarly, an economic argument can be made that fostering senior success after graduation may be the most significant intervention an institution can make in the name of alumni development and long-term institutional support (financial and otherwise).

The senior experience also frequently involves reexamination of the curriculum so that it intentionally leads toward goals and objectives that can be assessed, for example, through capstone courses, projects, and portfolios. This kind of rethinking of the educational goals and outcomes of baccalaureate education encourages faculty experimentation with different pedagogies and interdisciplinary topics, which can lead to greater faculty collaboration and stimulation. Finally, another beneficial outcome is the opportunity to take advantage of the captive senior population for purposes of assessment and continuous improvement by collecting information through such vehicles as senior satisfaction surveys, as a supplement to studies of alumni perception of success and employer feedback on performance of graduates.

Although more and more educators are asking what the institution can do to enhance chances for student success beyond the campus, because the senior experience movement is so new there is little empirical evidence to support the impact of specific interventions. However, there does seem to be evidence suggesting that opportunities for students to reflect on their experiences can help facilitate the transition to postcollege life (Cuseo, 1993) and that satisfied alumni are more likely to support their alma mater (Baade and Sundberg, 1993).

As a result of The Senior Year Experience conferences and research conducted by the chapter authors of this book, we do know that many campuses are instituting new and inventive interventions to address the needs of seniors. Initiatives such as capstone courses, alumni induction banquets, and "from backpack to briefcase" workshops illustrate the breadth and diversity of campus approaches. Institutions are implementing these kinds of efforts on campuses across the country (both small and large, private and public), but more research needs to be conducted to assess the impact each has on identifiable outcomes associated with a successful postgraduation transition. Although the range and scope of programs is impressive, in contrast to their institutionalization of the freshman year experience most colleges and universities have not yet developed comprehensive, strategic efforts to meet the needs of seniors.

CONCLUSION

The outcome of the undergraduate experience should be more than a framed diploma. We believe colleges and universities can and must intentionally and successfully influence and enhance outcomes in a variety of specific ways. Institutions committed to helping seniors achieve these outcomes, however, must subscribe to certain beliefs about their obligation to students and seek to understand the assortment of issues that converge during a student's final year. They need to revise their curricula, develop new programs, and allocate resources strategically to enhance senior success beyond the classroom. Most important, they need to work cooperatively across divisions and offices on campus.

The primary goal of any institution is to facilitate student learning, achievement of the goals of the curriculum and institutional mission statement, and student fulfillment of baccalaureate degree requirements. This involves everyone on campus, from the academic departments that confer degrees to the physical plant personnel who provide chairs and staging for commencement. The initiatives proposed within this volume cut across institutional divisions and involve multiple departments, services, and organizations. Ultimately, institutional commitment to a senior year experience requires every member of the campus community to recognize the role that he or she can play in enhancing the undergraduate students' final period and then acting accordingly. In a word, the successful senior experience and its outcomes require a partnership of all key campus constituencies. This is, of course, exactly what initiators of The Freshman Year Experience reform movement begun a decade or so before had already learned and agreed was necessary: a partnership of many people who work with students in transition on our campuses. This book, too, is based on that central philosophy.

CHAPTER TWO

Objectives and Benefits of
Senior Year Programs

Joseph B. Cuseo

Since 1990, The National Resource Center for The Freshman Year Experience and Students in Transition has sponsored four national conferences entitled The Senior Year Experience (SYE) and devoted exclusively to that concept, plus two national conferences entitled Students in Transition that included the SYE as one of their three major strands. This chapter provides a descriptive synthesis of the proceedings of these conferences, intended to supply the reader with an introductory overview of the essential goals of SYE programming along with illustrative practices designed to achieve these goals. Goals and practices are enumerated in a quasi outline format so that the overarching objectives and pertinent practices of the SYE movement can be readily identified and potentially implemented.

This chapter concludes with a narrative review of major reasons why the SYE, a student-centered movement, can also realize a number of institution-centered goals that serve the college or university engaging in SYE programming. It is beyond the scope of this chapter to provide an evaluative critique of the practices cited. The institutional programs identified in this chapter were chosen because they clearly illustrate or implement a major goal or intended outcome of the SYE movement. Empirical evidence for a program's effectiveness is cited if such data were published in the proceedings of the conference at which the program was presented.

PURPOSES AND GOALS

Review of the proceedings from The Senior Year Experience and Students in Transition conferences suggests that there are three major purposes of the SYE movement: (1) to bring *integration* and closure to the undergraduate experience, (2) to provide students with an opportunity to *reflect* on the meaning of their college experience, and (3) to facilitate graduating students' *transition* to postcollege life. More specifically, the SYE movement appears to be pursuing ten particular goals:

1. Promoting the coherence and relevance of *general education*
2. Promoting integration and connections between *general education* and the *academic major*
3. Fostering integration and synthesis *within* the *academic major*
4. Promoting meaningful connections between the *academic major* and *work* (*career*) experiences
5. Explicitly and intentionally developing important student *skills, competencies, and perspectives* that are tacitly or incidentally developed in the college curriculum (for example, leadership skills and character and values development)
6. Enhancing awareness of and support for the key personal *adjustments* encountered by seniors during their *transition* from *college to postcollege* life
7. Improving seniors' *career* preparation and *preprofessional* development, that is, facilitating their transition from the academic to the professional world
8. Enhancing seniors' preparation and prospects for *postgraduate education*
9. Promoting effective *life planning and decision making* with respect to practical issues likely to be encountered in adult life after college (for example, financial planning, marriage, and family planning)
10. Encouraging a sense of *unity and community* among the senior class, which can serve as a foundation for later *alumni networking* and future *alumni support of the college*

The remainder of this chapter attempts to (1) delineate specific objectives embraced by the SYE movement with respect to each of the foregoing goals, (2) showcase some of the movement's exemplary programs, and (3) highlight the movement's major advantages for both the student and the institution.

Goal One: Coherence and Relevance of General Education

The major vehicle used by SYE programs to bring coherence and closure to the general education experience is the senior year capstone course, designed to forge interdisciplinary connections among the liberal arts and sciences.

For example, Plymouth State University (Plymouth, New Hampshire) offers such a course as a required component of its general education curriculum (Lambert, 1991). At St. Mary College (Leavenworth, Kansas), the integrative capstone course is taught by three interdisciplinary faculty teams (Brinkman, 1991), as it is at Meredith College (Raleigh, North Carolina), where an interdisciplinary capstone course is taught by a triad of faculty from the humanities, natural sciences, and social sciences (Hornak and Shiflett, 1990).

Southwestern College (Winfield, Kansas) requires its seniors to enroll in Capstone Course: Responsibilities for the Future, in which faculty from diverse academic fields make guest presentations that relate to assigned course readings. As a course requirement, students engage in volunteer service for the local community, and they collaborate on team projects with classmates who have different academic majors. The projects are presented in class, and other members of the campus and local community are invited to attend these group presentations (Findley, 1994).

Another SYE programming strategy for promoting the coherence and relevance of general education is to provide seniors with an interdisciplinary learning experience centered around a relevant, contemporary issue. The University of Hartford (Connecticut) provides its seniors with the interdisciplinary, team-taught course Pluralism Revisited: Living with Diversity (Luebke and D'Lugin, 1990).

Other institutions have linked a travel-study experience to a capstone interdisciplinary course, thus extending the course to incorporate an experiential, cross-cultural dimension. The University Studies/Weekend College Program at Wayne State University (Detroit, Michigan) offers travel-study experiences for its reentry (adult) seniors in conjunction with interdisciplinary course instruction (Wright and McMahn, 1990).

Goal Two: Integrating General Education and Academic Major

One SYE strategy for realizing the goal of integrating students' general education and their majors is to provide a curricular anchor at the end of the undergraduate experience, in order to (1) allow general education to be experienced across the curriculum, (2) integrate coursework in the students' major fields of study, and (3) connect liberal education with preprofessional training by having students apply general-education principles and perspectives to content taught within preprofessional majors.

Marietta College (Marietta, Ohio) requires a capstone course within every major for all graduating seniors, designed to promote integration between the student's major and general education (Hartel, 1993).

Goal Three: Synthesis Within Academic Major

SYE programming has attempted to realize this goal of synthesis by requiring a capstone course in the major that is designed to promote intradisciplinary connections. For instance, Eastern Illinois University, with an enrollment of some 11,300 students, requires such a capstone course in the major for all its seniors, offering some fifty different sections, one for each academic major offered by the college (Whitley, 1990).

Goal Four: Connecting Academic Major and Work World

A variety of SYE strategies have been developed to provide students with opportunities for connecting their academic major with the "real world" of work, serving to link coursework with experiential learning and professional practice. SYE strategies for integrating the academic major and the work world include the following institutional practices:

- Senior courses in which potential employers and alumni in various careers serve as guest speakers or as resources for out-of-class projects

- Business professionals serving on college advisory committees, or faculty serving on corporate advisory committees

- Faculty development programs in which corporate professionals and faculty attempt to promote *positive transfer* between students' academic experience within their majors (for example, departmental curriculum and pedagogy) and their work experience in corporate organizations

- Research conducted jointly by faculty and business professionals (for example, joint data collection on the relationship between students' academic and professional performance; collaborative research on the relationship between specific college experiences and career success)

- *Linked* courses in the senior year designed to integrate theory and practice (for example, internship experience and senior seminar taken concurrently, which involves joint planning, coordinated topics, and mutually reinforcing assignments)

- Interorganizational exchanges between college faculty and corporate professionals that are designed to promote mutual understanding and appreciation of their respective practices

Goal Five: Developing Student Skills, Competencies, and Perspectives

Senior year programs have been consciously designed to promote the development of numerous student qualities.

Leadership skills are developed by means of special coursework, mentoring, and experiential activities. Regis College (Denver) offers an interdisciplinary course focusing on leadership that is reinforced with a series of out-of-class developmental experiences, including "outdoor challenges" (Jutras, 1990).

At the University of North Carolina, a senior year retreat is provided for selected students in the university's leadership program. During the retreat, students review and reflect on their leadership self-assessments reported during the freshman year and the leadership experiences they have had during their first three years in college. Seniors articulate how their leadership style compares and contrasts with the first-year assessments, how their style of leadership has evolved over the four years at the university, and how they see it in relation to their future leadership roles after college (Johnson and Edgerly, 1993).

At Purdue University, the Student as Mentor program has been developed, in which a senior (1) delivers an experiential leadership presentation to local high school students, (2) hosts potential first-year students during campus visits, (3) becomes a formal mentor for an incoming freshman, and (4) selects and trains college juniors to become the following year's senior mentors (Lybrook, 1995).

Character and values development are fostered by having seniors critically explore the ethical implications and consequences of decisions they will be making in their professional careers and personal lives after college.

Holy Family College (Philadelphia) offers a senior ethics course involving faculty and students from all disciplines that focuses on values education and applied ethics. The course is designed to assist students in establishing a foundation for decision making with respect to moral issues likely to be encountered in life after college (Hobaugh and McCormick, 1990).

Incarnate Word College (San Antonio) offers a senior capstone course in practical ethics that includes an "ethical court" in which students role-play defendants, prosecutors, and judges in ethical cases involving relationships, work, and political situations that may be encountered in postcollege settings (Doyle and Galloway, 1991).

The ability to work in small groups is developed by way of teamwork, problem-solving, consensus-building, and decision-making skills applied to real-world situations or issues.

At Keuka College (Keuka Park, New York), "team case-analyses" are conducted by small groups of students in its capstone management course (Breitling, 1991).

At Villa Julie College (Stevenson, Maryland), the capstone seminar teams up three or four seniors with different majors and personality profiles (as assessed by the MBTI) who then work together on tasks that require consensus building and decision making (Ellis, 1993).

Writing skills are promoted via the senior thesis, oral communication skills via oral reports and small-group exercises and projects. At the University of Wisconsin-Green Bay, each graduating senior is required to complete a major project or paper relating to a key issue in the senior seminar and is expected to demonstrate effective writing skills, small-group discussion skills, and formal speaking skills (Murphy, 1991).

Discipline-specific communication skills are developed, as in mastering the distinctive written and oral presentation styles peculiar to the student's major or professional field (for example, the business memo).

At Villa Julie College, all business administration majors are required to take the Senior Research Seminar in which they apply information search-and-retrieval skills to investigate a contemporary issue relating to business. Special emphasis is placed on the development of discipline-specific writing styles and oral presentation skills, which students use to present their research findings for critique by peers, faculty from business and other disciplines, and members of the business community (Ellis, 1993).

Goal Six: Enhancing Personal Adjustments

Toward the realization of this SYE goal, Mount Saint Mary's College (Emmitsburg, Maryland) has developed a self-assessment instrument (the Transition Style Indicator, or TSI) that is used to increase seniors' awareness of their "transition style" and its impact on how they handle transition to new situations (Beitz, 1993).

The University of Mississippi offers a senior-year transition course in which a needs assessment is administered on the first day of class in order to assess the work experiences and career knowledge of students enrolled in the course. The results of this assessment are used to modify the course syllabus in order to more effectively meet the particular needs of the enrolled students and to serve as a pretest against which posttest results are compared after course completion to show students how much personal insight and career-related knowledge they have acquired during the course (Nichols and Hood, 1993).

At Boston College, focus-group interviews are conducted with seniors who are asked open-ended questions designed to gather information on their final-year experience. Drawing on the ideas expressed during these interviews, senior year programming is planned by The Senior Year Experience Committee (comprising student development staff, college faculty, and currently enrolled seniors) with the intention of better meeting the transitional needs of graduating students. For instance, one planned program consists of a weeklong dinner series titled Senior Week: From Backpack to Briefcase, provided for seniors in response to their expressed need for a forum where they could discuss personal questions and concerns about their upcoming transition (Morgan and Armstrong, 1993).

Similarly, at the University of Maryland, the Senior Council has been established as a student organization for the purpose of providing information services and activities that are designed to "unify the graduating class and cultivate alumni involvement" (Van der Veer, Gast, Schmidt, and Lucas, 1993).

Goal Seven: Improving Career Preparation and Preprofessional Development

This general preparation and development aim of the SYE movement embraces a number of more specific objectives and practices.

Students can be helped to articulate a realistic, clearly defined career plan and a commitment to actualizing the short- and long-term goals of that plan. Kean College of New Jersey offers its seniors an elective course, Career Management, that requires them to complete a term paper including (1) personal reflection and response to the results of individual aptitude and interest tests administered by the college's career service center, (2) self-description of employment qualifications, and (3) a detailed plan for achieving career objectives (Casson, 1993).

Students' perspectives of a "career" can be broadened so that it is perceived as a lifelong activity involving continual choices and continuing educational or professional development (for example, via reading professional literature, participating in professional development workshops and seminars, becoming actively involved in professional associations and organizations).

At the University of California-Santa Barbara, the Professional Self career-counseling model developed for seniors describes career planning as an evolving process of "becoming" that continues throughout their professional lives. Students are equipped with an information package for lifetime career decision making that they can use at any point in their careers, returning to it whenever they need to reassess their work roles and make changes (Maestas, 1991).

At Presbyterian College (Clinton, South Carolina), a "transition module" has been developed to promote student awareness that first jobs are just the starting point of a lifelong career management and development process. The transition module is organized around the acronym PERFORM, a mnemonic for seven key elements of this lifelong process:

P = planning your career, a continuous process

E = education; it is not completed at graduation because lifelong learning is required to keep a career on track

R = relationships, which are essential to career development, so it is important to continuously build a network of contacts

FO = future opportunities, which must be monitored proactively so changes in career responsibilities and demand can be anticipated

R = reinvention, necessary for coping with change and developing flexible, transferable skills

M = marketing, important to be able to sell yourself to current and potential employers in order to maintain career mobility (Dupuy, 1996)

Practical experience can be gained through off-campus cooperative education, internships, field experiences, and work-shadowing opportunities that are built into or linked with an on-campus course, thereby providing students with a regular forum for discussing their off-campus learning experiences.

For instance, at Pine Manor College (Chestnut Hill, Massachusetts), internship students also enroll concurrently in a course with other interning students of the same major, during which time they come together to reflect on and discuss their internship or cooperative education experiences (Kutakoff, 1991).

Employment search-and-location strategies can be developed (for example, networking skills). At the University of the Pacific (Stockton, California), all students in the school of engineering are required to take the Professional Practice Seminar during the semester immediately preceding their first term in an off-campus, full-time co-op program. This course is taught by full-time faculty and covers a wide range of topics including résumé development, company profile research, personal job-search skills, and mock-interview exercises (Martin and Rosselli, 1996).

At Queens College (New York City) the basic elements of corporate outplacement career counseling and training services (traditionally designed to assist executives with career transitions) have been adapted and incorporated within an existing senior-level course (Simpson, 1994). Specific employment preparation and self-presentation skills can be learned (for example, résumé writing, interviewing skills, business etiquette).

At Slippery Rock University (Slippery Rock, Pennsylvania), students engage in videotaped "mock interviews" that are each evaluated by outside professionals from whatever career field the student intends to pursue (Walters and Hart, 1991).

Potential "job shock" can be reduced and students can be better prepared to function effectively in the real world of work by having students engage in simulated work situations. In the capstone course for business majors offered at the Mississippi University for Women (Columbus), the class is divided into small groups that simulate management teams of subsidiaries within a corporate conglomerate (W. Smith, 1991).

Mount Saint Mary's College (Emmitsburg, Maryland) offers a senior-seminar capstone course for business majors that simulates a business organization, Excellence Unlimited Incorporated. In this course, students are required to interview at least one practicing senior manager in a corporate organization and then provide their boss (instructor) with a deskside briefing and memorandum concerning their interview findings. The briefing is videotaped for later review by the students, who have been equipped with evaluative criteria for self-assessment. A number of video case studies of real workplace situations are also analyzed by students, and a panel of practicing managers comes to class for a discussion of what is expected of new professionals in the workplace (Beitz, 1993).

At Virginia State University, the Seminar in Marketing, consisting of three major units, is offered for seniors. The first unit of the course, Marketing and the Organization, provides students with a simulated corporate experience by structuring the class as a corporate organization; students then apply and interview for various positions within this organization. The class works with a real client (typically, a local business) to develop and assist in the implementation of a marketing plan.

The second unit of the course, Marketing and the Entrepreneur, requires each student to prepare a comprehensive business plan that is then presented to a panel of faculty and entrepreneurs for evaluation and feedback. The final unit, Marketing and the Self, involves investigation of an area of marketing that the student is interested in pursuing as a possible career. This requires each student to research a company of interest and prepare a letter of application and résumé specifically tailored to that particular company (Stitts, 1994).

At the University of South Carolina, journalism students enroll in the Senior Semester Experience in Journalism program during one of their final two semesters. As a capstone experience designed to prepare them for the real world of work in their chosen profession, seniors take a twelve-hour block of courses, during which time they produce a weekly newspaper. Students who graduate from this program with the intention of pursuing a career in newspaper journalism have a placement rate of almost 100 percent (Campbell and Turk, 1993).

At the University of Cincinnati, seniors majoring in engineering design take a capstone course culminating in creation of a design product (hardware, software, or both) that attempts to solve a real-world engineering problem. The course spans three terms. In the first term, students shape the design proposal; during the second term, the focus is research and design, resulting in a written design report; and the third term focuses on fabrication, testing, and debugging, eventuating in a formal presentation at a "product expo" attended by students, faculty, and members of the industry. The content of this presentation is eventually catalogued in the college library (Kreppel and Arthur, 1994).

Students can be familiarized with corporate life and culture by exposing them to practicing or retired business professionals who may serve as role models or career mentors for senior students. At the University of Minnesota-Duluth, each business student works with a retired executive on special projects (Falk, 1991). At the University of Idaho, The World of Corporate Business is offered as an elective course for students in all majors; it features guest presentations by fifteen to twenty corporate executives from leading firms in the Pacific Northwest (for example, Boeing, Hewlett-Packard, and Albertson's). Senior executives and CEOs selected from corporations with exemplary records on social issues discuss topics relating to management ethics and corporate social responsibility; students also have the opportunity to visit with these executives at luncheons and dinners. In addition to interacting with students, the visiting executives meet with interested faculty—who have found the meetings useful for keeping abreast of current business developments—and with administrators who use meeting time to apprise corporate leaders of current campus developments (Toomey, 1993).

Goal Eight: Enhancing Preparation for Postgraduate Education

Institutional practices that illustrate pursuit of this goal include the SYE program at American University (Washington, D.C.), where seniors in the School of International Service are linked with a beginning graduate student in the same school who has just gone through the process of applying to graduate school and gaining acceptance (Levinson and Skillings, 1993).

At Cazenovia College (Cazenovia, New York), the senior year experience embraces a two-semester sequence, the first of which offers the Senior Project class. The projects developed by students in this class lead directly to the Senior Seminar course, which is taken the following term. The latter class provides an opportunity for students to present their research in a setting that simulates a professional conference, but which is organized, promoted, and conducted entirely by the students (Buffalo, McLaughlin, Majorey, and Olin-Ammentorp, 1993).

At the University of California-Irvine, the Pregraduate Mentorship Program has been developed as a strategy for increasing the number of minority and women students in graduate school who may eventually become college faculty. The program provides students with stipends ($1,000–$3,000) for participating in faculty-sponsored research projects during the summer preceding their senior year and throughout their senior year. The research projects culminate with the Student Research Conference, at which time the seniors present their research to an audience of peers, faculty, and other members of the university community.

An additional element of the program is an elective two-unit course on contemporary postgraduate education in the United States, including such topics as GRE history and test-taking strategies, the graduate-school application process, and the graduate student experience. As a final component of the course, seniors complete a graduate school application and an accompanying statement of purpose (Martinez, 1993).

Goal Nine: Promoting Practical Life Planning and Decision Making

This broad-based goal of the SYE movement incorporates several specifically focused objectives and practices.

Financial planning can be encouraged (renting an apartment versus purchasing a home, budgeting, purchasing insurance, making savings and investments, effectively using credit, and developing a comprehensive financial plan). Assumption College (Worcester, Massachusetts) provides its seniors with *The Last Six Weeks Survival Handbook,* which is designed to provide students with practical suggestions for independent living after college (McCoy and Barnard, 1990).

Planning can be stimulated for active citizenship and community involvement (voting, governance, volunteerism). At American University, the Senior International Experience attempts to institutionalize students' commitment to service, through either part-time volunteer activities or full-time service (for example, the Peace Corps). This experience is designed to parallel the university's Freshman International Experience, which introduces beginning college students to volunteer opportunities relating to the study of international affairs (Levinson and Skillings, 1993).

Planning for lifelong learning (for example, developing strategies for continuing educational, personal, and professional development) can be encouraged. At Indiana University-South Bend, all seniors in the general studies degree program take a capstone course by the end of which they construct a written assessment of their academic work at the university and a future plan for lifelong learning that includes planning for career development, graduate study, and personal enrichment (Hengesbach, 1996).

Opportunities can be provided for "reality-testing" before leaving college by exposing students to realistic postcollege life experiences (for example, in-class simulations and role playing of soon to-be-encountered life situations). The Career Center of the University of Mississippi uses alumni programs to orient students to life after graduation. Seniors hear firsthand accounts of the postcollegiate experiences of alumni and acquire experience-driven advice about how to develop postcollege "life skills" (Busby and Nichols, 1996).

Goal Ten: Encouraging Sense of Unity and Community as Future Alumni

One institutional practice that illustrates pursuit of this SYE goal is a program initiated in 1994 at the Johns Hopkins University (Baltimore) and called Disorientation. It includes a collection of senior seminars complemented by a year-round series of social events (luncheons, dinners, "pub nights"), held on campus and off, designed to provide settings for seniors to meet and reunite with classmates, faculty administrators, and alumni (Boswell, Fraites, and Poonawala, 1995).

HOW THE SENIOR YEAR EXPERIENCE
BENEFITS THE INSTITUTION

As the ten foregoing goals and related practices strongly suggest, the SYE is a student-centered movement, the purpose of which is to support students in transition from college to postcollege life. However, graduating students may not be the sole beneficiaries of vigorous, comprehensive SYE programming. Such programming also has great potential for benefiting the institution itself. There are larger organizational goals and significant contemporary issues facing higher education that may be more effectively addressed by institutions making a strong commitment to the senior year experience.

Improving College-Business Relations

The SYE can stimulate partnerships between members of the college community and corporate employers on the issue of how to better prepare college graduates for work-related roles. A good illustration of such a partnership is at Kennesaw State University (Marietta, Georgia), where members of the management and marketing faculty have teamed with business leaders in both line and staff areas of corporate organizations to research and identify first those behaviors and skills demonstrated by graduates that differentiate effective from less-effective job performance and second how students could be exposed to and practice effective job-performance behavior while still in college (Lasher and Brush, 1990).

These sorts of partnerships serve to foster a more harmonious, collaborative relationship between the college and its corporate neighbors. This is a desirable end in itself, serving to improve college-community ("town-gown") relations, and it also may serve to lay the groundwork needed for securing future fiscal support from the business sector (for example, corporate funding for minority scholarships or paid internships).

The 3M Company (St. Paul, Minnesota) has provided such fiscal support by collaborating with the Minnesota State University system to develop the Minority Exposure to Corporate America (MECA) program. Designed for students of color who have achieved junior status in the state university system, the program has four major components: (1) $1,000 scholarships for MECA students that are awarded to them in both their junior and senior years of college, (2) paid internships at 3M for MECA students during the summer between their junior and senior years, (3) leadership development seminars for MECA students throughout their junior and senior years, which are jointly conducted by university faculty and 3M professionals, and (4) mentoring relationships between MECA students and 3M professionals who share similar cultural backgrounds and career goals (Beagle and Johnson, 1991).

Improving Alumni Relations

The SYE has encouraged alumni to become actively involved with their alma mater as career mentors for college seniors, guest speakers in the senior seminar, and consultants or advisors to faculty on matters concerning the relevance of the college curriculum to postcollege careers.

Departing graduates who have had a meaningful senior year experience may be expected to become more loyal alumni as a result of this positive last impression of their college, one in which the college conveys a final message of caring about what happens to its students after they cease to function as tuition-paying, revenue-generating customers. Such a final measure of support for departing seniors could yield more satisfied alumni who, by word of mouth, may become more effective recruiters for the college and, perhaps, more generous donors to their alma mater.

Empirical support for this contention is provided by preliminary research findings gathered at the University of Maryland, which suggest that increased institutional attention to serving the needs of graduating seniors results in improving their expectations of future success and promotes their ongoing commitment to the college as alumni (Van der Veer, Gast, Schmidt, and Lucas, 1993).

Promoting Faculty Development

The SYE has encouraged faculty to step beyond the boundaries of their circumscribed disciplines to collaborate with faculty from different academic areas (for example, via interdisciplinary team-teaching of the senior seminar) and professionals outside of academe (as in dialogue and cooperative education ventures with business professionals).

Forging Alliances Between Academic and Student Affairs

The senior seminar course has served to reduce the persistent gap between academic and student affairs by promoting communication, cooperation, and synergy among members in these historically separate units of the campus (for example, team-teaching unites college faculty and student development professionals in the areas of career preparation and leadership development, and guest lectures and workshops can be provided by student development professionals in faculty-taught senior seminars).

A good illustration of the partnership potential of SYE programming is the annual three-day career development conference offered by Elon College (Elon

College, North Carolina). Entitled Beyond Elon: Transition Tactics, this senior year transition program involves a working partnership that embraces student development professionals, college faculty, and community members from the local chamber of commerce who come together to jointly plan, organize, and deliver a comprehensive program for college seniors (Thompson, Highsmith, and Brumbaugh, 1993).

Enhancing Institutional Research and Student Assessment

As part of a comprehensive SYE program, student opinion or satisfaction surveys (senior surveys, graduating-student questionnaires) or graduating-student interviews could be administered for purposes of assessing final-year students' retrospective perceptions of the institution's key programs or services, their overall satisfaction with the college experience, and their future educational and professional plans. A profile of student persisters can be compiled from these assessments, which might then be compared with the results of exit interviews or surveys of students who have withdrawn from the college. These comparisons may uncover important differences between the perspectives of students who have completed college and those who have not.

Outcomes assessment also becomes more logistically feasible if it is conducted within the context of a capstone course, because there is a captive audience available for student assessment, thus circumventing the potential hassle and sampling bias associated with soliciting volunteers to come at their own time and expense. For example, King's College (Wilkes-Barre, Pennsylvania) has capitalized on this data-gathering potential of capstone courses by requiring all seniors to complete a faculty-constructed assessment instrument within one of their required major courses. This instrument is designed to assess discipline-specific knowledge and methodology as well as the liberal-learning skills of the graduating class (O'Hara, 1994). Similarly, the University of Nevada-Reno has integrated assessment of general education and assessment of the major within its senior year capstone courses (Nichols, 1994).

Moreover, if equivalent or parallel assessment instruments are used in both the freshman and senior seminars, then the resulting entry and exit data may be used to conduct *value-added* or *talent development* assessment, that is, to assess the degree of positive student change or development from the beginning to the end of the undergraduate experience. The University of North Carolina's leadership program approximates this assessment practice by having seniors reassess their leadership qualities relative to the self-assessments they reported during their freshman year (Johnson and Edgerly, 1993). Similarly, at Indiana University-South Bend, students in the general studies program take a "threshold course" during their freshman year in which they develop a written plan for integrating the university's curriculum and objectives with their personal goals and educational objectives. This same cohort of students takes a capstone course during the senior year, in which the students reflect upon and assess their educational experience at the university relative to the goals they initially articulated in their freshman-year threshold course (Hengesbach, 1996).

Also, as part of the capstone course, a senior thesis, senior project, senior portfolio, or senior self-assessment could be required and used as a source of outcomes assessment. For instance, St. Mary College (Leavenworth, Kansas) requires a final senior product defined as a "culminating performance, exhibit, or portfolio" (Brinkman, 1991). In its outcomes assessment of students majoring in education, Kean College includes three key components: a student portfolio, defined as a collection of documents and records from professional education courses and field experiences within the student's major; a written self-assessment by the student in response to her or his own portfolio; and a graduating-student interview (Prince, 1991).

Slippery Rock University uses off-campus professionals as assessors to evaluate the culminating portfolios of their communication majors (Walters and Hart, 1991). Copies of these final senior products might be saved for institutional research purposes (for example, to compare the quality of products generated by seniors before the introduction of a new institutional program or educational intervention with the products generated by seniors after the program or intervention has been implemented and experienced by its students).

Also, outcomes assessment of *alumni* could be conducted to evaluate graduating students' initial job placements, eventual career positions, and acceptance rates and performance levels at graduate or professional schools. The impact of specific senior year experience programs on these outcomes could be included as part of the institution's alumni assessment efforts. Michigan State University has engaged in such longitudinal research with its alumni and found that seniors who participated in its internship program had significantly higher rates of career placement and satisfaction than students who did not participate in its senior year internship program (Gardner, 1991).

However, it is noteworthy that two types of alumni assessment have received little attention at The Senior Year Experience and Students in Transition national conferences: preparation of seniors for graduate school, and preparation of adult students for reentry into the workforce. The paucity of conference papers pertaining to these types of transitional experiences suggests either they have yet to be carefully assessed or their assessment has remained at the level of local campus-specific institutional research and has not yet been shared systematically at national conferences sponsored by the National Resource Center for The Freshman Year Experience and Students in Transition. In either case, with increasing public demands for institutional accountability and more frequent questioning of the value of a college education, the need to conduct and communicate student outcomes assessment for the full range of postcollege outcomes and for key student subpopulations has become a national issue in higher education. Conducting such assessment as an integral component of a comprehensive senior year experience may represent a viable and timely institutional response to this national issue. (See Chapter Fifteen by Karl and Karen Schilling for additional detailed discussion of the senior year.)

CONCLUSION

The senior year experience has the potential for making significant contributions to four key areas of contemporary concern in American higher education:

1. The curriculum: by bringing needed coherence to both general education and the academic major, and greater connection between the college curriculum and the world of work

2. Student development: by fostering student growth in three areas that have been given relatively short shrift in postsecondary education: character, leadership, and teamwork

3. Campus community: by forging alliances between two key educational forces in the college community (academic affairs and student development) and by promoting partnerships between the college and two key members of its extended community (alumni and the corporate executives who employ its graduates)

4. Institutional accountability and quality: by providing a logistically feasible vehicle and context for outcomes assessment or for the exit component for value-added (talent development) assessment

Institutions may be reluctant to initiate or expand SYE programming, because at first glance it appears to be a high-cost, low-benefit endeavor that involves expenditure of institutional resources on departing students who will no longer be contributing to the institution's revenue base. However, the potential institutional advantages associated with SYE programming suggest that institutional commitment to the senior year experience is more likely to be an act of self-service than of self-sacrifice.

Most important, however, the senior year experience represents the institution's *last chance* to do something positive for its students. Moreover, if the senior year experience is combined with a substantive freshman year experience, the tandem can provide a meaningful introduction and conclusion to college life, serving to anchor the undergraduate experience with symmetrical support at its two most critical transition points, thus ensuring that students get this support both "coming and going."

CHAPTER THREE

Moving On

Seniors as People in Transition

Arthur W. Chickering
Nancy K. Schlossberg

We take the position that a critical purpose of higher education is to help students become effective agents for their own lifelong learning and personal development. The relationships faculty and staff have with students, the questions they raise, the perspectives they share, the resources they suggest, the short-term decisions and long-range plans they help students think through should aim to increase students' capacity to take charge of their own existence. The senior year, when students turn attention toward their futures, is the best opportunity to encourage that sense of agency and to supply experiences, concepts, and perspectives that help them move on energetically and enthusiastically.

When we were beginning work on *Getting the Most out of College* (Chickering and Schlossberg, 1995), which we draw on heavily here, we employed a George Mason University colleague, Susan Bourne, to interview a number of first-, third-, and fourth-year students. We also talked with six students six months after graduation. Their comments highlight many concerns, fears, and joys students experience as they head toward the future.

SIX COLLEGE GRADUATES

We basically asked the graduates how it had gone, and what insights they could offer.

37

Janice

Janice has a boy in middle school and two girls in high school. Her husband is a salesman. They married in their early twenties, and Janice has been a conscientious wife and mother. But then they realized they would need more income to help out with college costs when the kids finished high school. She worked so hard while in college, trying to keep up with classes and still doing most of the work around the house, she never had time to look far beyond it. After graduation she had two wonderful weeks of feeling great—no more piles of homework hanging over her head. After two weeks she began job hunting, but with no clear goal direction. Some places would not interview her until all her references were in; others interviewed her but never called back; and most places wouldn't even see her. She simply could not find a job. She complained, felt sorry for herself, and blamed the school. Eventually, she faced the facts. She realized that to move ahead she would need further training. She has enrolled in graduate classes in education and psychology and taken work as a part-time file clerk. She realizes she'll eventually have to work full-time but feels she needs focus, and with graduate training she will have that.

Abe

At twenty three, Abe was thrilled. If we had interviewed him a week—or even a month—after graduation, he would have seemed depressed and scared. Depressed because there was no structure in his life; he found himself living at home again, reporting his plans for dinner to his parents. Scared because he was worried that he might never find a job and that college education would prove to be a waste of time. However, after four months of intense job hunting, he landed an ideal job in the advertising division of a large company about two hours from home. He had a job with benefits and an apartment he could afford. He was far enough away from home to feel independent but close enough to go home for chicken soup when needed. The outcome was ideal. Wouldn't it be wonderful if we could assure everyone of a happy ending if they would only hang in there for four months?

Susan

Abe's twin sister, Susan, landed a job about a month after college—but she hated it. She felt it was menial, that all she did was sit at a reception desk and answer the phone. She had been a leader in college and expected that her first job would continue to build on what she had learned in college. She was unprepared for the realities of first jobs.

Lee

Lee, in contrast, enjoyed a month of getting himself together after graduation. Unable to find a responsible job, he volunteered at a hospital in which he eventually wanted to become a doctor. His plan to work as a volunteer while looking for a "real" job was short-circuited when the volunteer job turned into a paid job. Delighted and proud, Lee used this time to take the premedical course. After two months, he realized medicine was not for him. He now knows that he must face decisions about what to do with his future. Should he go to graduate school? Should he look for a job with benefits such as health coverage?

Sunil

Sunil graduated, moved home to live with his affluent parents, and worked out at the health club. His parents did not pressure him to move on, get a job, or begin to take responsibility for himself. However, Sunil was embarrassed whenever his friends asked what he was doing. As they began finding their niches, he became conscious that his behavior was inappropriate. He took a job at the health club where he worked out.

Nick

Nick knows exactly where he is going: to medical school. He has planned this for years. He is right on track.

Helping students move on after we have helped them move in and through college effectively can be one of our most satisfying yet challenging experiences. When students have defined a major that has worked for them, learned how to learn from both academic and extra-academic experiences, and developed a rich set of diverse and mature relationships, they are well positioned for work, further education, moving toward marriage, and starting a family. When adult learners have discovered a strengthened sense of competence, clarified their purpose or solidified an ongoing career commitment, and worked through new family roles and enriched perspectives with spouse and children, they are ready to put their newly developed competence and sophistication to work in a larger, more challenging life space.

Three sets of issues confront students facing such transitions:

1. Making a career connection
2. Clarifying their newer identity as it relates to vocation, avocation, and lifestyle
3. Developing a life-span perspective

MAKING A CAREER CONNECTION

Various studies concerning the work experiences of university graduates have found that:

- College and university experiences have not prepared students for the realities of the work world.

- The initial period after leaving college is often one of euphoria, what has been labeled the *vacation period.*

- The next phase is the *downward trend,* which produces feelings of discouragement.

Of course many students know exactly where they are going, but often it is a time of ambiguity. Perhaps this is the place for us to share the experience of chapter author Nancy Schlossberg after she graduated from Barnard many years ago.

Nancy's role model was the president of Barnard, who was married and the mother of five, a woman who could do it all easily. Nancy had the idea that women could do it all, and furthermore that graduating from Barnard was a ticket to success. Wrong! She pounded the pavements for four months and only then landed a job as a salesperson in a bookstore. It was December. She was stationed by the door. She was very cold and mentioned to her supervisor that perhaps the store should invest in a storm door. He smirked, "Well, you'd better dress more warmly." She did just that, wearing ski clothes to work the next day. She was fired.

Nancy's next job was an even worse fit for her. She became a file clerk in a huge company, and the job lasted ten days.

She remembers walking up and down the streets of New York wondering if, when, and how she would ever fit into the world of work. She might have realized that:

- Transitions can be difficult.

- When you are leaving a secure place and moving into an uncertain world, things can feel very unsettled.

- How you feel today is not how you will feel forever.

- You have potential resources to deal with transitions.

Many students find it difficult to leave the structured world of school and move into a world with no organized plan, no admissions directors, no counselors, no student development educators. As one student told us, "I am trying to decide whether I will live at home and get a job, or whether I will move out of the house for good and then get a job. It sure would be nice to graduate from college and have a serious relationship and not have to worry about going out and trying to find somebody out there." Another student said she was sad and scared about "leaving behind the involvement with the university, the organizations, the faculty." Another said, "I'll be leaving behind all the people who gave me support—the entire university, my friends, my fraternity." And yet another senior reports, "I feel like I am leaving behind a safe haven to continue to experiment and grow. Once I get out, there will be a smaller margin of error."

College is promoted as the route to success. Clearly, college graduates do much better in the world of work than those who do not go to college. But most college graduates are not helped to set *realistic expectations* about the next steps. Yet realistic expectations are essential for this next phase of life.

Realistic expectations include knowing that life is full of *discontinuities.* Mary Catherine Bateson, in *Composing a Life* (1989), described the discontinuities in the lives of five adult women. This view of adult development contrasts with the popular model of the successful life: an early commitment that launches one on a single rising trajectory. She points out that a recurring issue for adults is the need to leave a structured, safe environment for the unknown. In fact, every time one makes a change, that is what happens.

Realistic expectations also include realizing that there might be a temporary period of *downward mobility.* Many young college students, especially those who have assumed leadership roles, have had access to power. If they want to become powerful, by and large they can, by participating in student activities and student government. Once into the "real world," that is no longer true. They start at the bottom again. The lack of congruence between what they had and what they expected can be discouraging. It feels like downward mobility; they have fewer resources, less access, less power.

One senior says that she feels bad, in fact distressed, that she does not know exactly what she is going to do once she graduates. She is afraid about the immediate future—getting the next job and a career direction. This sentiment is echoed by others. As one young man said, "I'm sure on my abstract goals. I want to get a job that I feel comfortable with. But I'm mixed up about what that's actually going to be. I'll probably be waiting tables after college because I am so unsure of my career direction."

The job search is a search to connect with, or change your relation to, the world of work. Realizing that it takes time to find the right spot for yourself— that there are periods of downward mobility and discontinuities—helps ease this period between the relatively secure world of college and the ambiguous world of work.

CLARIFYING THE NEW IDENTITY

Daniel Levinson's book *The Seasons of a Man's Life* (1978) describes the early adult transition for men. This process of entering adulthood takes many years. It is the time when the young man is "creating a basis for adult life without being fully within it. . . . His tasks are now to explore the possibilities of this world, to test some initial choices, and to build a first, provisional life structure." Levinson continues: "The primary, overriding task . . . is to make a place for oneself in the adult world and to create a life structure that will be viable" (pp. 71–72).

There are two main tasks in this period.

One deals with separating from the family of origin. This requires more independence, more autonomy. If, because of special circumstances, the young person still lives at home, according to Levinson he (or she) can work on separating and differentiating from parents and siblings. Of course separation from parents is a lifelong process. To summarize: "During the Early Adult Transition, he has to separate from the family in a new way. He must remove the family from the center of his life and begin a process of change that will lead to a new home base for living as a young adult in an adult world" (p. 75).

Several students specifically mentioned the psychological and financial separation from family. Arthur said, "I will be moving. I don't know where. Hopefully, I will be moving to what I consider home. I know I have to establish a life without my parents. I have always lived with them. I will be leaving my family, in a way. I will be establishing new work. I am excited about proving to myself that I can survive on my own. I have always been protected by my parents. It is time to prove to myself that I can do everything that I have done before and take on additional roles." Another senior said, "With leaving, I will be taking on more responsibility for being independent. I will be leaving the life of being dependent on parents."

The second task, according to Levinson, is to get grounded occupationally and develop a permanent relationship. This task has two contradictory parts to it: continual exploring of new possibilities while trying to make more permanent commitments (p. 29).

This contradiction was reflected in interviewees' following comments dealing with fear of the unknown future and the desire to have closure and at the same time being afraid to close options prematurely. One senior said:

> I am looking at joining the Peace Corps. It is a different learning experience than college, and I can still go off from it and get a job. I want to keep open different options and opportunities. Maybe later I will go to graduate school. Now I can go off and explore the world. But maybe I'm wrong. I read marketplace surveys which predict that if you don't get involved or get a job immediately or have something that is directed towards your education, they will start questioning whether you are ready to deal with life. I am ready to deal with life. But the marketplace won't comprehend that I want to delay committing to a career. I want to spend this period discovering the world.

Maggie, a senior, said she felt no pressure to make either a career or relationship commitment:

> I am still thinking about do I want to teach or do I want to work in an office or whatever. I feel I can still explore different options. I am excited about going into the world on my own, living without Mom. Now I won't have to go back home on breaks. My only fear is not getting a job or not making it. I want to be happy

and successful. Coming to college was the hardest thing I ever had to do. Now I am ready to leave. I only wish my advisers had given me more insight into different jobs.

Another young woman told us: "My roommate wants to travel. Her boyfriend, probably her fiancé by Christmas, hates traveling. He despises going any place more than an hour from his home. I wonder why she is limiting herself. She has the rest of her life to be married. But she does not see that. She will marry him and maybe in fifteen years regret it. It is going to be hard for me to tell my roommate I'm so happy for her when she gets engaged. In a way I am happy for her, but I'm scared she is limiting herself too early."

Arthur talked about this also. When asked what he feared about leaving college, he answered, "Not finding a job. Maybe I should go to graduate school, but I want to keep my alternatives open."

His World, Her World

Despite the fact that Levinson and his colleagues concentrated on men, his description of the tasks of this period apply also to women. Both women and men are concerned about their emerging identities, how to build a life that enables them to work at the level they want and in an area that interests them, and how to establish a meaningful relationship.

However, it is important to point out that though women and men are dealing with the two issues Levinson identified—separating from the family of origin and fashioning a life structure—they go about it in different ways.

Dreams influence the unfolding of one's life structure. Many men's dreams are primarily vocational; they see their wives or partners as helpmates. In contrast, many women have *split dreams* that include career and relationships. These dreams play out differently.

In a longitudinal study of thirty-four women, Josselson (1987) concluded that the different pathways women follow in identity development tell more about women than looking at their roles does. In other words, what is relevant is not whether a woman is a mother, a worker, a single parent, or childless, but rather how the woman separates from family and anchors or commits to the adult world. Although there is no pure type, Josselson identifies four general categories of women:

1. *Foreclosures* are those women who stick with their family's expectations. These women often adopt their parents' standards and follow their career directions.

2. *Identity achievers* are those who have tested new waters, are forging their own identities, and keep focusing on the future. These women are more concerned with their own view of themselves than are the foreclosures, who are more concerned with their parents' expectations.

3. *Moratoriums* are those who struggle to make commitments but have not found the right niche. Although open to choice, they fear too many options. They are struggling to find their own identities.

4. *Identity diffusers* are those who are drifting and avoiding an identity. This group has the most difficulty forming stable relationships. They are the most troubled.

Although Josselson was writing about and for women, we think these categories are applicable to men also. Everyone is struggling with identity issues. Some stick close to home; others go in new directions. There are many ways to live out a life. We recall a young man who wanted to write, who wanted to create. When he graduated from college, he resisted pressure to enter the family insurance business. In fact, he broke with his parents and went to work for an advertising company as a copywriter. Then he met a young woman with aspirations for money and community status. She pushed him to return to his family, so he entered the business and became very successful. In his fifties, he began volunteering with a local community theater group, never giving up his role as president of the insurance company. By the time he reached sixty, he had built the community theater into a major force in the city, was president of that board, and was still in the insurance company.

Another young man who wanted to be a writer turned out differently. He married a woman who encouraged him in that direction. His wife went to work and earned the money; he wrote. At age forty he is now witnessing the production of two of his plays.

Many women have ideas and dreams of what they want and are either subverted or encouraged by their partners. Choice of a partner influences the direction identity—and the dream—takes. Though this is changing somewhat, women's dreams have generally been subsumed, taking second place to men's dreams.

Carolyn Heilbrun (who also writes as Amanda Cross), points out in *Writing a Woman's Life* that to be a woman in previous generations was to put a man at the center of one's life. "If he notices me, if I marry him, if I get into college, if I get this work accepted, if I get that job, then I will know who I am. There always seems to loom the possibility of something being over, settled, sweeping clear the way for contentment. This is the delusion of a passive life" (1988, p. 130). Although this book was written for and about women, the need to define oneself by a relationship or by a job, the need for closure, applies to both genders among those we interviewed. This need can lead to the panic some feel when they leave a structured environment.

In a recent speech to graduating senior women at Scripps College, Naomi Wolf, author of *The Beauty Myth*, provided a survival kit for women:

- Refuse to have your scholarship and gender pitted against each other.
- Don't be afraid to ask for money for your work.
- Never cook for or sleep with anyone who routinely puts you down.
- Become goddesses of disobedience. . . . Young women tell . . . of injustices, from campus rape to classroom sexism. But at the thought of confrontation, they freeze into niceness. . . . And at last you'll know . . . that only one thing is more frightening than speaking your truth. And that is not speaking [Wolf, 1992, p. 19].

We think men and women both need the same advice. It is important to know yourself, your partner, your boss; speak the truth and not be put down; be intentional about your futures by articulating your dreams; and be aware of how your dreams might subvert someone else's.

Any orientation toward the future always involves a number of interacting questions. How important are the expectations others hold for us: parents, partner, spouse, children? How much risk are we willing to take? Do we need some time out? How solid or open is our own identity?

Developing a Life-Span Perspective

Life and learning do not stop with graduation. We don't get grown up once and for all, at any particular point in time. If we become static, in some ways we die. Career success and a good life depend on continuous learning and self-development. Going to college, taking courses, investing in other activities and organizations, getting a job, establishing new relationships, building relationships with faculty, coping with a frustrating institutional bureaucracy—all these stimulate significant learning. Such experiences, positive and negative, are what keep us alive and growing. Leading a rich, full life often depends on our capacity to put ourselves in new, challenging situations and then to learn from them.

For students to stay in charge of their own learning and development and to keep their own development under way, two things are helpful. First, it is useful to have some perspective on what lies ahead, what some have called the *adult life span*. Second, it is useful to be clear about the knowledge, competence, and personal characteristics you are taking with you. We asked senior students what they were taking with them from their college experiences. Their responses covered a wide range of knowledge, abilities, and personal characteristics. An extended look at what one student, Robin, had to say is illuminating.

ROBIN: What I've gained is a better understanding of how the system works, how politics goes, how the world is interdependent. Much of what I learned has come from outside the classroom. I have learned a lot of business information. I have learned how to write contracts that protect the contractor and contractee. I have probably learned more about computers than I ever care to know because I had to work with them. A lot of the stuff I am taking with me is practical that will help me support myself while I am waiting for a real job.

INTERVIEWER: What are some things you have learned that are most important for your future?

ROBIN: Time management is a big one. How I can fit all the things that I do into my life? So I am taking away knowing how to manage myself— through time, through business, through personal relationships. I am taking away a great knowledge of how the world runs through governments, because that is what I have studied. I am taking away a greater knowledge of business systems because that is what I have worked in. I am also taking ideas of the way organizations work. I will be able to apply those things no matter where I go.

INTERVIEWER: What have you learned about transitions?

ROBIN: Never be afraid of change. Change can be bad. There is no doubt that change can be bad, but it doesn't mean you have to be afraid of it. A transition is merely a challenge. It is very important to go in with the attitude that I can handle this. It is not going to take me over. It is not going to stop me. I am going to conquer whatever is out there. I think [my father's being in] the Army had a lot to do with that. I had to move. I had to meet new people. At one point in time, I was a shy person that hid behind my mother's skirts. In Germany, because of transitions, every summer I would have friends come and go. I learned not to be afraid of it and not to worry about it. It was something I could deal with.

INTERVIEWER: How do you deal with stress?

ROBIN: When I am upset I just send the world away, close myself in my room, and close myself within myself. I go inward. I figure out what I have to do to achieve what I am going into. I refuse to let it get the best of me. I stay on top of it. There will be times when a transition is given to me and I have to work through it. I understand that and it doesn't bother me. Somebody else can tell me where to move and when to move, but I am in charge of that transition.

INTERVIEWER: What have you learned about taking charge of your own learning and future?

ROBIN: I didn't take charge of my own learning until I had to complete the general education requirements. I learned to develop my own agenda, my own program. I was not only an international studies major, but I was the first to have a minor in history and in European studies. I believe you cannot be a diplomat without knowing the history, and

Europe is my area of study. There is a lot I developed on my own just because I needed to.

INTERVIEWER: What have you learned about your approach to learning?

ROBIN: I had to learn how to study. I went through high school with a 4.0 average. I didn't have to study. It was a breeze. I got to the university and there was no structure. No one checked my homework. No one took attendance to make sure I was in class. No one told me I had to do something. There were no quizzes on the readings. I did not work well with this lack of structure. It took my first year and a half to learn to deal with it. But I just had to teach myself to manage my time. I had to teach myself how to study. I had to teach myself how to learn in a different environment.

INTERVIEWER: What have you learned about relationships?

ROBIN: I learned not to compromise myself. I have done that before and [it] ended up hurting me. I learned that no one out there is more important than my own feelings. That may be selfish, but that is the truth to me. But I learned to compromise, also. I learned how to come out of a fight and still turn around and say, "I'm sorry." I learned how to have fun with a large group of people. I had groups of friends before but I always felt on the outside, on the fringes. I learned how to manage a relationship that is real personal and a relationship which is profes-sional. I learned to separate the two, which I never had to do before. You can have one person you work with in a professional way and in a personal way, and separate the two without compromising yourself or your ideals, without conflict of interest entering into the relationship. I learned to deal with many aspects of one relationship.

It sounds as though Robin has achieved significant learning and personal development during her college years. She now has some practical skills that can help her get immediate employment as she pursues her long-range career plans. She has broad-based knowledge about political systems, historical per-spectives, and Europe that is pertinent to those plans. She has developed more sophisticated understandings about how organizations and businesses work that will serve her well across a wide range of possibilities. She has developed strong self-discipline, the ability to manage her time and herself, and to get where she wants to go. She has a sense of competence that lets her welcome change and tackle transitions, confident that she can handle them in ways consistent with her own purposes and needs. She developed her own program consistent with her particular needs for learning and personal development, and she knows how to take charge of her own learning. She has become sophisticated concerning per-sonal and professional relationships. She can handle relationships and maintain her own identity and integrity. She respects individual differences; she appreciates encountering and learning from persons different from herself. Robin has made good progress in several key developmental areas and has a good sense of how to tackle her future.

The Adult Life Span

But one thing Robin has not learned in any systematic way is the adult life span. Neither has Janice and the other adult learners with whom we talked. So on this topic we have no personal voices to share from our interviews, despite the fact that all these persons will face many changes throughout their lives, encountering work, family, and personal situations that call for new learning.

The adult life span is not a new idea. Philosophers, poets, playwrights, and novelists have given us ancient and modern descriptions. In Shakespeare's *As You Like It,* Jacques sets forth seven acts, from "the infant mewling and puking in the nurse's arms," through "the whining schoolboy . . . creeping . . . unwillingly to school," "the lover sighing like a furnace," the soldier "jealous" and quarrelsome, the "capon lin'd" justice, and the aging shrunken person to the final scene of "second childishness, and . . . oblivion." These artistic descriptions singing down through time suggest fundamental chords that underlie the melodies, harmonies, and overtones found by current scholars, whose research findings and theoretical perspectives can help students anticipate some of their future challenges for learning and self-development. With that knowledge they can assess which of those challenges they have already met and dealt with, which may be coming at them soon, and which are still over the horizon.

Levinson describes a general pattern that begins with the transition from adolescence to adulthood, leaving the parents and getting out into the adult world, during the late teens and early twenties. Leaving one's family and establishing a new home base can be a time to discover and stretch one's newfound independence.

When we asked another senior if it would take long to get settled after graduation, he said, "No. I've been fortunate. I prepared myself for that. A lot of people are on campus for four years and after that they're kind of in shell shock. They have to find a place to live. They have to learn to start, you know, buying groceries. I mean just the simplest things. I moved off campus for my senior year. I have a place to live, shop for myself, the whole thing. So for me the biggest change will be the work world, the nine-to-five concept, overtime, and all that sort of stuff." Moving off campus into his own apartment helped this student move one basic step away from family and on his own.

During the mid-twenties—a period of *provisional adulthood*—each of us explores first commitments to work, marriage, family, and other adult responsibilities. Then we face another transition, from the late twenties to the early thirties, when these initial commitments may be reexamined and their meanings questioned. The long-range implications of continuing with our current work, spouse, community, and lifestyle become apparent. At thirty-five, one or more of these may look less challenging or satisfying than it did at twenty-two. We may change one or another: our work, our community, our spouse. Or we may simply flirt with other alternatives and recommit ourselves to the current combination.

The thirties are typically a time when we settle down and focus on achievement and becoming our own person. But as we move into our forties or fifties, time becomes more finite. During these years we may begin taking responsibility for aging parents while responsibilities for children often continue. We become more aware of the likely limits for our career success and achievement. We examine major questions concerning values and priorities for the future. If we don't make a career change now, we continue our current work until we retire. Most persons stick with their general career orientation, but with moderated expectations and drive. A marriage may be temporarily or permanently upset. Friends, relatives, and spouse become increasingly important as we *restabilize* during the late forties and fifties. We begin to give more time to interests and activities that have been set aside as we invested heavily in work. During our fifties, we increasingly invest more time and energy in personal relationships.

Women's situations differ from Levinson's findings for men. For women, the first stage, leaving the family, may be aborted when they leave parental constraints only to enter the family constraints of a husband and children. Similar constraints may work for men, though typically not as powerfully. Leaving parents and college, establishing one's own base, can be a time for experimenting with different jobs, a career, developing individual talents. But independence, experimentation, and self-development are *not* usually very congruent with the expected roles of wives and mothers when they exchange being dependent on parents for being dependent on a husband. Older women, going back to college—or to college for the first time after raising a family—often encounter, a decade or so later, some of the experiences Levinson describes for the men he studied when they were young adults. We suggest that young women need to think through the consequences of first choosing the role of wife and mother and pursuing a career later, or making a career a significant part of their life and their identity immediately as they move on from college.

We need to understand that all these research findings and theories reflect our particular historical period. If current social conditions persist—with dual-career families, with women moving into an increasingly wide range of careers and occupations, and with continued legal and public concern for equal rights for women—a study forty years from now of persons whose lives started during the 1970s will reveal very different patterns. But even though conditions are changing, these findings provide a useful perspective as students think about the mix of family, work, lifestyle, community responsibilities, and avocational interests they want to create during their own adult lives. We know that women who find rewarding work and education, as well as the rewards of sharing child-bearing and homemaking, enrich their own lives as well as their spouses'. They become stronger, more able to make their own decisions and take charge of their own existence.

CONCLUSION

Faculty members, advisers, and student services professionals can be mightily helpful to students of whatever age who are facing the graduation transition. We can be sounding boards for thoughts concerning refashioned identities; we can help persons integrate information from the career planning center, job interviews, and conversations with family, friends, faculty members. We can introduce them to pertinent literature concerning the adult life span, help them identify developmental tasks they have completed and those coming at them, and help them identify further learning that may be required or that they will want to initiate. By so doing, we can help students leave college with optimism, enthusiasm, and the sense of being in charge of their own futures. Not only will we have helped them move into college effectively, we will have helped them move through and then move on with energy and enthusiasm, ready to take charge of their own lifelong learning and self-development.

CHAPTER FOUR

A President's Personal
and Historical Perspective

Arthur Levine

Twenty-seven years ago, I was a college senior. The year was 1970. The economy was strong; few students were worried about getting jobs. (The men were more concerned about the draft.) I was a biology major; I had long planned to become a doctor. During the summer between my junior and senior years, I had decided not to apply to medical school. The biggest issue in the fall was whether to complete a major in biology, which I no longer cared for, or to change to a more truncated program in general science. I worried whether general science would be as good a credential.

One night in February, my friends went to a movie, and I decided I would give up the film and plan the rest of my life. An hour later, the assignment was completed. I was disappointed I'd missed the movie.

I applied to VISTA and the Teacher Corps. I thought I might be a psychobiologist, so I took the GREs. I had already taken the medical boards. Then I decided, no, I would become a lawyer, so I took the law boards. Better yet, I would be a teacher, so I took the National Teachers Exam. No, I would go to graduate school in education, so I took the Miller Analogies Test. No, I would head off to Washington, so I took the civil service executive management test. No, I would go to business school, so I took the management boards.

This chapter is based on a speech I presented at the Second National Conference on The Senior Year Experience, sponsored by the University of South Carolina, San Antonia, March 17, 1991.

I was ETS poster boy for 1971.

Academically, my senior year held little meaning for me despite a multiplicity of interdisciplinary courses, opportunities to create my own major, and the possibility of writing a senior thesis. I was simply completing courses, gathering the final credits with disinterest.

Yet I had a marvelous senior year. I fell in love with a field and found a calling. In the first term, it was entirely cocurricular. I chaired the student educational policy committee. I read everything I could find about higher education. I had never been as intellectually turned on at any point in my college career. During the second term, I took an independent study in the philosophy of education, reading Dewey, Whitehead, Cardinal Newman, Paulo Freire, Paul Goodman, Maria Montessori, and Robert Paul Wolfe. I audited a course on the history of higher education while slogging through my required science courses.

I thought it was all for fun. I didn't know it could be useful. I extended it into a second year—a friend and I trekked across the country studying how the various forms of undergraduate curriculum we had examined in the educational policy committee actually worked.

For most students today, their senior year is like mine was *in some respects*. Formally, it lacks focus. It is merely a time of finishing up; it provides no conclusion to the college education and little preparation for life after college.

But their senior year is different from mine, too. Some students take fewer tests than I did (to the chagrin of the College Board). Most are much more anxious about jobs. They live in a different time, and most never find the direction or excitement I did. Many do not receive hands-on work experience like mine. Most do not have a chance to integrate life inside and outside the classroom.

But this is not the case for all students. Across the country, colleges and universities are increasingly concerned about the senior year. There is a sense on many campuses that the final year of college needs to be different in some fashion, that the time in which students exit college should be as special as the time in which they enter. One of the devices institutions are using to establish that specialness is the capstone experience.

The capstone can be used to mark the final year of college as either a transition or a conclusion. The aim is to give students an experience or exercise which is retrospective—tying the four or more years of college together—or prospective, preparing the student for the next phase of life after undergraduate education. In the main, colleges and universities have used three very different mechanisms for these purposes: a course, a project, or an examination.

None of these approaches is particularly new or innovative. In fact, all of them were employed in the medieval university. For example, a millennium ago, students who entered the University of Paris, at an average age of fifteen or sixteen, undertook a six-year course in which they studied under several scholars, wrote and defended a thesis, became an apprentice teacher, studied with a master, and passed a public examination. In essence, there was a senior project, a senior exam, and a senior master class.

In one form or another, each of these practices migrated to the American college. By 1646, a decade after its founding as the first college in what would become the United States, Harvard required both entrance and graduation examinations. The senior exam asked students to read and translate from Latin editions of the Old and New Testaments. The examination was oral, public, and conducted by outside examiners. It was not a terribly rigorous assignment.

The graduation examination gradually gave way to the in-class test. Yale, for instance, began with a procedure much like Harvard's. In 1762, in the first known student revolt in America, seniors refused to take the graduation exam. By 1804, Yale had moved to daily quizzes. In 1815, there were annual tests. By 1830, this was replaced by biennial exams at the completion of the sophomore and senior years.

It was the University of Michigan, in 1882, that ended common tests for each class and introduced the in-course test at the direction of an instructor. The decision was driven by the increasing specialization of the undergraduate course of study; the rise of electives, which meant students were studying different subjects; the growing gap between external tests and student coursework; and the fact that written exams preserved a public record of student achievement.

Nonetheless, the senior year exam has not disappeared. Seemingly in waves, institutions have regularly reintroduced it. During the 1920s and 1930s, for instance, Swarthmore College created an honors program dependent on external examination prior to graduation, and the University of Chicago tied its degree to passing fourteen examinations. The 1960s brought similar innovations at schools such as Hampshire College, which linked graduation to six exams, and New College, now at the University of South Florida, which required a senior oral exam for its degree.

The story of the senior seminar is not very different. It too can be said to have roots in the earliest colleges, which had a distinct curriculum for each class. By the close of the eighteenth century, this produced a capstone course for seniors, on a topic ranging somewhere between philosophy and religion and typically taught by the college president. Mark Hopkins at Williams offered the most celebrated version of the class to every senior for four decades, inspiring a future U.S. president, James A. Garfield, to say the ideal education was a log with a student at one end and Mark Hopkins on the other. Ultimately, this course was a victim of increasing collegiate specialization and changes in the job of the president that removed him from the classroom. Like the comprehensive exam, the senior seminar has continued to reappear regularly in progressive-era schools such as Reed College, depression-era colleges such as the University of Chicago, and 1960s-era institutions such as Justin Morrill College at Michigan State University.

The history of the senior project is less certain. It was not imported to the colonies by the first colleges, which traced their roots to the English rather than the French universities. The English university, more collegiate in orientation than its continental counterpart, did not require a thesis. A number of institutions take credit for introducing the senior thesis to the United States, but what seems clearest is that it was a product of the German research university, which began to influence American higher education in the 1820s. In 1876, with the founding of the Johns Hopkins University, the United States invented its own prototype of the research university. Hopkins began with a thesis requirement. Over the years, the thesis project has gone through periods of shifting popularity as have the other capstone approaches, serving as a distinctive element in the curricula of a number of institutions, such as Reed, Bard, Bennington, and Bradford colleges.

CURRENT PRACTICE

What follows is a brief look at three important forms of capstone experience.

Senior Seminar

Historically, fewer than one college in twenty offers a senior seminar, though they are being talked about and adopted on a rising number of campuses. Their purposes differ dramatically. For instance, the University of Nevada at Reno has two different seminars, one used as a capstone to general education and the other as a finale to the major. The focus at Mercer University is on ethics. In contrast, Virginia State University offers a final seminar in its marketing concentration that extends the major into the real world via a field experience. The University of Cincinnati takes an opposite approach to the major and attempts to go beyond the traditional engineering practice question to the more fundamental issues of what and why. Marietta College has chosen an entirely different direction. It offers a short seminar to seniors entitled, "Wine, Dine, and How to Act Fine," which teaches eating, business, and international etiquette via lectures, role plays, and practica.

Perhaps the most extensive senior seminar program in recent years was attempted at Bowdoin College in the 1960s and 1970s. It was part of a comprehensive senior program housed in a senior center, a small complex of dormitories with facilities that housed the entire senior class as well as a small number of faculty. The center contained a dining room, guest apartments, recreation rooms, and common rooms. Activities taking place in the senior center included concerts, lectures, classes, and many of the senior seminars.

The seminars, with which professors were encouraged to experiment, all had roughly the same general structure: a few weeks of class meetings at the start of the term, then a lengthy period in which each student worked on a topic-related project, either individually or as part of a group, and then further class meetings, where students discussed their work or the projects. Coordination of seminars was achieved through staff meetings held twice a semester. Seminars were limited to fifteen students and graded honors, pass, or fail. Some twenty to twenty-five seminars were offered each year for the approximately two hundred seniors. Faculty participation was voluntary.

So what can one conclude about senior seminars? Maybe simply that they are more different than alike. They are disciplinary or interdisciplinary or theme based. They involve lectures, discussions, practica, independent study, and every conceivable combination thereof. They are taught by individual faculty, faculty teams, off-campus professionals, students, and anyone else you can imagine. What they share is that when they are good, they are very, very good; when they are bad, they are horrid. In my time, I've seen more of the latter. In the seminars I have studied, students often give them low marks—a poorly understood course dwarfed in a year spent fulfilling remaining requirements. Faculty find the seminars hard to teach, generally requiring teachers to move beyond their specialties and demanding much preparation time. In curricular terms, the seminars are largely unconnected to the rest of the senior year or the prior three years of college. However, when they work, students praise them as exciting and offering new perspectives. Faculty find them invigorating, fun to teach, and a laboratory for trying new ideas. The keys appear to be clarity of purpose, active learning, adequate resources, excellent teachers, and newness. In general, the success of these courses has tended to be short-lived, with the faculty growing tired of them after only a few years.

Comprehensive Examinations

This is the rarest form of capstone experience. In recent years, few institutions have moved in this direction, though King's College is an exception. It introduced something called the senior integrated assessment, requiring students to demonstrate competence in the subject matter and methodology of both general education and the major.

The design of senior exams has varied widely from school to school. For example, at Reed College graduating seniors have been required to take a two-hour oral exam based on their entire college experience but focusing on a senior thesis and their senior year coursework. According to Reed's registrar, no one has failed the exam in years, making it primarily a psychological hurdle.

The University of California, Santa Cruz, also started with a required senior comprehensive administered by the academic departments. In some instances, a thesis was substituted for the exam. The exams were graded honors, pass, or fail; those who failed were required to retake the test. Two failures would keep a student from graduating. Few students did. The format varied by subject; for example, students in the fine arts had to assemble a one-person show, those in the sciences engaged in research activities, and those in literature took a test based on a list of thirty to forty books.

Interviews with individuals involved with senior comprehensives reveal some very real strengths. They force students to integrate knowledge from a number of courses. They build a period of introspection and review into a college education. They provide students with a broad general faculty assessment. They are popular with the faculty at the schools using them. But there are also some considerable negatives associated with the senior comprehensives. Students generally despise them. They raise anxiety levels among students substantially. They tend to be ritualistic because few students fail them. They increase faculty workloads, particularly in departments with large enrollments.

Senior Theses or Projects

In recent years, more than two-fifths of colleges and universities have employed this most common of capstone approaches. At some, such as Princeton, it is required; at others, such as Harvard, it is principally an option for honors students.

At Bradford College, the senior project is intended to be a vehicle for applying the prior three years of study. Students must demonstrate that they are capable of carrying out an independent project: formulating a question, developing a method for answering the question, and finally producing a project to respond to the question. Working with a faculty adviser, students have engaged in projects ranging from producing plays and directing movies to writing theses and composing music. A week in the spring, called Academic Celebration, is reserved for public presentation of the senior projects.

Across the country, California State University-San Marcos has taken a rather different approach to the senior project. The College of Business requires an eight-credit course, two credits in the fall and six in the spring. During the fall students take a class on critical thinking, problem solving, and decision making. The spring course divides students into four-member teams, which either individually or in groups carry out projects in areas such as manufacturing and service industries. The students are required to produce a reading list, write a proposal, develop a final plan, prepare a report, and make a presentation.

According to instructors and participants, as a capstone the senior project has many pluses. It provides students with an opportunity for sustained independent study. It raises self-esteem by giving students a chance to complete a major work of their own (since most projects are successful). It succeeds with students of varying ability levels. It is regarded by employers as excellent practice for jobs. Both faculty and students regard the experience positively.

There are negatives, too. The senior project is faculty intensive. It tends to make undergraduate education more specialized and extends the major. It can be a very routine exercise. It pushes graduate school into the undergraduate years. Students don't fail.

CONCLUSION

So which of these capstone approaches is best? What should colleges and universities do to guide the senior year?

To answer these questions, let's consider who our students are. The majority of college seniors today were born after 1977. They were born after John Kennedy was murdered and Lyndon Johnson's Great Society ended. They were born after Robert Kennedy and Martin Luther King were assassinated, after men landed on the moon, and after the Watergate break-in. They were not yet born when the last U.S. troops left Vietnam or when Jimmy Carter was elected president or when the hostages were taken in Iran. They were one year old when Ronald Reagan was voted the fortieth president, six when Mikhail Gorbachev came to power in the Soviet Union. They were nine when George Bush beat Michael Dukakis for president, and thirteen when Bill Clinton defeated George Bush for the presidency.

In 1993, I surveyed a nationally representative sample of 9,100 college students, conducted focus-group interviews with students on thirty campuses, and surveyed a representative sample of three hundred chief student affairs officers. I asked the students what social or political events most influenced them. They answered: the *Challenger* explosion, the fall of the Soviet empire, the Iraq war, the *Exxon Valdez* disaster, the Rodney King trial, and the AIDS epidemic. The students viewed each of these events as at least partially negative. Even the fall of the Soviet empire was seen ambivalently. Communism had been vanquished, but its decline left a loose nuclear arsenal, a destabilized Russia, and civil wars in Central Europe.

The students felt the United States was troubled. They were critical of America's social institutions. More than three out of four criticized Congress, the media, corporations, and the family. Their harshest criticisms were reserved for government, politics, and politicians. Most believed that people only looked out for themselves.

The students resented the fact that their generation had been handed huge social problems—ranging from the environment and racism to a national debt and a poor trade balance—that were created by previous generations. They felt they did not have the luxury of withdrawing from problems and tending to themselves, as the yuppies did, because the problems were growing worse and were overwhelming them. The students rejected quick fixes and broadscale solutions. They thought government was incapable of solving these problems.

The students are responding to this situation in two very different ways. First, they are deeply concerned about their futures. Will there be good jobs available to them when they graduate? Can they pay back their student loans? Will they be able to afford a home or to have a family? Can they have a good marriage? Many of the students say they have never seen a successful adult romantic relationship. They worry a lot about the possibility of divorce in their own lives.

Second, they are becoming socially engaged. Their focus is local: their community, their neighborhood, their block. Almost two-thirds of college students (64 percent) are now involved in community service. As one young woman at the University of Colorado put it, "I can't do anything about the theft of nuclear-grade weapons materials from Azerbaijan, but I can help clean up the local pond, work at the community homeless shelter, or tutor poor kids in my neighborhood."

Today's seniors also have heroes. In contrast to the students of the late 1970s who said they had no heroes, a majority of current students (55 percent) report having at least one. The most common choices are local and personal—mom, dad, or Jesus Christ—as are the activities in which the students are engaged.

The inescapable conclusion is that this is a generation of seniors torn between doing well and doing good. Three out of four college students say it is essential or very important to be very well off financially. In contrast, five out of eight want a career that will make a meaningful social contribution. These are not wholly compatible goals. At bottom, today's college students are confused about the future. They do not want to be Donald Trump, but the thought of being Mother Teresa is not all that appealing either.

These realities have large implications for the senior year of college:

- *Integration:* pulling together the four years of college
- *Breadth:* taking students beyond the increasing specialization of the major by offering a final general education experience
- *Application:* using student expert knowledge to examine a discrete issue and produce a substantial product
- *Transition:* preparing students to move from college to the world beyond

I suggest that the senior year is too late for real integration, though integration is desperately needed. If a college is committed to this goal, integration has to be built into the curriculum throughout four years. The same is true of general education. It does make good sense to extend it throughout a college career, not to concentrate it entirely at the beginning of that career with a dollop of the same at the end. I confess a prejudice: I believe undergraduate education is already too specialized and students sufficiently career and professionally oriented to warrant a senior experience that emphasizes greater specialization.

Instead, I suggest that campus efforts focusing on the senior experience should emphasize transition to life beyond college. Today's seniors are uninformed or misinformed about careers and career choices. They are longing to make a difference, but uncertain about whether they can or whether it would be worth the risk. The senior experience should seek to respond to these needs.

This might be accomplished principally by means of a senior seminar and a senior project. The seminar could focus on *career* in the broadest sense of the word: work, family, civic involvement, and everyday coping. It would examine each of the components of a career and a full life through readings, field experiences, simulations, and guest speakers. It would consider the choices students need to make and how those decisions might be made.

The accompanying senior project might be somewhat different than the format commonly used by colleges today. The aim should be to give students an experience in applying their education to a real-world problem or, alternatively, to applying their education in an extended field experience or internship. Both would serve in this manner as transitional devices for students.

Colleges could render these initiatives even more effective with supplementary extra- or cocurricular activities. For instance, they might add a senior parents' weekend on careers, career counseling and assessment, career workshops, alumni and senior counseling sessions, volunteer opportunities, and awards for career achievement. This could be a very powerful set of activities.

The senior year has had a mixed record in higher education. But rethinking the senior year to meet the needs of current students could be very useful. When it is more than an additional set of requirements in the final year of college, the senior experience has the potential to assist students in making better life choices and in making the transition to the world beyond college.

CHAPTER FIVE

Are College Seniors Prepared to Work?

Philip D. Gardner

Few noticed the wisps of change blowing through the economy in the early 1970s, but to the careful observer the signs were evident. Experiments were being tried by various companies on team-organized processes, quality circles, and restructuring work assignments. Some succeeded, such as TRW's oil well cable division plant (Boyett and Conn, 1991), and others failed, including People's Express Airline. Each success and failure contributed momentum to the changes in the structure of work, workplace arrangements, and career progression that burst forth at gale force by the late 1980s.

Global competition has been identified as the major impetus for change. Globalism, however, embraces many smaller forces that have converged at the end of this century. Consumer expectations have shifted to customized products, selected on the basis of quality and just-in-time delivery. Production systems are being restructured from linear and plodding assembly lines, based on large economies of scale and requiring low-level skills, to flexible and weblike arrangements that cater to smaller-production specialized systems requiring highly educated workers. This new arrangement was unleashed as businesses realized that technology removed constraints of place and time: capital could be transferred in nanoseconds, workers could be assembled from around the world, and any location could be a potential worksite. A major force behind this new economy was the realization that economic activities were no longer merely driven by the production of products; instead they were engaged in the production, dissemination, and use of knowledge. As the knowledge-based economy has emerged, employers face a major problem: many workers are unprepared to handle the new tasks associated with their work assignments and processes.

Criticism of new-worker preparation was at first targeted toward high school graduates. After a vast number of production jobs suited to people completing high school were eliminated during the early 1980s, high school graduates now enter labor markets with access primarily to minimum-wage employment opportunities. "Good jobs" now require competencies in mathematics, language, computers, and science at levels that exceed many high school students' abilities. College students avoided this first barrage of criticism; but by the end of the 1980s, college advisers and faculty began hearing similar criticisms of their students' skills and workplace competencies from employers.

Much of the criticism has passed through the media in the form of anecdotal comments. Few analytical studies have examined the issue closely. Thus the question remains largely unanswered whether students are prepared for the workplace. This chapter probes the question from two viewpoints: the employer's and the new college graduate's. Exploring evidence from several research efforts, this commentary identifies a consistent theme that transcends both groups. College students show strength in their content or academic skill base but lack competencies to handle successfully the principal complex issues of work: interpersonal communication, teamwork, applied problem solving, time management, setting priorities, and taking initiative.

These competencies are never developed solely in the classroom. The broader experiences that engage students both on and off campus contribute to the growth and maturity of these competencies. Students, however, have few opportunities to reflect on the development of these competencies, which would allow them to connect their student experiences to the world outside the campus. The Senior Year Experience model provides the student with the type of opportunity that stimulates reflection. This chapter concludes with a modular approach that connects the freshman and senior experiences.

THE WORKPLACE: A NEW CONTRACT BETWEEN WORKER AND EMPLOYER

The restructuring of U.S. companies has been ongoing for nearly a decade. Each day seems to bring still more announcements by highly identifiable prominent corporations that to enhance their responsive capabilities they must reduce their workforces and adapt new principles of organization. The new structures have been characterized by Handy as "shamrocks" (organizations of "essential executives and workers supported by outside contractors and part-time help"; 1989,

p. 32) or as enterprise of global webs (Reich, 1991), that is, each is a strategic center connected to a wide array of units that can be combined to address various problems or contribute to production or service. In each case, these new organizational arrangements link smaller units that can respond and adapt to changing consumer expectations and global economic conditions. The signals that stimulate the linkages depend on acquisition, utilization, and expansion of knowledge. As Allan Bird (1994) explains, organizations have become boundaryless: their shapes and structure extend beyond the confined limits of walls, to expand, contract, or rearrange as their environment changes.

These structural changes have direct implications for the human resources employed by organizations. The workplace has also become boundaryless, with elimination of hierarchial positions (many at middle management) and deemphasis of job titles. This dynamic has had and will continue to have profound impacts on careers, which are no longer shaped by organizational hierarchies and bounded by roles, positions, or job titles (Arthur and Rousseau, 1996; Bridges, 1994). As Bird observes, "recent developments in information and telecommunications technology, organizational forms, labor markets, and changing personal values suggest that a view of careers as taking place solely within organizations may no longer be sufficient to encompass the ever increasing work experiences that many people currently encounter" (1994, p. 157). From another perspective, the implicit contract between employee and employer has been rewritten, now emphasizing a package of skills required to manage and enhance knowledge rather than the ability to perform simple repetitive tasks over a long tenure with the organization.

Table 5.1 compares the characteristics for workplaces of the 1980s with those emerging today. Our perception of a linear, hierarchial system of work has been anchored in the belief that an employee enters a company out of high school or college and makes a long-term commitment to that employer, and vice versa. Advancement and status in the organization have been a function of longevity, and values have centered around loyalty, endurance, and the personal relationships among employees. Actual work assignments have been narrowly focused on technical specialties or administrative procedures. Advancement may require a broader range of knowledge, but this expansion of specialties has often occurred within a functional area. Specialties have allowed workers to control selected pieces of information. Because access to information gains power for the holder, information has been guarded and given forth frugally. Evaluative feedback has been infrequent and seldom tied to compensation, which increased annually irrespective of performance. The system has depended on managerial control, which promotes competitiveness among employees at the expense of collaboration with coworkers.

In the new workplace, flexibility and creativity have pushed aside loyalty and endurance in the new workplace. Employers now desire workers who can

Table 5.1. Comparison of Characteristics for the Traditional Workplace and the New Workplace.

Traditional	New
Tenure: long, steady	Tenure: short, not guaranteed
Advancement: a function of loyalty, relationships	Advancement: few opportunities
Technical specialty	Breadth of knowledge with specialty
Control information for power	Enhance flow of information; analyze; conclude; recommend
Feedback: limited	Feedback: constant
Status: based on longevity and relationships	Recognition: based on performance
Compensation: increase annually	Compensation: small base with incentives and pay for knowledge
Managerial control	Peer pressure and employee self-control
	Team membership with individual assignments
	Unemployment: part of process
	Emphasis on flexibility and creativity

Source: Adapted from Reich (1991); Boyett and Conn (1991).

quickly adapt their work schedules and tasks to accommodate new initiatives. They place increasing emphasis on workers who creatively apply current products and services to new opportunities, even if the endeavor involves risk. Workers now regularly handle knowledge by analyzing, drawing conclusions, and presenting recommendations for the purpose of enhancing the flow of information to all organizational members. This requires workers to have a broad knowledge perspective (knowledge of their competitors; knowledge of what consumers are doing; and knowledge of how national, regional, and global events may affect their organization), as well as specific knowledge for task performance. Compensation is largely based on performance incentives and the cost of acquiring new knowledge. Recognition is also earned through performance. Although certain tasks are individually accomplished, much of the work now takes place in a team setting. Teams remove the need for managerial control, replacing it with peer pressure and employee self-control. There are few advancement opportunities; workers even encounter periods of unemployment as they navigate to new positions. For some companies, longevity and loyalty remain important assets, but for others, the employment contract between employer and employee is being rewritten—no longer guaranteeing a job but promising challenging positions that provide access to new skills.

These dynamics require employees to have a new mix of skills and competencies. The list is familiar to most readers but is worth repeating. Academic skills that provide this cornerstone include reading comprehension, writing ability (increasingly technical), numerative literacy (mathematics), science (especially applied physics), computer literacy, and domain skills specific to a student's academic major. Balancing these skills are reasoning competencies, which focus on problem solving and critical thinking (most important, learning to learn); interpersonal communication and teamwork skills; and personal skills, including time management, goal setting, commitment to quality, entrepreneurialism (which encompasses creativity and risk taking), flexible attitude, and openness to new ideas and processes.

Bridges (1994) and others argue that of the total jobs available, 75 percent will require general skills and knowledge (a good liberal arts education) and 25 percent will require specific skills and knowledge (technical competencies, programming skills). Yet even highly trained technical employees have to possess a broad set of general knowledge and personal skills to complete their job assignments successfully. The bottom line finds workers in need of a different mix of skills and competencies, in addition to more of them, to remain competitive and employed in the new economy.

EMPLOYERS: "NEW COLLEGE GRADUATES ARE NOT READY TO WORK!"

Corporate views on workplace competencies of college students have been captured in various ways. A rich textual picture of employer perceptions of the new economy's impact on entering professionals has been drawn through detailed focus-group discussions conducted by the nonprofit RAND research institute for the College Placement Council Foundation (Bikson and Law, 1994). Corporate representatives from senior management, human resources (personnel), and line management as well as newly hired professionals reflected on the various skills and experiences that contribute to successful work performance (measured on a 5-point Likert scale). Ten clusters of skills or factors that were attributed to performance were rated. Domain knowledge (knowledge in academic major) turned out to be only moderately important in comparison to more general cognitive, personal, and people-related skills and traits (Table 5.2).

An interesting dimension of this study was the elicitation of views from a group of academic representatives (senior institutional administrators, academic faculty, and career services staff). What is striking, as Bikson and Law pointed out, is the similarity and consensus in the ratings, although academic participants tended to rate these clusters higher than corporate participants, par-

Table 5.2. Skills and Other Factors Contributing to Successful Work Performance: RAND Study.

Skills/Other Factors	Corporate Respondents (mean)	Academic Respondents (mean)
General cognitive skills	4.7	4.8
Social skills	4.7	4.7
Personal traits	4.3	4.3
On-the-job training	4.1	4.2
Knowledge in academic major	3.9	4.1
Prior work experience	3.6	4.0
Firm's recruiting practices	3.7	3.6
Cross-cultural experience	3.2	3.8
Foreign language competency	3.0	3.9
Attributes of educational institution	3.2	3.7

Note: Scale: 1 ("not very important") to 5 ("very important").

Source: Adapted from Bikson and Law, 1994, p. 10. Used by permission.

ticularly in areas closely associated with their institutional mission: domain knowledge (academic), cross-cultural experiences (study abroad programs), and foreign language training.

Domain knowledge—knowledge attributed to the academic major—stands as the doorkeeper, however. To get through the employment door requires strong domain skills (often assumed to correlate with grade-point average); yet job success is predicated upon a combination of social, personal, and applied cognitive skills (Kelley and Caplan, 1993). Employers identified specific competencies that included teamwork, effective written and oral expression, interpersonal communication, flexibility, an understanding of quality, and producing innovative (entrepreneurial) practices. Employers acknowledged that these competencies were a consequence of the changing demands in the workplace and realized that they were more behavioral than knowledge based. Nevertheless, the concern expressed by many employers was that students arrived at their organizations unprepared in these areas.

More familiar to the public, because of their media appeal, are snapshot surveys of employers, which direct respondents down a checklist of possible skills, rating each item. Scales can be anchored by terms such as *level of importance* or *adequacy of training. Recruiting Trends,* an annual survey of employers by Michigan State University's Career Services and Placement (Scheetz, 1993), serves as an example. In the 1993–94 edition, employers were asked to rate the importance of sixty-five different characteristics to job performance; this was a departure from similar studies that focus on a more limited list. From this example, personality traits emerged at the top of the list, intermingled with content and knowledge skills. These questions are often followed with queries whether seniors are adequately prepared (Scheetz, 1994). The results generate a list of concerns (much seen in the media), including attitude, work ethic, communication skills, and unrealistic expectations.

The problem with this latter approach is that the categories are often very general. For example, what does communication encompass? Three forms of reading and writing exist (Daggett, 1992): personal response, report or research, and technical. Employers could apply a different definition than the one assumed by educators. Thus it is important to define clearly the skill components being evaluated.

Work done by Elizabeth Jones (1995) serves as an excellent example. Jones discovered that employers and educators differed over components of critical thinking as it applies to college graduates. For example, initially faculty and employers disagreed over detecting indirect persuasion (interpretation skill), detecting and analyzing arguments (analysis skill), and reflection (presenting argument skill) while agreeing on the importance of other critical thinking skills (evaluation and inference, as examples). The two parties were able to reach consensus on several of these skills after repeated discussions. The value of Jones's contribution was the understanding that critical thinking takes place in context. The academic environment differs contextually from the environment of work; how one adjusts critical thinking skills to accommodate to a new environment becomes a key attribute of a newly hired college-educated worker.

Very few studies, however, track new graduates into the workplace, measuring the performance standards required for a given competency against the workers' educational preparation. A thorough study of high school graduates by Daggett (1992) illustrates how important context can be. Breaking each of the skill areas into its basic components, Daggett observed new hires working in various positions and was able to identify the skills actually being used and how prepared the individuals were. Through this method, his research team identified, for example, that technical reading and writing were the communication skills lacking among new high school workers. At the same time, educators were responding to the demand for better performance by increasing personal response and research or report reading and writing.

Modifying Daggett's approach, the Collegiate Employment Research Institute developed a performance and preparedness inventory of key competency areas for college students. The major competencies expected of college graduates were broken into specific subskills. Each subskill was rated twice. The first rating asked for the performance level required of that skill in a typical entry-level position. A 6-point scale was adapted from Bloom's Taxonomy (1956) that organizes learning into how it is utilized, from awareness (lowest level) to evaluation (highest level). At the middle region of the scale, between application (3) and analysis (4), were the performance levels new graduates would be expected to meet upon entry into their job.

A 5-point Likert scale was used to capture the employers' perceptions on the educational preparedness of college students, from 1 ("not at all prepared") to 5 ("superbly prepared"). Employers were further asked to distinguish between technical employees (for example, engineers, computer scientists, and accountants) and nontechnical employees (generally students from the liberal arts disciplines and general business).

A pretest of the instrument with ninety-four employers revealed that a reasonably high level of performance, approximately 4, was expected in each skill area. Differences existed between technical and nontechnical positions on skill levels in some areas (Table 5.3). Technical positions placed more emphasis on domain skills—primarily mathematics, technical reading, managing data systems (information systems)—and thinking skills (problem solving, reasoning). Receiving more emphasis on the nontechnical side were organizational skills (interpersonal, conflict handling, cooperative working), thinking skills, job skills (coping with deadlines, setting priorities, following directions), and speaking and listening skills.

Ratings on preparedness clustered around the midpoint of 3, "adequately prepared" (Table 5.4). Technical graduates were likely to be "highly prepared" in mathematics and information systems; their lowest preparation was found in the area of writing. Nontechnical graduate scores were fairly consistent, being better prepared in reading, speaking, and listening and in information systems more than in mathematics and writing.

Standard Z scores were tabulated to permit the two scales to be compared. Comparisons between performance and preparedness could indicate whether graduates were underprepared (overprepared was possible, but not found) for the performance levels required. While students seemed to be well prepared in the domain skills, they fell short in areas related to the context of work and applying their knowledge in work environments. An exception found technical graduates underprepared in several key domain areas of reading and writing. This list contains those individual competencies where significant differences between performance required and level of preparedness appeared.

Through these employers' eyes, a fairly consistent picture emerged on college students' preparedness for work. Students were perceived as well prepared in their academic or content areas. The exception appeared among technical graduates, whose reading and selected writing skills needed improvement. The majority of competencies where students failed to be adequately prepared involved skills needed to handle the context of work. These skills are particularly relevant to liberal arts graduates, as these are the very skills employers expect them to bring to the workplace.

Table 5.3. Differences in Skill Levels Expected of Technical and Nontechnical Graduates.

Technical Graduates	
Reading	Differentiating fact from inference
	Summarizing main and subsidiary ideas
	Understanding technical and abstract material
	Locating specific facts and details
Writing	Composing letters, reports, and memoranda
Speaking/listening	Presenting oral information and directions
	Participating in discussions
Thinking skills	Problem solving
	Decision making
	Reasoning
	Creative and critical thinking
Organizational skills	Interpersonal skills
	Handling conflict and criticism
	Leadership skills
	Working as a member of a team
Job skills	Setting priorities
	Coping with deadlines
Personal skills	Workplace values and ethics
	Ability to negotiate the system
	Adaptability
Nontechnical Graduates	
Speaking/listening	Observing verbal and nonverbal cues
Thinking skills	Problem solving
	Decision making
	Reasoning
	Creative and critical thinking
Organizational skills	Handling conflict and criticism
	Interpersonal skills
	Working as a member of a team
	Leadership skills
Job skills	Goal setting
	Setting priorities
	Coping with deadlines
Personal skills	Workplace values and ethics
	Initiative
	Adaptability
	Personal work habits
	Ability to negotiate the system
	Self-esteem

Source: Information prepared by the author from original resources.

Table 5.4. Level of Skills or Competencies Required for Entry-Level College-Educated
Positions and Level of Educational Preparedness (Mean Score).

Major Competency Areas	Technical		Nontechnical	
	Performance	Preparedness	Performance	Preparedness
Reading	4.13	3.26	3.70	3.29
Writing	3.50	2.88	3.43	3.04
Speaking/listening	3.91	2.98	4.01	3.29
Mathematics	4.16	3.72	3.44	3.02
Thinking skills	4.34	3.11	4.25	3.15
Organizational skills	3.95	2.95	4.26	3.23
Information systems	4.33	3.59	3.76	3.28
Job skills	4.06	3.16	4.21	3.12
Personal skills	3.99	3.16	4.08	3.16

Source: Information prepared by the author from original resources.

GRADUATES: "WE ARE EAGER TO WORK BUT FIND THE WORKPLACE CHALLENGING"

To balance the above picture, student experiences during the transition from college have been captured in various studies that have focused on students' socialization into the workplace (Table 5.5). Recent technical graduates (engineers and computer scientists) were asked to identify the skills or competencies that they felt were best prepared by their college education. A subsequent question asked for areas they felt were inadequately prepared (Gardner and Motschenbacher, 1993). Their educational strengths centered around the specific technical skills that pertained to their academic major and the problem-solving processes emphasized by faculty. Because engineering is a demanding field, the students believed that their education instilled discipline and enhanced their work ethic. On the negative side, these graduates identified deficiencies in their oral and written communication skills; their struggle to work in teams, which also involved their inadequate interpersonal skills; and their undeveloped leadership and management skills. Many young engineers were troubled by their inability to apply theoretical engineering knowledge to real work situations.

In a similar population of liberal arts graduates who have been participating in a longitudinal study of their transition experiences, graduates remarked that most employers attributed their success to being able to think independently and creatively and to solve problems effectively. They viewed themselves as possessing strong communication (verbal and writing) and interpersonal skills. They also commented that their general knowledge allowed them to participate

Table 5.5. Self-Evaluation of College Education: Strengths and Weaknesses.

Technical Graduates' Strengths	Technical Graduates' Weaknesses
Problem-solving skills	Oral communication skills
Technical (theoretical) skills	Written communication skills
Computer knowledge	Applying learning to real work situations
Report writing	Interpersonal/teamwork skills
Discipline/work ethic	Leadership/management skills
Liberal Arts Graduates' Strengths	**Liberal Arts Graduates' Weaknesses**
Thinking independently/problem solving	Understanding world of work
Communicating: verbal and written	Applying theory to practice and hands-on experiences
Learning to learn	Specific content knowledge
General knowledge	Understanding of office politics, ethics, and business viewpoint
Interpersonal skills	Computer skills
	Flexibility

Source: Based on Gardner and Motschenbacher (1993); Lunney, Gardner, and Williams (1996).

in a variety of workplace activities. Their employers felt their most appreciated strength was their attitude toward learning—being continuously willing to learn new skills and applications (Lunney, Gardner, and Williams, 1996).

Weaknesses for liberal arts graduates dealt more with the context of work: not knowing enough about the workplace, which resulted in more time required to socialize into the work environment, and learning how to deal with the subtle, implied aspects of the work, such as office politics and ethics. They also realized they needed to be more flexible as job assignments changed frequently in comparison to tasks in their structured academic environment. Like their technical counterparts, they had trouble applying their theoretical knowledge to work situations and wished they had had more hands-on experience before entering the workplace. They felt they lacked the depth of content knowledge in some areas; finance would be an appropriate example. One skill that nontechnical students identified as being particularly deficient was an understanding of computer technology.

An exploratory study into the workplace readiness of college students, currently under way at Michigan State University, looks at student preparation in the noncontent areas that both employers and graduates have identified as problems. Because it was deemed important to place students in context, a simulation that engaged the student in real workplace situations was preferred. Wilson Learning's Success Skills 2000 (Wilson Learning, 1992) met both conditions: a visually driven assessment that covered the competencies involving applied problem solving, interpersonal effectiveness, and accountability. Approximately two thousand students have been tested in this exercise. These preliminary findings point to some specific weaknesses, as well as strengths, that lay the groundwork for helping students in their preparation for transition.

The Wilson assessment is a criterion-referenced tool for which a national norm (50) has been established using a group of 350 recent graduates evaluated as performing above average on a common job-assessment instrument. In addition, the competencies have been weighted, reflecting the emphasis the benchmark employers placed on them. For example, among the eight interpersonal effectiveness competencies, the three teamwork skills have greater weight than the other interpersonal communication skills. Thus the assessment can be termed high stakes in that the expected level of competencies have been set to a high standard.

Table 5.6 presents the overall and class-level mean scores. Students appeared able to adapt their critical-thinking and problem-solving skills from the classroom to the workplace. Students demonstrated that they know how pieces of information are interrelated but did not do as well in accessing the accuracy of their information by using other references, or in evaluating the usefulness of information in the context being applied. They chose the appropriate strategy that achieved the organization's goals, but they often failed to consider all the options, limiting the possible solutions available to them. Comparisons across class levels found little change in mean scores over the four years. Students who demonstrated effectiveness in using these competencies have probably been actively using these skills for a long time.

Students showed less proficiency in their interpersonal effectiveness skills, particularly teamwork-based competencies. Students were frustrated in trying to identify options that reduced conflict among team members and often failed

Table 5.6. Scores on Workplace Readiness Assessment for Undergraduates (Mean).

	All Participants	First Year	Sophomore	Junior	Senior
Total score	25.89	24.30	25.30	28.72	30.92
Applied problem solving	43.24	41.08	42.60	44.42	43.30
Interpersonal effectiveness	32.39	28.56	28.33	31.24	36.18
Accountability	31.50	28.17	29.47	31.54	33.54

Source: Information prepared by the author from original resources.

to work in a manner that contributed to the unity and success of the team. Their strongest communication skills centered on influencing others by communicating in ways that gained acceptance, and on being able to justify their position. Their inability to persuade or convince others to support their position, through a presentation or effective discussion, was evident, particularly among first- and second-year students. When building rapport with others, students were sensitive to other people's feelings, but they did not always act positively with others to ensure that their organization was represented well. These skills improved over their college tenure, as seen by the nearly 10-point difference between seniors and first-year students.

The area in which students showed themselves least prepared for work was their personal accountability or self-management, most noticeably their ability to take initiative in the workplace and management of their work efforts (time management and setting priorities). Taking the initiative was an area that needed improvement, though students demonstrated they could work with little or no guidance and would voluntarily assist their coworkers without being ordered by their supervisors. A major shortcoming found students unable to manage their time so as to handle multiple tasks and meet expected deadlines while successfully avoiding burnout or high levels of stress. Another problem concerned their tendency to be inflexible in modifying their work assignments to complete challenging tasks. Finally, their understanding of what defines quality work and their use of workplace systems to ensure quality needed more development. Accountability scores improved only incrementally over the four years.

THE WORKFORCE READINESS OF COLLEGE STUDENTS

As companies strive to maintain a critical advantage through creative problem solving, rapid introduction of new products, and redesign of product and service processes, their success depends on a commitment to learning (Garvin, 1993). Garvin's definition of a learning organization focuses on contextual experiences: "a learning organization [is an organization] skilled at creating, acquiring, and transferring knowledge, and at modifying its behavior to reflect new knowledge and insights" (p. 80). Five key skills are required of employees in learning organizations: (1) systematic applied problem solving, (2) experimentation and creativity, (3) learning from one's own experiences and organizational and societal history, (4) examination of best practices, and (5) ability to transfer knowledge for understanding throughout the organization. Employees who portray these skills—the *new learning employees*—balance expertise in their content knowledge with strong interpersonal communication, teamwork, and self-accountability skills.

New college workers appear to be better prepared in content- or academic-related work competencies while they show deficiencies in people-related competencies that augment their formal education. In the old, hierarchical economy, where academic skills were the critical (and often sole) employment-selection criteria, young workers had the luxury of extended time in their first position to develop interpersonal, applied-reasoning, and self-management skills. Within the last decade, however, the average tenure in one's first position has decreased by two-thirds, from approximately forty-two months in 1980 to fourteen months in 1990 (Gardner and Motschenbacher, 1993). The complex demands and pace of the new economy require college students to attain a better balance between their academic skills and people-related applied competencies before graduation. This balance, however, eludes many college graduates.

Students demonstrated modest success in applying their learning processes in contextual situations. The failure to engage fully in contextual learning arises from two related barriers to the balancing of skills. Schroeder (1993) has argued in the first case that the majority of today's students possess learning styles that are different from those of the faculty who teach them. Faculty are drawn to the teaching profession because this environment values independent thought, autonomy, and appreciation for abstract concepts (that is, it stresses intuitive learning). Their teaching approach emphasizes theory-to-practice—dealing initially with broad conceptual ideas and worldly issues before focusing on concrete, specific examples. Using the Myers-Briggs type indicators, Schroeder found that only about 40 percent of students were compatible with this style of learning. The majority of students, 60 percent, were concrete learners who expect sequential learning environments that delineate a practical rationale for doing something, accompanied by structured, practical experiences; this combination stresses sensing and kinetic learning. The motives for learning for these two groups are out of sync. The practical students seek information that can be collected for later use in their work or life (practical), while intuitive faculty find pleasure in the stimulation and exchange of ideas and concepts (intrinsic).

From a different perspective, Baxter-Magolda (1992) has posited that students move through four phases of learning: absolute, transitional, independent, and contextual. Absolute learners view their instructors as the sole purveyor of factual information; these learners often dismissing divergent opinions as coming from individuals who are misinformed. Instructors provide information that is assumed to be accurate, with that accuracy being confirmed through feedback on tests. In the transitional phase, learners realize that uncertainty exists; not all information can be acquired or remembered, and this fact requires understanding and application of knowledge. Independent learners accept the fact that learning has multiple sources, including peers and themselves (self-initiated). This stage marks a shift from waiting for information to be given by faculty to exploring for knowledge with faculty serving as mentors and coaches. The final phase, contextual learning, introduces judgment, which recognizes that knowledge interpretation can change with context. The task becomes one of applying knowledge to different situations and reflecting on the consequences of possible solutions.

Normal progression through these stages would be expected or at least assumed to occur between the freshman and senior years. Surprisingly, Baxter-Magolda found in her six-year longitudinal study of college students, most students failed to reach the independent stage by their senior year; only 18 percent did so. Most students transitioned into independent and contextual learning stages only after graduation.

Additional barriers that may present themselves are a function of institutional characteristics such as mission and size. Communication that emphasizes justification and persuasion takes practice within a supportive environment, typically the small class. Large classes seldom provide opportunities to craft writing skills beyond the occasional research paper. Students' interpersonal communication skills may also be reduced to one-on-one experiences, as a result of circulating within a small circle of friends and associates while avoiding situations regularly infused with new individuals.

Teamwork skills are only marginally addressed by the "team projects" that seem to have proliferated in response to the cry for these skills from business. Teamwork requires a contract between members on expectations and performance (goals), agreement on how decisions are made and conflicts resolved (control), and the roles each member has (membership). Instructors give little time in class to maintaining an environment for teams to function. Rather, teams are shuffled together with only the class assignment as a goal. Nothing arouses the ire of students more than random shuffling of a class. Without being able to select their friends, they find their difficulties with the assignment compounded by imposing dialogue with unknown people, which challenges even the best communicators in the class.

Self-management starts with the basics, such as attending class and turning in assignments on time. Faculty believe they are dealing with adults, and the decision to attend class is up to the adult. For some faculty, taking attendance means taking on a parental role. At the same time, faculty can be "softies" on extending deadlines and accepting excuses for missed assignments. Students take these behaviors into the workplace with severe consequences. A recent study of employers by Johnson and Wales University found the leading reasons why employees who are new college graduates are fired included poor attendance, failure to follow instructions, and lack of initiative ("Companies Seek Same Qualities in Job Applicants," 1995). Today's fast-changing economy requires higher standards of self-management; student expectations with regard to their behaviors must be raised. Being held accountable for class attendance and all deadlines is a small start toward better self-management.

Many undergraduates fail to acquire expert practice using their academic knowledge in various contexts. Although internships, service learning, and cooperative education engage some students, faculty often view these as vocational endeavors that should not be a part of the academic experience. Yet all faculty have participated in expert practice while obtaining their advanced degrees. Young doctoral students are given progressively more difficult research assignments until they can demonstrate to the satisfaction of their advisers that they are prepared to undertake a dissertation. Throughout the process, mentors and peers offer assistance and insight; failures and mistakes are viewed as necessary steps to success. Undergraduates, especially the 85 percent who do not immediately pursue graduate school, need similar opportunities to practice their craft. Waiting until after graduation to gain experience places graduates in difficult situations; failures and slow adaptation often lead to termination of employment.

OPPORTUNITIES FOR WORKPLACE READINESS ENHANCEMENT

Schroeder contends that mismatches in learning style contribute to students' inabilities to master critical-thinking skills, as they fail to become engaged in the learning process. The question shifts from viewing students as having "deficiencies" to understanding "natural differences" in how someone learns (Schroeder, 1993, p. 25). It would be futile to change learning styles by making faculty more practical or students more abstract. Bridging these differences involves several activities, according to Schroeder, among them designing learning opportunities that accommodate the spectrum of student learning styles. These opportunities could center on active, applied experiences and projects that stimulate senses, such as case studies and sequential learning assignments. Baxter-Magolda similarly found that as students gained experience through work and practice (for example, community service), they moved quickly toward becoming contextual learners.

Not every class can be restructured to accommodate a variety of learning styles. Students should understand their individual learning styles, as well as the various stages in the learning process. In addition, strategies that allow them to adapt their learning styles to new situations need to be identified or presented to them. Schroeder recognized the need for personalizing the learning experience. Faculty can provide immediate feedback on course content, but only a few opportunities exist that offer students the opportunity to reflect on their total set of collegiate experiences in relation to their postgraduation expectations.

For students to gain relevancy in their academic training and reflection on how their experiences affect their career and life expectations, faculty and student support staff have available other options—none of which are particularly new:

- *Credit classes that emphasize leadership, teamwork, and communication skills.* Seldom are these skills incorporated across the curriculum. Having faculty highlight these skills in their courses removes the category of skill classes as single, one-stop experiences, moving instead to observing the skill being used universally.

- *Expert practice.* Although faculty do not have to be involved in administering experiential programs, they do need to give the programs validity by relating their importance to students. They also have to provide a venue for reflection upon these experiences when students return to campus. Their insights as to how experiential learning meshes with a student's academic training provides useful feedback essential for student development. Faculty also can exert influence by setting rigorous standards and evaluation criteria for internships, as they do for co-ops. An internship that merely allows a student to file papers offers little expert practice and should not be viewed as acceptable.

- *Out-of-class enrichment.* A variety of activities that engage students in skill development can be made available. Student design competition in many engineering programs stimulates teamwork, communication, and responsibility. Another example is seeking community projects either through class or service learning. Both bring students together in new contextual situations.

- *Evaluation experiences.* Workplace readiness assessments, like Wilson Learning's Success Skills 2000, offer feedback to students on their ability to adapt their competencies to new situations. A portfolio is an excellent device to encourage students to reflect on their experiences, skill acquisition, and application of education or academic training to future work and life situations. Institutions could provide each first-year student with a portfolio to be developed during his or her stay at the institution and, it is to be hoped, beyond. A successful portfolio endeavor requires structured opportunities for the student to explore and reflect on personal development.

BRIDGING THE FRESHMAN AND SENIOR YEARS

Across the four years of college, students can prepare for their eventual transition by regularly exploring their activities and behaviors in relation to what they anticipate will engage their life after graduation. Three central areas of development—intellectual, professional, and personal—can be presented in various formats at four key access points: freshman, sophomore, junior, and senior years. The intellectual component would address critical thinking and problem solving; the professional would include interpersonal communication, leadership, teamwork, and ethics; and the personal would encompass time management, self-evaluation, and stress management.

During a freshman year experience course, a learning style inventory could be introduced that provides insights on individual learning styles and on approaches for dealing with other learning styles encountered in the classroom. Students could explore critical thinking in various disciplines. Strategies for organizing team projects, developing leadership, and practicing ethical behavior in the classroom could be introduced. To integrate these experiences and articulate their expectations, a professional portfolio covering major skill and competency areas could be started and utilized over the next four years.

The second module, encompassing the same themes, would occur during the second half of the sophomore year. This module would be organized around a workplace readiness assessment, similar to Wilson Learning's workplace assessment. This engages students in behaviors expected in the workplace. Students become aware of their ability to adjust their skills to different contexts and have the time to practice and develop skills through a variety of experiences during their junior and senior years (experiential learning, out-of-class enrichment).

In the junior year, the focus shifts to making preliminary steps to transition. The same three development areas are emphasized, but the instruction takes place in contexts removed from the classroom. Students visit various workplaces to observe applied critical thinking, teamwork, and project management, for example. By this time, students should have enough on- and off-campus experiences to begin to understand what the transition from college entails, as well as the expectations that society (work and community) holds as they anticipate leaving college.

The senior year course prepares students to actually leave the campus. This course would be merged with or accompany an academic capstone course, integrating the content domain with real-world situations. Attention does need to be paid to life skills, particularly time management, stress, or finances. These topics appear to be critical for many graduates; many reported that they had difficulty budgeting their income. They also need time to prepare mentally to leave their college community. For many students, this mental release can be very difficult, causing them to contrive ways to delay their leaving. Students also need to begin to realize that there will not always be someone available to handle their concerns. Answers come through their own efforts, such as being able to use a telephone book's Yellow Pages or develop a network of friendships and professional support.

CONCLUSION

The materials prepared by Employment Technology Corp. and Wilson Learning that accompany their assessment present an analogy between a bicycle and the means by which the student moves into the workplace and a career. The back wheel represents the student's academic or content skills; being attached to the chain, these skills are critical to getting a career started. The front wheel represents the applied people skills that are necessary to navigate the bike around potential roadblocks and even change direction to a new position (Sefchik, 1995). Most students graduate with a well-developed back wheel; their front wheels, however, are not well formed, causing problems during their early career.

As of this writing, there is no institutional model that utilizes all the proposed modules. The freshman and senior courses, particularly the former, exist on many campuses, with a great variety of content offering. The sophomore and junior experiences, however, are absent on college campuses; the challenge for those faculty and staff committed to students' development and successful transition to a life beyond campus is to design the appropriate programs to achieve this success. The modules that link the freshman, sophomore, junior, and senior experiences lay out a scheme for fruitful discussion on enhancing student readiness and eventual successful transition.

PART TWO

ENHANCING THE
SENIOR YEAR EXPERIENCE

Although the concept of the senior year experience is relatively new to higher education, the practice of providing specific programs and services for seniors is not. Many colleges and universities have long-standing traditions in using senior capstone requirements, special career programs, or graduation celebration activities to mark the close of the undergraduate experience. Many of these programs are highlighted in the chapters of Part Two. What is new, however, and one of the purposes of this part is the emphasis on approaching the senior year from a comprehensive perspective and the need for various campus units to work together to improve the overall quality and nature of the final quarter of the student's baccalaureate educational experience.

The four The Senior Year Experience national conferences and two Students in Transition (including seniors) conferences have brought together educators from differing campuses across the country to share best practices and help create this new movement. Part Two draws on what we have learned from these conferences and other sources about exemplary programs and provides both qualitative and quantitative information on the theme areas associated with the senior experience.

Further, Part Two provides a more in-depth discussion about such issues as how to build a cumulative curriculum to integrate student learning in the senior year and the role of higher education in enhancing seniors' preparation for professional success beyond the classroom. Authors also challenge faculty and administrators to pay more thoughtful and deliberate attention to cultural events and rituals, both institution and student initiated, in the senior year because of the potential of these activities to serve as important vehicles for reflection and closure.

In spite of the fact that most seniors already have some work experience, research suggests that the transition from undergraduate to postcollege employment situations can be difficult. Findings presented by chapter authors reveal that many graduating seniors lack competencies in key areas necessary for success in the professional workplace. As a result, examples of various curricular and cocurricular approaches needed to address this deficiency are discussed.

Another thesis presented in this part of the book shows the development of civic virtue to be affected by a variety of college environments and student experiences. Implications suggest specific ways for institutions to enhance the citizenship development of graduating seniors through integrating service learning into the general education program, establishing community service initiatives, implementing comprehensive leadership education programs, providing opportunities for students to experience and understand how a democratic political system is supposed to operate, and embracing diversity and multiculturalism on campus. Finally, Part Two encourages us to give more thought and action to the process of intentionally preparing successful undergraduate students to become successful graduate students.

CHAPTER SIX

Curricular Structures
for Cumulative Learning

Barbara Leigh Smith

S ome students graduate from college with a strong sense of personal transformation and a feeling of engagement and curiosity that will carry them forward the rest of their lives. Not only do they feel competent in their particular fields of inquiry, but they also have a sense of coherence about their undergraduate experience. It adds up.

As one senior said in speaking of an integrated studies model of senior year instruction, "I began to learn new ways of thinking. . . . This is the first place . . . where I had the opportunity to integrate bits and hunks of information . . . and synthesize them into a new understanding of the world, of myself, and of my role in society. It's like the difference between collecting a pile of bricks and building a house." For other students, the opposite may be true. Their undergraduate experience feels like fragments, a series of unrelated courses and relationships.

Creating an educational environment that cultivates a sense of coherence and personal empowerment is not simple. A growing literature suggests that effective learning environments result from the complex interplay of many factors: the academic culture and scale of an institution, the peer group, the form and content of the curriculum, and the pedagogy and value system that prevail (Astin, 1993b; Pascarella and Terenzini 1991; Barr and Tagg, 1995; National Institute of Education Study Group, 1984). Students thrive in challenging academic environments characterized by active learning and frequent interaction between students and faculty, but the political economy and structure of many institutions frustrates these practices.

In recent years, a number of promising approaches have emerged to build reflective practice and cumulative learning experiences into the curriculum in the senior year. Institutions that do this well have a clear point of view about institutional goals, student development, curricular structure, and pedagogy, and they usually make a substantial commitment to staff and faculty development.

Without this broader point of view, these approaches, like many others, can easily become simply another add-on, another "pile of bricks, rather than a house."

In the following section of this chapter, I discuss the state of the undergraduate curriculum and some of the explanations that are given for its widely perceived problems. Understanding the barriers to coherence in the curriculum is the key to making improvements in the future. Progress depends, I contend, on reconceiving faculty roles and rewards *and* rethinking the structure of the curriculum. It requires reexamining fundamental values and raising our expectations. A substantial number of institutions are doing just that. This chapter goes on to present a variety of ways in which curricular structures and faculty and student roles and practices are being rethought to enhance cumulative learning.

RECENT STUDIES OF THE CURRICULUM: A PILE OF BRICKS OR A HOUSE?

In the last decade, there has been considerable discussion about the need for higher education reform (National Institute of Education Study Group, 1984; Barr and Tagg, 1995; Wingspread Group on Higher Education, 1993). Critiques have been wide ranging. A generally convergent set of recommendations calls for reform in the undergraduate curriculum, rethinking faculty roles and rewards, more sharply focusing institutional missions on teaching, taking values seriously, and pushing for higher standards and expectations. General education has received the lion's share of the attention (Gaff, 1991). National surveys indicate that as many as 90 percent of the nation's colleges have recently reviewed their general education programs, but progress has been uneven. Many commentators note a long-standing and continuing disjuncture between general education and study in the major (Boyer, 1987). The overall undergraduate degree and the major have received less scrutiny, but several recent studies pursued these issues in detail.

The 1985 Association of American Colleges (AAC; now called the Association of American Colleges and Universities, AACU) study *Integrity in the College Curriculum* offered an extensive critique of the undergraduate curriculum: "The major in most colleges is little more than a gathering of courses taken in one department, lacking structure and depth, as is often the case in the humanities and the social sciences, or emphasizing content to the neglect of the essential style of inquiry on which the content is based, as is too frequently true in the natural and physical sciences" (p. 36).

Integrity in the College Curriculum also noted an ethos of self-containment that draws a sharp demarcation between general education and the major, a demarcation it regarded as increasingly problematic. This observation about the marginality of general education has become a byword in most studies of general education.

Subsequent AACU work raised additional issues. A study by Robert Zemsky of seniors' transcripts at thirty-five institutions showed a pattern of taking advanced subjects for which they had little or no prior experience. This study raised substantial questions about the extent to which there was study "in depth." Another AAC project conducted in 1986–1989 used external evaluators to assess learning in the major. It reached similar conclusions, finding many students less skilled than their instructors expected (Association of American Colleges and Universities, 1991, p. vii).

In 1989, the AACU took this work one step further and initiated a detailed study of the undergraduate major in conjunction with various disciplinary associations in the fields of biology, economics, history, mathematics, philosophy, political science, psychology, physics, religion, sociology, and women's studies. This study found that many majors lacked principles of organization and structure. Little attention was paid to sequence and progression. Reform efforts tended to be piecemeal, focusing on the beginning and end of the major, but "what falls in between—the bulk of the work of the major—is all too often haphazard, at times exhibiting only numerical or political principles of organization" (Association of American Colleges and Universities, 1991, p. 9).

The AACU concluded that the curriculum needed a deeper, better articulated framework than simply a major and a list of general distribution courses. The association argued that coverage and study in-depth were too limited notions of what students need. Instead, it proposed that "the major should be a matrix for integrative and collaborative learning, not a cocoon for premature specialization. . . . Majors must teach students how to work with others to explore significant questions, how to test the limits of any initial perspective, and how to integrate different parts of their learning, within and beyond the academy" (Association of American Colleges and Universities, n.d.).

Boyer's seminal work *College: the Undergraduate Experience in America* (1987) raises similar issues and conclusions. In a study of thirty campuses, Boyer found confusion over goals, a fragmented and overly specialized curriculum, divided loyalties among the faculty, and a mismatch of faculty expectations and student preparation. Much confusion centered on the relationship between liberal education and specialized study. Boyer argued for an "enriched major" whereby students experience study-in-depth but also learn to put their specialty in context. In many fields, Boyer found that skills had become the ends: "We are turning out technicians. But the crisis of our times relates not to technical competence, but to a loss of social and historical perspective, to the disastrous divorce of competence from conscience" (p. 111).

In 1993, another prominent study group convened at Wingspread to discuss the state of American higher education. Its report, *An American Imperative,* was a clarion call for a recommitment to values, higher expectations, and educational improvement (Wingspread Group on Higher Education, 1993). Like Boyer, the study group found the academy deeply divided and disturbingly silent over fundamental goals.

WHY ISN'T THERE MORE CUMULATIVE LEARNING?

Various explanations are offered about why the faculty have not deeply engaged questions about the undergraduate degree as a whole. The AAC's *Integrity* study "argued that the chief cause for the disarray of the curriculum and the demise of good teaching was the increased professionalization of the professoriate and the faculty members' development of primary loyalties to their disciplines rather than to the institutions where they taught or to their students" (Association of American Colleges and Universities, 1991, p. 20).

Broadening faculty dialogue and interest in the student's overall work is a major challenge in a culture that values departmental specialization, a national rather than a local sense of connection, and faculty autonomy. An ethos of specialization and narrow conceptions of faculty roles increase the distance between the norm of "doing my own thing" and the value of creating a larger sense of community and common enterprise. Faculty have a sense of responsibility to their own courses and, to a lesser degree, to their departmental majors, but few feel any personal obligation for the undergraduate degree as a whole. As the scale of institutions and the number of part-time faculty have increased, the sense of personal connection and individual responsibility has diminished even further.

The curricular structure and the nature of the student body also make it difficult for faculty to engage these larger issues about the shape of the overall degree. Many institutions have highly diverse student bodies. Large numbers of transfer and part-time students make it difficult for baccalaureate institutions to design coherent degree programs that work for everyone. In many states, public higher education systems have been purposely built in two tiers—large numbers of students do their lower division work in a community college and then (it is hoped) transfer to a four-year institution. Student mobility and heterogeneity complicate efforts to design programs that bring general education and study in the major into concert.

PROGRAMS THAT ENCOURAGE CUMULATIVE LEARNING

Fortunately, a variety of innovative approaches are emerging to build a more coherent undergraduate experience. Strategies to encourage cumulative learning include a senior thesis or a senior project, an internship or a community service project, a senior capstone seminar, or a student learning plan, among others. At many institutions, these options are available to honors students even when they are not available to the senior class as a whole. In some institutions, the curricular options for seniors are well grounded in some larger rationale that is linked to institutional mission, a specific educational philosophy, and a particular view of student development. At their best, these innovations represent a genuine change in the institutional culture and not simply a new "pile of bricks."

Learning Communities:
The Importance of Structure and Pedagogy

Many institutions are using learning communities to create a more coherent curriculum and to address issues such as student retention and academic achievement. The term *learning community* as I am using it refers to a variety of curricular models that reconfigure traditional three- or four-credit courses into larger blocks of coursework so students have the opportunity for deeper understanding and integration of the material they are learning and more opportunities to interact with their peers and their faculty (Gabelnick, MacGregor, Matthews, and Smith, 1990; B. L. Smith, 1991; Smith, 1993). Proponents of this approach argue that the way the curriculum is divided up and taught is a root cause of many educational problems. Getting beyond the current division of the curriculum into small and fragmented courses is the key, but rethinking the pedagogy and the content connections is also essential. Until we begin to reconfigure educational structure, learning community proponents argue, attempts to build cumulative learning experiences will be frustrated by the way the curriculum divides up space and time.

The Evergreen State College represents one of the institutions most committed to learning communities, but other institutions such as Cornell College in Iowa and Colorado College also use curricular restructuring around the idea of having students take one course at a time. Literally hundreds of other colleges are now using course-clustering models to promote curricular coherence, a sense of community, and active learning. Major efforts are under way at institutions such as Temple University, the University of Washington, the University of Oregon, Seattle Central and North Seattle Community Colleges, Skagit Valley Community College, Illinois State University, George Mason University, the University of Houston, and La Guardia Community College, to mention just a few.

Learning communities often combine academic and student life to create living-learning environments. Notable efforts include the programs at St. Lawrence University and University of Michigan. There are also hundreds of successful learning community efforts on commuter campuses, where learning community programs help create a sense of academic community. On these campuses, in particular, learning communities have significantly improved student retention. The work of Vince Tinto, Anne Goodsell Love, and Pat Russo has been instrumental in carefully assessing the impact of learning communities and collaborative learning (Tinto, Goodsell Love, and Russo, 1993; Goodsell and others, 1992).

The learning community work is continuing to expand with assistance from organized dissemination networks and national funding agencies. With a grant from the Fund for Postsecondary Education, the Washington Center for Undergraduate Education, which is located at The Evergreen State College, recently launched a national learning community dissemination project. The Washington Center serves as a platform for learning community efforts in the state of Washington that now involve more than two dozen institutions (B. L. Smith, 1991, 1993).

Institutions often develop their own language to name their learning community efforts. Evergreen's curriculum is organized around "coordinated studies programs." Students enroll in one year long thematically integrated interdisciplinary programs rather than twelve separate courses. The programs are team-taught, and there is a heavy emphasis on active and collaborative learning in the delivery of the curriculum. Since team-teaching and designing integrated curricula are not usually learned in graduate school, The Evergreen State College has devoted considerable resources to faculty development to support its approach to teaching and learning. Most other institutions using learning communities also find it important to invest heavily in faculty development.

At The Evergreen State College, senior students might enroll in a program called Computability and Cognition, for example, which probes the scope and limits of formal systems and the implications for the nature and limits of human reason. This program draws upon various areas of inquiry, including formal language theory, mathematical logic, cognitive science, computer programming, and philosophy of the mind. In another advanced program, Politics, Power, and Media, students explore relationships among political events, social change, and the media. The students learn to integrate theory and practice by developing interdisciplinary collaborative film and video projects; they finish their senior year with a portfolio of work that demonstrates their capabilities as film and video makers, skilled writers, and individuals who know how to collaborate.

Evergreen's structure is based upon a philosophy that emphasizes specific educational principles: uniting theory and practice, collaboration, interdisciplinary education, exploring significant differences, and personal engagement in learning. The founding faculty believed that altering the structure of the curriculum was a fundamental prerequisite to putting these principles into action.

Many colleges across the United States have now adopted the learning community approach through various course-clustering models, usually in the form of quarter or semester rather than yearlong programs. Although there are community-building benefits from simply having students spend more time together in clustered courses, what really makes learning communities pay off is the close integration of the curricular material and learning in settings that are active and collaborative. Learning communities can provide the platform for powerful and transformative education, and they provide a natural way of bringing the curriculum together around larger themes than the individual course can accommodate.

Ability-Based Education: What Defines an Educated Person?

If altering structure is one way of enhancing cumulative learning, outcomes-based or ability-based education represents another powerful approach through a redefinition of student learning. This approach turns away from the notion of progression in college as measured by the accrual of credit hours, moving instead to a deeper notion of student learning in terms of developing and demonstrating certain abilities or competencies. Leading the effort in this area is Alverno College, a Catholic women's college of twenty-four hundred students located in Milwaukee, Wisconsin.

In the early 1970s, Alverno reconstituted itself around a radical redefinition of the college experience. Alverno requires its students to develop and demonstrate various abilities that provide a natural framework for integrating general education and the major. As one Alverno faculty member put it, "the ability framework serves as a consistent framework and pathway for the students throughout their college career, cutting across disciplinary content both horizontally and vertically" (Steve Sharkey, personal correspondence with author, July 18, 1995).

The Alverno faculty currently defines certain specific abilities as central:

- Communication
- Analysis
- Problem solving
- Valuing in decision making
- Social interaction
- Global perspectives
- Effective citizenship
- Aesthetic responsiveness

Each ability is defined in terms of a sequence of developmental levels that the student must eventually master. These abilities are taught and assessed throughout the curriculum in both general education courses and those in the major. The abilities become an integrative cross-curricular element bringing the major and general education together. But they are not an end in themselves. Alverno sees these abilities as *a means to help* students become independent lifelong learners, so a premium is placed on students' being able to transfer specific abilities from one arena and course to another (Alverno College, 1994a).

Alverno takes the job of defining these abilities and assessing them very seriously. Issues of teaching, learning, and assessment became natural complements of one another. Majors consciously employ a somewhat more discipline-oriented version of the abilities. As Steve Sharkey (personal correspondence with author, July 18, 1995) points out, in the social science major one of the departmental outcomes is that the student "effectively conducts social research." This departmental ability builds upon a variety of the general education abilities and places them in the more specific context of the major.

As students mature and move toward their senior year, they become more autonomous learners; they set their own standards as they encounter new situations and as the assessments become more holistic and situational (Loacker, Cromwell, and O'Brien, 1985). An example demonstrates this: "biology students extend the communication of their investigative thinking processes from lab partner and instructor as audience to a small group or team to an entire class, to the natural sciences division, to students and faculty from other disciplines, as well as to off-campus groups. Each movement represents a need to rethink how to clarify ideas for a group with a new set of assumptions, understandings, and interests" (Alverno College, 1992, p. 16). Here is a further example:

An English student . . . would be given a weeklong simulation exercise. . . . Working two or three hours a day with several peers as the staff of a fictitious community cultural center, she handles a variety of problems. While planning an upcoming literary festival, she might be asked to step in as emergency substitute teacher in a class on Elizabethan plays. She may have to deal personally, in a videotaped interaction and in writing, with a benefactor's repeated attempts to influence the poetry selections for the festival . . . she is called on to apply her literary knowledge, her ability to define and defend criteria for judging works, and her understanding of the impact of literary art on its audience. At the same time, she must frame and deliver complex messages to varying audiences using several media [Alverno College, 1979, p. 16].

Business or management students might have another type of assessment experience: "In their small business course, each student designs a business plan for a proposed small business venture. In addition to their instructor's and a peer's assessment, each takes her individual plan to a local bank, where a commercial loan officer, previously contacted by the instructor, has agreed to assess it" (Alverno College, 1994b, p. 73).

Students find the Alverno approach transformative, as the following senior's comment indicates:

The concept of values has taken on new meaning for me. I have had to work at identifying the sources of my values and the relationships among them. I have had to develop the ability to discern the influence values have on the systems in my environment. Through this evaluation process, I have had to confront value problems raised by change. This increased self-awareness has not only allowed me to act on my value judgments, but it is also allowing me to better understand and respect others for their value judgments. Therefore, by having a better understanding of myself, I am now better able to understand others—a critical asset in the practice of nursing [Alverno College, 1994b, p. 66].

The abilities framework creates a whole new understanding about what it means to be a teacher and serve students, as faculty member Steve Sharkey puts it. A variety of organizational structures and institutional practices develop and sustain this commitment, such as an interdisciplinary committee structure, an ongoing weekly program of college institutes where faculty meet regularly and share ideas, and workshops where faculty learn to adapt their teaching to the ability framework.

Over the years, Alverno faculty have designed ingenious ways of assessing what are often regarded as difficult-to-measure, though important, liberal arts goals. The approach draws deeply on the creativity of the faculty and the students and does an admirable job of placing the major in the context of liberal learning. The Alverno faculty refine this approach by continuing to ask themselves how the curriculum is improving student abilities and in what ways it needs improving.

Though no other institution has so thoroughly adopted ability-based learning and assessment, Alverno College has widely influenced higher education, especially as assessment has become a national issue.

Notable pathways of influence include a robust program at King's College, Clayton State College, and Central Missouri State University, among others. Alverno has also influenced others through its annual summer workshops on teaching and assessment for faculty from around the nation and through various networks on assessment supported by the Fund for the Improvement of Postsecondary Education, the American Association for Higher Education, and other organizations. In 1994, Alverno was recognized for its outstanding faculty development efforts by winning the prestigious Hesburgh Award.

Alverno offers a sophisticated prototype for defining what cumulative learning can mean as a student moves from the freshman to the senior year. It pushes us to ask: What are the abilities we are trying to cultivate in an undergraduate? And how do we define an educated person? How do these abilities develop over time?

Thinking about abilities and outcomes often helps faculty clarify the goals of undergraduate education. It also pushes us to more closely link our educational goals with our teaching practices and assessment approaches. In defining progress in higher education, this approach takes us considerably beyond simple notions of accumulating knowledge; it provides a natural way of integrating liberal arts goals with study in the major.

Capstone Courses

Capstone courses and senior seminars are growing in popularity as a means of enhancing the senior year. In Chapter Four, Art Levine distinguishes four major purposes for capstone courses: integration (pulling together the four years), breadth (giving a final general education context on top of specialized study), application (providing the opportunity for advanced research), or transition (a capstone focusing on the transition out of the academy). Clearly, the purpose of a capstone seminar should be defined in light of each institution's purposes.

Capstones are often used as a means of integrating general education and the major. Institutions that receive a large number of transfer students often struggle with the question of how to integrate general education with study in the major. An increasing number are turning to capstones. At the University of Wisconsin-River Falls, seniors take at least one interdisciplinary capstone course. Eastern Washington University now requires its transfer students to take upper-division theme-based integrated courses. Senior students also do a community problem-oriented capstone course. The University of North Carolina-Asheville offers a senior capstone titled The Future and the Individual. It recently added a ten-hour community service component focusing on contemporary issues and ethical issues. At Lynchburg College, students take a senior capstone course focused on great issues and great books. The capstone provides seniors the opportunity to bring their specialized knowledge and their breadth of experience to bear on perennial issues and questions. With a similar purpose, Lafayette College offers seniors a variety of theme-based interdisciplinary seminars with such titles as Politics and the Arts, Freedom of Expression, and Changing Roles in the Third World.

At the University of South Carolina, several types of capstone courses are available. One, pioneered by John Gardner, focuses on issues of life transitions and draws heavily upon the discipline of psychology (see Resource B for the course syllabus). At The Evergreen State College, a pilot project for part-time students includes a capstone course that asks the students to examine both what they have accomplished and their future. Portfolio projects, autobiographical writing, and career planning and counseling are typical parts of these capstone experiences.

Many institutions also offer capstones focused around applications projects, major research projects, and collaborative or independent study options in the major. At the University of South Carolina College of Journalism, for example, senior students take a course that involves producing a weekly newspaper. Brigham Young University has a large capstone program in engineering that involves more than twenty faculty and 170 students with projects coming from industrial partners. Students at Marietta College in the management program work in teams to provide business consulting and technical assistance to small businesses. At Miami University, students in the Western College program complete a yearlong senior project culminating in a public conference in a professional meeting format.

Community Service, Internships, and Experiential Learning: Situating the Self in the World

A number of colleges have adopted community service and experiential learning as an integral part of the senior year (Kendall and Associates, 1990; Ehrlich, 1995). Experiential learning is valuable in promoting personal, social, and intellectual development in students (Kendall and Associates, 1990). A number of institutions have a long history of integrating service and experiential learning into their curricula. Especially notable are Antioch College, the "work colleges"— Berea, Blackburn, and Warren Wilson—the Fielding Institute, and Manchester College. There is now a substantial literature on the positive contributions of service learning in this arena. Kendall and Associates provide an excellent compendium in their three-volume *Combining Service and Learning* (1990).

The rationale for using experiential learning varies. A number of institutions, grounded in the educational philosophy of John Dewey, embrace this approach simply because it promotes student learning. Internships are seen as a valuable means for combining theory and practice.

Students often comment that internships help them see that their undergraduate work has indeed prepared them for the world of work. As one senior student noted: "They talk about combining theory with practice. Well, that is exactly what an [internship] does. But it also familiarizes the student with the demands of the working world. So, while you're still in school, you realize what kinds of skills you're going to need when you graduate" (Tommerup, 1993, p. 90).

At Portland State University, community service is also seen as an integral part of the institution's self-definition as an innovative urban university. Resulting from a recent curriculum reform, senior students complete a six-credit capstone course based on a collaborative community service project. Unlike conventional individualized internship programs, the Portland State program is organized around long-term projects developed in collaboration with the city of Portland and various community agencies. The program uses the metropolitan area as a "learning lab for students to apply the expertise they gained in their major. The capstone has two additional objectives: to give students experience working in a team context necessitating collaboration with persons from different fields of specialization and to provide the opportunity for students to become actively involved in this community" (White, 1994).

The Portland State community service project provides an ideal vehicle for integrating general education goals such as understanding ethical issues and social responsibility, communication, and human experience with study in the major.

Long-term projects developed in concert with various academic departments will cycle generations of students through them. One such project includes an annual ecological survey done in conjunction with the City of Portland. Another, developed in collaboration with the Washington State Historical Society, focuses on the culture, economics, and environment of the Columbia River. The Portland State model is unusually ambitious since it will involve two thousand students each quarter. Portland State has developed an extensive implementation and faculty support system to carry out the new reforms.

At Seattle University, community service is also seen as an integral part of its mission as an urban Catholic university. Service learning is integrated into a variety of courses throughout the university. Students work with immigrant groups in literacy programs, at shelters, in community food programs, and in nursing homes with the elderly. In their classes, they reflect on these experiences through journals, papers, and seminar discussions. The community service work is seen as an important way of integrating general education with work in the major and giving students the opportunity to test classroom learning in the real world. Goshen College is another church-related institution with a mission-driven notion of community service, but in this case the service is done abroad. Goshen maintains a series of overseas sites for its students, many of whom spend at least one semester there working in local communities.

Summative Self-Evaluations: Developing Self-Reflectiveness as a Lifelong Learner

Student self-evaluations are another approach being used at a number of institutions to promote self-reflection and integrative thinking in students. At some colleges, such as The Evergreen State College, students do self-evaluations throughout the undergraduate career. Looked at over time, these student self-evaluations provide a vivid portrait of student intellectual development (MacGregor, 1993; Thompson, 1991, 1992). Student self-evaluations are especially valuable in the senior year as a vehicle for students to reflect on what they have learned and to think about next steps.

At Fairhaven College at Western Washington University, all students write a senior summative self-evaluation, a particularly appropriate step in a college that emphasizes individual choice and responsibility. Fairhaven supports the process of writing these self-evaluations through a seminar, which has become an important rite of passage. All senior students take this capstone seminar at the end of their senior year. It provides an opportunity for discussing and presenting one's work and reflecting on it as a member of the college community.

The seminar concludes with a formal summary and evaluation paper written by each student. The paper asks students to look at their *entire* undergraduate career—the general education program, the work in the major, internships and community projects they might have done, and their cocurricular involvements—and write about what it has meant to them. What did the choices and pathways they chose mean? How does it fit together, and where does it take them? This is much more than a chronology and a list: at its best, the summary and evaluation paper is a deeply reflective synthesis.

Many students find this self-reflective opportunity meaningful, as the following student notes: "The seminar provided a wonderful structure within which I have been able to thoroughly look back over my four years, reviewing, questioning, bringing to articulation a portrait in words of my experience here. . . . Writing my 'Summary and Evaluation' was a chance for me to come to a sense of completion with what I have accomplished at Fairhaven College and to also see I take with me much work still to be done" (MacGregor, 1993, pp. 29–30).

Another student noted the overwhelming nature of writing the self-evaluation and the deep questions it raises: "I sit in a heap of journals, evaluations, papers, notes, books, scripts, ditto sheets . . . proof of my college career . . . and I ask myself, 'what does it all mean? What have I learned? How do I know what I know? How have I changed? What tools have I acquired, and how will they help me live my life? As an educated person, what responsibilities do I now have and to whom, and to what extent will I be responsible? How have my subjects of study affected my life as a woman? Where do I go from here?'" (MacGregor, 1993, p. 38).

Assessing one's education can be an overwhelming task, but it is an essential part of making that critical transition to becoming an autonomous lifelong learner.

Many other colleges also use student self-evaluations. Interest in this approach is growing and often connected to work with student portfolios. At Sonoma State University, students in the Hutchins School write a summative evaluation. Student self-evaluations are also used at Antioch University-Seattle, Alverno College, and a number of other institutions (MacGregor, 1993).

CONCLUSION

In this chapter, I've described a number of promising curricular approaches for making the undergraduate experience more coherent. All of these approaches take the student to new levels of self-reflectiveness about his or her educational experience. At the same time, they provide a useful vehicle for students to start the transition out of the academy, to begin planning ahead and thinking about their role in the larger society. Unfortunately, in most institutions students still do simply accumulate a pile of brick-credits. The approaches described in this chapter reach beyond and require the student to make something out of it— through a summative self-evaluation, a demonstration of having learned certain abilities that link general education and the major, a community service project that serves the community while also testing the student's ability to link the field of specialization with others in working collaboratively on a community project. The approaches represent new ways of thinking about teaching and learning for both students and faculty, and a shift in institutional culture. These senior year initiatives ask faculty and students to situate the college experience in the real world, to articulate a point of view over time, and to think about how the bricks do in fact make a house.

CHAPTER SEVEN

Preparing Students for Life Beyond the Classroom

Elwood F. Holton III

I'm really stunned," said John, a new college graduate just into his second month of work with a major corporation. He had just had a meeting with his boss and was discussing it with a fellow new hire. "I really thought I was doing well. During my first week, I found a mistake my project engineer had made. Then in the staff meeting last week, I spent twenty minutes talking about a new technique I learned in school that could be helpful. In the meeting with the vice president, I was careful to keep quiet and let my boss do the talking. Now she tells me I'm too cocky, that my attitude is irritating others and I need to be more of a team player. And the vice president thinks I'm a wimp. I was only trying to do my best to help. Where did I go wrong? Why didn't my boss tell me earlier what I was supposed to be doing?"

It is increasingly clear that as this scenario drawn from multiple student experiences illustrates, the transition to work can be a difficult process for new college graduates. Philip Gardner's chapter in this volume (Chapter Five) and work by others (Arnold, 1985; Gardner and Lambert, 1993; Holton, 1995; Keenan and Newton, 1986; Nicholson and Arnold, 1989, 1991; Richards, 1984a, 1984b) clearly point to the need for increased attention to preparing seniors with the full range of tools needed for professional success. What these studies demonstrate is that most colleges and universities are strongest at providing discipline-specific knowledge and skills necessary to accomplish work tasks (Philip Gardner's *content skills*) but are weak at providing non-task-specific professional skills to enable students to apply their knowledge and skills in a work context, succeed as professionals, and build a new life as professionals after they leave college. New employee development programs in industry are little different, remaining focused mostly on training new graduates in the basic skills to accomplish tasks they encounter in their first jobs (Holton, 1996b). It seems clear that these efforts have not been adequate to make the transition successful.

A variety of external forces are converging to spotlight this weakness in the higher education system. As Gardner outlined in Chapter Five, today's graduates face a new workplace with lower job security, pressure for high productivity, and constant change. This has led to increased pressure from students and alumni for colleges and universities to change their curricula to better prepare students for successful careers. Employers voice similar concerns, demanding that graduates be better prepared. Few employers have the luxury of long-term, expensive new employee development programs. Increasingly, they are pushing new employees to become productive more quickly and asking institutions to give them better-prepared graduates. Not surprisingly, parents are increasingly concerned about career preparation for their children, particularly as college costs have escalated and job markets tightened. Parents want to see their kids graduate, but more important, they want their graduate to find a good job and become successful in that job.

In Chapter Two, Joseph Cuseo outlined a variety of initiatives underway on college campuses to improve seniors' transition out of college in an effort to respond to these pressures. The common thread in these initiatives is that institutions must be more accountable for outcomes beyond graduation and assume more responsibility for the career success of their graduates. Most of the debate on undergraduate curricular reform has embedded in it some type of linkage between higher education and the so-called real world (for example, Brand, 1993; Johnstone, 1993; Mooney, 1992). Equipping seniors with a broader range of workplace skills is one means of being more responsive in preparing them for postgraduation success.

The notion that colleges and universities should be more closely connected to the world of work and better prepare students for professional roles in society is not a universally popular one. Some faculty strongly believe that the university's or college's only role is to foster academic learning and educate citizens. The very idea of relating academics to work may incite accusations of "vocationalism." While I am sensitive to the deep academic traditions represented by this argument, colleges and universities cannot hide from the reality that most students pursue academic degrees as preparation for careers. Given this reality, it seems myopic and ill-advised for institutions to pretend that they are not accountable for work-related outcomes of education. Imagine parents' reactions to that idea! It is appropriate to debate the balance of academic versus work-related preparation, but it is this author's position that higher education must be more accountable for preparing students for professional life.

What is not completely clear are the mechanisms by which nontask professional skills can be integrated with task skills to prepare seniors for work, and the respective roles for higher education and employing organizations in ensuring a successful transition from college to work. This chapter offers a prescriptive look at the role higher education should play to enhance seniors' preparation for professional success. The first part of the chapter examines some of the research and theoretical underpinnings from organizational research. Then a conceptual framework of learning during a successful transition to work is described and used to specify how higher education should expand its role. Next a four-part partnership model outlines a means of implementing changes on campuses. Finally, career-related life issues that may arise during the transition to work and for which graduates need to be prepared are discussed.

BACKGROUND FROM ORGANIZATIONAL RESEARCH

The importance of the transition to work cannot be underestimated, and it is clear that there are real career and performance issues to be addressed. Studies have reported unusually high turnover for new employees, usually around 50 percent (Leibowitz, Schlossberg, and Shore, 1991; Wanous, 1980). Job satisfaction studies have shown lower satisfaction among new employees (Morrow and McElroy, 1987) and higher satisfaction when the socialization process leads to greater person-job congruence (Richards, 1984a; Stumpf and Hartman, 1984). Higher job satisfaction may lead to higher performance (Petty, McGee, and Cavender, 1984). Studies of organizational commitment have shown a link between organizational commitment and work experiences during organizational entry and the first year on the job (Meyer and Allen, 1988). Commitment has been shown to be linked to turnover (Mobley, Griffeth, Hand, and Meglino, 1979) and performance (Meyer and others, 1989). Organizational entry also has a lasting effect on a person's career (Bray, Campbell, and Grant, 1974). However, most newcomers undergo reality or culture shock because they do not understand the culture very well before joining the organization, making "fit" problematic (Taylor, 1988).

Feldman (1989) noted two perspectives in the organizational literature. Human resource development scholars have focused mostly on skill development for job task competence. Socialization research has focused on the nontask aspects of the entry process, such as acquiring success-related attitudes and values, learning one's work role as a new employee, adapting to the organization's culture, earning respect and credibility, and becoming a member of the organization's social system. This split is unfortunate because a new employee becomes an outstanding performer through a process of acquiring *both* task-related competence from job training and non-task-related competence from socialization; neither should stand alone (Feldman, 1989). Outstanding task performance cannot be achieved without effective socialization because few employees perform their tasks independently of the organizational milieu of norms, values, relationships, and culture. Most of the difficulties new graduates encounter during the transition to work, as well as the complaints employers have about new graduates, fall in the category of socialization because it deals with the context of the job.

A variety of research directions have been undertaken, but unfortunately, socialization research remains somewhat fragmented and incomplete (Feldman, 1989; Fisher, 1986). Recent research developments point to an expanded role for those involved in developing new graduates for work, including higher education. It is now clear that for newcomers socialization is fundamentally a process of learning and change (Fisher, 1986; Louis, 1980; Morton, 1993; Ostroff and Kozlowski, 1992). It is primarily a social learning process involving supervisors, coworkers, and other key persons in the organization (Reichers, 1987). Furthermore, socialization-related learning is significantly associated with important employment outcomes (Ostroff and Kozlowski, 1992). It appears that socialization is little different from any other work-related learning need. The only difference is the content, not the learning objectives and methods. Unfortunately, there has been little focus on solutions to the learning challenges.

Earlier conceptualizations of socialization viewed it largely as a reactive process on the part of newcomers, who were seen as passive recipients of socialization. Recent studies (Morrison, 1993) have shown that newcomer proactivity can enhance outcomes of the socialization process, which has led to a more dynamic conceptualization of the newcomer and raised new research questions about the content of socialization (Chao and others, 1994). Instead of asking *how* the process affects newcomers and what the outcomes are, socialization researchers are raising new questions about *what* newcomers need to learn and how they can best learn the content.

It has also become increasingly clear that socialization is an important concern for any person crossing an organizational boundary (Van Maanen and Schein, 1979). Although many studies have used new college graduates entering their first work organization, recent studies have included more-experienced employees entering new organizations (Adkins, 1995) and changing roles within an organization (Chao and others, 1994). Adkins reports limited relationships between previous work experience and socialization outcomes, suggesting that socialization is a recurring phenomenon. Chao and others (1994) found that experienced workers went through resocialization as they changed positions in their company. It is now clearer that enhancing graduates' skills to make the transition from college to work also builds lifelong career skills.

HOW MUCH RESPONSIBILITY
DOES HIGHER EDUCATION HAVE?

These new perspectives lead to a reconceptualization of the transition, from one of a two-stage process (college student to professional) to a three-stage process (college student to new employee to professional; see Table 7.1). Whether intentionally or not, the new-employee stage and the associated skills needed to break into an organization are generally overlooked by colleges and employers. The breaking-in stage should be considered a distinct and unique career stage with special rules and special relationships. It is only by viewing the new-employee stage as unique and requiring special skills and special strategies that we can help new graduates succeed at it.

A central question, then, is, Whose responsibility is this new-employee stage: higher education's or employers'? The basic premise of this chapter is that it is a shared responsibility between higher education and employers. The goal of preparing graduates for professional success is not a new one for higher education. What is new is the realization that subject matter knowledge and skills are but part of the necessary learning. The academic model must be extended to accept partial responsibility for the new-employee stage and give graduates all the tools to succeed. This enlarged toolkit includes the traditional subject matter knowledge and skills, but it must also encompass the skills to use them in organizational settings for professional success. This is much more than just applied learning because it embraces the socialization notions of learning to succeed as a professional.

Achieving an outstanding level of work performance requires a combination of job task and nontask proficiencies. Traditional college curricula focus heavily on task-related theory, knowledge, and skills and prepare graduates very well to perform the basic tasks of their jobs. As a result, new graduates focus heavily in the same area and may be insecure, worried, or anxious about their abilities.

Table 7.1. Three Stages in the Transition from College Student.

Stage	Primary Challenge	Responsibility
College student	Acquiring knowledge and skills	College or university
	Finding a job	
New employee	Breaking in	College or university
	Fitting in	Employer
Professional	Getting ahead	Employer

Employers, however, are more concerned about such things as a new employee's willingness to learn new things, fitting in to the culture, earning respect and credibility, learning the politics of the organization, building effective working relationships, becoming accepted as a member of the organization, learning the informal structure and methods of the organization, discovering what the unwritten expectations are, understanding the power and reward structure, and learning how to get things accomplished within the organization. Most employers (particularly large ones) are good enough at hiring new people to be reasonably assured that graduates have the raw talent and ability to perform the basic tasks of the job. This is not to say that task performance is unimportant but rather that it is less variable and easier to predict. What employers cannot assess very reliably and find more variable in their college hires are the nontask skills. Graduates often fail to realize that the nontask or professional skills are equally important as task skills. It turns out that they are the key in the employees' gaining opportunities to demonstrate their full task capabilities. Field interviews with managers indicate that outstanding performance on the basic tasks of the job usually earns an employee only an average performance rating (Holton, 1991).

THE PARADOX OF ACADEMIC PREPARATION

At the heart of the problems most new graduates (and their mangers) experience during college-to-work transition is the failure to recognize how much the educational culture has shaped their attitudes, expectations, behaviors, and overall view of organizations. Today's traditional-age baccalaureate graduates have spent most of their lives (a minimum of seventeen years) in educational institutions by the time they go to work. Educational attitudes, expectations, and behaviors become so deeply ingrained in them that many are not even aware of how much they have been shaped by the education experience.

New graduates then face a dramatic culture shift when they move from college to the professional world. The work world is so fundamentally different from the world of education that it requires an almost total transformation on the part of the new graduate. And organizations want employees who fit (Schein, 1992; Deal and Kennedy, 1982) their culture, and are quick to look for confirmation that a new employee will fit. Even students who have jobs throughout college (and many do) find the shift to the postcollege professional world a significant transition because of the new roles and expectations they encounter. Simply working in an organization (for example, part-time during college) only minimally prepares a student for professional life.

The paradox is that although the *knowledge* acquired in college is critical to graduates' success, the *process* of succeeding in school is very different from the process of succeeding at work. Many of the skills students developed to be successful in education processes and the behaviors for which they were rewarded are not the ones they need to be successful at work. Worse yet, the culture of education is so different that when seniors continue to have the same expectations of their employers that they did of their college and professors, they are greatly disappointed with their jobs and make costly career mistakes. Despite their best attempts to make adjustments, they cannot adjust for educational conditioning because they are not conscious of it.

If seniors do not undergo interventions and instead do what comes naturally, they unknowingly continue to expect the workplace to be like college. Many of the behaviors that managers label as "immature," "naïve," or not "fitting in" and that keep newcomers from being successful are simply behaviors education has not only tolerated but rewarded and encouraged. In many cases, new graduates are simply doing in the workplace what they have been conditioned to do for seventeen or more years. They do it simply because they are not being taught any differently, not because they are naïve or unwilling to adapt. To compound the paradox, the graduates whom employers seek the most are the ones who have best learned the educational system. Not surprisingly, they may have the most difficulty unlearning the highly internalized educational process.

Table 7.2 presents some of the key differences that new graduates talk about.

Here are a few examples of how this can hurt them. In college, students usually receive a lot of direction about what to do and how to do it. The curriculum tells them what courses to take, and professors tell them what is expected of them. If the professors do not give a clear syllabus or tell them what to study for an exam, students are probably entitled to get upset. However, they rarely get that type of direction at work and are likely to complain. Some have become so accustomed to being told "how they're doing" that they frequently ask their managers for feedback—leaving the impression that they are insecure. Other new graduates are so used to growing and developing through education that they get very upset when their boss does not send them to much training during the first year. Still others cannot understand why they are not getting to do work that stretches their minds and challenges them, not realizing that work seldom mimics college. Some new graduates are faulted for not using good judgment because they are too quick to challenge established practices in the organization. Yet didn't they spend most of their college careers doing just that? I have heard managers complain that new hires "don't respect their superiors" enough. But how many times do you think they were rewarded in college with "class participation points" for challenging a professor (their "superior") in class? The list of examples could go on and on.

Clearly, there are pedagogical advantages to some of the practices described previously when learning performance and graduation are the goal. However, if the goal is extended to include professional success, educators must realize

Table 7.2. College Graduates' Perceptions of Differences Between College and Work.

College	First Year of Work
Frequent, quick, and concrete feedback (grades and so on)	Infrequent and less precise feedback
Highly structured curriculum and programs with lots of direction	Highly unstructured environment and tasks with few directions
Personally supportive environment	Less personal support
Few significant changes	Frequent and unexpected changes
Flexible schedule	Structured schedule
Frequent breaks and time off	Limited time off
Personal control over time, classes, interests	Responding to others' directions and interests
Intellectual challenge	Organizational and people challenges
Choose your performance level (A, B, and so on)	A-level work required all the time
Focus on your development and growth	Focus on getting results for the organization
Create and explore knowledge	Get results with your knowledge
Individual effort	Team effort
"Right" answers	Few "right" answers
Independence of ideas and thinking	Do it the organization's way
Professors	Bosses
Less initiative required	Lots of initiative required

Source: Adapted from Holton, 1991.

that many helpful practices embedded in the academic culture have the unintended effect of hurting graduates in the workplace. Higher education must strike a better balance between the supportive processes that aid learning and the less supportive, more ambiguous, and somewhat messy real-world processes that prepare graduates for work.

CONCEPTUAL FRAMEWORK FOR UNDERSTANDING ADAPTATION TO WORK

A central problem in addressing this issue has been the lack of a conceptual framework to guide interventions. Without such a framework, it is difficult for employers or educators to identify their respective responsibilities, audit devel-

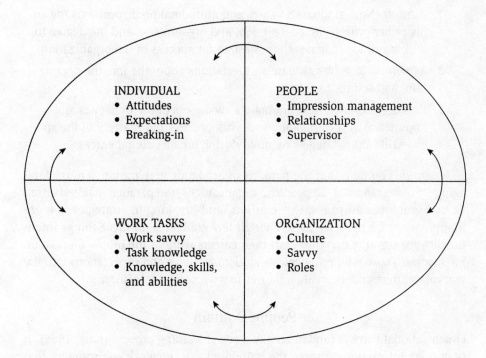

Figure 7.1. New Employee Development Learning Tasks.

opment processes, and design interventions. In this section, a taxonomy of learning tasks during successful organizational entry is reviewed to provide a conceptual basis for understanding higher education's role.

The taxonomy, outlined in Figure 7.1, most closely follows Fisher (1986) in conceptualizing four content learning domains: *individual, people, organization,* and *work tasks.* The first three domains constitute what has traditionally been called socialization; the last domain consists of learning that is traditionally called job training. Each domain is further subdivided into three learning tasks, for a total of twelve learning tasks. (For a more complete description of this taxonomy, including supporting research, see Holton, 1996b.)

Individual Domain

All new employees, regardless of experience level, bring with them accumulated learning, attitudes, and values that have been shaped by previous cultures and work experiences. It is these prior experiences that can serve as either a foundation for or a barrier to early success.

The *individual* domain encompasses three learning tasks: attitudes, expectations, and breaking-in skills:

1. *Attitude.* New graduate's values and attitudinal predispositions toward his or her professional career, job, and organization and the degree to which attitude matches those desired for success in the organization

2. *Expectations.* New graduate's expectations about the job, the organization, and self in the job

3. *Breaking-in skills.* New graduate's awareness of the dynamics and importance of the adaptation-to-work process and mastery of the special skills and strategies required during organizational entry

It is in this domain that the paradox of academic preparation is most damaging for new graduates. To people in organizations, the paradox manifests itself as new-employee attitudes, expectations, and breaking-in strategies that are inappropriate for professionals. Though few graduates do these things intentionally, the result is that they start their careers without the proper foundation for success. Those who bring college student attitudes and expectations into the workplace immediately create a barrier to a successful transition.

People Domain

Organizational entry is fundamentally a social learning process (Katz, 1985). It is through interaction between the individual and the work environment that much of the information about the organization is obtained, acceptance is gained, and roles are learned (Ashford and Taylor, 1990; Louis, 1990). In fact, only a small amount of newcomer learning occurs in formal training or from written materials. More learning comes from sources such as feedback, initiation rites, on-the-job training, and informal conversations.

4. *Impression management.* New graduate's awareness of the role impressions play in establishing the organization's initial evaluation; his or her understanding of the impression management process, ability to learn what impressions are viewed most favorably in the organization, mastery of the skills and strategies necessary to manage the impressions created

5. *Relationships.* New graduate's understanding of the role relationships play in organizational success and the kinds of relationships that should be built, the skills necessary to build and maintain effective professional relationships and networks, effective teamwork strategies

6. *Supervisor.* New graduate's awareness of the importance of the supervisor-subordinate relationship and their respective roles, the skills needed to be an effective subordinate and to manage the supervisor relationship for mutual gain, effective strategies for building a strong working relationship with a supervisor

If the first three tasks are not mastered and new graduates enter the organization with inappropriate attitudes and expectations, poor impressions result. This in turn discourages people from building the strong relationships that lead to the types of organizational learning crucial for early success. Relationships with supervisors are also immediately strained, potentially reducing opportunities for success-creating assignments.

Organization Domain

If strong, effective relationships are established with people in the organization, a newcomer can learn the complexities of the organization itself (Feldman, 1989), represented by the *organization* domain. Recent studies have found a significant relationship between learning about non-task-related dimensions of the organization and entry outcomes (Chao and others, 1994; Copeland and Wiswell, 1994; Holton and Russell, 1997). This reinforces the notion that developing high-performance new employees is a combination of task knowledge and knowledge about the organization, acquired through social learning processes.

7. *Organizational culture.* New graduate's understanding of the elements of organizational culture and how it affects performance; his or her awareness of the importance of fitting into the organization's culture and of the skills needed to learn the key elements of the culture not explicitly taught

8. *Organizational savvy.* New graduate's awareness of the informal organization and success factors in the organization; his or her understanding of appropriate means for getting results through the informal organization and of the skills to learn the informal organization and effectively use it to achieve desired results

9. *Organizational roles.* New graduate's ability to locate himself or herself in the larger perspective of the organization's mission, to understand the role and identity of a new graduate in the organization, to learn what appropriate expectations and activities are for that role; his or her ability to accept the limits and realities of that role and reconcile role conflicts and ambiguity

Work Task Domain

The fourth domain is the most familiar and need not be discussed in detail. There is no question that understanding the tasks of the job and having the correct knowledge, skills, and abilities are essential to new employee success. As stated earlier, it is in this domain that employers, colleges, and newcomers focus most of their attention. It should be clear, though, that new graduates have less chance of success in this domain without a foundation of success in the previous three.

10. *Work savvy.* New graduate's understanding of how to apply the realities of organizational life in a specific job, to apply skills to the job; his or her acquisition of generic professional skills (for example, communication, time management, and so on) necessary to function in the job

11. *Task knowledge.* New graduate's understanding of the basic tasks he or she is required to perform in the job and how to perform the tasks successfully

12. *Knowledge, skills, and abilities.* New graduate's ability to identify the knowledge, skills, and abilities needed to perform tasks successfully, now and in the future; his or her knowledge of the formal and informal learning skills necessary to acquire such knowledge, skills, and abilities

WHAT IS HIGHER EDUCATION'S ROLE?

Using this model as a framework, higher education should assume responsibility for four key aspects of development for graduates, beyond the task-related knowledge currently provided:

1. Developing fully the individual domain (attitudes, expectations, and breaking-in skills)
2. Teaching basic skills in the people and organization domains
3. Building awareness of the entire scope of learning tasks after employment
4. Developing organizational learning skills to enable graduates to complete the learning

Developing the Individual Domain

There is little reason that higher education cannot take full responsibility for developing in graduates sound professional attitudes, realistic expectations, and an understanding of how to enter an organization. Clearly, there are certain organization-specific components that may need adjustment later, but the difficulties during the transition are more basic ones. For example, attitudes such as flexibility, commitment to quality, working for the good of the team, willingness to pay one's dues, desire to learn, and and the like are missing in many graduates. Most have very unrealistic expectations about the type of work they will be doing early in their careers, what organizations should be doing for them, the role of a new employee, the pace of promotions, and other matters. Few understand that proposing significant changes is not smart until you have earned acceptance and respect, that earning acceptance and respect is just as important as task performance, and that impressions count more when you do not have any track record. All of these are examples of individual domain learning tasks that are well within the capability and mission of higher education and should be more fully developed in graduates.

Teaching Basic Skills in the People and Organization Domains

Because these two domains are much more organization specific, higher education has a more limited role. However, basic skills in each domain should be taught to enable graduates to focus on the organization-specific components. For example, in the people domain, seniors can be taught principles of impression management and how to determine effective strategies in their new organizations. They should certainly be taught how to build work relationships and networks. And they can be taught the basic skills of being an effective subordinate, how to determine effective subordinate skills in the new organization, and how to manage a boss.

In the organization domain, every graduate should understand what organizational culture is, how it affects her or his career, and how to decipher it. Every graduate must understand something about organizational politics, how informal systems work in organizations, and how to use those systems to get results. Finally, graduates can be taught what the role of a newcomer is and how to make sure they meet role expectations.

Building Awareness of the Entire Scope of Learning Tasks After Employment

In learning tasks where students cannot be given all the answers, such as learning about organizational culture or organizational savvy, colleges can at least teach students the questions to ask for advanced learning. For new graduates unaccustomed to work organizations, the scope of learning is usually not immediately apparent. In addition, from college they are more accustomed to being told what the learning agenda is. Graduates need to realize what they do not know about being successful in an organization, know what questions to ask, and be motivated to engage in the new learning. Colleges should accept responsibility and focus on developing a learning plan or agenda for seniors. One effective approach is literally to develop lists of questions graduates need to answer once on the job.

Developing Organizational Learning Skills

Awareness is only part of what seniors need as preparation for advanced learning. Frequently overlooked is the fact that most of the learning that occurs during organizational entry requires fundamentally different learning skills than are cultivated in college. First, many things can be learned only by interacting with other people, so *social learning* skills are most important. Second, the learning process at work is usually an *experiential* one, as the learning occurs while one is engaged in work projects. Third, *self-directed learning* becomes the norm, because newcomers have to take the initiative to learn much beyond the task knowledge to do their jobs. Fourth, the learning is *unstructured* in that it has no definite beginning and ending points. And it is *indeterminate* in that it may be difficult to tell when one has the "right" answers or when learning is completed, especially when dealing with complex or unusual problems. In short, it is a messy, and continuous, process.

Contrast this learning model with the educational model, which is predominantly book learning in formal classrooms led by instructors in neatly packaged courses. The learning skills for college success bear little resemblance to those needed in organizations. Unless students are taught new ways to learn, they may be unable to adapt, even if they have the awareness of the learning required. Educational programs have not traditionally embraced these objectives as part of their curricula, which accounts for part of graduates' transition difficulties. It appears that successful people have acquired their awareness and learning skills from other places, usually from role models, mentors, or prior work experience. Individuals who have not naturally had access to other sources of learning are at a decided disadvantage when entering the workplace. It is not surprising that co-op and internship programs have been found to be an effective means to teach these skills (Ashford, 1988).

CHANGING HIGHER EDUCATION

The potential exists for colleges and universities to radically alter and improve preparation of graduates for work. At one level, institutions can respond with courses and workshops that address some of these subjects. These can be initiated by academic departments or student services organizations. Workshops can be quite helpful in at least building awareness among seniors, while courses can have a broader impact—particularly if required for graduation.

These interventions are an important tool, but higher education cannot fully address the problem without broader and more comprehensive initiatives. Because transition difficulties come from the tremendous differences between college and work cultures, culture change is required in higher education. Changing the culture is most effective if built upon campuswide partnerships incorporating key groups that influence seniors' development. These partnerships should focus on four key areas: expanding career and co-op services, changing the classroom experience, faculty initiatives, and institutional policy changes.

Expanding Career and Co-op Services

Career and co-op service groups on campus are unique in that they have a strong linkage to employers *and* have responsibility for aiding the transition out of college. It seems logical, then, that they should play a key leadership role in providing services to seniors. However, little impact can be expected from simply implementing voluntary workshops such as those provided for job searches. Until graduates enter the workplace, it is very difficult if not impossible for them to recognize the need to learn about the transition to work. In addition, it is unreasonable to expect even several days of workshops to undo years of continuous acculturation.

This presents both a problem and an opportunity for career planning and placement. On the one hand, career services offices often struggle to maintain close relationships with academic departments, so that leading change with them may appear intimidating or impossible. Many departments are strapped for resources and can hardly imagine taking on another initiative. On the other hand, this presents a golden opportunity to force partnerships to develop where they do not now exist. For many career service offices, this may be just the lever needed to enhance their status on campuses. The key link that career services offices can provide academic departments is access to a broader range of employers than most can access by themselves. If academic affairs officials are sold on the benefits, additional resources are likely to be available.

To anticipate the cases made by Smith and Gast in Chapter Twelve and Bates Parker, Jordan, and Keeling in Chapter Thirteen in this book, a comprehensive career services program should include the following:

- Structured partnerships with employers to identify key competencies
- Workshops and seminars offered to students directly and through academic departments
- Counseling for transition to work and work entry
- Structured partnerships with academic departments to design and implement transition programs
- Provision of access to employers (for faculty lacking organizational experience
- Opportunities for seniors to receive mentoring from recent graduates
- Resources to develop professional skills
- Strong co-op and intern programs

Changing the Classroom Experience

Perhaps the most controversial and difficult part of this undertaking is the need to change the classroom experience. It is in the classroom that much of educational acculturation takes place, so even the best workshops and courses are ineffective if no changes occur in the classroom. Educators must come to grips with the fact that many faculty efforts to make the learning process easier actually *hurt* graduates' preparation for professional life. The paradox of academic preparation may be difficult for many educators to accept, but it is one key to improvement.

It is difficult to convince colleagues that allowing students to struggle in their learning process may teach them more than does preparing additional handouts to make the learning easier. Teachers certainly have a responsibility to help students learn, but in terms of real-world preparation, too much support is actually a disservice. Ideally, the curriculum should evolve so that students become comfortable in work environments by graduation. Somewhere between the sink-or-swim real-world approach and a let-me-help-you higher education approach, there must be a balanced, workable solution.

In general, freshman and sophomore courses should continue to be supportive and assist students in learning how to learn at college. To a certain extent, these courses prepare students for learning in their major fields. By the junior year, though, classes should start to shift their focus to preparing students for work that lies beyond. Part of that preparation should be making the classroom more like a work environment. Ideally, there should be progression so that as students work toward graduation they are slowly moved from a supportive climate and encounter more real-world-like learning environments.

Practically speaking, teachers should bring an organizational culture into the classroom as much as possible. Consider some of the following steps:

- Expect professional attitudes and behaviors from students at all times.
- Introduce more uncertainty to wean students from the comfort of educational structure.
- Create simulations and role plays that mimic interactions between people in organizations.
- Require a high level of teamwork and interpersonal interaction to build interpersonal skills.
- Teach students to expect and manage change.
- Let students experience ambiguity and uncertainty.
- Require more self-directed learning.
- Use learning activities that present real-world complexities.
- Set higher standards.
- Hold students more accountable (deadlines, attendance, late work, and so on).
- Expect students' quality of work to be as high as what jobs require.
- Create many opportunities for students to interact with practitioners in the field.
- Create appropriate expectations about the workplace.
- Constantly remind students of differences between education and field practice.
- Spend time in the field yourself so you can inject realism into the classroom.

The classroom needs to become not only a setting for acquiring knowledge but a laboratory for experientially learning how to learn in work settings. The learning *process* becomes just as important as the course content.

Would these changes be popular with students? Not likely. In fact, many of the changes would bring quick complaints from most undergraduates accustomed to traditional methods. If the changes were made overnight, something close to mutiny might result! To make it work, the changes must first be properly implemented. For example, faculty should involve students in the process by explaining why changes are being made; they should use student frustration as part of the learning. Alumni and employers can meet with students to reinforce the need for different approaches. Students can thus come to understand the reasons and eventually appreciate them. Clearly, this is a more difficult approach than a traditional class, but there seems to be little choice.

Faculty Initiatives

The key to changing the classroom experience is to involve teaching faculty in the partnership. One issue that arises is the competence of faculty to implement the new teaching model. For one thing, most faculty are not trained teachers but rather specialists in their fields who need to be trained how to teach differently. Also, faculty who have not worked in noncollegiate organizations (there are many) have no clear picture of what organizational learning and professional life may be like. The solution is to locate faculty who have field experience and the ability to develop new learning models. Then they must be given release time and support to develop new models and help other faculty implement them.

A major barrier to faculty buy-in is the teaching evaluation system. The first issue is simply whether teaching is rewarded. This is a huge issue beyond the scope of this chapter, but suffice it to say that few faculty will make the changes if there is no payoff. The second issue is the teaching evaluation mechanism prevalent in most institutions: the student rating form. As long as faculty are rewarded based on student opinions of their teaching, they have little choice but to teach in ways that are more popular with students. It is difficult to see how changing the classroom experience to be more worklike will be popular with students (at least initially), so faculty run the real risk of lowering their teaching evaluations. Even those faculty who know and believe in the need for different learning models may be reluctant to make changes and endure low evaluations, particularly if teaching evaluations are used in decisions on promotion, tenure, or pay.

Research in human resource development indicates that self-reported reactions to learning experiences have little validity in predicting learning or performance after learning (Alliger and Janak, 1989; Dixon, 1990; Holton, 1996a; Warr and Bunce, 1995). Although reactions to learning certainly have some influence on the outcomes, they are not very effective as primary evaluation measures. In addition, heavy reliance on student evaluations for faculty assessment may be partially responsible for creating the paradox of academic preparation by discouraging learning experiences that are not popular but necessary. Other evaluation mechanisms have to be used, such as teaching portfolios, peer review panels, employer reviews, and so forth, to assess aspects of courses that are expected to be beneficial but not popular. The student rating forms also need to be changed to include responses to items such as "this course has helped prepare me for work" instead of "I enjoyed this course."

Institutional Culture Changes

Whereas some changes can be made at the departmental and classroom levels, the importance and impact of the transition to work demands an institutional-level commitment for lasting change. It should be apparent that meaningful change only results from long-term changes in institutional culture. Particular attention should be paid to the following components of culture.

Mission and Goals. An institution's vision and mission define the guiding lights for institutional activities; they set expectations for and shape student behavior (Kuh and others, 1991). Institutional leaders need to alter their institutions' mission so that it includes not just preparing graduates to find jobs but providing them with the full range of capabilities to succeed at work. Although few chief academic officers and presidents would disagree with this statement, in reality institutions tend to see graduation, and perhaps placement, as the end product. Leaders need to set institutional goals that clearly reflect this changed mission. This means identifying the professional capabilities as well as the occupational knowledge and skills that graduates need.

Leadership. Two types of leadership are needed: formal and emergent. An institution's formal leaders (that is, senior management) must demonstrate that preparing seniors is a priority concern. Their commitment must be clearly expressed and unequivocal. Without the demonstrated commitment of formally designated leaders, little can be expected to happen. One administrator should be given oversight responsibility for all efforts in this area, campuswide.

The most effective formal leadership is a partnership between the chief academic officer and the chief student affairs officer. Unfortunately, these two parts of the campus are often divided by organizational politics, status, and resource issues. Student services is charged with developing the students' lives outside the classroom, while the academic organization is responsible for classroom learning. As has been discussed, effective interventions address both; this requires close collaboration between the two groups, which must start with the senior officer in each unit.

Equally important, though, is emergent leadership, which can occur at all levels of the organization. Extending the mission requires champions who believe in the idea and take risks to promote new approaches to preparing seniors. Reluctant faculty and department heads must be convinced and shown how to implement new practices. These champions may emerge from any part of the institution and may or may not hold administrative positions. They should be located, nurtured, and rewarded.

Accountability. Goals are worthless unless institutions hold themselves accountable for achieving them. Higher education in general has struggled with the whole notion of outcomes assessment, due in part to the many different outcomes expected from a college degree. In the case of professional preparation for work, concrete goals can be defined and outcomes measured. Leaders must hold departments accountable for not only graduating students but preparing them for a successful transition to their chosen paths after college.

Resources. Resources must be made available to support programs and initiatives. Initiatives without resources tend to be viewed as unimportant and are unlikely to be effective. Although some changes do not require additional money, others do. On-campus grant programs can encourage new initiatives. Faculty may need release time to revamp courses or develop partnerships with employers.

Rewards. To facilitate change, individuals and departments should be rewarded for accomplishments in this area. Faculty in particular need to see that efforts are recognized and rewarded.

EMERGING CAREER-RELATED LIFE ISSUES

A new employment contract has emerged in the work world that is radically different from the paternalistic lifelong one prevalent in years past. This new contract requires employees to assume much more responsibility for their own careers, offers little in the way of long-term job security, and changes the nature of employee benefits. It also requires expanded skills for a successful transition to professional life, primarily because of increased responsibility placed on the individual. Anecdotal evidence suggests that new college graduates are often ill prepared to deal with such issues, which may increase stress during the transition and decrease overall satisfaction with their new life. These skills are not directly related to organizational performance, but graduates who are struggling with personal transitions that accompany going to work tend to underemphasize work issues until their personal life becomes more stable. Thus to increase personal satisfaction during the transition and remove barriers to professional transition success, it may be important for colleges to provide training in these topics:

Career planning. The common theme today is that graduates, not their organizations, are responsible for their own careers. It is not uncommon to find significant career issues emerging even within the first year. Graduates need to know how to identify career goals, make career choices, pursue new opportunities, and in some cases find new jobs.

Financial and retirement planning. Because of the new contract, graduates face completely different financial decisions than their parents did. Many graduates have to make investment decisions on 401(k) plans within the first few weeks of joining an organization. Some companies have completely abandoned their traditional defined-benefit pension plans in favor of other options that put all the responsibility on the employee. Graduates need the skills to make informed choices about their financial future.

Employability. The watchword for many employees today is to "stay employable, not employed." This means that employees have to build skills that are in high demand, build a network of contacts within the organization, make contacts in other organizations, be visible among important people, and so on. New graduates usually have golden opportunities during the early months to build new skills and make contacts, but they may not realize the importance of starting early. They should be taught how to stay employable.

Organization benefit plans. Along with retirement decisions, new graduates are also faced with an array of decisions about organization insurance and benefits plans. Larger companies may offer a cafeteria plan, where graduates can choose from a confusing array of health insurance plans. Graduates joining smaller companies may face the opposite problem and have to find their own sources of health insurance.

Personal business. New jobs often require graduates to face for the first time issues such as apartment leases, home buying, auto loans, mortgages, car and home insurance, and budgeting. These issues can be perplexing and time consuming when first encountered.

Relocation. Many graduates relocate to new cities as part of their transition. If so, they face the formidable challenges of locating housing, commuting in a new area, finding personal services (doctor, pharmacy, shopping, and so forth), and meeting new friends. The transition to a new city can be difficult and adversely affect work and personal life.

CONCLUSION

The responsibility for preparing students with nontask professional skills has traditionally been left to employers, who under the old employment contract were more willing to accept it. Higher education can no longer take this approach. The academic model must be extended to encompass—as a central part of the institution's mission—providing the full range of skills necessary for the transition to work and early career success. The short-term consequence of not doing so is that graduates are ill prepared for professional life after graduation, resulting in lower career satisfaction. In the long run, this reflects back on the campus. The long-term consequences to the institution of not embracing transition issues are the opposite of the benefits outlined by Cuseo in Chapter Two, which is to say, poor college-business relations, worse alumni relations, lost opportunities to develop faculty, fewer alliances between academic and student affairs, and lower-quality student assessment. Most important, graduates are not well prepared for their careers.

Although some educators may argue that this is too "vocational," the reality is that most students today look to a baccalaureate degree as a foundation for some form of work. The role advocated here is not one of job-specific preparation but of providing a foundation of lifelong career skills. This is entirely consistent with higher education's traditional mission. It is also an opportunity for higher education to strengthen its role and respond to many of the pressures it faces. Higher education can ill afford to ignore this critical issue.

CHAPTER EIGHT

Leadership Education
in the Senior Experience

Stephen W. Schwartz
Nance Lucas

Leaders must help bring younger leaders along," John W. Gardner has said in *On Leadership*. Leaders "can create the conditions of challenge, expectation and opportunity. They can remove the obstacles, unearth the buried gifts and release the work-renewing energies. . . . Given the mysteries of human development, the role of luck, and the many paths to failure, we shall never succeed in devising a program of training that will with certainty turn a promising youngster into a leader. We can, however, produce a substantial cadre of young potential leaders from which the next generation of leaders will emerge" (1990, pp. 161–162).

We live in an age that nurtures the growth of cynicism, abounds in antileadership sentiment aimed at political and corporate leaders here and abroad, and dampens people's desire to assume leadership roles. Although many cry out for more effective leadership, they are ambivalent; they appear to be uncertain of the kind of leadership necessary for a world of rapid change and for a public that is increasingly disenchanted with our national leaders, no matter what their philosophy or affiliation. In the face of such ambivalence, educators today ponder their responsibility for preparing students for leadership roles and citizen involvement. Educators recognize that they must continue to feed the stream of leaders in order to ensure that the highest values of democracy are sustained, and they are prepared to meet the challenge by providing well-designed programs of leadership education.

This chapter underscores the responsibilities of higher education to provide increased opportunities for students to realize their leadership gifts and potential. As our world changes, so do the many ways in which we prepare young people for leadership responsibilities, especially for the roles they assume after completing their baccalaureate education.

Colleges and universities, with their constant influx of students from the freshman to the senior years, provide a fertile ground for leadership education and citizen preparation. As the perfect setting for the generative process of leadership development described by Gardner in *On Leadership*, higher education offers the right opportunities for realizing leadership potential both in and out of the classroom. Senior faculty and staff have the opportunity to mentor not only their junior colleagues but also graduate and undergraduate students. Upper-class students, especially seniors, can, as part of their civic campus duty, mentor and coach incoming students and encourage them to get involved and make a difference. Collectively, everyone on the campus can play a role in nurturing the next generation of leaders and in encouraging what Derek Bok (1990) regards as quintessential, the higher standards of ethics and social responsibility.

The catalogues of today's colleges and universities reveal that education for leadership is part and parcel of a contemporary liberal arts education, even as it was in the late eighteenth-century Western Reserve and Northwest Territory. Between the Revolutionary and Civil War eras of U.S. history, graduates of America's colleges were expected to assume positions of leadership in all walks of life, especially in the rapidly developing communities of the Northwest Territory, and colleges were expected to prepare students for these roles. William H. Heid describes this preparation as "a blend of emotional and intellectual qualities combined into a broad moral approach to life" (1993, p. 164). The curriculum, particularly that of the senior year, was thus focused on the development of moral character required for leadership.

In contrast to the leadership curriculum of the nineteenth century, and in spite of highly rhetorical statements that proclaim important leadership missions, colleges and universities of the twentieth century have until recently ignored the teaching of leadership. For the most part, development of leadership skills in college graduates has been seen as a by-product of the educational process and not the result of well-designed deliberate interventions. Perhaps inherent in this neglect is a tacit acceptance of trait theory, the belief that leaders are born and not made. In addition, the belief of some college faculty that leadership cannot be taught has delayed the entry of leadership education into the contemporary curriculum.

In the past several years, however, the leadership mission of the American college and university has been resurrected in programs designed for deliberate cultivation of leadership abilities and habits. For whatever reason—and one can speculate in a variety of directions—the 1980s saw the development of many carefully articulated leadership development programs in both academic and student affairs divisions. (For an extensive listing of such programs, see Freeman, Knott, and Schwartz, *Leadership Education 1996: A Source Book*, published by the Center for Creative Leadership, 1996–1997).

To explore the recent renaissance of leadership education, this chapter provides an overview of leadership education program models, including contemporary theories and definitions of leadership, and gives examples of comprehensive leadership education programs that stress fundamental components, model good practices, and include a senior year focus. The chapter closes with an enumeration of good practices of leadership education programs.

CONTEMPORARY LEADERSHIP EDUCATION IN HIGHER EDUCATION

Leadership is a fluid concept, the meaning of which has evolved throughout history. Consider Joseph Rost's survey of definitions in *Leadership for the Twenty-First Century* (1991). Just as postindustrial organizations have changed since the Industrial Revolution, so has the concept of leadership. According to Rost, how we lead in the twenty-first century will look drastically different from how we have led in the twentieth century. Our assumptions and beliefs about leaders and leadership continue to change, and we envision a different type of leadership as we prepare for the new millennium. To a great extent, the trend today in America is moving away from hierarchical leadership toward more collaborative models of shared leadership. The relationship and interactions between leaders and followers are changing from an authoritarian model to a more inclusive, empowering leadership style. In the field of leadership studies, more attention is devoted to the interactions between leaders and followers than to the traits of the positional leader.

These changes are relevant to higher education as colleges and universities rise to meet the challenge of preparing tomorrow's leaders, for as leadership itself changes so must the programs that teach leadership. The content and emphasis of most leadership programs prior to 1985 look drastically different from today's programs. Early leadership training—both in the academy and in corporate America—emphasized self-promotion and success, ambition, excellence, taking charge, goal attainment and bottom-line results, and the spirit of enterprise, to name just a few overarching themes.

DeMott (1994) observes that today's leadership programs are marked by "a new consciousness." This new consciousness includes the "(1) capacity for vital response to values issues, especially the issue of the common good, (2) assurance that, in this country, reaching an adequate concept of the common good requires ceaseless experiment with democratic process, and (3) belief that genuine fulfillment for democratic man and woman is unattainable save through direct, lifelong participation in democratic experiment" (p. 6). DeMott further observes that leadership education today generally "manifests a firm bias against the notion that the common good can be reached through the pursuit of purely private gains. The stressed meanings of 'to lead' are *to include* and *to be included*; leader-like behavior is thought of less as 'influential' than as 'comprehensive'" (p. 7).

It should be obvious that the new consciousness of today's leadership programs requires new pedagogies. How does one teach the concept of the common good to a society preoccupied by individual rights? Why should students be concerned about leadership for social change? How do we prepare students— who are exposed to empowering and inclusive leadership models during their college years—to enter organizations that still employ traditional, hierarchical, industrial models of leadership?

Good Practices of Comprehensive Leadership Education Programs

Leadership development is a lifelong process, beginning before the collegiate years and continuing throughout adulthood. Elementary school children learn early leadership lessons at home and in school, about issues of fairness and notions of right and wrong. Children are exposed to simple yet powerful themes of leadership in fables and other children's books. In Margery Williams's classic children's book *The Velveteen Rabbit* (1983), Rabbit learns about hope, the process of becoming real, caring for others, and experiencing change. This children's book underscores Gardner's concept of the generative nature of leadership development: leadership is a lifelong journey, full of transitions and change.

Higher education serves as a vehicle to foster students' leadership development from the point of matriculation to graduation—from beanie to mortar board. The preparation of students for responsible citizenship and leadership is a process that should span the entire undergraduate experience. First-year students should be engaged in educational and developmental activities focusing on personal leadership development combined with an introduction to leadership studies. Students should be provided with traditional and experiential educational opportunities to learn about and practice leadership through the senior year. Several of today's colleges and universities offer full-stream leadership programs stretching horizontally from first year through graduation.

Comprehensive leadership programs are defined as offering multiple learning environments and initiatives beginning in the freshman year and continuing through the senior year experience. In keeping with the idea that leadership development is a lifelong journey, comprehensive leadership programs span students' college careers and encourage them to continue focusing on their leadership development beyond graduation.

Five Model Senior-Based Leadership Programs

Common to these comprehensive programs is the belief that leadership is the nexus of behaviors that can be taught. Based on the behavioral approach and research from Ohio State and Michigan studies, Karen Klenke relates that these behaviors can be categorized as "concern for the welfare of followers, including supportive behavior, information sharing, delegation and participative decision making; and concern for the task, including patterns of work organization, clear channels of communication, structuring of the role of leaders, and task and goal attainment" (Klenke, 1993, p. 115). In addition, many of these programs grow out of a commitment to the liberal arts and, rather than focus on the fields of social psychology and management, take a multidisciplinary approach. Here are five programs that can serve as models.

Leadership Program, Duke University. Among these programs is the Leadership Program at Duke University, begun in 1985 on the belief "that the country has urgent needs for abler and more ethical leadership, and that students might become better leaders through more active, imaginative, and experiential kinds of learning" (Clark and Freeman, 1990, p. 160). In many respects, the program proceeds on premises similar to those of the nineteenth-century institution of higher education, that is, developing the character of students for enhanced awareness of other people and the processes around them. Through a combination of courses, campus and community service, internships, and mentoring relationships, this program attempts to enhance understanding of democratic and civic values, develop conscience as an internal guide, instill the confidence necessary to tolerate ambiguity and take risks, establish a balance between the students' needs as individuals and as members of a community, and hone the skills that make citizens effective members of their communities: communication, negotiation, problem analysis, and problem solution. In short, the program hopes to bring out "the best that American students have to offer: energy, hope, intelligence, and earnest desires to do something of value for others" (Clark and Freeman, 1990, p. 160).

Jepson School for Leadership Studies, University of Richmond. As ambitious as the program at Duke is, it is less a program than a series of courses and opportunities for experiential education. Four other programs—at the University of Richmond's Jepson School for Leadership Studies, Marietta College's Bernard P. McDonough Center for Leadership and Business, the University of Maryland's Academy of Leadership, and St. Norbert College—offer students the opportunity to major or minor in leadership studies. The programs are structured in such a way that students have the opportunity to develop an under-standing of the complexities of leadership and the habits of mind and heart needed to assume the responsibilities of leadership. In general, these four programs look forward to the behavior of students as they take their places in communities after their graduation.

The Jepson program offers Richmond students a major in leadership studies. Because of its abiding commitment to the belief that real-world problems are complex, the program eschews as inadequate a one-dimensional social-scientific approach to leadership, providing instead a blending of the humanities and social sciences. Its aim is to educate *for* and *about* leadership so that students understand the moral obligations of leadership and are prepared to assume the ethical responsibility of serving society either as leader or follower. To be effective in serving in a democratic society, students must learn certain skills by observing and practicing leadership outside (as well as inside) the academy. Having completed the major, students are expected to be able to reflect on experience in such a way that they come to a sophisticated understanding of their theoretical assumptions and personal views of leadership.

The leadership studies major at Jepson seeks to produce three student outcomes, which are cognitive, affective, and behavioral in nature. The means for achieving these outcomes are four central curricular components that govern the design of leadership courses: core leadership knowledge, knowledge of leadership contexts, development of leadership competencies, and leadership experiences.

To establish core leadership knowledge, courses introduce students to theories of leadership and their historical evolution, modes of thinking critically about leadership, the ethics and moral perspectives of leadership, and leadership as a group enterprise. These courses provide the foundation upon which other components are built. Components concerned with leadership context introduce students to four organizational types (formal organizations, social movements, community organizations, and political systems) and demonstrate that leadership is determined by organizational context. Jepson students are asked to recognize that leadership is not monolithic, that no one notion of leadership serves across the full range of situations facing leaders. Courses also serve to develop in students the competencies that leaders need: the agreement-and-institution-building competencies outlined by John W. Gardner (1990) as well as workplace and marketplace competencies (seizing opportunities, crossing boundaries, and developing cultural sensitivity and such interpersonal skills as conflict resolution and decision making). Finally, the leadership major requires that students practice leadership through service, internships, foreign study, and assignments that require application of leadership principles. It is the hope of the Jepson School that this curriculum produces "ethical, imaginative, compassionate leaders who are critical, visionary thinkers . . . prepared to serve effectively in formal and informal leadership roles in a variety of contexts; to think critically and creatively about leadership theory and practice; to apply multiple knowledge bases to the study, observation, and practice of leadership; and to demonstrate moral judgment, imagination, and courage in the exercise of leadership" (Klenke, 1993, pp. 125–126).

McDonough Center for Leadership and Business, Marietta College. Similar in its commitment to a multidisciplinary liberal arts approach to leadership education as well as to a developmental model seeking changes over time, Marietta College's McDonough Center for Leadership and Business, located in Marietta, Ohio, offers a minor or certificate in leadership studies as an adjunct to the traditional academic major. Although the program is open upon application to all students on campus, most students entering the program make their decision prior to matriculation at the college. The minor requires the completion of twenty credit hours of course work, one hundred hours of community service, and a senior internship. Students may choose an alternative to the minor, the certificate in leadership studies, which requires only fifteen credit hours and fifty hours of community service.

Although the name of the McDonough Center might suggest a concentration on leadership for and in business, as at Richmond the Marietta faculty have chosen to focus their efforts on education *for* and *about* leadership in a variety of contexts, and a chief aim of the center is to develop in its graduates the values and skills required for effective citizen leadership. By the time they graduate, candidates in the program are expected to have acquired the values and skills that position them for leadership in their homes, communities, and workplaces. They have also acquired a definition of ethical leadership, the inclination to be involved rather than disengaged from the problems—both large and small—that face them, the ability to view problems from community and multicultural as well as individual perspectives, and the ability to use a wide array of group skills.

The first year begins with a special, weeklong orientation designed to introduce new candidates to upper-class candidates, to faculty and administrators who work in the center, and to the concepts of leadership that inform the work of the McDonough Center. Among other things, the orientation prepares candidates for the intensive yearlong leadership seminar that lays the foundation for further growth.

Although the two-semester seminar in leadership changes every year as new faculty teach it, the core of the course helps students become comfortable with the concepts and elements of leadership and introduces them to several conflicting definitions. Definitions are viewed in the context of the seminar's major theme: the relationship of the individual to the community and the understanding that this relationship is at the heart of leadership, which is, first and foremost, about people in groups. In addition, students should develop an appreciation for followers and the skills that enhance the effectiveness of followers.

The sophomore year offers students a second yearlong seminar focusing on theories and models of leadership and the organizational models in which leadership occurs. In the first semester, students are introduced to important leadership theories (trait, situational, contingency, transactional, charismatic and transformational, followership, and power and empowerment). In the second semester, they study the organizational contexts in which the theories play themselves out, especially with reference to enacting change in a variety of organizations.

By the end of the semester, students have gained the basis for "reading" an organization, with all that that implies about understanding the role of leaders and followers in enacting change. They should understand that different organizational contexts constrain behavior in specific ways and that leadership styles must therefore be appropriate to their contexts.

Throughout both the freshman and sophomore years, instruction aims at developing in students a number of small-group skills. Attention is given to collaborative projects, and instruction is provided to make the collaborations effective. (This is not unlike the training undertaken in corporate and institutional settings as traditional work processes shift to self-directed work teams.) Courses therefore stress such skills as active listening, giving and receiving feedback, effective positive confrontations, and conflict resolution.

Juniors devote themselves to preparation for the senior internship (undertaken during the summer between the junior and senior year) and completion of leadership-designated courses across the curriculum. A one-credit-hour internship preparation seminar covers two topics of importance: developing internship-seeking skills and developing the skills of participant observation.

Students begin with an introduction to the Career Center and its many reference works on internships, but they move quickly to exercises intended to help develop self-awareness and self-expression. Skill assessment leads to developing a vocabulary for communicating one's personal traits and ambitions to potential employers. This vocabulary is used almost immediately in preparing a résumé and letter of application tailored to specific internship possibilities discovered in the Career Center. It is then used in exercises intended to enhance the students' interviewing skills.

The second course module focuses on the skills of participant observation needed to make the internships a learning experience and not just another summer job. Class exercises require students to write critical-reaction papers about organizations they are involved in; the lens through which students observe these organizations has been created from the course materials of the first four seminars on leadership. That is, students describe the organizations with specific issues in mind—the relationship of the individual to the group, for instance—and with attention to a variety of leadership and organizational models. In short, it is expected that students use the issues, theories, and models studied in previous courses systematically and analytically. During their internships, students maintain a journal based on their observation; the journal is the basis for their reflections on the internship in another one-hour course, the postinternship seminar.

As for the internships themselves, students are encouraged to go far afield from what is most routine and normal in their lives. Because only a minority of students are inclined to tackle the unknown, the majority seek internships related in some way to their academic majors. Psychology majors, for example, seek research or clinical internships, and business majors seek internships with strategic planners or venture capitalists. In contrast, some students are willing to travel to foreign countries (Britain, Australia, and China), and others work in rural Appalachia or urban San Francisco.

Juniors also complete two leadership-designated courses offered by departments and including a leadership focus. Leadership-designated courses include those created especially for the leadership program—for example, Leaders in Protest (history), which examines counterculture leaders such as Mother Jones and Emma Goldman—as well as existing courses enhanced for the leadership program—for example, Native American History, which compares Native American models of leadership and community with mainstream models, and The Presidency and Executive Leadership (political science), which uses biographies of presidents to illuminate the nature of presidential leadership. Among other things, these courses help highlight leadership issues in a wide array of contexts.

The senior year is one for reaching conclusions about the nature of leadership and the readiness of the students to practice leadership after graduation. The postinternship seminar asks students to share their internship experiences with each other within the context of leadership topics. For instance, one discussion may be devoted to the culture of the sponsoring organizations, and the part played by culture in shaping the organization. Another discussion might focus on different strategies for change. In addition, students write an extended paper in which they attempt to answer some of their unanswered questions about leadership. Finally, the students engage in some serious self-assessment, in which they analyze their ability to use an array of group skills, work with others to solve real problems, perceive and respond appropriately to different cultures, operate from a personal working definition of leadership and from an understanding of the needs of a pluralistic democracy. In short, students are asked to assess the degree to which they find themselves "positioned for leadership." The assessment is anything but scientific, and the program will ultimately undertake a longitudinal study of its graduates.

Academy of Leadership, University of Maryland. The Academy of Leadership at the University of Maryland offers an extensive and multifaceted set of leadership education initiatives, beginning at the high school level and continuing through the graduate level. The academy's mission is to foster future generations of public leaders through education, research, service, and training. The theory of transforming leadership of the eminent leadership scholar James MacGregor Burns serves as the academy's guiding leadership philosophy. The academy's programs and research are founded on the idea that "leaders and members raise one another to higher levels of morality and motivation" (Burns, 1978, p. 20).

A comprehensive leadership program, the academy offers a unique two-year residential leadership program for first- and second-year students, entitled College Park Scholars Public Leadership Program. Based on a multidisciplinary curriculum, the program engages students in multiple learning environments: classrooms in their residence halls, field trips, community service, internships, and team projects. Students, faculty, staff, and alumni from various academic majors and disciplines such as government and politics, business, journalism, psychology, computer science, history, education, and engineering define the program's multidisciplinary approach. Students who complete the required nineteen academic credits at the end of their sophomore year receive an academic citation on their transcript.

The curriculum centers around four major themes: public leadership, social justice and law, public policy, and ethics. Each semester's theme is explored through either a three-credit or a one-credit colloquium complemented by out-of-class activities. The colloquium brings together students, faculty, and leaders to engage in a series of leadership inquiries related to the program's four academic themes. Students prepare to participate in a number of internships offered by the Academy of Leadership in local, state, federal, and international government or in a community service project. Students intern in public service fields or community service sites to learn firsthand about public policy issues or social problems and to experience and practice leadership in different settings.

The Leadership Laboratory, designed for public leadership students, includes leadership and personal skill training, self-assessments, and a library of leadership resources. In addition to the curriculum, students participate in retreats, actively practice leadership in committees and teams, interact with prominent leaders and scholars, and attend field trips to places such as the nation's Capitol, museums, and the statehouse. Students also have opportunities to apply what they learn in the classroom through service learning projects. Themes such as the ethics of reciprocity, empowerment, coalition building, advocacy, social action, and grassroots organizing are explored through service learning activities.

Beyond the College Park Scholars Public Leadership Program, upper-class students, including College Park Scholars graduates, can enroll in academic courses through the academy. Courses include Political Advocacy, History of Social Movements, African Americans in the Political Process, Women in Politics, Group Relations and the Politics of Identity, and Politics and the Media, to name a few. The academy also offers internships in public leadership and community service. Internship placements include the White House, Congress, and the Office of the Governor. The academy's internships carefully match students with prominent mentors who are committed to the empowerment of young leaders. Typically, junior and senior students elect to participate in the internship program. An academic course on leadership theory and practice is offered to support each of the internship experiences. Seniors are encouraged to apply to serve as teaching assistants for the academy's courses and to serve as mentors to younger students in the College Park Scholars Program and internship students. Teaching assistant and mentor programs allow senior students at the academy to experience the idea that leaders are both teachers and learners, and leaders have a responsibility to mentor others and prepare individuals for leadership and service.

The faculty of the Academy of Leadership partners with local John F. Kennedy High School to create and implement a four-year leadership curriculum at the secondary school level. Understanding that an individual's leadership development begins prior to collegiate years, the faculty and high school teachers designed a comprehensive curricular and cocurricular leadership program entitled the Leadership Training Institute (LTI). Fifty students from each class (ninth through twelve grades) are selected to participate in the LTI, which engages young students in coursework, committees, internships, grassroots organizing, lobbying, and partnership programs with the University of Maryland. The academy also cosponsors with Kennedy High School a regional leadership education training summer program for elementary and secondary school teachers. The teachers, who can receive continuing education credits for the training, attend seminars, work in teams to design curriculum modules, and meet again midyear to assess their work and exchange ideas.

St. Norbert College. Another college offering a minor in leadership studies is St. Norbert College in De Pere, Wisconsin. The minor grows directly from the college's mission in several ways: first, the mission emphasizes the intellectual, personal, and spiritual growth of students; second, the minor is informed by the college's notion of leadership as citizenship; finally, the minor is consistent with an interdisciplinary approach to education and a belief in the importance of sound scholarship while adhering simultaneously to a belief in the importance of practice. Moreover, the minor is well structured to accomplish its purposes.

Inspired by the Norbertine tradition of service, the minor emphasizes ethical commitment linked to action. Consider the objectives of the minor: to understand leadership within the context of the global common good; to recognize and appreciate theories and styles of leadership, including culture and gender issues; to examine leadership from varied perspectives, including the historical, literary, and sociological; to understand the impact of leaders on organizations and communities; and to exercise socially responsible leadership within the local, national, and international communities. In light of these objectives, the minor emphasizes the Norbertine belief that leadership is *first and foremost* a commitment to civic responsibility, moral integrity, and respect for gender and cultural diversity leading to acts of service to the community. To the end of rendering effective action, leadership is a set of skills involving goal setting, communication, and persuasion.

The minor involves completing five courses chosen from both core courses and electives organized by category. Specifically, the minor requires (1) Introduction to Leadership Studies, a team-taught course examining leadership in terms of communication, psychology, political science, philosophy, and ethics, focusing on what leadership is and how it works; (2) Leadership Studies Capstone, a capstone course combining skills development and practical application on campus and in the community with theories and concepts of leadership; and (3) the student's choice of three electives from the following categories and courses:

- *Ethics.* Courses focus on theories of human good and norms of conduct: Ethics, Business Ethics, Ethics: International Issues, Ethics in Society.

- *Interpersonal or small group.* Courses address the relationship between a leader and a small group, with attention to the influence of the leader on the individual members of the group and the dynamics of interpersonal relationships: Group Dynamics, Small Group Communication, Business and Professional Speaking, Persuasion.

- *Institutional or societal.* Courses explore the interactions of leaders and followers in societal entities and large organizations: Behavior in Organizations, Organizational Communication.

- *Leadership in context.* Courses examine leadership in a variety of contexts, for example, a discipline, political system, culture, historical period, institution, gender, or ethnic group: Leadership and Society, Leadership in Modern Mass Movements.

A combination of theory and practice, the minor helps students understand leadership's infinite variety and applicability to life. In discussing the commonplace notion that leadership involves "a great man," students in the introductory course come to recognize that leadership embraces more than a set of abilities inherent in one person, that it is about groups rather than individuals, and that it must be viewed in terms both of process and relationship. Moreover, they recognize that commitment is prior to skills, which fall into place after commitment. The following definition comes to spring easily to their lips: "leadership is service for the global common good."

Perhaps more than anything else, students are aware of the delicate interplay of theory and practice and of "self" and "other" in courses like Leadership and Society and Leadership Studies Capstone. Both courses employ readings and experiential exercises (for example, on- and off-campus group and individual projects) and emphasize the self and the other. Consequently, students have ample opportunity to think as much about their own leadership development as they do about leadership in general. The emphasis on self in relation to other works wonderfully in the leadership studies capstone. One student's comments are representative of the group reaction: "I've gotten more out of this class than any other single class I've ever taken." More than anything, St. Norbert students have gained the knowledge of self that Warren Bennis (1989) believes is the necessary prerequisite to significant leadership.

The Student Life Division of St. Norbert College sponsors a cocurriculum leadership program through the college's Citizen Leadership Development Center. The Citizen Leadership Development Center boasts a full-stream, comprehensive cocurricular leadership program. The center sponsors numerous programs ranging from tailored workshops on rudimentary leadership topics such as goal setting, meeting management, and organizational diversity to service learning projects and scholars-in-residence. In contrast to some full-fledged comprehensive leadership programs, which offer quantity but fall short on quality in merely scratching the surface of leadership education at the expense of achieving depth in content, the Citizen Leadership Development Center delivers on both program quantity (breadth) and quality (substance). Characterized by an enriched and creative content, the center exposes students to cutting-edge leadership themes and is inclusive in its approach to involving students in planning and implementing the many programs and services.

The center's mission is "to exist to sustain the needs of society for thoughtful citizens and productive professionals who will serve communities and organizations as catalysts for voiced and necessary change. Through the programs, experiences, and services offered, participants will gain an understanding of the leadership process by the sharing, development, and enhancement of knowledge necessary for the practice of collaborative, effective, just, and ethical leadership. The center encourages participants' growth through self-understanding and the understanding of others different from themselves, skill assessment, experiential learning, and recognition" (St. Norbert College, 1996).

The mission statement reflects the array of leadership program and service offerings by the Citizen Leadership Development Center. It is no accident that "development" is a part of the center's title and that programs such as Genesis,

Outreach Interns, and the Leadership Advisory Committee have a distinctly developmental focus.

The center sponsors various programs and services:

Teaching and Learning Together. Leadership consulting services.

Tailored Workshop Series. Leadership workshops tailored to student groups.

Student Events Calendar. Monthly information on student-centered programs.

Leadership Resource Center. Library housed at the center that contains over four hundred books on leadership, organizational and human development, and organizational management.

All-Campus Leadership Conference. Annual thematic conference planned by various student groups and campus departments. (Another good example of collaboration between the center and other campus partners.)

Campus Community Service and Leadership Awards Recognition Program. Campuswide recognition captures the community esprit de corps for those serving and leading as citizens in the St. Norbert College community.

Becoming a Citizen Leader at St. Norbert College. Designed for all new students to expose them to the value of social action in the community and what it means to be a responsible member of the community.

Citizen Leaders. Senior service learning project implemented and designed by graduating seniors and cosponsored by the Alumni Association.

Genesis. Leadership peer mentoring program where new students are paired with juniors who serve in leadership capacities at St. Norbert College.

Scholars-in-Residence. Two scholars annually visit the college to share their leadership knowledge and experiences during a three- or four-day visit.

National Student Leadership Recognition Review and Referral. Students are provided with award announcements ranging from the *USA Today* Award to Who's Who Among Students in American Universities as well as regional, state, and national leadership program awards.

Cocurricular Transcript. Service for students to document their campus involvement, leadership and community service experiences, and activities.

The Bridge. Semesterly leadership newsletter, edited by an undergraduate student intern, contains information on upcoming programs and spotlights student leaders, announcements, and reflections.

What is apparent from this survey of existing collegiate leadership study programs is that they are addressing, very deliberately, the contemporary call for more and better leadership and that they are developing standards of excellence by which such programs can be measured.

GOOD PRACTICES

Based on the programs previously mentioned, these *good practices* of leadership programs emerge:

- Embedded in the teaching of leadership should be the notion that leadership is about responsible citizenship (which includes effectiveness in the workplace), social change, leading with integrity, and leadership for the public good. Programs should help students answer the questions: Leadership for what purpose? How can this purpose bring about positive change for the public good?

- Programs and courses should focus on values exploration and formation. Students should be provided with opportunities to reflect on their values and personal mission in life and how they relate to the leadership process. Leadership programs themselves may embrace particular values in program content and delivery.

- Comprehensive leadership education should begin in the first year and continue through the senior year. Leadership programs should be based on the developmental patterns and growth of college students from the first year of college to the senior year.

- Programs and courses should have clear objectives and outcomes. Program planning should include creation and articulation of program objectives and learning or behavioral outcomes.

- Programs and courses should involve partnerships with faculty, student affairs professionals, alumni, and community leaders. A good practice of administrators of leadership programs is to model an inclusive approach that involves collaboration with other campus units, the local community, and external agencies and organizations.

- Content should include a survey of the field of leadership studies with emphasis on contemporary leadership definitions, theories, models, and practices. Students should learn about leadership theories and models that are congruent with the kinds of leadership called for in modern organizations. It should be noted that leadership programs must also prepare students to enter hierarchical organizations in which leadership is viewed according to the traditional industrial paradigms. Leadership programs should prepare graduates to measure leadership on a continuum from leader centered and hierarchical to relationship centered, inclusive, and nonhierarchical.

- Programs and courses should move from theory to practice, both in and out of the classroom, providing ways for students to think critically and imaginatively. Theory should inform practice, and practice should inform theory. Programs should provide opportunities for students to apply what they are learning and to reflect on how their leadership practices reflect theory. Experiential learning initiatives should provide avenues for reflection on leadership philosophies, assessment of self and others, and feedback.

- Programs and courses should receive ongoing evaluation and assessment. Program staff should design the evaluation methodology during planning stages and prior to implementation. A variety of evaluation and assessment interventions should be used, such as focus groups, traditional written methods, external evaluators, and pre- and post-assessment, to name a few examples. Evaluations should focus not only on how well participants liked the program but also on how much the students learned or changed as a result of their participation.

CONCLUSION

Whatever the current state of success of collegiate leadership programs, it is safe to say that leadership is being taken seriously today at a number of colleges and universities across the country as a way of preparing students for life after college. Colleges that wish to begin leadership courses and programs no longer have to labor as pioneers. Irving Spitzberg's 1987 article "Paths of Inquiry into Leadership" provides a starting point, as do articles by Thomas Wren (1994, 1995) and Karen Klenke (1993) in the *Journal of Leadership Studies*. The Jepson Leadership School, the McDonough Center, and the Academy of Leadership stand ready to lend their expertise and years of experience. In addition, the University of Maryland's National Clearinghouse for Leadership Programs is a reliable source of information on college-based student leadership programs.

Our belief is that more programs are needed to develop more and better leaders and that providing this development in a well-structured program eases the transition of graduates to nonstudent roles as citizens, both in the workplace and in their domestic lives. Building on the foundation laid during the early years of college, senior year practicum experiences allow students to test competencies considered critical to success in the workplace, such as the ability to work in teams; interpersonal communication; problem solving; and management of time, priorities, and initiative. Moreover, the same experiences prepare graduates for social responsibility and civic virtue.

The experience of one Marietta College student who completed his senior internship with a group of community organizers in a neglected section of the South of Market district of San Francisco is illustrative. This student spent the summer of 1991 polling the residents of the area to determine the housing needs of the community following the 1989 earthquake and prior to the construction of a single room occupancy hotel. As he made the rounds of one SRO hotel, he found himself on the third floor, talking to an old man in a wheelchair. What he discovered was that the man had not left the floor of the hotel for two years because the elevator shaft had been damaged in the quake. The internship brought home to that student something about the nature of human suffering that he had never known before. It provided for him the opportunity to consider the nature of his responsibilities as a citizen in twentieth-century America.

Anecdotes abound, and all suggest that carefully articulated leadership programs help prepare college graduates who are ready to join the workforce as well as increase the ranks of community leaders who make such a difference in the lives of their communities—as teachers who continue to challenge their students, members of the chamber of commerce, representatives of the city council, scout leaders, political and social activists, and company presidents. Some believe that the concern in preparing young leaders today is "not that we need to develop better leaders, but we need to develop more leaders" (Tyree, 1996, p. 32). Contemporary collegiate leadership programs are doing both.

CHAPTER NINE

Developing "Civic Virtue"
Among College Students

Linda J. Sax
Alexander W. Astin

Each spring, at commencement ceremonies across the country, graduating seniors are typically charged to use their college education to "become good citizens," "make a difference in society," "become the leaders of tomorrow," or simply "get out there and do something." Such graduation rhetoric has become so commonplace one hardly questions whether college actually prepares graduates to meet the challenges of citizenship.

College mission statements testify to the fact that higher education is publicly on record as committed to promoting good citizenship. College mission statements promise, for example, to promote "responsible participation in a democratic society," "encourage student leadership, volunteerism, and community service," and "prepare individuals for fulfillment of their roles as productive and responsible members of the local, state, national, and world communities." Given the promise of such statements and the exhortations of commencement speeches, it is reasonable to question the extent to which colleges actually work to instill a sense of civic virtue in their graduates. Improving higher education's ability to promote citizenship is in fact a top priority of current movements to enhance the senior year experience. A recent Wingspread Conference challenged higher education to produce "graduates who will perform as informed and involved citizens ready to assume leadership roles in American life" (Wingspread Group on Higher Education, 1993, p. 2). The responsibilities of citizenship may range from behavioral (for example, voting) to intellectual (consciously becoming informed about political and social issues) to humanitarian (helping others in difficulty). Citizenship development is particularly important during the senior year, as it marks a period of transition into adulthood—a time when many students are deciding what to do with their lives as well as how to live their lives. The senior year is therefore an opportunity for colleges to provide students with the guidance and direction to help make the responsibilities of citizenship central to their lives.

Recent data from the Cooperative Institutional Research Program (CIRP) at the University of California-Los Angeles suggest that colleges and universities face an increasingly difficult task of producing model "citizens" by the senior year. Higher education's ability to produce graduates with a strong sense of civic virtue is, of course, dependent on how civically virtuous students are when they come to college. Indeed, results from the latest annual Freshman Surveys show that political apathy is on the rise and that college students feel increasingly disconnected from civic life (Sax, Astin, Korn, and Mahoney, 1995; Dey, Astin, and Korn, 1991). The percentage of entering college freshmen who report frequently discussing politics has dropped from a high of 30 percent in 1968 to an all-time low of 15 percent in 1995. The percentage of freshmen who believe that it is very important or essential to keep up to date with political affairs has dropped from 58 percent to 28 percent in the past thirty years. Student involvement in political campaigning is equally dismal: only 7 percent of 1992 freshmen worked on a local, state, or national political campaign, compared with 16 percent in 1969.

Given incoming students' apparent disinterest in civic affairs, it is important to ask whether colleges and universities can "reconnect" students to civic life and promote their sense of civic virtue by the end of the senior year. In an attempt to answer this question, we begin this chapter with a review of literature and previous research on higher education's role in citizenship development. Next, based on the results of a national study of college impact (Astin, 1993b), we summarize how civic virtue is affected by a variety of college environments and student experiences. Finally, we offer policy perspectives that higher education faculty, administrators, and staff should consider in their efforts to instill a sense of civic virtue in students by their senior year.

CITIZENSHIP AS A GOAL OF UNDERGRADUATE EDUCATION

The development of citizenship is a long-standing goal of higher education in the United States (Boyer and Hechinger, 1981; Finkelstein, 1988; Ketcham, 1992; Morse, 1989; Newell and Davis, 1988). More than two hundred years ago, Thomas Jefferson touted education for citizenship as essential to the development of a well-informed and critically thinking citizenry (Morse, 1989). Although nineteenth-century industrialization and educational specialization downplayed the role of civic education (Morse, 1989), citizenship reappeared as a priority of higher education through the general education movement of the early twentieth century. At that time, general education was seen as the means for providing the basics of civics education and a common understanding of society and culture that were apparently becoming lost in an increasingly overspecialized college curriculum (Ketcham, 1992; Rudolph, 1962).

Although many continue to believe that civic education can be achieved through transmitting a core set of information, traditions, and values (Bloom, 1987; Hirsch, 1987), the increasing diversity of race, ethnicity, religion, and heritage in the United States makes it unrealistic for higher education to impart any notion of a "common" culture (Strike, 1988). Indeed, reformers emphasize that civic education is not about educating students to have certain partisan political views, but about enhancing students' ability to gain "perspective" (Boyer, 1987), make "responsible judgments" (Ketcham, 1992), and become active and proactive citizens beyond merely voting (Newell and Davis, 1988). As noted in a Carnegie Foundation report, "If there is a crisis in education in the United States today, it is less that test scores have declined than it is that we have failed to provide the education for citizenship that is still the most important responsibility of the nation's schools and colleges" (Newman, 1985, p. 31).

PREVIOUS RESEARCH ON CITIZENSHIP AND VALUES DEVELOPMENT IN COLLEGE

Despite the widespread belief that citizenship development is a critical function of higher education, previous research suggests that the development of civic virtue among college students is modest at best (Pascarella and Terenzini, 1991). What modest change does occur, however, tends to be toward greater liberalism, civic responsibility, and social conscience (Astin, 1977; Bowen, 1977; Hyman and Wright, 1979; Jacob, 1957; Pascarella, Smart, and Braxton, 1986; Pascarella and Terenzini, 1991).

In exploring the issue of *how* colleges promote citizenship, research has examined the impact of institutional characteristics as well as measures of the student experience. The weight of evidence suggests that the type of institution attended is a relatively unimportant factor in citizenship development (Jacob, 1957; Pascarella, Ethington, and Smart, 1988; Pascarella, Smart, and Braxton, 1986; Pascarella and Terenzini, 1991). Instead, it is the nature of the individual student's experience that seems to have most influence on the development of civic values.

Aspects of the college experience that most effectively promote civic values include living in a residence hall, majoring in the social sciences, interacting with faculty, and gaining leadership experience (Pascarella, Ethington, and

Smart, 1988; Pascarella and Terenzini, 1991). These findings support the notion that civic outcomes, like other college outcomes, are dependent on students' degree of "involvement" in the college environment (Astin, 1985; Tinto, 1987), particularly when that involvement fosters learning in a social and cultural context (Jacob, 1957; Morrill, 1980; Morse, 1989; Newell and Davis, 1988).

Despite the useful information on citizenship development provided by previous studies, such research has also faced important limitations. The early works of Jacob (1957) and Hyman and Wright (1979) were comprehensive, but they were cross-sectional instead of longitudinal. And even though the research of Pascarella, Smart, and Braxton (1986) was longitudinal, it did not explore the effects of student involvement. Finally, although Pascarella, Ethington, and Smart (1988) conducted a longitudinal study with numerous involvement measures, they measured change more than nine years after college entry and therefore could not determine whether students had changed during college or in the years after.

OBJECTIVES AND APPROACH

Using a national four-year longitudinal database of college students, this chapter examines four questions:

1. To what degree do students develop citizenship qualities between their freshman and senior years of college?

2. How is citizenship development affected by characteristics of the college environment (for example, size, type, control, faculty, and peer groups)?

3. How is citizenship development affected by students' involvement in the college experience (courses taken, time spent on various curricular and extracurricular activities)?

4. What are the implications of these findings for higher education?

To answer these questions, we analyzed data from the CIRP's 1985 Freshman Survey and 1989 Follow-Up Survey. This particular longitudinal sample includes 27,065 college freshmen, at 388 four-year colleges and universities, who completed both the Freshman and Follow-Up Surveys. The Freshman Survey, which focuses on first-time, full-time college freshmen, has been conducted annually since 1966 and includes information on students' personal and demographic characteristics, high school experiences, and expectations about college as well as their values, life goals, self-concepts, and career aspirations. The 1989 Follow-Up Survey includes information on students' college experience and their perceptions of college as well as posttests of many of the items that appeared on the 1985 Freshman Survey. In addition, data from CIRP's 1989 Faculty Survey (35,478 faculty at 392 institutions) were used to create measures of the faculty environment at each institution.

Finally, although the student follow-up data are now nearly eight years old, the findings should nevertheless be a reliable indicator of the present-day impact of college. First, to the extent that today's college students differ from students entering college in 1985, this study controls for dozens of entering-student characteristics. Second, the college environment changes relatively slowly over time, as evidenced by the general stability of the faculty labor force, curricula, and institutional structural characteristics.

Our study examined the impact of college on nine measures of *citizenship* or *civic virtue.* Although the following list does not include all possible measures of civic virtue, it does encompass key aspects of Bowen's definition of citizenship as the "commitment to democracy" and "the disposition and ability to participate actively in civic, political, or other voluntary organizations" (1977, p. 57):

- Social activism
- Leadership
- Cultural awareness
- Commitment to environmental involvement
- Commitment to racial understanding
- Belief that individuals can change society
- Tutoring others
- Participating in campus demonstrations
- Voting

Social activism is defined in terms of the importance the student assigns to each of four life goal items: participating in community action programs, helping others who are in difficulty, influencing social values, and influencing the political structure. Each of these values suggests high activity, assertiveness, and social involvement (participating, helping, influencing). All four components of the social activism measure are pretested in the 1985 Freshman Survey.

Leadership is defined in terms of three self-ratings—leadership ability, popularity, and social self-confidence—and whether or not the student was elected to a student office. All components of the leadership factor are pretested in 1985 except being elected to student office.

The cultural awareness factor encompasses the student's self-rated degree of change (from freshman to senior) on two self-change items: "cultural awareness and appreciation" and "acceptance of persons from different races/cultures." The student's cultural awareness score thus consists of the simple sum of responses to these two questions. No pretests exist for this item, although the notion of change is inherent in the way the question is worded: "Compared with when you entered college as a freshman, how would you now describe your . . . cultural awareness and appreciation . . . acceptance of persons from different races/cultures?"

Commitment to environmental involvement is defined as the importance the student places on "becoming involved in programs to clean up the environment." Similarly, commitment to racial understanding is defined as the importance the student places on "helping to promote racial understanding." Both of these items are pretested on the 1985 Freshman Survey.

The belief that individuals can change society is based on the student's level of *disagreement* with the statement "Realistically, an individual can do little to bring about changes in our society." Students who disagree with this item are seen as exhibiting greater civic virtue. This item is also pretested on the 1985 Freshman Survey.

Finally, three behavioral outcomes refer to activities engaged in during college: tutoring others, participating in campus demonstrations, and voting in the 1988 presidential election. Tutoring others has an identical pretest from the 1985 Freshman Survey. Participating in demonstrations does not have a direct pretest, although the 1985 Freshman Survey asked students to indicate their likelihood of engaging in this activity during college. Finally, voting in a presidential election does not have a direct pretest in the freshman survey because most college freshmen in this sample were younger than voting age in the November before they entered college.

CHANGE DURING COLLEGE

Table 9.1 displays students' scores on each of the citizenship items in 1989, with 1985 scores listed when available. The top portion of the table lists the outcomes for which we can examine changes over four years. The bottom portion of the table lists items for which direct pretests are not available.

For each of the pretested items, students' scores reflect a modest increase in civic virtue during college. Within the social activism factor, students become more committed to helping others in difficulty, participating in community action programs, influencing the political structure, and in particular influencing social values. Similarly, students show increases in all three self-rating items in the leadership factor: leadership ability, popularity, and social self-confidence. Students also experience strong gains in their commitment to environmental involvement, and more moderate gains in their commitment to racial understanding and their time spent tutoring others. Finally, there is a small increase in student belief that individuals can bring about changes in society.

Table 9.1. Citizenship Outcomes: Change During College.

Change Outcomes	Percentage		
	1985	1989	1985–1989
Items with direct pretests			
Social activist			
Helping others in difficulty[a]	65.2	71.6	+ 6.4
Influencing social values[a]	35.8	50.4	+ 14.6
Participating in community action programs[a]	27.4	34.9	+ 7.5
Influencing the political structure[a]	18.9	23.7	+ 4.8
Leadership[b]			
Leadership ability[c]	57.9	63.3	+ 5.4
Popularity[c]	47.0	49.2	+ 2.2
Social self-confidence[c]	50.0	54.7	+ 4.7
Becoming involved in programs to clean up the environment[a]	20.6	34.9	+ 14.3
Helping to promote racial understanding[a]	35.3	39.4	+ 4.1
Tutoring others[d]	49.6	53.5	+ 3.9
An individual person can do little to bring about changes in society (disagree)[e]	67.2	68.9	+ 1.7
Items Without Direct Pretests			
Participated in protests[f]	7.4	24.8	+ 17.4
Cultural Awareness[g]			
Cultural awareness and appreciation	—	78.1	—
Acceptance of people of different racial/ethnic group	—	61.9	—
Voted in presidential election	—	69.2	—

[a] Goals rated as "essential" or "very important."

[b] The item "elected to student office" has been omitted in order to make the 1985 and 1989 measures comparable.

[c] Self-rating of "above average" or "top 10 percent."

[d] Student's behavior done "frequently" or "occasionally."

[e] Percentage who "disagree strongly" or "disagree somewhat."

[f] 1985 percentages refer to self-rated chances of behavior as "some chance" or "very good chance." 1989 percentages are those reporting that event actually occurred during college.

[g] Percentage reporting self-rated change of "stronger" or "much stronger."

Among items that do not have direct pretests, findings still suggest some degree of citizenship "development" during college. For example, although only 7.4 percent of freshmen believed there was at least "some chance" of participating in protests during college, 24.8 percent participated in protests by their senior year. Further, when asked to self-report change during college, 78.1 percent felt their cultural awareness and appreciation had become stronger during college (as compared with 20.6 percent reporting no change, and only 1.3 percent reporting that their cultural awareness had become weaker). Similarly, 61.9 percent felt their appreciation of people from different races and cultures had become stronger during college (35.0 percent reported no change and only 3.1 percent reported becoming weaker in this area during college). Finally, 69.2 percent of students reported voting in the 1988 presidential election, compared with 36 percent among all eighteen-to-twenty-four-year-olds (U.S. Bureau of the Census, 1993).

As a whole, the findings in Table 9.1 suggest that students do indeed gain in their civic virtue during college. By their senior year, students become more concerned with helping others in need, more committed to effecting social and political change, and more confident in their leadership ability.

ENVIRONMENTAL EFFECTS: RESULTS OF MULTIVARIATE ANALYSES

Now that we have demonstrated that students develop a greater capacity for citizenship during college, a more important issue, at least from a practical perspective, is *how* college promotes citizenship. We are interested in knowing how citizenship outcomes are affected by characteristics of institutions, curricula, faculty, and peer groups. We are also interested in the effects of place of residence, choice of major, and various forms of involvement. In doing so, we first need to exert as much control as possible over self-selection (that is, over potentially biasing entering-student characteristics) before examining the possible effects of the college experience. The technique chosen for this task is blocked, stepwise multiple regression analysis.

The basic idea behind this type of causal modeling is to control different blocks of variables according to their known or assumed order of occurrence. Described as the "input-environment-outcome" (I-E-O) methodological framework (Astin, 1991), analyses examine the impact of various college environments and experiences on student outcomes, after controlling for students' precollege characteristics and experiences. Thus, because entering characteristics of the 1985 freshmen are known before these freshmen have any significant exposure to college, student input characteristics are controlled before examining the effects of the college environment.

Analyses then examine the effects of 192 measures of the college environment. These include 16 measures of the characteristics of the institution attended (size, control, and so on), 15 measures of the curricular requirements, 35 measures of the student's peer environment, and 35 measures of the freshman's place of residence, financial aid, and choice of major. In a final block, an additional 57 "involvement" measures have been included to assess environmental experiences that occur only after the student has been enrolled in college for a period of time. These include the quantity and quality of student involvement in academic work (22 measures), faculty (6 measures), the student peer group (14 measures), work (4 measures), and miscellaneous other nonacademic involvements (11 measures). See Astin (1993b) for a complete description of independent variables.

ENVIRONMENTAL EFFECTS ON CITIZENSHIP DEVELOPMENT

The remainder of this chapter focuses on the effects of college on the development of citizenship. The variables presented in this chapter were significant predictors of citizenship development *after* controlling for salient precollege characteristics of citizenship outcomes (as determined by regression analyses). Input characteristics that are most predictive of citizenship outcomes include:

SAT scores

Intellectual self-confidence

Parental education

Family income

Early commitment to political and social change

Participating in volunteer work during high school

Being African American or Chicano (predictive specifically for the outcomes of social activism and participating in protests)

Social Activism

Social activism, as we discussed regarding Table 9.1, refers to the student goals of participating in community action programs, helping others who are in difficulty, influencing social values, and influencing the political structure.

College Environment Influences. Not surprisingly, the faculty's social activism and community orientation has a positive effect on the student's social activism score. This environmental factor measures the extent to which the institution is perceived as concerning itself with producing student leaders who become agents of social change. Here we have clear-cut evidence that institutional values or priorities can have a direct effect on students' values. One peer environment factor also enters the regression equation with a positive weight: the mean socioeconomic status (SES) of the peer group. Development of social activism is also positively affected by majoring in the social sciences, and negatively affected by majoring in the natural sciences, engineering, or business.

Student Involvement Activities. The involvement measures showing the strongest relationships with social activism (after controlling for input and environmental variables) all have to do with activism or diversity issues: discussing racial and ethnic issues with other students, taking ethnic studies courses, socializing with students from different racial and ethnic groups, attending racial and cultural awareness workshops, and participating in campus demonstrations. Social activism is also related to hours per week spent in volunteer work. We cannot always be sure of the direction of causation in these "intermediate outcome" relationships, but it is interesting to consider the possibility that students' commitment to social activism can be reinforced through such activities.

Social activism is also related to student-student and student-faculty interaction. It also has positive relationships with the number of history or writing skills courses taken, and a negative residual relationship with number of mathematics or numerical courses taken.

Leadership

As we defined it earlier, the leadership measure comprises self-ratings of leadership ability, popularity, and self-confidence; and election to a student office.

College Environment Influences. The sole positive environmental influence on undergraduate development of leadership skills is leaving home to attend college. One peer group factor—the percentage of students who are engaged in outside work activities—has a significant negative effect on leadership. In all likelihood, when many members of the peer group are engaged in employment off campus, leadership opportunities may be curtailed and the incentive to seek leadership positions reduced.

But the largest environmental effect on leadership, in this case a negative one, is associated with a faculty environmental factor: the "research orientation" of the faculty. Why the development of leadership qualities among undergraduates should be attenuated when the faculty is heavily engaged in research and scholarship is not immediately clear. Because involvement with faculty tends to be closely associated with the development of leadership qualities, it may well be that heavy faculty commitment to research simply reduces the amount of time and energy that faculty members can devote to those student-faculty activities that facilitate leadership development.

Student Involvement Activities. As might be expected, changes in leadership (after controlling for student input and environmental effects) are associated with more involvement measures than any other single student outcome. The effects of student-student and student-faculty interaction are particularly strong. Larger-than-average increases in leadership scores are also associated with being a member of a social fraternity or sorority, playing intramural sports, hours spent in volunteer work, tutoring other students, participating in a group project for class, and making presentations to class. Not surprisingly, substantial *negative* effects are associated with hours spent watching television and hours spent commuting. Clearly, both of these activities would serve to limit student opportunities for participation in leadership activities and the development of leadership skills.

Cultural Awareness

Awareness, appreciation, and acceptance of persons from other races and cultures showed one of the highest numbers of influences, positive and negative, among the nine measures.

College Environment Influences. That self-reported growth in cultural awareness is positively affected by going away from home to attend college reinforces the idea that one of the benefits of the residential experience is to enable the student to become familiar with a greater variety of racial and cultural groups. A similar argument can be made to explain the positive effect on cultural awareness of having a college work-study assignment; in other words, having an on-campus job tends to bring the student into contact with a wider variety of fellow students and staff.

The strongest positive effects on cultural awareness, however, are associated with two environmental measures from the Faculty Survey: faculty diversity orientation (the extent to which faculty incorporate issues of race and gender into their research and teaching) and institutional diversity emphasis (the institution's concern with and commitment to diversity issues). In other words, students report greater increases in cultural awareness when they attend institutions where race, ethnicity, and gender are valued in the curriculum, in research, and in admissions and hiring.

The degree of concern with materialism and status among the peer group, conversely, has a negative effect on cultural awareness. Majoring in any of three fields of study also produces negative effects on cultural awareness: engineering, physical science, and business. These negative effects reinforce the belief that peers and faculty in the sciences, engineering, and business give low priority to issues of cultural awareness and diversity.

Student Involvement Activities. As might be expected, the involvement measures having the strongest partial correlations with self-reported increases in cultural awareness all have to do with diversity issues: discussing racial and ethnic issues, attending racial and cultural awareness workshops, socializing with people from different racial and ethnic groups, participating in campus demonstrations, and enrolling in ethnic studies courses. Weaker positive effects are associated with participating in a study abroad program, hours per week spent attending religious services, number of history courses taken, and holding a part-time job on campus (other than work-study). Two involvement measures produce negative partial correlations with cultural awareness: hours per week spent watching television and working full-time while enrolled as a student. Both of these activities may well serve to limit students' exposure to persons from other cultures. It is also interesting to consider the possibility that the *content* of television programming might have something to do with this negative effect.

Commitment to Environmental Involvement

Commitment to the environment refers to the student's personal goal of becoming involved in programs that help clean up the environment.

College Environment Influences. Student commitment to involvement in programs to clean up the environment is affected by a rather unexpected set of environmental variables. Positive effects are associated with the percentage of faculty involved in team-teaching, perceived racial conflict on the campus, and majoring in natural science. Faculty use of graduate teaching assistants and the percentage of students majoring in physical science fields both have negative effects on students' commitment to the environment.

One can only guess at the meaning of these effects, although several explanations are possible. Courses that are team-taught, for example, may often focus on issues having to do with ecology or the environment. Ecology may well lend itself to team-teaching, since ecological issues cut across several disciplines. At the same time, many courses on ecological issues are taught in natural science departments. These interpretations, if correct, suggest that one way to encourage more student interest and involvement in environmental issues would be to require more team-taught courses on the subject.

Student Involvement Activities. A substantial number of involvement variables are associated with commitment to getting involved in environmental programs. Many of the variables having positive associations suggest that environmental and diversity concerns are linked: discussing racial and ethnic issues, participating in campus demonstrations, attending racial and cultural awareness workshops, taking women's or ethnic studies courses, and socializing with persons from different racial and ethnic groups. Other positive associations involve hours per week spent in exercise or sports, hours per week spent talking with faculty outside of class, number of science courses taken, number of history courses taken, hours per week spent reading for pleasure, and hours per week spent in volunteer work. Involvement factors showing negative associations include hours per week spent socializing with friends, attending religious services, and watching television.

Promoting Racial Understanding

As mentioned earlier, civic virtue is also measured in terms of students' personal commitment to help promote social understanding in society.

College Environment Influences. Commitment to racial understanding is positively associated with the following environmental variables: going away from home to attend college, the humanities orientation of the college environment, the socioeconomic status of the peer group, and the institutional diversity emphasis. Commitment to promoting racial understanding is negatively affected by majoring in business, nursing, science, or engineering.

Student Involvement Activities. As might be expected, most involvement variables that are still correlated with commitment to promoting racial understanding after entering student and environmental characteristics are controlled relate to diversity issues: discussing racial and ethnic issues, attending racial and cultural awareness workshops, socializing with people from different racial and ethnic groups, participating in campus demonstrations, and enrolling in ethnic studies courses. Although it is entirely possible that some of these involvement variables are the *result* of increased interest in promoting racial understanding rather than the cause of this increased interest, it is important to keep in mind that promoting such activities on campus may well enhance students' commitment to promoting racial understanding. Three academic variables also have positive partial correlations with this item: hours per week spent studying or doing homework, number of foreign language courses taken, and number of history courses taken. Two involvement variables have negative associations with commitment to promoting racial understanding: number of mathematics or numerical courses taken and alcohol consumption.

Belief That Individuals Can Change Society

As described earlier, *disagreement* with the notion that the individual is relatively powerless to bring about social change is taken as exhibiting greater civic virtue.

College Environment Influences. Students' belief that individuals can bring about changes in society is positively affected by going away from home to attend college, majoring in business, and by an environmental emphasis on social activism and community; the belief is negatively affected by majoring in science or engineering.

Student Involvement Activities. Involvement variables positively associated with the belief that individuals can effect social change include the diversity activities of socializing with persons from different racial and ethnic groups, discussing racial and ethnic issues, participating in campus demonstrations, and taking women's or ethnic studies courses. Additional variables positively associated with this belief include hours per week spent talking with faculty outside of class, number of writing skills courses taken, hours per week spent participating in religious services, and hours per week spent in volunteer work. This belief that individuals can change society is negatively associated with only one involvement variable: hours per week spent watching television. It proves to be the strongest association with any involvement variable.

Tutoring Other Students

Tutoring is the first of the three behavioral outcomes we look at as evidence of students' civic virtue.

College Environment Influences. Tutoring is positively affected by leaving home to attend college and receiving a grant from the college. The frequency of tutoring is negatively affected by the research orientation of the institution and by the percentage of students who are receiving merit-based aid.

Majoring in physical science increases the student's likelihood of tutoring other students, whereas majoring in social science decreases that likelihood. In all probability, the differential effects of majors reflect differential *demand* for tutoring in various subject matter fields.

Student Involvement Activities. Tutoring is positively associated with a substantial number of involvement variables, after the effects of input and environmental variables have been controlled. Notable among these is assisting faculty in teaching a class, hours per week spent talking with faculty outside of class, and being a guest in a professor's home. This pattern suggests strongly that faculty may well serve as "brokers" between their best students and those who are experiencing academic difficulties. Tutoring is also positively associated with enrolling in an honors program, hours per week spent in volunteer work, holding a part-time job on campus, working on a group project for a class, number of math courses taken, and number of foreign language courses taken. These latter effects may reflect the fields in which students are most likely to be tutored by other students. The only involvement variable entering the regression equation with a significant negative weight is, once again, hours per week spent watching television.

Participating in Campus Protests

Another behavioral indicator of civic involvement is students' participation in campus protests and demonstrations.

College Environment Influences. One peer group measure, political liberalism (versus conservatism), has a positive effect on the likelihood that the student will participate in campus protests. Participation is also positively affected by institutional diversity emphasis, racial conflict, the percentage of students majoring in the humanities, and attendance at a nonsectarian four-year college. In short, it would appear that a student's chances of participating in demonstrations or protests while in college are maximized if the student lives away from home and attends a nonsectarian college where the peer group is politically liberal, the curriculum is strongly oriented toward the humanities, and there is a strong campus emphasis on diversity issues. Not surprisingly, majoring in engineering reduces the student's chances of participating in campus protests.

Student Involvement Activities. Several involvement variables turn out to be associated with participation in protests, once the effects of student input and environmental variables are taken into account. The strongest positive associations involve discussing racial and ethnic issues, attending racial and cultural awareness workshops, socializing with people from different racial and ethnic groups, enrolling in women's studies courses, hours per week spent in volunteer work, hours per week spent in student clubs or organizations, receiving personal or psychological counseling, and being elected to a student office.

Voting

The final measure of civic virtue is having voted in the 1988 presidential election (the vast majority of the 1985 freshmen had reached voting age by the time of the 1989 Follow-Up Survey).

College Environment Influences. The strongest positive environmental effect on voting is associated with the intellectual self-esteem of the peer group. Other positive environmental influences include the diversity orientation of the institution and having a high percentage of men in the student body. Students who leave home to attend college are less likely to vote in a presidential election. (Resident students apparently are unlikely to register in their college towns or to vote by absentee ballot.) The percentage of faculty involved in teaching general education courses also has a negative effect on voting.

Student Involvement Activities. Involvement factors that are positively associated with voting in the 1988 election included number of history courses taken, hours per week spent attending religious services, taking essay exams, participating in campus demonstrations, discussing racial and ethnic issues, socializing with students of different racial and ethnic groups, enrolling in women's or ethnic studies courses, and attending racial and cultural awareness workshops. These latter two factors, together with the positive effects associated with the diversity orientation of the institution, suggest that the student's level of political involvement can be increased by encouraging students to take an interest in political or racial issues. The only involvement variable showing a negative association with voting in the 1988 election is participation in intercollegiate athletics.

Summary

Across the nine outcomes assessed in this chapter, more than fifty different variables emerge as significant predictors of citizenship development. Among these, a few stand out with particularly strong and consistent effects: the positive ones of diversity activities, volunteer work, and leaving home to attend college and the negative one of watching television.

The positive effects of diversity activities are numerous. By the end of the senior year, students are likely to increase their level of civic virtue if they engage in socializing with someone of a different race or ethnicity, attend racial awareness workshops, take ethnic studies or women's studies courses, discuss racial and ethnic issues, and participate in campus protests or demonstrations. Similarly, students are more likely to gain in civic virtue when they attend institutions that are committed to policies such as increasing the representation of minorities in the student body, increasing the representation of women and minorities on the faculty, and emphasizing multiculturalism.

The positive effects of volunteer work on civic virtue are also quite interesting. Controlling for students' precollege disposition toward service, students who spend time volunteering during college (compared to those who do not volunteer) become more convinced that individuals can change society, are more committed to personally effecting social change, and develop stronger leadership skills. These effects are particularly interesting because they suggest that students' actual *participation* in community service or volunteer activities ("involvement") helps reinforce the notion that they can do something about society's problems.

Leaving home to attend college also produces positive effects on the development of civic virtue during college. Except for the fact that students living away from home are less likely to vote in a presidential election, leaving home to attend college produces positive effects on five citizenship outcomes: leadership, cultural awareness, commitment to promoting racial understanding, tutoring other students, and the belief that individuals can change society. Further, Astin (1993b) found that students who leave home to attend college are more satisfied with the college experience; specifically, those who live in campus residence halls are more likely to finish college. Clearly, leaving home to attend college provides students with experiences and opportunities that encourage them to be more concerned with the welfare of others and more committed personally to making changes in society.

The only measure to produce consistently strong and negative effects on citizenship development is hours per week spent watching television. Students who spend more time watching television are less likely to develop leadership skills, become culturally aware, tutor other students, or engage in environmental cleanup, and—perhaps most interestingly—they become less likely to believe that individuals can bring about changes in society. Our earlier research (Astin, 1993b) also showed uniformly negative effects of watching television on a variety of other outcomes: college grades, self-reported growth in most areas of academic and personal development, and nearly all aspects of satisfaction with college. Additionally, watching television seems to encourage the development of materialistic values, that is, placing high priority on being well off financially and believing that the chief benefit of college is that it increases one's earning power.

This pattern of results closely parallels the findings from studies done at the precollegiate level on the effects of television-viewing habits (Huston and others, 1992). Why should television have such effects? There are several possible explanations. The most obvious, of course, is in terms of the involvement concept: watching television is a passive activity that can isolate students from each other and take time away from the activities that are more conducive to citizenship development, such as volunteering, attending diversity workshops, holding an on-campus job, and interacting with students and faculty. At the same time, the content of television programming tends to be heavily materialistic, which may help to account for the tendency of television viewing to encourage development of materialistic values among college undergraduates.

In sum, the findings presented in this chapter support Boyer's assertion that "the quality of the undergraduate experience is to be measured by the willingness of graduates to be socially and civically engaged" (1987, p. 278). The consistent positive effects of volunteering, diversity activities, and leaving home to attend college are underscored by the many other forms of involvement that promote civic virtue, most of which involve students' social *and* academic interaction with faculty and students. Conversely, time spent in activities that disengage students from the college environment—watching television, commuting to campus, and working full-time off campus—serves to limit the development of civic virtue.

CONCLUSION

During the 1994 election campaign, Representative Bernard Sanders of Vermont observed that *"the United States is fast becoming a nondemocratic country. We have the lowest voter turnout of any major industrialized country on earth. . . .*

The simple fact is that the majority of Americans . . . no longer believe that the government is relevant to their lives" (Sanders, 1994). Whereas some of our faculty colleagues may argue that the failure or success of our system of representative democracy is not higher education's responsibility or concern, they forget that promoting "good citizenship" is one of the most commonly stated values in the mission statements of most colleges and universities. We are, in other words, publicly on record as committing ourselves and our institutions to the value of promoting good citizenship.

If institutions are truly committed to educating students for citizenship, they have numerous opportunities to fulfill this commitment. First, colleges and universities can explore how to integrate *service learning* into the general educational program—beyond the scattered courses or internships in which it may be emphasized now. Service learning can be integrated directly into the curriculum by offering courses in all disciplines that combine classroom learning with a community service component. Colleges may also establish community service centers where the skills and interests of student volunteers are matched with the needs of community agencies. Ideally, such centers would maximize student learning by engaging students in reflection activities that help illuminate the meaning of their service involvement. On campuses around the country, service learning has proven to promote students' commitment to their social, cultural, political, and natural environments; it has also been found to promote academic achievement (Astin, 1993b; Astin and Sax, 1996).

Second, we need to help all students—not just political science majors—understand how our democratic system actually works. Take the most basic of all ingredients in any functioning democratic system: *information*. Even the most elementary understanding of how a democratic political system is supposed to operate recognizes the central role of information, in that a democracy works only to the extent that the voter is well informed. Our students, then, need to be taught how to inform themselves so that they can formulate the right questions.

Third, institutions can enhance citizenship development by embracing diversity and multiculturalism on their campuses. It is important for campuses to realize that simply *having* a diverse campus is not the key to promoting civic virtue among students; citizenship development stems from institutional efforts to understand and appreciate local, national, and global diversity. Citizenship development is enhanced by such activities as attending multicultural awareness workshops, discussing racial and ethnic issues, interacting with people of different races and ethnicities, and enrolling in ethnic studies courses. Citizenship development also stems from an institutional commitment to increasing racial and ethnic diversity among students and faculty. In addition to promoting civic virtue, an emphasis on diversity is positively associated with students' cognitive development as well as overall satisfaction with college (Astin, 1993a).

Educating students about diversity is particularly critical in the senior year as students begin the transition to graduate school and career environments that only benefit from a greater respect for and understanding of diverse people, ideas, and perspectives.

Finally, in light of the reduced budgets and other external pressures that institutions face today, it is fair to ask whether higher education has the wherewithal to undertake any such initiative as citizenship development. Arguably, most of the educational resources and personnel needed to develop greater emphasis on educating students for citizenship already exist on campus; educators just need to recognize that they have the capacity to draw those resources and personnel together in new and creative ways. Citizenship development should not be considered an add-on, to be pursued only if new money ever becomes available. Rather, it needs to be viewed as an integral part of the educational program. If we want our students to become good citizens by acquiring the virtues of honesty, tolerance, empathy, generosity, cooperation, and social responsibility, we have to demonstrate those qualities not only in our individual conduct but also at all levels of institutional policy and practice. Particularly in this time of college students' increasing disconnection from civic life, it is in higher education's interest to produce seniors who leave college with a greater sense of civic duty and social responsibility than when they entered.

CHAPTER TEN

Strengthening the Ties That Bind

Cultural Events, Rituals, and Traditions

George D. Kuh

As a student carries out the final tasks of the senior year and looks ahead to graduation, he or she is likely to become retrospective. This mood and thought process is well articulated by a Stanford University senior:

I'm going to spend some time during these last few weeks getting in touch with the people I knew when we were frosh. It's amazing how quickly the four years have gone by and how many of the people who were really important to you in those first few weeks go their own way. . . . But before it's too late I want to touch base with them, see how they are doing, tell them how important they were to me—how important they *are* to me. . . . I wish we had something like frosh week at the end, too, when everybody could spend time together again.

The sentiments expressed by this student are important to this book in general and this chapter in particular for three reasons. First, many others can identify with what this student is saying, especially those who left home to attend college right after high school. The words convey a powerful human need—a yearning to "close the circle" (Kluge, 1993) by acknowledging the importance of people who were very important at an especially vulnerable time: those first few weeks of college. Second, the reference to four years flying by represents not only passage of time but accomplishment; those four years stand for a college degree, the number of years being much less significant than the achievement. Finally, the student recalls the role of the institution in providing opportunities to satisfy affiliation and other needs at the beginning of college and wisely asks whether the university can do more to bring closure to the baccalaureate experience.

This chapter examines institutionally sponsored and student-initiated cultural events that commemorate the conclusion of college and the transition to the next phase of one's life. First, the various forms of cultural expression used in events common to the senior year are described. Then the effects of these events are considered. The chapter concludes with some suggestions for increasing the desired impact of cultural events for both the institution and students. Many of the activities used as examples occur near the end of the senior year, such as farewell banquets and commencement. However, events at other times during the year also serve important purposes and are mentioned on occasion herein.

TRADITION AND RITUAL AS CULTURAL EVENTS

Culture represents the values, beliefs, customs, and normative patterns developed by groups of people over time. Therefore, to understand the meaning of cultural events during the senior year, one must understand the institutional context. Particularly important are the institution's espoused values and aspirations for its students, the cultures students themselves create, and the beliefs and expectations of the faculty and administrators.

Most cultural events combine expressions of different aspects of a group's culture. For example, ceremonies such as baccalaureate and commencement comprise rituals, traditions, symbols, stories, and physical settings (Kuh and Whitt, 1988) arranged in an evocative and sometimes exaggerated manner in order to command audience attention and participation. Many aspects of these events are scripted so as to be similar in content and setting from one year to the next (Myerhoff, 1977). That is, most commencement ceremonies include some variation of "the formation of candidates for degrees into one or more lines, the procession of faculty and students, the commencement address, the conferral of honorary degrees, the conferral of various degrees (baccalaureate, master's, and so forth), the hooding of doctoral degree recipients, the alumni association's welcome to those receiving degrees, the tossing of mortar boards into the air at the conclusion of the formal event, and the recession from the site of commencement" (Kuh and Whitt, 1988, pp. 16–17).

For spectators, the central meaning of commencement and other cultural events may be fairly simple. For some parents of traditional-age students, commencement symbolically represents achievement of an educational goal. For students, the event may have additional, more subtle meanings: ending a unique period in one's life, leaping into an uncertain future, separating from friends, and becoming independent from parents, to name a few. For older students, the conferral of an earned degree may be the instrumental lever to a better job. While consumed with these thoughts and others, people nonetheless participate in a synchronized cooperative way in what are often elaborately staged events (Burns and Laughlin, 1979).

CULTURAL PROPERTIES

Among the more visible cultural properties are physical, verbal, and behavioral artifacts. Physical artifacts "surround people physically and provide them with immediate sensory stimuli as they carry out culturally expressive activities" (Kuh and Whitt, 1988, p. 19). They include indoor and outdoor spaces, art, architecture, and attire (Kuh and Hall, 1993). For example, the academic gowns worn by faculty and students during commencement are silent reminders to all present that American colleges and universities have their roots in medieval Europe (Manning, 1993).

Ceremonies "when they are well chosen and understood . . . do their work unnoticed" (Myerhoff, 1984, p. 160). At Montgomery County Community College (Pennsylvania), commencement is held in a tent, a practice that began because "there was no building on campus large enough to allow more than 400 people to gather at once. Now, even though more accommodating facilities are available, the tradition of commencement in a tent behind College Hall persists" (Carnegie Foundation for the Advancement of Teaching, 1990, p. 58). The tent is an annual reminder of the college's founding mission: to offer a bootstrap opportunity for first-generation college students who desire to develop their talents and increase the quality of their lives.

Examples of verbal artifacts include the language used in stories told and scripts read during baccalaureate and the conferring-of-the-degree ritual at commencement. One commonly used verbal artifact is the symbol of the year of the graduating class. Speakers and university officials typically refer to graduates as "members of the Class of [fill in the year]." No matter when a student might have started school—four, eight, or fifteen years earlier—the year that one graduates marks that person as a member of that year's class. Such language carries expectations for an enduring link among members of the class, and between students and their institution.

Behavioral artifacts include rituals: activities that connect the past to the present and translate beliefs into action (Masland, 1985). They create occasions for people with common experiences and interests to commune (Kapferer, 1984), thus maintaining normative practices and social structure. When rituals are public, as with senior dinners, they communicate to others the values and expectations of certain groups, differentiating them from members of other groups, and allow participants to make meaning of milestones in the company of others who understand the importance of the experience. Given the increasingly complex nature of the world and the decay of values that is inevitable over time (Gardner, 1990), rituals such as those common to the final weeks of the last year of college serve "to bring some particular part of life firmly and definitely into orderly control" (Moore and Myerhoff, 1977, p. 3).

One ritual that occurs at virtually every commencement exercise combines physical, verbal, and behavioral artifacts. Near the end of the ceremony, usually in an indoor auditorium or outdoor amphitheater-type setting, graduating students are directed to move the tassel on the mortar board from right to left, signifying that they have met all the requirements for the degree to be conferred. This pronouncement, coupled with the moving of the tassel, takes about fifteen seconds and symbolically connotes the conclusion of baccalaureate study. For traditional-age students who have pursued their studies full-time, commencement signals a major transition, "the beginning of adult life" (Hedges, 1989, p. A32). For others, such as older students who worked while going to school part-time, commencement commemorates a milestone achievement, often against great odds.

Individuals also can be symbols (Dill, 1982). For this purpose, outstanding senior awards are made to recognize students who have excelled academically or made substantial contributions to the quality of campus life, calling attention to efforts worth emulating by others. In *Alma Mater,* Kluge (1993) describes the uplifting effect that Stone, a senior dying from cancer, has on the community. Stone knows full well he has but weeks to live and chooses to spend his final days pursuing his intellectual interests and completing the requirements for his degree.

FIVE PURPOSES OF CULTURAL EVENTS IN THE SENIOR YEAR

Cultural events can be divided into three categories: (1) institutionwide events to which all members of the graduating class (and occasionally their loved ones) are invited, (2) institutionally sponsored events to recognize the achievements of specific groups, and (3) both formal (for example, student government) and informal student-generated events. Some of the latter events are sponsored by the institution; others are initiated by students in order to demonstrate independence from the institution and, in some instances, appreciation to family members for their support. Each of these events serves a somewhat different purpose.

In this section, five potentially important outcomes of cultural events in the senior year are considered: (1) recognizing achievement, (2) encouraging students to reflect on the meaning of their college experience, (3) cultivating loyal graduates, (4) unifying the senior class, and (5) easing the transition to life after college. In addition, cultural events often have multiple purposes and result in some combination of these outcomes.

Recognizing Achievement

Certain cultural events in the senior year are designed to acknowledge the academic achievements and other accomplishments of graduating students and the support of loved ones who made the achievements possible. Among the most common are induction ceremonies into senior honoraries. Another less formal but much appreciated symbolic recognition of achievement is permitting seniors to register first for classes. Commencement weekend probably provides the best example of a formal institutionalized effort to signify the educational achievements of students.

At a commencement weekend event at Dartmouth College, the dean presents awards for outstanding achievement (for example, highest grade point average). Some institutions, including large ones such as The Ohio State University, attempt to personalize the event by handing diplomas to students. At some small colleges, such as Hanover (Indiana), Kenyon (Ohio), and Luther (Iowa), following commencement the graduating class files through a "gauntlet" formed by faculty and staff who applaud continuously until the last graduate has exited. In this way faculty and staff pay tribute to the achievements of another group of rising alumni and alumnae, acknowledging their passage into the "real world."

At Reed College, seniors must complete an oral examination as well as a senior thesis. Seniors celebrate the completion of the thesis by marching en masse from the library to the president's office (Mitzman, 1979).

Not all the achievements worthy of recognition are academic in nature. For example, St. Olaf College (Minnesota) undergraduates host a party for seniors who participated in the Winter Songfest, a major cultural event on that campus organized around themes of the Christmas season (J. Lyons, personal communication, Dec. 3, 1994). In addition, such student groups as fraternities and athletic teams sponsor commemorative activities, often banquets, to acknowledge their departing senior leaders; athletic teams frequently salute their graduating players and even families before the final home game.

Encouraging Students to Reflect
on Their College Experience

Reflection is a key factor in fostering intellectual development (Cross, 1993; King and Kitchener, 1994), a goal of every college or university. Senior seminars sometimes are intentionally organized to address this goal. Cultural events can also be used to help students understand the changes they have experienced during college (Kuh, 1994). Unfortunately, rituals and traditions are not often designed for this purpose. Institutions with a religious heritage may have an advantage in this regard because they have such activities as convocations and chapel built into the regular rhythms of campus life, to structure occasions for students to think about their experiences in a suitable public forum.

Stanford University provides an opportunity for seniors to consider what they were like when they first arrived on campus. During Frosh Orientation, Stanford provides a long roll of paper on which newcomers record their initial impressions and expectations for college. At commencement, the roll is displayed again so that students can see what they were thinking at that point in their lives and reflect on how they are each different from the person who wrote those impressions. At this time, Stanford also replays the videos taken during Frosh Week.

At Dartmouth College, the Saturday before commencement is Class Day. A morning session features remarks from class officers and a faculty member selected by the class. When the college was all-male decades ago, following the morning session seniors would gather at the Lone Pine, a large old pine tree on campus, to smoke their pipes together one last time and reflect on their college experiences. The significance of the pine was that as students left the college they would be like a prominent pine tree in a forest: strong, able to bend without breaking. The ceremony concluded with students breaking their pipes and exchanging pieces with peers to symbolize enduring friendship; that is, though classmates might go in different directions, the shared fragments symbolized their being together in spirit. In a subsequent iteration of the event, students would take a piece of wood from a ring of cedar, go to the pine, and break off pieces for classmates, to symbolically cement the bond created through their shared Dartmouth experience. Several years ago, Dartmouth introduced a midnight candlelight march from the center of the campus to the Lone Pine for all seniors (T. Moore, personal communication, May 18, 1995).

Cultivating Loyal Graduates

Students who see their institution as "special" tend to become loyal supporters after college. Rituals and traditions such as alumni initiation meetings and senior class gift (for example, a class scholarship) are instrumental in cultivating the loyalty necessary to ensure an institution's long-term vitality. By creating deep emotional attachments, students indeed feel special and sense that their institution is unique: "There is a feeling that there is the small world of the lucky few and the large routine one of the rest of the world. Such belief comes from a credible story of uncommon effort, achievement, and form. . . . Such an emotional bond turns the membership into a community. . . . Enduring loyalty follows from the collective belief of participants that their organization is distinctive, [causing] individuals to stay with the system, to save and improve it rather than to leave to serve their self-interests elsewhere" (Clark, 1972, p. 183).

Some institutions provide students with cameras to use in the last few weeks to create a lasting photographic record of friends and favorite campus haunts. The photos are a permanent reminder of the link between graduates and their institution and this important period in their life. This expression of interest by the institution is much more meaningful than simply announcing to students that they are now members of the however-many-thousand graduates of Old Siwash.

Another way institutions engender loyalty is to involve seniors in a philanthropic activity, such as a senior challenge or senior class gift project. These activities are consistent with an institution's humanitarian values and promote interaction among class members who might not otherwise have contact with one another. Such events also further solidify the emotional attachment between participating students and the institution.

Unifying the Senior Class

The student quoted at the opening of this chapter indicated a strong desire to close the circle before leaving college (Kluge, 1993). Although many students do this on their own, the institution can structure activities to promote such behavior. (At institutions that attract large numbers of part-time and older students requiring six or more years to graduate, this goal is much less important to students and the institution.)

At residential colleges, one approach to closing the circle is to designate the few days prior to commencement as senior week. At small liberal arts colleges, "the graduating class has the campus to itself, just as it did when it arrived for freshman orientation four years ago. The circle closes" (Kluge, 1993, p. 240). Students spend their last days in college together, feeling that the institution belongs to them. At large, state-assisted colleges and universities, seniors sometimes complete their final exams early so that their academic commitments are over a few days prior to commencement. The intention is for students to touch base with acquaintances, reminisce, and say goodbye (as was in the mind of the Stanford student), to their friends and classmates but also to the institution and its faculty and staff.

To keep students occupied, numerous events and activities are typically scheduled: trips to amusement parks, dinners, picnics, and banquets. At Canisius College (New York), for example, faculty and administrators host a quad party and champagne brunch for graduating students (T. Miller, personal communication, Dec. 3, 1994). Indeed, senior week often is the first time students and faculty interact more or less as equals.

Mount Holyoke has a series of events: Survival Night, Picnic, Barbecue, Tree Planting, Alumnae Parade and Laurel Chain, Phi Beta Kappa initiation, President's Reception, Canoe Sing, Baccalaureate Service, and Commencement Day Buffet. All but Senior Survival Night and the Barbecue take place on the weekend of graduation (Manning, 1989) to build momentum for the culminating event, the commencement exercise (K. Manning, personal communication, June 28, 1995).

For years, the psychology department at Hope College (Michigan) has sponsored a senior recognition dinner. The awards ceremony is the highlight. In a parody of the end-of-term honors convocation, each graduate is presented with an "award" that pokes good humor at the recipient, often focusing on a particular event or exaggerating a personality characteristic of the student. The warm, lighthearted combination salute and send-off for students on the verge of graduation brings out the best in faculty creativity (C. Greene, personal communication, Jan. 26, 1995).

Easing the Transition to Life After College

Cultural events help people negotiate orderly transitions from one type of situation to another, thereby providing a sense of continuity to one's life. "Ritual inevitably carries a basic message of order, continuity, and predictability. Even when dealing with change, new events are connected to preceding ones, incorporated into a stream of precedents so that they are recognized as growing out of tradition and experience" (Myerhoff, 1984, p. 152). In fact, taken together, the rituals practiced during the last few months of the senior year through commencement can be viewed as a rite of passage, "ceremonies whose essential purpose is to enable the individual to pass from one defined position to another which is equally well-defined" (van Gennep, [1908] 1960, p. 3).

Rites of passage have three stages: separation, transition, and incorporation (van Gennep, [1908] 1960).

Separation is when the individual or group is symbolically or physically set free from the present situation. For example, years ago at Wichita State University the senior class president passed "the lamp of knowledge" to the junior class president (Kuh and others, 1991). The formal transfer of the lamp (a symbol of leadership and achievement) from seniors to juniors acknowledged that the seniors had accomplished their goals and that now the juniors were expected to exert leadership and do the same. At the University of Maine at Orono, one residence presents graduating seniors with a T-shirt that proclaims, "I'm outta here!" (K. Douglas, personal communication, June 16, 1995). At some institutions with nursing programs, graduating students tear up their scrubs and loop them around trees near their classroom building to symbolize their completion of rigorous training as health care providers. Such off-campus events as picnics are another way to symbolize the separation by using a physical setting some distance from the institution. Some expressions of separation can be quite routine and mundane but meaningful nonetheless, such as packing the car for the last time, turning in residence hall room keys, paying graduation fees, and joining the institution's alumni association.

Transition is a time of flux between the existing and future states of affairs, such as the yearlong placement activities many business programs provide to prepare their graduating students for finding a job. Other transition experiences include taking a summer job following graduation while seeking a career opportunity, or simply taking a year off before beginning graduate study.

Incorporation occurs when a new position or status is acquired, such as beginning full-time work in one's chosen vocation following graduation. Graduation then not only symbolically represents completion of degree requirements but also signifies movement from the "bubble" of college life into the "real world." The pivotal moment is the moving of the tassel.

College seniors do not necessarily recognize that they are moving through these stages; too many administrators and faculty also seem to be oblivious of the process. But when cultural events are intentionally organized to address these transitions, students are able to discern and reflect on their importance.

Institutions understandably differ with regard to how they deal with such transitions. For example, students attending the service academies often have the next phase of their life relatively well defined; that is, the majority know what they will do next and that their undergraduate training has prepared them for such experiences. A state university graduate with a liberal arts degree whose career goals are unclear faces a far more uncertain future. In both cases, however, transition issues warrant attention by the institution.

Most institutions emphasize separation and pay less attention to the transition and incorporation phases. As with new student orientation, staff can be assigned to help students move through these stages, as when career services staff offer transition workshops for seniors. However, such programs do not always have the desired impact. In part this is because mixed messages are sent ("graduation means you will be leaving, but by joining the alumni association you can stay 'connected'"). The more effective approaches ritualize the placement process, periodically updating students on their classmates' progress in obtaining jobs. Although this approach can fuel a competitive ethos, it also can instill an additional measure of loyalty as students see that prestigious firms are seeking people from their institution.

Multipurpose Events

"The final steps where seniors passed on their power to the class beneath them, the senior play, festive dinner, and finally commencement itself celebrated the success of a graduating class and framed their transition to the world outside" (Horowitz, 1993, pp. 172–174). It is misleading to associate a single purpose or effect with a cultural event. Most events have multiple outcomes, and no matter how tightly it is scripted, participants and spectators experience and interpret the same event differently.

Manning's firsthand account of the Alumnae Parade and Laurel Chain Ceremony at Mount Holyoke College captures the flavor of these multiple meanings and purposes:

Any negative feelings that the students had about their struggles with the academic rigor, the loneliness of the non-existent social life, and doubts whether they could get through the challenge of the intense intellectual challenge . . . faded as alumnae gathered with old friends, made new ones, and continued to build the fierce devotion to the community and college. The Alumnae Parade was great entertainment . . . walking canes, hats, umbrellas, and t-shirts coordinated by class color. . . . Balloons and lettering of the placards announced both the color of that particular class and the events which made up their history. The symbols of the individual classes were incorporated into the signs, costumes, and parade paraphernalia. The colors and symbols stayed with a class from freshman year through reunions as alumnae. . . .

The newest group to experience the pageant that transformed students into alumnae were gathering at the end of the line. Excitement grew as an alumna . . . rolled out the Laurel Chain. . . .

Three members of the class of 1908 participated in the parade. . . . Dressed in white with blue ribbons in their hair they rode in antique automobiles. . . . Blue balloons decorated the cars and flew alongside as they drove along. . . . Although a student joked about being on the "wheelchair brigade," it was evident in the way that she spoke of their accomplishments that she admired the stamina and tenacity of these centenarians [who] showed a fierce devotion. . . . [They] were symbols of the strength and tenacity of the college.

The applause and excitement of the crowd grew as the seniors appeared with the Laurel Chain [at the grave of the founder, which] represented the presence of her founding ideals. . . . Alumnae . . . stopped and lined the road in a double row through which the seniors as rising alumnae would pass. The line of seniors, waving to those gathered on the roadside, marched through the towering trees up the rise to the founder's grave. . . . Continuous clapping sounded as an outpouring of support and understanding rose from the alumnae. . . . The president of the college, the alumnae president, and the president of the senior class joined the class of 1988 at the gate of the grave. A ripple of excitement and cheer went through the seniors. The Laurel Chain was being passed overhead and draped over the fence. The white dresses, generations of students, pageantry, and fun of it all was "amazing" [1989, pp. 176–189].

The significance of the Alumnae Parade, Manning explains, is that graduating students experience the bond shared among the previous generations of Mount Holyoke alumnae and the pride these accomplished women have for their college. The graduating seniors are now becoming part of this history. The Laurel Chain Ceremony symbolizes and actually builds the unity of many generations of Mount Holyoke graduates.

The "P-rade" at Princeton is similar. Alumni return en masse each spring to march with graduating seniors: "The procession is led by members of the 25th-year reunion class, followed by the oldest alumni, known as the 'Old Guard.' Strung out behind the 'Old Guard' are classes of more recent vintage, in descending order, with the seniors bringing up the rear. Carrying class banners and dressed in colorful costumes and special blazers to distinguish each class, the alumni and their families and the seniors—some 10,000 strong—march through the campus to Clarke Field. The ceremony binds the youngest graduates to the generations preceding them" (Carnegie Foundation for the Advancement of Teaching, 1990, pp. 58–59).

Viewed from a cultural perspective, senior seminars and theses also can contribute to several of the purposes mentioned above. They can be transition-facilitating experiences, promote student-to-institution bonding as a result of interacting with small groups of faculty and students, and provide opportunities for seniors to reflect on what they have learned.

OTHER TYPES OF RITUALS AND TRADITIONS COMMON TO THE SENIOR YEAR

Up to this point the discussion has focused on activities that are institutionwide in scope and purpose. Some other types of events are also particularly meaningful for certain groups of students and their families.

The School of Education at Indiana University hosts a buffet luncheon including a brief ceremony for graduates and their families and friends following the all-university commencement exercise in the football stadium. Every year the featured speaker is a recent recipient of the school's teaching award, a fitting symbolic reminder for education majors about the value of instructional excellence. Before this event was initiated several years ago, the master's students in student affairs administration would reserve a residence hall lounge and provide a light lunch for graduating students, their families, and the faculty following the institutionwide commencement ceremony. In this setting, family members were able to meet the people who were instrumental in their loved one's personal and professional development. Both the school event and the smaller informal group-sponsored event are examples of efforts to counter the anonymity so often associated with large university graduation exercises and to recognize that graduation is more than an individual milestone; it can be an accomplishment for one's family as well.

In a similar vein, the four ethnic community centers at Stanford (American Indian Program Office, Asian American Activities Center, Black Community Service Center, and El Centro Chicano) sponsor celebrations for graduating students and their families in addition to the all-university event to affirm their achievements and heritage. For example, at the dinner hosted by the American Indian Program Office, the event begins with a prayer offered in the tribal language of one of the graduates. After dinner, each graduate is introduced and his or her achievements and contributions to the community described. Then a

Pendleton blanket is wrapped around the shoulders of the graduate—a gift to honor that student's role in the community. At that point, family members or friends are invited to share their thoughts, and the graduating student has a chance to thank those who have been instrumental to his or her success (J. Larimore, personal communication, June 9, 1995).

Whether such events should be discouraged or promoted as a "natural" phase in the evolution toward a multicultural campus can only be determined on a case-by-case basis (Kuh and others, 1991). In such instances, faculty and staff must be sensitive to the possibility that the expressed need for such events may reflect growing frustration with an institution's inability or reluctance to embrace people of all groups as full members of the institution. At the same time, resistance to ethnic graduation ceremonies is not uncommon, especially when it appears that such events are competing with the institution's graduation exercises.

Not all the events that occur during the senior year are consistent with the institution's espoused values. On occasion, events evolve unintentionally to become inappropriate and offensive. Such events are countercultural because they are at odds with the espoused values of the institution (Kuh and Whitt, 1988). Most of these events are student initiated.

On occasion, students interrupt a carefully scripted ceremony with pranks, perhaps in an attempt to establish or become part of tradition themselves. For example, at Brown, as at many other universities, being selected to speak at the commencement is a coveted honor. In 1798, Brown students were upset at how college officials determined which students would have speaking parts at commencement. Some students put lead into the locks of the doors to the bell room. This delayed the ringing of the bells by the person responsible, so that students could sleep in on commencement day morning (Steinberg, 1992).

Some institutions combine alumni events with senior week or commencement to symbolically connect the newest class with all graduates. At Amherst College the institution's statue goddess, Sabrina, was a popular guest at class dinners that accompanied graduation in the 1930s and 1940s. Over time, it became a source of pride to see if the graduating class could remove her from her secure resting place before she could be put on display at the dinners. In 1951, Sabrina was stolen just a few hours before commencement by a dozen members of the graduating class. "By secretly making clay impressions of all the curator's keys and carefully timing the watchman's rounds, the conspirators were able to create the two keys needed to enter the memorabilia room" (Steinberg, 1992, p. 132).

Today such elaborate schemes are rare. However, students frequently interrupt commencement exercises by decorating their mortar boards, tossing beach balls, popping champagne bottle corks, setting off firecrackers or other noisemakers, and squealing and shouting when friends receive diplomas. This behavior seems to be contagious, as family members in the audience frequently exhibit similar behavior.

Occasionally, students adapt an event so that it becomes antithetical to the institution's mission and values. At Dartmouth, institutional aspirations changed without concomitant changes in the institutional culture. For example, part of the oral history of the previously mentioned Lone Pine tradition was that at one point a Native American student smoked a peace pipe at the pine and then broke it, giving pieces to his classmates. Recently, Native American students challenged the story, saying it had become twisted over time and inaccurately depicted their cultural heritage. At that point, the ring of cedar was introduced to turn what had become a negative tradition for some into a positive tradition for all, thus preserving the symbolism of class unity (T. Moore, personal communication, May 18, 1995).

At some colleges, certain senior week activities are out of control. This fact has prompted some institutions to banish underclass students from the campus during this period in part because of liability issues, and in part as an effort to extinguish such behavior in the future. Consider Kluge's description of one such event:

> The evening started with a party at a farm. . . . I left early [for] Lewis Hall,
> watched television in the lounge. A couple seniors came by, lugging a case of
> Old Milwaukee [beer]. . . . I learned the whole senior class was invited to return
> to the freshman dorms, back to where it all began for them. Closing the circle.
> The idea was, they'd have an ice cream party. The food service was just setting
> it up when I went to bed, an ice cream buffet, all sorts of flavors and toppings,
> all you could eat.
>
> Or throw. I was asleep when all hell broke out: screams and shouts, alarms,
> doors slamming. Slipping into my bathrobe, I stepped out into a hall that was
> one long puddle. They got to the fire extinguishers. Water and beer cans every-
> where: the smell of a flooded brewery. Around the corner, where a security
> guard was talking into a crackling radio, another smell assaulted me, that of ice
> cream, melting into the lounge carpet and starting to stink. Later, it's discovered,
> someone went into the toilets and kicked a urinal to pieces [1993, p. 241].

Such destructive behavior is all-too-common at some predominantly residential colleges and well out of line with what one reasonably expects of college graduates. One interpretation is that students view these final few days of their collegiate careers as the last chance to act irresponsibly. This also illustrates how "participants depart from the controlled ceremonial 'script' the organizers provide and embark on their own, anti-structural drama" (Mechling and Wilson, 1988, p. 316). It is rare that senior week is the first evidence of such behavior. If assertive action is not taken from the first day of orientation to discourage such irresponsible conduct, then the institution reaps what it sows.

IMPLICATIONS

This section offers some ideas for institutions desiring to maximize the impact of cultural events in ways that are advantageous to both students and institutions.

1. *Assign some individual or group responsibility for oversight of cultural events that involve graduating students.* Several offices usually are directly involved in staging all-institution ceremonies such as commencement. But most institutions do not hold any one individual or office accountable for the quality of the range of cultural events and the impact on the behavior of students or the institutional climate. In order to maximize the impact of such events and to discern how students are interpreting their participation, somebody must be responsible for evaluating and coordinating these events. This person or group must become familiar with the institution's culture and how ritual and tradition presently are being used.

The University of Arizona is an example of a specific office taking responsibility for a cultural event and having a positive influence by collaborating with students and others. Some years ago, commencement at that institution was out of control. That is, students were constantly interrupting the ceremony by tossing beach balls and waving signs. The dean of students established a community standards committee, composed mainly of students along with a few faculty and administrators. One of the group's agenda items was to examine how to restore dignity to the commencement exercise. Subsequently, commencement was improved to everyone's benefit (E. Foley, personal communication, June 15, 1995).

2. *Encourage one or more faculty and staff members to become "cultural practitioners"* (Lundberg, 1990). To become familiar with the institution's culture and how cultural events affect seniors and the institutional climate, people must be able to think and talk in cultural terms. Therefore, some administrators and faculty must become cultural practitioners, people who are familiar with concepts and language that communicate various cultural properties and who actively seek out connections among these events, actions, language, and physical settings.

Learning how to speak in public and knowing when and how to invoke history, institutional symbols, and heroes and heroines to underscore the importance of certain behaviors are important skills to cultivate. Often people find it awkward to use the symbolic power of language in the service of institutional values and aspirations. Some background reading may help (Kuh, 1993; Kuh and Whitt 1988; Masland, 1985; Tierney, 1988). As more people at an institution begin to think in these terms, the influence of cultural events on seniors and institutional learning environments becomes more apparent.

3. *Conduct a systematic study to discover the effects of cultural events on seniors and the institutional goals.* Understanding how such subjective elements of institutional life contribute to instilling loyalty in graduating seniors is essential. Students in advanced seminars in anthropology or sociology could assist by examining these events as a class project, to determine how traditions and rituals are used and their impact. The methods to "discover" the rituals and traditions are many and varied. Here are some suggestions in this regard:

- Conduct a yearlong observational study of how the institution uses cultural events to attain the five purposes of senior year cultural events, described earlier.

- Compile a comprehensive inventory of the rituals and traditions that have the potential to affect the institution and graduating students positively or negatively. Included in the inventory should be academic activities such as senior seminars and theses.

- Examine newspaper accounts and videotapes of informal events and ceremonies during the senior year to understand the messages sent and received by various groups (Manning, 1993).

- Talk with institutional historians (perhaps a long-time faculty member, or some graduates from different decades) to develop a perspective on how events during the senior year have changed over time.

- Develop lists of student-initiated or informal events and formal institution-sponsored events. What values are expressed? Who participates in which events? To what extent are the events consistent with the institution's values and aspirations for its graduates? What are the reactions of students, faculty, and administrators to the various types of events?

- Take several walking tours of campus during senior week to determine how students are spending their time. Be sure to vary the time periods of the observations, and try to put into words what you feel as well as what you see.

- Observe commencement from the perspective of a parent or family member. Then observe commencement from the perspective of a graduating student. What values are expressed? Is the language inclusionary or exclusionary (Manning, 1993)?

- Review the list of recipients of honors and recognitions to determine whether students from all backgrounds seem to have a fair chance of meeting the criteria (Manning, 1993).

4. *Periodically assess the impact of cultural events.* Like it or not, formal institutional programs and events are always laden with symbolism. An annual eval-

uation should be conducted of how cultural events are being used and whether the messages that these events communicate are those that the institution intends to send. What messages are being sent? Are these the messages that are received? How can these messages be communicated more clearly? An example is the P-rade at Princeton. "When the class had first opened its ranks to women marches [sic] along the parade route" (Carnegie Foundation for the Advancement of Teaching, 1990, p. 60), there was cheering and dancing to celebrate the significant change in the direction of the institution after women began to be admitted.

Rituals and traditions that no longer attract student interest should be officially discarded. Of course, some disappear without any institutional effort. The ritual passing of the lamp of knowledge at Wichita State mentioned earlier died out for lack of student and administrator interest. That traditions disappear is not tragic; the tragedy is that they are not replaced with something similar so as to serve the purpose for which the previous ritual was developed.

The most troubling aspect of trying to renew the significance of a cultural event such as baccalaureate services is that often the legitimizing moral and value bases are no longer present; for example, the religious beliefs of the institution's founders may no longer be integral to the college's mission and philosophy. Thus it is important to develop rituals and traditions that are rich enough to command interest and loyalty.

Special attention should be given to those events that have become countercultural or have a negative influence. Sometimes events become countercultural because the purpose for which they were originally established is no longer compelling. Some cultural events lose their appeal because of changing student interests and needs. In the latter case, a think tank of students, faculty, and staff should be charged with determining appropriate responses, one of which is to consider the introduction of activities that are consistent with current students' psychosocial development and transition needs.

Cultural events are more likely to have desired effects when they are context specific and take into account the backgrounds, experiences, and realities of the students and their supporters—families, partners, children, siblings, coworkers, and others. For example, at many residential colleges enrolling primarily full-time traditional-age students, senior week activities are important to completing the circle. But this outcome is much less significant at an institution with many "new century" students, those who commute, are enrolled part-time, are over twenty-five, or come from historically underrepresented ethnic backgrounds (Plater, 1995). For many of these students, even commencement is "less a rite of passage for students and more a public-relations event for the university" (Hedges, 1989, p. A32). Department-based events that include family members are often more meaningful than institutionwide activities.

Similarly, the status of various groups is often reflected in institutional traditions. Some traditions demean the worth and dignity of certain groups because they trivialize their experiences and backgrounds. The messages sent by both institutionally sponsored and student-initiated rituals, and the responses of groups to these messages, need to be examined to gain a better understanding of the institution's character (Kuh, 1993) and to develop strategies that communicate to all students that their accomplishments are deserving of recognition by the entire academic community (Kuh and others, 1991).

5. *Make cultural events in the senior year educationally purposeful.* It is little use for an institution to stage cultural events in the last few weeks of school if such events have not attracted student (or faculty!) interest up to that point. Certainly in the last few days of college, students think about their experiences and the institution somewhat differently from earlier years, as the Stanford student's comments showed. But the cultivation of loyal alumni and alumnae begins with matriculation. That is, a college cannot wait until the senior year to make cultural events a meaningful part of the undergraduate experience or to make students feel they are important and expected to be loyal to their alma mater. The institution must assiduously attempt to cultivate loyalty from the students' first days on campus; it is too late to express interest in the well-being of students in the last few days or at any single event!

If events are not carefully staged, nurtured, and taken seriously by the institution and by students throughout their undergraduate experience, they do not have the desired effects in the senior year of establishing loyalty, uniting the class, and encouraging reflection on the impact of college. Thus senior year activities should lie near the far end of a continuum of cultural events that instill loyalty and encourage reflection. At the same time, every opportunity should be used to send such messages about loyalty, accomplishment, and transition to ensure the welfare of graduating students and the long-term vitality of their college. One way to address these important matters is to have a prominent graduate speak at commencement, or some other event where all seniors are gathered, about transition issues and the responsibilities of alumni and alumnae to their alma mater.

Reserving a few days between final examinations and commencement recognizes the importance of having some special time for seniors prior to their leaving the institution. A balance must be struck, however, between how this time is spent and how much time is allocated. Whether a full week is needed warrants consideration: What is the relationship between senior week and the institution's educational mission? What is the obligation of senior week to the institution? What is the institution's obligation to senior week? What is the obligation of senior week to graduating students and returning students? Should the philosophy of senior week be to encourage students to do whatever they want, or should the institution delineate what constitutes acceptable behavior for the academic community? And if senior week must be reinvented, how should it be structured so that both the institution's goals and students' interests are served?

Awards celebrations always should devote some time to activities that address the transitions facing seniors. Transition issues become much more important the closer one gets to commencement day. It is, therefore, important to identify issues and address them in different settings over the course of the last few months, to be sure that seniors hear them more than once.

The key to successfully fostering reflection during a cultural event is to provide enough structure and clearly explain expectations for what the event is designed to produce. For example, students might be asked during the senior dinner or departmental function to write down a half-dozen ways they have benefited from attending the institution. As students begin their final year of study, advisers and senior seminar leaders could ask in what ways the students' experiences thus far have been powerful in shaping their personalities and values. One option might be to require that students write an essay on how they have changed and what their institution has contributed to these changes.

6. *Do not underestimate the difficulty of changing or eliminating countercultural traditions.* Cultural roots run deep into the psyche of a group of people. Students often initiate countercultural events to demonstrate their independence from the institution. As a result, it is particularly difficult to stamp out student-initiated traditions that are antithetical to the institution's goals. Just when it appears that the countercultural senior week behavior of a student group (such as that described by Kluge earlier) has been eliminated, make no mistake—modifying the most debilitating aspects of a culture demands constant attention over more than a few years.

CONCLUSION

Cultural events are commonplace in colleges and universities. As a result, they are frequently overlooked as potentially powerful influences on the quality of student experience and campus life in general. But such events, when carefully planned and orchestrated, can have positive side effects for both individuals and institutions. They provide occasions to address such important community challenges as affirmation of different groups of students and collective as well as individual achievements. When used properly, they can encourage students to reflect on what they have learned. They also are vehicles permitting people to thank those who have made special contributions to their education and affirm commitments, thereby further knitting seniors to one another and the institution. In such efforts, the institution must model what it expects from its students: authenticity, integrity, wisdom, high moral standards, and compassion.

In the final analysis, a college or university is what its graduates and others believe it is (Wilkins, 1989). Thus graduates must have faith in the ability of their college to prosper, develop, mature, and remain viable. To nurture such faith, a college must clearly communicate its vision and aspirations and graduates' responsibilities to the alma mater. When appropriately scripted and staged, cultural events are an essential vehicle for engendering loyalty and easing the transition from college to the next phase of life.

CHAPTER ELEVEN

Creating Pathways to Graduate School

Richard B. Lawhon

American graduate schools are the envy of the world. They have earned that respect by consistently offering challenging instruction, maintaining comprehensive facilities, and demanding high standards of performance. They also have been fortunate. A steady stream of talented applicants allows graduate programs to be highly selective about enrollment.

But the flow of students coming out of undergraduate schools has changed greatly in the past few decades. Consequently, graduate schools need to examine seriously whether traditional methods of graduate instruction will work with contemporary seniors and others who might pursue advanced degrees in the near future. However, graduate schools make changes slowly. Therefore, those of us who wish to improve the performance of the next generation of seniors who become graduate students must not wait. We must examine attitudes and behaviors exhibited by the best graduate students and consider ways to teach those habits to our seniors—before they leave us.

CHANGES IN TODAY'S SENIORS

Not only does the face of the senior of today, the potential graduate student of tomorrow, show more variety of racial and ethnic hue, but the percentage of women enrolled essentially matches that of men. Great differences among their social and cultural practices significantly alter the way contemporary seniors approach graduate study. For example, their learning styles demand more instructional variety than is found in the traditional lecture, seminar, and laboratory, complemented by long hours of individual research. Because they have done so as undergraduates, seniors want to work collaboratively with each other when they enter graduate school. Some want to conduct research under more than one adviser or major professor. They ask for such alternative assignments as projects and internships instead of lengthy research papers. Often more gifted with oral skills than with writing abilities, they want to produce their scholarly work through a variety of interactive media in which older faculty (including graduate faculty) are not always well trained—media that such faculty might even think are not appropriate for the field. Working seniors with family responsibilities need more flexibility in course scheduling, and growing numbers of seniors who want to enter graduate study have disabilities requiring accessibility in ways that old buildings and crowded facilities have trouble providing.

THE RELATIVELY NARROW PATH TO GRADUATE SCHOOL

As we consider the questions involved in helping contemporary seniors visualize themselves as happy, productive graduate students, we should remind ourselves of the role of graduate study in the overall enterprise of higher education. Graduate school serves many purposes, but none is more critical to higher education than preparing the professoriate of tomorrow. Doctorates or other advanced degrees that unfortunately we usually refer to as *terminal degrees* are now standard requirements for tenure-track positions in American colleges and universities. Community colleges and technical schools also want their faculty to have graduate degrees.

Despite dramatic increases in graduate school enrollment over the past quarter century, only a small percentage of our population holds master's degrees or doctorates. The *Digest of Educational Statistics* (U.S. Department of Education, National Center for Education Statistics, 1995b) reports that only 5.1 percent of the U.S. population aged twenty-five and over hold master's degrees, and less than 1 percent hold doctorates. Such degrees maintain their high professional and social status, and doctoral degrees especially have the cachet of exclusivity. This prestige attracts larger and larger numbers of students to graduate education, but too many fail to complete their training and consequently never receive their degrees. Anyone who attempts to measure graduation rates or time to degree for graduate students soon becomes familiar with the complexity brought to the task by such issues as full-time or part-time status, when to start counting years, changes from master's to doctorate, program or other major changes, and program interruptions. Bowen and Rudenstine's thorough 1992 study *In Pursuit of the Ph.D.* shows that doctorate completion rates over a ten-year period among such popular areas as the sciences, social sciences, and humanities ranged from a high of 75.3 percent (achieved only by our best students at some of our finest institutions) to a low of 39.2 percent. For most universities, doctoral program completion rates probably are much lower, even if we look at data with the time-to-degree variable lengthened. See also the second chapter of *The Path to the Ph.D.*, the 1996 report of the National Research Council (NRC), for an informed discussion of the problems encountered and results developed in other studies that sought to measure attrition among graduate students. Similar doctoral completion rates (approximately 39 percent to 72 percent) are reported in the NRC work, though the composition of the graduate student cohorts examined varies somewhat from the Bowen and Rudenstine study. The more recent publication features comprehensive bibliographies at the conclusion of each chapter.

Not only are we losing too many graduate students before they complete their work, but there also are problems with the pipeline through which talented undergraduates are funneled into master's and doctoral programs. Not enough minorities and women enroll in graduate study in fields other than education, nursing, public health, social work, and library and information systems. Talented undergraduates in the sciences and engineering routinely choose good-paying jobs over graduate school. Familiar to graduate recruiters are these sentiments expressed recently by a black engineering student at my university: "I can make real good money with the B.S. degree I'm getting after five *long* years; why should I go to graduate school?" Even more troubling are comments like this one from a computer science major about to graduate with her bachelor's degree: "Graduate school? That seems like delaying my *life* for two or three more years."

There is no antagonism in these sentiments, merely ignorance. Educators have not made the case for graduate school to broad groups of undergraduates. Instead, our very modest recruiting efforts have been directed at a relatively few easily identified students for whom we compete vigorously with other graduate schools. These students usually are seniors who can be distinguished by their B+ or better GPAs, unusually high GRE scores, or repeated demonstrations of leadership in extracurricular activities. Though we recruit specifically for minorities and women in some areas, we still seem to enroll more middle- and upper-class white males—especially in doctoral programs. The National Research Council (1995) reports that from 1978 through 1993, the gap between the number of doctorates earned by white men and those earned by white women steadily declined in size. During that time, the margin in favor of men decreased from about eleven thousand more degrees in 1978 to about four thousand in 1993. In 1978, white men earned four times as many doctorates as all other racial groups (male and female combined), and by 1993, although the discrepancy was considerably reduced, they still earned several thousand more doctorates than all other racial groups combined.

WHAT WE SHOULD BE SAYING TO SENIORS

For the most part, undergraduates—especially seniors—who are not top-ranked achievers do not hear warm stories of the close mentoring relationships graduate students establish with their professors. Graduate school recruiters, on severely restricted budgets, do not describe for them the small classes and long-term personalized intellectual guidance that characterize graduate study—at least at our better universities. Not unless they are seniors in the top 10 percent of their classes.

But far more seniors than this small group deserve to be in graduate school; thus it is our responsibility to increase the number of seniors who become successful graduate students. Consider for a moment the reaction of seniors who were not only told about these aspects of graduate school but also were able to experience this kind of treatment while still pursuing their bachelor's degrees. Their appetite for graduate study would increase as they gained firsthand appreciation for the excitement and opportunities awaiting them.

We should also tell them about the highly personal relationships that graduate students form with small numbers of their peers, the relationships that truly define collegiality. Many seniors have not thought much about this type of collegiality, because it has not been critical to their success as undergraduates. Instead, their undergraduate years may have seen collegial small-group participation in cocurricular contexts (especially social fraternities and sororities), but not in the curriculum. They seldom have experienced small-group collegiality with people sharing their intense interest in the same academic field.

Seniors need our help to realize that graduate school is different. There they will find that they have little time or inclination to participate in strictly social organizations, replacing those instead with friendships with other graduate students studying in their fields. Seniors need to be shown that this phenomenon is inevitable; shared interests and responsibilities lead them into close friendships with other graduate students. Moreover, these relationships provide them with academic and emotional support throughout their graduate careers—often to an extent that family and friends are not able to understand or duplicate.

This area of institutionally facilitated ways to provide social and emotional support for students is one in which undergraduate and graduate administrators need to learn from each other. Although membership in social clubs would detract too much from academic concerns, there are organizations that help graduate students perform better by helping them maintain their enthusiasm. For example, associations that promote collegiality and help students create professional networks can benefit students' emotional well-being and their academic achievement. Graduate students should become involved in one or two professional organizations, but they remain reluctant to do so unless encouraged by faculty and administrators—or unless they have participated in such groups as undergraduates.

For the same purposes, seniors should be encouraged to spend less time in social or recreational activities and instead to become active in professional associations. There they can experience relationships similar to the type they will enjoy as graduate students. Ideally, we would have graduates and undergraduates interacting more with each other in professional associations focused on academic areas. But as I discuss later, such involvement remains sporadic unless faculty and administrators promote it.

HABITS AND ATTITUDES OF SUCCESSFUL GRADUATE STUDENTS

The observations made thus far about student behavior are necessarily general. No specific set of behaviors can guarantee that seniors will succeed in graduate school. There is too much variety among the backgrounds of today's students and in the requirements found among the plethora of graduate programs offered by the contemporary university. However, we do know several characteristics and behaviors of graduate students who successfully complete their studies. Reviewing these, and proceeding cautiously with our inferences about their generalizability, we can devise a set of guidelines for reviewing the demands of graduate programs that seem to appeal to our seniors. We also can consider the teaching methods our seniors are likely to encounter in graduate school. Finally, we can look at ways to prepare our seniors better to excel in graduate study.

GRADUATE STUDY VERSUS UNDERGRADUATE EDUCATION

Developing high levels of overall academic skill and learning advanced research methods are the two primary concerns seniors should have if they are contemplating graduate school. They also need to develop a more narrowly focused set of academic interests. Courses in the majors in which they are completing bachelor's degrees were only part of their academic work. Outside those majors, they studied many subjects they may or may not have enjoyed but to which they were exposed in required courses. Most seniors realize that all undergraduate majors require such compromises: they took some courses they chose, but they took even more courses that were chosen for them. Seniors normally enroll in twice as many courses as graduate students take, or so we hope, and undergraduate courses frequently are designed to educate them broadly instead of training them specifically. At the end of a typical 120-hour curriculum, seniors have spent between one-third and one-half of those hours in their majors and the rest in arts and sciences core courses, minor areas of interest, and electives.

When they go to graduate school, things are different. They do not have to compromise as much. Graduate study finds them training almost exclusively in fields or areas of study they can approach more as labors of love than as efforts to obtain job credentials. As graduate students, they conduct much more extensive research, and the volume of reading and writing they do in a single course is usually much greater than what they have experienced thus far. To do well under these conditions, they have to love their work—or at least like it very much. Other motivations for graduate study—increased income potential, for example—may be present, but those do not fend off loneliness, fatigue, and boredom nearly as well as does love of one's work.

Seniors may already think of their bachelor's degrees not just as necessary career training but also as important social and cultural achievements. A graduate degree, however—especially in such professional fields as medicine, law, and teaching—may be necessary career training, but social and cultural pressures are no longer really issues. Few people are expected to earn graduate degrees to be considered good citizens or to satisfy behavioral norms.

This shift from studying what is required to what is loved is not known to most students until they experience it, that is, once they enroll in graduate school. If seniors could be convinced before the fact that they would experience this pleasant change of attitude, more would seriously consider graduate school. This is especially true of the brightest, most creative seniors; the ones that graduate schools covet; the same students that schools must win over by competing heavily with the job market. Graduate schools cannot take this competition lightly—or wait in confidence that such seniors will seek them out.

Beginning with their undergraduate coursework, what do we look for in seniors we want to see in graduate school? We know that good graduate students are well prepared. But do we know whether that preparation includes extensive coursework directly related to the graduate field? Or should it include broad general knowledge and limited coursework in the field itself? Graduate programs in English, psychology, and history operate on the premise that the enrolling students must have considerable familiarity with those fields—specific prerequisite courses in many cases. Conversely, graduate programs in business administration, education, and journalism frequently make it clear that they prefer students who do not have extensive undergraduate coursework in those fields.

Our experience as educators has shown us that successful graduate students usually chart their courses toward the middle of these two opposite points. The best graduate students have more-than-adequate undergraduate preparation in their fields. However, they do not bring so many preconceived notions and ideas that they spend their first year in a potentially disillusioning fight for authority with their graduate faculty. In other words, they do not overestimate the value of their undergraduate training. Frequently, the better graduate students appear to have made a point of broadening their undergraduate education to include as much general knowledge as possible—and of spending some time considering the relationship of that general knowledge to their chosen field for graduate study.

Such reasoning shapes their attitudes toward graduate study. Successful students begin their graduate work with tempered enthusiasm: a combination of fascination for discovering and mastering the secrets and skills of their fields and a reasonably sober assessment of the possible contributions and limitations inherent in viewing the world from the more narrowly focused perspective of their chosen disciplines. Their attitudes include self-confidence but not arrogance, and they have a reasonably good idea of the difference between skepticism and cynicism.

Although parents, friends, and peers can shape their attitudes, usually none can have the intellectual influence on those attitudes that faculty can exercise—especially key advisers and major professors. The most successful graduate students choose their mentors early and spend time with them weekly or even daily, if possible. Since these faculty (should) also teach undergraduates, we ought to increase the opportunities for talented seniors to interact with them as well. Even simple conversations, over a brown bag lunch for instance, help seniors develop attitudes that encourage them to enroll in graduate school with improved chances for success.

Helpful attitudes easily observed among impressive graduate students and successful seniors include those regarding studying, reading entire assignments, and completing homework and projects on schedule. The good study habits that are so essential in graduate school can be acquired by seniors, if they have not already been formed. Once those habits are practiced regularly, they markedly increase seniors' optimism about continuing into graduate school. Students who bring excellent study habits into graduate work are less likely to exhibit the kind of emotional stress that causes them to make extraordinary demands on family, friends, or whatever social support network they use.

Contrary to some ideas, social support is clearly visible in the routines of the best graduate students. They do not spend all their time alone. In fact, the long hours in the library or laboratory drive them to seek the company of family or friends whenever they can work social hours into their schedules. A popular myth about graduate school holds that the student inevitably neglects a spouse or partner so much that marriages and long relationships are severely strained and often break apart. At best, such claims are exaggerated; if such things occur, they rarely happen to well-prepared students with good attitudes and good habits. A better reason to encourage graduate students to have strong social support is the great emotional lift that family and friends can provide by being interested listeners who are willing to modify their social schedules to include the graduate student whenever possible.

A final but critical observation about successful graduate students involves money. Simply put, they do not have to spend much time worrying about it. Graduate school is extremely expensive, but graduate students plan ahead. They secure fellowships or assistantships, they arrange for student loans (if they need them), and they attend to such things as summer employment, financial support from family or spouse, and one or two sources of emergency loans for contingencies they cannot afford from their regular sources of support. Attitude is important here, too. The best students know they will have limited resources for the years in graduate school, and they make up their minds to live within their means through those years (and six months beyond, because paychecks from full-time employment do not always begin coming in right after graduate school ends). If transportation, such as a used car, is necessary, the best students take precautions to see that the car is mechanically sound enough to last without the likelihood of major repairs. Although it's not often possible to retire all debts (undergraduate loans, for example) before entering graduate school, these students reduce their indebtedness as much as possible. If deferred payment on existing loans is possible, they request it before enrolling in graduate school. When it comes to money, successful graduate students do what is necessary to keep it from being a significant distraction.

IMPROVING GRADUATION RATES AND TIME TO DEGREE

Before considering more specific suggestions for increasing seniors' interest in graduate school and preparing them better for graduate study, we need to ask ourselves what improvements we can realistically expect from our efforts. There are too many variables affecting graduate students' work to permit us to believe that across-the-board, general changes and new techniques are going to make precisely measurable differences.

Rather than provoke (appropriate) misgivings among faculty and administrators with claims about improving the academic performance of graduate students, let us instead look at two aspects of graduate training that probably could be positively influenced by the suggestions that follow in this chapter. From the observations we have made thus far about behavior and attitudes among successful graduate students, we should be able to see the possibilities of improving graduation rates and shortening time to degree in many programs.

During my years in graduate education, I have noticed an apparent correlation between graduation rates and the level of faculty involvement with graduate students. In even the toughest Ph.D. programs, when faculty-student ratios are kept low, classes and seminars are small, and frequent scheduled as well as unscheduled interactions occur between faculty and students, graduation rates as high as 90 percent are attainable.

There is also an observable relationship between conviviality—yes, friendliness—and the persistence shown by graduate students. Faculty and administrators who organize and attend social events for graduate students increase the loyalty and motivation of those students. Consciously or unconsciously, such faculty model a life that they find satisfying personally, encouraging graduate students to believe that such a life is desirable and attainable for them too. If they are ever tempted to leave graduate school for attractive jobs or social distractions, graduate students who frequently see their mentors actually enjoying life—academically as well as socially—will resist such temptations more effectively.

Faculty behavior is critical to student persistence, but administrators must be careful not to undermine the faculty's efforts by less-than-careful enrollment management. Such management must be based on regular monitoring of the market for the graduates, the demographic mix of the students in the program, and the financial resources available to the department to support the faculty and the students. Support in this context means a number of things. Faculty need adequate salaries, workspace, equipment, travel funds, and staff assistance. Support for graduate students includes fellowships, assistantships, workspace, equipment, and occasional travel funds. These are not luxuries; they are necessities.

Though invariably pressed for resources, administrators can help increase their support for better preparation of seniors for graduate school in several ways. They can solicit money from professional associations and such other external sources as national eleemosynary groups interested in improving postsecondary education and tap into funds generated by student activity fees. They can increase the number of paid internships and traineeships available to seniors, appeal directly to alumni who have gone on to graduate school, or create formal credit-bearing capstone courses (paid for through tuition fees). Depending upon the location of the school, administrators could ask local business and public institutions to finance special seminars for graduating seniors and even offer their seniors weekend and summer programs for an additional fee (over and above their tuition).

PROGRAM IDEAS FOR SENIORS

Old ideas that still have currency, new ideas that have not been fully developed, and other suggestions that have not been given enough time to prove themselves are all included among the things we might find effective in helping more seniors become better graduate students. Many such efforts began life during the 1960s and 1970s as federal programs to encourage and prepare minority students to enter graduate study in larger numbers. Regrettable victims of recent changes in federal spending priorities were programs such as the Minority Excellence in Graduate Education grants to expose minority undergraduates to advanced research methods, Patricia Roberts Harris fellowships for women and minorities, and the Ronald E. McNair Program of summer programs to prepare minority undergraduates for graduate study, especially in engineering and the sciences. These programs were never properly evaluated, but those of us who observed some of them in action saw successful use of a wide variety of teaching methods, including individualized instruction, sensitivity to multiple learning styles, and alternatives to "major paper" assignments. I have seen most of these ideas tried at my institution, but many were underfunded and not given what I consider to be adequate time to have their maximum impact on graduate students. Seldom have I seen them tried with seniors, but on the campus today there is considerable interest in improving the preparation of seniors for graduate study; thus some of the programs and services may receive a much-deserved second look. Thus some of the best of these ideas are included among the suggestions that follow.

An important requirement to the success of most of these ideas is active participation of faculty—especially graduate faculty whenever possible. The benefits of their participation are numerous. Seniors would have extensive personal contact with researchers and writers whose articles, monographs, and books have been, and will be, used by these students as texts and reading material. Having such distinguished faculty direct them in graduate-level research—or simply spending time with them in conversation—increases motivation, interest, and understanding among both groups: the seniors and the faculty who teach them in graduate school. If the graduate faculty are willing to meet with the undergraduate faculty and administrators who plan and implement programs built on these ideas, the seniors who join them are much more assured of being involved in activities that are truly rewarding.

In no particular order, then, here are some ways we could better prepare seniors for graduate study.

Summer Workshops

Ranging in length from one to six weeks, summer workshops, taught by graduate faculty assisted by graduate students, offer one of the best opportunities for intensive preparation of seniors. Graduate research methods; overviews of outstanding universities and their programs; career counseling; practice and assistance with applications; tips on improving entrance exam scores; and practice with writing, computer use, and public speaking are some of the areas or ways in which undergraduates can be helped in summer programs. These programs could be designed for any graduate students or restricted to those whose interests are similar—engineers, for example.

Early Orientation

Many graduate schools do not offer formal orientation. Most rely on the individual departments or colleges to provide necessary information and welcome new students. These sessions can be outstanding, but many are superficial and hurried. Consequently, early orientations organized while students are still undergraduates are especially helpful to students who plan to travel far to school and to those who have never attended a large institution. Probably best targeted toward students planning to study in the same field, early orientations could use faculty, administrators, and graduate students currently studying in the areas of interest to the seniors who attend the sessions. The programs should be available to manageable numbers of students, to permit as much small-group work and one-on-one discussion as possible. Issues should be restricted to those specific to the institution(s) the participants plan to attend.

A special orientation for minority graduate students may prove effective, especially if faculty role models representing various racial and ethnic groups can be brought in to talk to individuals or small groups. Campus organizations and programs designed to meet the special needs of minority graduate students should be represented at the orientation.

Shadowing

At institutions with both graduate and undergraduate programs, arranging for seniors to follow graduate students around for a few days is no problem. Even at colleges without graduate programs on campus, limited shadowing of graduate students at nearby universities could be arranged. To be most effective, such programs should include individual planning between the senior and a faculty member before the shadowing takes place. Following the event, reasonably extensive discussion of what was observed should also include the faculty member, and a paper or other presentation of findings before other seniors would be a good idea.

Offices of Fellowships and Summer Programs

Establishing an office that gathers information about distinguished fellowships and helps selected seniors (and other undergraduates) apply for them can greatly enhance students' chances of winning them. Assistance should include helping students complete the application—especially required essays—and rehearsing them for required interviews. Undergraduate institutions whose students enjoy the greatest success in winning such prestigious awards as Rhodes, Truman, Marshall, or Fulbright scholarships have such offices in place. Student affairs personnel working together with faculty advisory groups seem to be the key to staffing such services.

Preprofessional School Advising Service

A fairly new service that promises to ease the entry of seniors into law or medical school as well as various graduate professional programs is a preprofessional school advising office. Helping seniors understand the rigorous schedules they will face and making sure they know all the career possibilities associated with their chosen profession are two important ways a skilled career counselor can increase seniors' chances of success. Help with applications, advice about taking entrance exams, writing applicant essays, and deciding how to pay for professional school are other services this office could offer. The National Academic Advising Association (NACADA) is a valuable national resource on improving academic advising for students, in this case seniors who wish to attend graduate school.

Mentoring

Frequently used at graduate schools to orient and train new students, mentoring is more intrusive than shadowing, requiring frequent discussions between the parties involved. Seniors could be mentored by an available graduate faculty member or graduate student. The process could occur as part of a summer program or a semester-long weekend program, where the mentoring could occur during the week and discussions of its results could be held on weekends. Mentoring could also be part of a capstone course for seniors.

Tutoring

Seniors whose skill levels are not quite up to graduate school standards yet would benefit greatly from tutoring sessions with graduate students. The best sessions would find the students working one-on-one, but small groups of seniors with rotating graduate student mentors also could work. Social interaction would be fostered more by the latter format. Tutoring should take place over an extended period, perhaps a full academic term.

Professional Association Seminars

Even if they occur only two or three times during the senior year, regularly scheduled meetings with professionals already in the field, graduate students, and graduate faculty can have a powerful impact on seniors. Recruiting is the primary goal of such events, but collegiality can be so much in evidence that seniors' appetites for such relationships are whetted. Realistic presentations by professionals make the field come alive, stir the imagination of seniors, and give valuable insight into the realities of careers in a field.

Faculty-Student Lunches, Forums, Panel Discussions, Social Events

Sometimes seniors need relief from formal presentations and pressure from recruiters. Lunches, or even occasional informal dinners, at which seniors and faculty are both guests of administrators (who might be present) introduce students to the satisfaction that comes with collegiality based on common intellectual interests. Seniors learn that people with advanced degrees are not at all stuffy, and they become less self-conscious about telling friends and family of their own plans to enter graduate study.

Classroom Visits from Outstanding Graduate Students

Visits from articulate, enthusiastic graduate students can be fairly easily accommodated in senior seminars to create excitement among seniors who may be considering graduate school—and provoke at least mild curiosity among those who are not. Caution should be taken to ensure that the visiting students are energetic, capable speakers who share anecdotes, give "inside advice," and avoid technical explanations. A question-and-answer session should always be a part of such visits, and the faculty member should prepare the class to ask a variety of interesting questions. These visits help recruiting more than anything else.

Visits to Graduate Classes and Laboratories

Even if logistics restrict seniors in a capstone course to just one or two visits to graduate classes or laboratories, the results are usually worth the planning and effort required. A key to their success is the preparation of seniors for the visit. They need to be given specific assignments—what to look for during the visits—as well as ample time to investigate on their own and ask whatever questions occur to them. These visits help seniors who are trying to choose between certain fields they may be considering, and they make more credible the efforts of faculty who teach them special skills in workshops back at their undergraduate institutions. Summer programs and early orientation also can use these visits effectively. Shadowing and mentoring take individuals into graduate classes, but visits can complement these activities too.

Distribution of Printed Guides, Reminders, Planners, and Tip Sheets

Advice about choosing a school, applying to graduate programs, looking for fellowships and other forms of funding, and planning budgets is another approach that can be covered with handouts customized to each area. Rather than simply placing a graduate studies catalogue in front of seniors, administrators and faculty should try to get graduate schools to prepare brief reference materials for seniors. If that is not possible, faculty and administrators should prepare their own excerpts and summaries of important application, enrollment, or matriculation issues for seniors to refer to during discussions. These materials are needed in summer programs as well as capstone courses.

CONCLUSION: IMPLICATIONS FOR IMPLEMENTATION AND PRACTICE

Radical reform is not needed in the way we prepare and place seniors in graduate school. Modest efforts such as those mentioned in this chapter go a long way to preserve the necessarily high standards of quality in graduate training while simultaneously improving the performance and persistence of graduate students. These ideas help keep more students in graduate school, and they make students more attentive to their responsibilities while there, which permits them to finish their work in less time. To be effective, these ideas must have the leadership of faculty and administrators who prepare seniors for graduate school and the cooperation of graduate faculty and students. These people understand the aspirations of today's seniors, and they know that habits and traditions still current in graduate school can be modified to better serve the needs of today's seniors.

Changing the process of graduate study—especially to permit current seniors to earn degrees in less time—will not be easy, and more money for graduate study is essential. But tough questions must be asked before increased spending produces the desired results, such as exactly what changes should be made, who must make them, and how long the changes will take to be put in place. Part of the problem is the lack of agreement among faculty about whether graduate programs can maintain their traditional standards if changes are made in teaching methods and as they add the new courses, traineeships, and internships that are necessary as new degrees are offered and older degrees modernized. An equally vexing concern is that increasing numbers of nontraditional seniors do not always bring with them the types or levels of academic skills that graduate faculty are trained—and expect—to work with.

We do not have to answer all these questions thoroughly before beginning to try some of these ideas. There is little chance these activities could adversely affect any seniors who wish to pursue a graduate degree. There is every chance that we will help seniors—especially nontraditional students who do not fit the somewhat narrow definition of undergraduate most often sought by our graduate schools. We should try things, and we should tell each other what happens when we do. Our work may even speed up the slow pace of change in graduate schools.

PART THREE

DEVELOPING SPECIAL SUPPORT SERVICES FOR SENIORS

In Part Two, we explored the broad themes of the senior experience that cut across both the curriculum and the cocurriculum. In Part Three, we focus on specific support services for seniors and the roles that certain offices and campus units can play in organizing to address issues related to the senior year.

Believing that traditional career counseling and job placement efforts are no longer sufficient, in this section we propose an expanded role for the career center on campus. We also examine the college-to-career transition issues facing multiethnic and disabled college seniors and provide specific recommendations for targeted programs to prepare and address these students' unique transition issues.

Because alumni can serve as bridges to the future for anxious graduates entering new communities and workplace situations, chapter authors also suggest an enhanced role for the alumni and development offices. The authors believe that most colleges and universities can no longer afford to take future alumni support for granted. Therefore, these offices need to provide leadership for the rest of the campus in cultivating loyal alumni while students, especially seniors, are still on campus.

CHAPTER TWELVE

Comprehensive Career Services for Seniors

Denise Dwight Smith
Linda K. Gast

Today's graduating seniors face important transitions in their lives, filled with anticipation, panic, hope, and fear. Yet they respond quite differently.

This senior majoring in English is overwhelmed and approaches graduation and the task of finding a job with denial, procrastination, and avoidance:

> I really don't have time to be bothered with looking for a job. I will wait until I go back to Raleigh and then look for a job this summer. I am not sure what I want to do anyway, and the placement office didn't have any of the public relations companies coming to campus that I was interested in. Maybe I will just go to graduate school.

This senior psychology major is obsessed with doing everything right and preoccupied with finding a good job, especially since she found her first career unfulfilling:

> I need to get in to see a counselor right away to review my draft of my résumé. I am worried that I do not have any experience to compete with the other students who have had an internship. I need to send this off this weekend to my friend's dad for the positions he told me about. I will also look at the papers for ads. What else can I do? . . . I am just scared I will not have a job to pay off my loans, which are soon going to be due. . . . I also am worried that I will have to take a position that is so boring. That was why I got out of teaching. One of my sorority sisters did that last year. She is still so unhappy and still looking for another option.

This third senior, a computer science major, seems in control of his career future. He has prepared ahead of time, has gained experience in his field, and is now demonstrating behaviors indicative of constructive career planning:

> I am ready to participate in the on-campus interviews now that I have attended the orientation and interview workshops offered by the Career Center. . . . I am hopeful that I can have an opportunity with one of the top three companies I have targeted. I also know that I will get an offer from the company I co-oped with. I have always been interested in computers and problem solving, so I am eager to get a good job.

Shipton and Steltenpohl (1981) submit that "all persons need to define the meaning of work for themselves in terms of its importance in their lives, the satisfaction, or dissatisfaction it brings to them, and its relationship to their leisure interests. . . . If colleges are to truly enhance individual development and prepare students to cope with succeeding stages of development, faculty, staff, and counselors need to be prepared to assist students of all ages in clarifying their life, career, and academic purposes" (p. 690).

In this chapter, we look at the career needs and experiences of seniors and how institutions can support them. We argue that colleges and universities must reformulate the goals of education to embrace career development as integral to the undergraduate experience. The chapter outlines how this comprehensive and integrated approach directly supports institutional missions and current priorities for higher education. We also describe the roles of faculty, staff, and administrators as collaborators in this new educational approach. A feature that receives emphasis in this chapter is the role of experiential learning in helping move students to higher levels of career understanding and academic integration. Lastly, we argue that a paradigm shift must occur in how campuses view *career services,* including coming to see the career center as a vital link between academia and the employment community; we describe a conceptual framework for the delivery of campus career services that creatively engages faculty, alumni, parents, and employers; and we recommend organizational structures for the new comprehensive career center.

HISTORICAL PERSPECTIVE ON CAREER DEVELOPMENT

Economists, psychologists, counselors, sociologists, and others have been studying how people choose careers and the paths they pursue since the beginning of the twentieth century. Early career theory suggested that a clear understanding of one's abilities and interests paired with knowledge of occupations that "matched" one's abilities and interests would lead to a reasoned occupational choice and therefore greater work satisfaction and productivity (Parsons, 1909; Williamson, 1939). This approach to career decision making created the need to counsel individuals about their abilities and interests and to provide vocational education beginning in the high school years. In 1951, Ginzberg (an economist), Ginsburg (a psychiatrist), Axelrad (a sociologist), and Herma (a psychologist) radically departed from prior thinking and posited that occupational choice was a developmental process that occurred over a number of years, culminating in early adulthood. Ginzberg later revised this thinking (1972, 1984) and stated that *"occupational choice is a lifelong process of decision making for those who seek major satisfactions from their work. This leads them to reassess repeatedly how they can improve the fit between their changing career goals and the realities of the world of work"* (Ginzberg, 1984, p. 180; Ginzberg's emphasis). Here the emphasis is on learning and understanding career development as a continual process, not a static point in time or series of events. Contemporary approaches to career development remain rooted in the life-span process approach but are seeking broader application as differences among gender, race, and socioeconomic class have been noted in both how and why individuals make various career choices.

As career theory evolved into a lifelong developmental concept, campus career services evolved from matching persons and jobs into offering comprehensive career services. Through the 1960s, counseling students about careers took place predominantly in counseling centers, quite apart from the job assistance being provided by campus *placement bureaus.* When lifelong career development became preeminent in the 1970s, career counseling and job placement functions were combined in *career planning and placement* offices. Although missions differed, the majority of these offices embraced the need to work with students prior to the senior year to clarify career plans and to provide assistance with finding a job or applying to graduate school. During this same time period, the notion of experiential learning—exploring and actively participating in career fields through internships, cooperative education, and volunteer service—was taking hold on many college campuses, sometimes within the career office and sometimes within academic units.

The 1990s have brought tremendous changes in how career services are viewed and delivered on college campuses. The dual roles of career counseling and job placement are being replaced by a comprehensive approach to career development that seeks to be fully integrated into the traditional academic curriculum. The new comprehensive career centers have strong career development foundations, with missions explicitly tied to institutional goals. They assist students from all academic disciplines, adult learners as well as those eighteen-to twenty-two-year-olds, graduate students as well as undergraduates, international and multiethnic students, alumni, and sometimes even faculty and staff.

Comprehensive career centers assist with student retention efforts through early career clarification, teach the importance of networking as a lifelong career skill, increase student career awareness by disseminating career information via the World Wide Web and other technological advances, and help students see connections between their academic studies and employment or volunteer experiences through experiential learning and other curricular programs.

While the American academy does not focus on careerism per se, the relationship between academic study and career future is paramount from the viewpoint of students and their parents or families. More than at any other time in recent history, today's student expects college to prepare him or her for a better job and to increase lifelong earnings (Astin, 1993b), whether the job is a first-career position or a career change. Parents and families expect the same. Graduating seniors are experiencing a work world that is radically different from that of past decades. This nation's marketplace is international; its GNP is service based and increasingly provided by small entrepreneurial organizations; the workforce is increasingly made up of part-time, contractual, and flexible-hours workers of both genders who are diverse in age and culture; and the use of technology is common to almost all professions. Today, graduating seniors can expect to change careers as many as five times and have ten to fifteen different jobs over the course of their working lifetimes.

Yet in a 1994 national survey conducted by the College Placement Council (now the National Association of Colleges and Employers), nearly two thousand seniors cited "defining career options," "lack of knowledge of the career planning process," and "lack of experience" as the biggest hurdles to finding a job after graduation. Although today's economic revolution is creating a multitude of new jobs, predictions are that 25 percent of the college graduate labor force will find jobs that have traditionally required less than a college education (Shelley, 1994). As the U.S. Department of Education, National Center for Education Statistics sees things, "Although about three-fourths of recent graduates who were working full time . . . reported their jobs were related to their field of study, only 60 percent reported a college degree was required to get their job" (1996, p. 108). Career counselors and faculty are facing new challenges in educating students for a society in which work is no longer defined by traditional career paths but instead focused upon short-term project assignments and keeping oneself employable. In fact, several organizations no longer use job descriptions or career paths but rely more on project team assignments (Kirby, 1996). Traditional campus career counseling and job placement are no longer sufficient. It is essential that the undergraduate experience help students of all ages and backgrounds make informed and personally meaningful career and job decisions; help them learn vital lifelong skills to plan, manage, and change careers; and accomplish these goals through coordinated curricular and cocurricular efforts on college campuses.

THE SENIOR YEAR AND CAREER DEVELOPMENT

There is a great myth that all seniors are ready for graduation and their impending transitions into careers or graduate education. A student's state of readiness for a successful transition is not realized simply by the timing of graduation. In fact, many seniors are unclear about their goals, confused by the graduate school and job search processes, and worried about their future. Data from the Senior Transition Survey at the University of Maryland (*Senior Transition Survey*, 1993) indicated that 76 percent of 970 survey respondents were concerned about finding a job and adjusting to work, 40 percent were concerned about getting into graduate or professional school, and 47 percent indicated that they were still uncertain about their career choice. A 1996 survey by the National Association of Colleges and Employers found similar concerns, reporting that a significant number of graduating students (36.7 percent) find "competition for jobs is their biggest obstacle to finding a job" (Collins, 1996, p. 41), despite an improved economy. The same survey also found seniors' lack of experience (21.1 percent) and uncertainty about what they wanted to do (13.3 percent) as the second and third most frequently cited obstacles to finding a job (Collins, 1996). And several recent publications attest to the fact that seniors and recent college graduates experience heightened anxiety surrounding their transitions from college to career because their expectations of the workplace (and their lives) do not match reality (Ellin, 1993; Holton, 1993; Sullivan, 1993).

Similarly, Andrew Wolvin, leader of The Senior Year Experience Implementation Team at the University of Maryland, reports that "the desire for career assistance is one of the most common threads running through every aspect of our work with seniors thus far. Time and time again in survey responses, focus-group conversations and weekly team meetings, discussion of career development has appeared as a major concern" (personal memo to W. L. Thomas, June 23, 1996).

Like the three students presented at the beginning of this chapter, college seniors exhibit varying degrees of readiness to engage in career-related activities and display a range of behaviors and emotions. And they often underestimate the time, energy, and dedication needed to carry out career planning for their future. Despite services of the campus career center, counseling center, academic advisers, and faculty to help with career questions and concerns, too many students approach graduation without having taken advantage of such supports. Still others delay any career-related activities until impending graduation, thus missing opportunities and important building blocks in the preceding years.

Career development emphasizes the importance of engaging in successive activities in order to establish clear career goals throughout one's lifetime: understanding oneself (abilities, values, interests); targeting occupations that reflect one's interests, values, and abilities; and gaining experience (Super, 1969; Holland, 1973; Tiedeman and O'Hara, 1963). Students should experience all such activities during the college years (as was exemplified by the computer science major at the beginning of this chapter). Students who have failed to engage successfully in these activities prior to the senior year find the transition to work, a second career, or graduate school even more difficult.

Career planning activities, however, should be accompanied by development of job and career skills that can benefit the work world of today and tomorrow. Seniors may be ill prepared for the job search and transition process and also lacking in critical skills for employment. Philip Gardner (Chapter Five) and Elwood Holton (Chapter Seven) point out that students possess few of the contextual work competencies needed such as interpersonal communication, teamwork, applied problem solving, and self-management. Seniors often are unaware of the importance of such basic skills in the workplace.

Assisting seniors with career development should not be limited to the goal of full-time employment following graduation. A significant and increasing number of graduating seniors plan to attend graduate or professional school, return for a second baccalaureate degree, or combine postbaccalaureate jobs with simultaneous coursework to increase their employability. According to the U.S. Department of Education, National Center for Education Statistics (1995b), enrollment in graduate school rose approximately 23 percent between 1985 and 1993, and enrollment in first professional degree programs rose 7 percent between 1990 and 1993. Yet seniors too often select graduate or professional school as a delaying behavior rather than a conscious career choice. The academy can take advantage of these career trends as a time to reinforce the notion of lifelong learning. By reconceptualizing the senior year experience, specific career development activities inside and outside the classroom can help focus and encourage student interest in further education. Seniors can develop a more realistic picture of graduate or professional education and at the same time focus their career interests through increased opportunities to engage in research projects with faculty, capstone classes that incorporate modules on current research in the discipline and opportunities for graduate study, and faculty colloquia and other cocurricular "career" events. (Lawhon discusses this issue in greater depth in Chapter Eleven.)

Perhaps the greatest challenge for college campuses in assisting students with their career needs lies in dealing with the shifts in attitudes and values among so many college students in comparison to the previous baby boomer generation. Many traditional-age college students want information immediately, succinctly, and clearly. They are more demanding, less introspective, and less tolerant in some ways than prior generations (Cannon, 1992). Neil Murray (1993) suggests that educators acknowledge this new generation of students and respond to their different needs and demands. One of these apparent needs is the desire for a lifestyle with more focus on leisure-time pursuits and less focus on work. Today's seniors, traditional-age and older alike, have experienced rampant corporate downsizing and restructuring and, as a result, are less trusting of corporate America. In increasing numbers, they are relying more on themselves, starting their own businesses (Lane, 1995), and engaging in community service work in an apparent attempt to gain greater control over and balance in their lives.

Finally, a look at the senior year and career development would not be accurate without paying attention to the changing nature of the student population. Increasingly, college students are women, older, and more racially and ethnically diverse; they work at least part-time throughout their college education experience. And students matriculate with a wide range of abilities, disabilities, and demands for services. Some research suggests that the career needs of a more diverse student body may be different from those of the traditional white male population upon which most of our career theories and educational foundations have been based. For instance, extensive reviews of the research document that women restrict their career choices more than men (Betz and Fitzgerald, 1987; Fitzgerald and Crites, 1980). Women also are less likely to advance to higher levels in their occupations, experience more conflict between work and family roles, and have different career patterns than men (Betz and Fitzgerald, 1987). Providing career development support on campuses today requires more complexity and flexibility than in the past, with increased attention to differing needs and lifestyles.

CAREER DEVELOPMENT AS AN INTEGRATED EDUCATIONAL COMPONENT

In most institutions of higher education, among other things the goals of undergraduate education include graduating students who are self-aware, who "know how to acquire knowledge and how to use it" (Dressel, 1968, p. 210), and who can make meaningful contributions to society through their work and community involvement. Career development directly contributes to each of these goals by helping students explore, clarify, and implement decisions about academic majors, postbaccalaureate education, and career choices.

There is compelling evidence to suggest why it is vital for colleges to pay attention to the career development of students. First expressed by an undergraduate in the level of comfort with his or her choice of academic major, clarity of career choice has been linked to higher rates of retention and academic performance (Astin, 1993b; Maryland Longitudinal Study Steering Committee, 1986). When students in the Maryland Longitudinal Study were grouped by both academic and career-clarity dimensions, patterns emerged: (1) the higher the academic performance and the higher the vocational identity, the more likely students are to remain in the university experience; (2) the lower the student performance on both dimensions, the more likely students are to drop out of the university; and (3) high academic performance alone cannot ensure the level of career clarity that facilitates transition to the world of work or graduate study. Similar findings have occurred in campus-based research across the country.

A second compelling reason for colleges to embrace the importance of career development in the educational experience is to fully prepare students for the new global workforce. A 1994 study released by the National Center for Education Statistics, "was the first broad-based study to document the degree to which education is directly linked to (workplace) productivity" (Applebome, 1995, p. 49). Yet many institutions do not acknowledge the workplace as a potentially rich and valuable source of learning, despite the fact that the majority of today's college students (46 percent of full-time and 85 percent of part-time students) work while obtaining their undergraduate education (U.S. Department of Education, National Center for Education Statistics, 1995b, p. 142). The U.S. Department of Education, National Center for Education Statistics says that "among 16–24 year old college students in 1993, almost half of full-time students and 85 percent of part-time students were employed" (1995b, p. 15). Although some institutions allow credit for work-and-learn opportunities (experiential learning), obtaining faculty sponsorship is frequently difficult for students (Bikson and Law, 1994). A recent report on higher education from the Wingspread Group on Higher Education (1993) proclaims that America's ability to compete in a global economy is seriously at risk unless higher education produces "graduates who will perform as informed and involved citizens ready to assume leadership roles in American life" (p. 2). If higher education is to fulfill its long-held mission to society, the current chasm between student employment and academic learning must be bridged.

In our opinion, bridging the gap between employment and academic learning, and responding to increasing student, parent, employer, and legislator criticisms of higher education, requires a metamorphosis of current undergraduate education. In Alexander Astin's *What Matters in College?* (1993b), several research findings seem central to our arguments for a new approach to undergraduate education: (1) "the student's peer group is the single most potent source of influence on growth and development during the undergraduate years" (p. 398); (2) "next to the peer group, the faculty represents the most significant aspect of the student's undergraduate education" (p. 410), particularly interaction with faculty outside the classroom; and (3) working full-time as a student or working off campus in part-time jobs with no relationship to academic study have significant negative correlations with student retention (p. 196). A recent article in the *New York Times* quotes Peter Likins, president of Lehigh University: "These corporations are ever more competitive . . . and they are saying 'We can't afford to hire someone and then take two years training them how to function—you have to do it.' I've been in higher education a long time, and I've never seen such fundamental change in undergraduate education as what I'm seeing now" (Johnson, 1996, p. 28).

Contrary to popular fears of corporate involvement in higher education, Likins has found strong support from corporate executives for traditional liberal arts education and a renewed interest in ethics. The new educational model, then, must be one in which curricular and cocurricular components are partners in an integrated approach to undergraduate education and in which career development is an integral part of both components. As long as student career development and undergraduate education remain disconnected processes, the effectiveness of the undergraduate experience continues to be compromised.

FACULTY INVOLVEMENT AND THE NEW CURRICULAR MODEL

Career center professionals have long seen the value of integrating career development with classroom learning, but it should be even more important to faculty today than in the past. Increased pressures on higher education to become more accountable and the almost universal need for increased institutional funding are being felt by the individual faculty member, too. These pressures can be eased, if only in part, by faculty's active participation in student career development. Faculty connections with students, in and out of the classroom, have been shown to positively affect student retention and academic performance, indicators increasingly used to differentially allocate institutional resources. Accountability measures often call for "placement rates" by programmatic area (Joint Commission on Accountability Reporting, 1996) as a measure of program viability. Faculty who are involved with student career development activities can gain increased exposure to possible outside funding sources from organizations hiring their students.

Faculty can integrate career development into the curriculum by offering capstone courses at the senior year that emphasize application of domain knowledge in the workplace, designing innovative curricular interventions such as "minimester" courses, undergraduate research projects, and course modules in theoretical or foundations classes that help students clarify career goals and apply the discipline to challenging real-world situations. Faculty carry on integration as well by developing experiential learning programs prior to the senior year.

The National Society for Experiential Education (NSEE) has adopted this definition of experiential learning: "learning activities that engage the learner directly in the phenomena being studied" (Kendall and others, 1986, p. 1). As Smith noted in Chapter Six, experiential learning opportunities can encompass a variety of experiences for students prior to graduation, including structured internships for credit, cooperative education, nursing clinicals, student teaching, certain research projects, team intern projects, graduate assistantships, practica, and field studies. Other experiences may be less academically based and more career exploratory (such as externships, mentorships, part-time employment, or community service) but can benefit greatly from faculty support and involvement. In the federally funded school-to-work projects, students are paired with sponsoring community agencies to help deal with social issues such as crime, the environment, teenage pregnancy, and health problems (Commission on National and Community Services, 1993). Many universities have established prework seminars that help students prepare for issues such as work habits, safety, organizational politics, ethics, employment of work-related expenses, and sexual harassment. Campus career centers can be invaluable partners with faculty in developing and delivering such curricula and programs.

Key benefits of experiential learning to students include (1) increased awareness of skills and competencies and their application, (2) relevant professional experience that increases the quality and quantity of job offers upon graduation, (3) increased understanding of the need or desire for graduate or further education, (4) greater understanding of work cultures, and (5) development of quality work habits that facilitate the transition from college to work (Shea and others, 1995). The subject matter itself is not always the important information for the student, but how it is delivered and integrated into the problems of today's society does make a difference. For example, students taking a required course in Spanish or Chinese benefit in their civic and work responsibilities if they have learned in class the need for understanding and applying foreign language to business and political problems endemic to a global society.

There are several essential elements to developing high-quality experiential learning opportunities that ensure students' integration of academic learning and workplace application, as cited in the Experiential Learning Council Report from the University of North Carolina at Charlotte (Shea and others, 1995).

Faculty Involvement

Faculty support and respect is crucial to the administration of quality experiential learning programs that best prepare the student going through his or her senior year. David Kolb's theory of learning emphasizes a cycle of experience, reflection, conceptualization, and application or experimentation (McKenzie, 1996). His theory shows the importance of having faculty incorporate and support experiential education as part of any teaching model. Faculty benefit because in so doing they develop reflective learners: "The development of a reflective learner is an essential integrative tool. It can help us as educators to wed the practical and philosophical goals of experiential learning, moral and ethical development, and servant leadership with the academic curriculum itself" (Goldberg, Golden, and McGillin, 1996, p. 29).

The level of faculty involvement can vary, from total academic department control and accountability to program sanctioning and referral support. Faculty can serve as advisers; seminar leaders; reviewers of internship objectives, plans, and job descriptions; members of advisory boards and experiential learning policy committees; job developers; site visitation coordinators; reviewers; and record keepers. The depth and breadth of faculty involvement in experiential learning programs is dependent upon the philosophy, administration, and promotion and tenure practices of the institution.

Faculty who incorporate experiential learning programs into their curricula can greatly support broad educational missions: "Developing reflective learners can, in the end, be one important part of higher education's contribution to a more ethical and prosperous America of citizen-learners" (Goldberg, Golden, and McGillin, 1996, p. 29). However, faculty also can be direct beneficiaries of such initiatives. Some of these benefits are special curriculum development grants; release time for research and development of experiential learning courses or programs; international travel, when such programs are coordinated with other countries; expanded research and consulting opportunities; special research grants, equipment donations, and other resources from employers and alumni; and classroom environments enriched by real-world applications of the subject matter that elicit students' becoming actively engaged in the learning process (Shea and others, 1995). Faculty involvement can boost institutional retention rates, enhance institutional accountability, and increase revenue. They also become invaluable advisers and educational partners with career center staff in helping students explore, clarify, and implement their career plans. By the senior year, students benefiting from faculty support of their career development inside and outside the classroom, coupled with career counseling and guidance, are much more likely to enter professions or graduate study with focused career objectives and the desire for continued lifelong education.

Learning Objectives Grounded in Fields of Study

Students, faculty, and employers all need to be clear about the expressed intent of the experience (objectives), the need to relate the experience to academic study (learning), and what tasks or responsibilities are undertaken to meet the objectives (experience). Many campuses have developed formats for *learning proposals* written by the student, reviewed by the site supervisor (employer), and approved by the faculty sponsor or career center. Such proposals should specify the duration of the experience and amount of credit or remuneration to be granted the student. Experiential learning programs that are integrated into the academic experience are more likely to have structure and guidelines that facilitate greater learning and awareness, especially if the rigors of academic credit are involved.

Reflection Component

Experiential learning has at its core a component of reflection in order to aid in integrating work and academics; increase student understanding of self, skills, and competencies; and hone work habits and work culture awareness. Reflection can take many forms such as a personal journal, essay or final report, panel presentation, video or creative project, group project, or seminar discussion. The best prepared senior is one who has experienced a sector of the work world, been intellectually challenged to see the relevance of academic study to work situations, and begun to understand how he or she fits into the needs of the workplace.

Clear Expectations for Employer or Site Supervisor

Employers are often eager to obtain free or inexpensive labor, but they may not comprehend the responsibility of supervising and teaching a student about their culture, expectations, work processes, and project outcomes. Although the written learning proposal can serve as a guideline, many institutions have developed separate documents outlining expectations for supervision and evaluation, compensation requirements, and student worker benefits. It is also recommended that each employer or site be visited and evaluated periodically. Career centers can play an invaluable role in setting expectations and disseminating them to employers and evaluating sites.

Evaluation

All experiential learning opportunities should have an evaluation component. The best evaluations engage all participants (student, employer, and faculty). Student achievement of learning objectives should be evaluated, as should general feedback to the student, the worksite and supervisor, and the institution and faculty sponsor. Evaluations of the student's performance can be a component of grading, and site reviews can play a key role in maintaining quality experiences.

CAPSTONE COURSES AND INNOVATIVE CURRICULAR INTERVENTIONS

Other curricular interventions can provide critical support to the career development of students, particularly to seniors. Recent undergraduate education reforms have seen many campuses establishing or reestablishing capstone courses to integrate general education and academic discipline learning and to introduce important dimensions such as ethics, current trends, and research or creative innovation in the field. We would argue that such capstone courses are ripe for career development infusion. (See John Gardner's capstone course syllabus in Resource B as an illustration.)

In order for seniors to fully integrate their undergraduate experience, they must see its application and relevance to their immediate future. Integration can be assisted by introducing career components into capstone courses. The chemistry department at the University of Maryland has done just that. Chemistry 398 has members of the profession, faculty, and career center staff visiting the classroom to address issues such as career opportunities and employment trends, requirements for admission into graduate or professional school, industry applications of chemistry, innovative research in the field being conducted by faculty and private industry, and ethical issues in the form of case studies. This three-credit course is required of all chemistry majors prior to graduation. Other curricular innovations might include specific career planning classes, cotaught by career center professionals and department faculty, and teaching seniors job search and interviewing skills as well as how to plan for and make informed career decisions for the future. At Indiana University, the School of Business requires all seniors to enroll in a noncredit course of this nature. Many institutions offer mini-mester courses, brief and intensive over a period of a few weeks. Such academic terms are appropriate for senior transition classes, preferably with designated sections for specific academic majors or colleges, focusing on postgraduation plans and lifestyles, or for certain senior research and creative projects with the specific intent of providing an experience students can immediately apply in their first professional position or in graduate or professional school. As part of the senior year capstone experience, students at Wheaton College are given copies of their original admissions essays and asked to review them in the context of the intervening years. They are asked to reflect upon changes in their career aspirations, how college helped them achieve their goals, and how the college could have done a better job in preparing them (Goldberg, Golden, and McGillin, 1996).

CREATING COCURRICULAR PARTNERSHIPS FOR ENHANCED CAREER DEVELOPMENT

Career information and career planning assistance are being sought by admissions offices in their recruitment efforts; by various student affairs units, advising offices, and academic departments during the college years; and for career changers, by the alumni office after the college years. Although many career centers have been providing such outreach assistance for several decades, the depth and breadth of service now required is far greater than in the past. Additionally, if career development is to be a truly integrated component of the undergraduate curriculum, then cocurricular programming also needs a more comprehensive, developmental approach involving career centers, student affairs units, and academic departments.

Professionals in student affairs ardently strive to create programs, extracurricular activities, services, and living environments that foster appropriate and healthy learning, growth, and development. These activities help shape the formation of student values, interests, and skills, as well as abilities to learn from and interact with others. Student development services are concerned with the total person: social, moral, emotional, spiritual, intellectual, physical, and vocational. Similarly, career development and career planning focus on work values, interests, and skills, but they do so with respect to the "total person." Opportunity therefore exists for cocurricular programs to become more multidimensional by engaging student affairs staff, faculty, and career center professionals in collaboration. For example, a program entitled Women and the Glass Ceiling in the Workplace could examine career, social, and emotional issues; International Careers: Facts and Fiction could address personal, career, and cultural issues in working for a foreign company.

Traditionally, institutionwide attention has been paid to career development at the freshman year in many freshman seminars and especially at the senior year through career centers, with the intervening years largely missed except for experiential learning programs and services offered by career centers or academic departments. Cocurricular programs focusing on career needs of students should be evaluated to ensure a comprehensive approach during all years of the undergraduate experience—with particular emphasis on the senior year, where so many transition issues are related to student career needs. With the expertise and guidance of career center staff, important campus units such as academic advising, residence life, student activities, the health center, the counseling center, and others can be brought together to develop a cocurricular plan for the undergraduate experience. A Women's Week cosponsored by the career center, the student activities office, and relevant student organizations for women or an International Job Fair cosponsored by the career center and the international students office would be much more effective than similar programs offered only by the career center or a single campus department. During the senior year, the finance department, financial aid office, and career center might sponsor a series of workshops on the theme of financial management, including how to develop a personal budget, manage credit card expenses, save, and invest for the future. The career center, organizational behavior and psychology faculty, alumni office, and center for multiethnic students might sponsor a Changing Work Cultures speaker series, where alumni speak about the traditional, Eurocentric work ethic, issues for workers of different racial and ethnic backgrounds, and new model programs that embrace diversity. The list is limitless.

THE NEW CAREER CENTER: STRATEGIES FOR A PARADIGM SHIFT

A case has been made in this chapter for a metamorphosis in the undergraduate education experience. This metamorphosis seeks to fully integrate curricular and cocurricular activities, particularly in the interests of student career development, toward a more comprehensive and responsive preparation of students for future society and a global workforce. Central to the achievement of this new model is the involvement and expertise of the campus career center. However, the career center of the future also must undergo a paradigm shift, which requires that career center professionals and institutions totally reconceptualize the career center's role within the institution and the programs and services the center delivers.

The new career center should hold on to lessons learned over the past fifty years while moving ahead in bold, new directions to develop programs, services, systems, and methodologies that better serve the needs of an increasingly diverse student population and a rapidly changing, global society. The new center should reflect established standards for professional practice published by the Council for the Advancement of Standards (CAS) (1997) and by the National Association of Colleges and Employers (NACE) (1997). Such standards emphasize the importance of understanding career development as a lifelong process and integrating career planning and employment services and also the need for graduate-degreed staff with appropriate background and training, ethical and legal guidelines for programs and service delivery, and program evaluation. The 1997 NACE standards, in revision, expand upon the CAS standards by providing specific guidance in the areas of assessment, program management, faculty relations, employer relations, and organization and mission. Emerging roles for the new career center include being a *catalyst* for the use of technology to assist student career planning and employment needs; a *collaborator* with faculty, parents, alumni, employers, and members of the community in the delivery of programs and services; an *educator* for the campus community about student employment trends, work values, and other career-related issues; and a *consultant* on outcomes assessment to support institutional accountability.

Catalysts for the Use of Technology

The use of technology to deliver career and employment services has burgeoned in the last few years. The operations of career centers are information intensive. Recent software developments and the exponential growth of Internet use have made career resources, job listings, student résumé and credentials databases, and employer databases much more accessible to students and staff and made internal operations management much more efficient. Today's students want information quickly and easily, and computer applications are helping career centers meet those demands. Career centers are creating home pages on the Internet, allowing students remote access to campus interviewing and job opportunities, putting career resource catalogues online, and creating discussion groups. A new consortium of twenty-one career centers in the Atlantic Coast and Southeastern Athletic Conference universities have joined forces to create SEACnet, the Southeastern-Atlantic Coast Career Network, with a home page where employers can locate job candidates from twenty-one institutions with a few keystrokes and students can view career and employment information from multiple institutions. SEACnet also broke new ground by providing videoconferencing capabilities to employers as a consortium. An employer located in Atlanta can travel across town to the Student Success Center at the Georgia Institute of Technology to interview students at Duke, the University of Maryland, the University of North Carolina, and the University of Tennessee— saving thousands of dollars in travel and lost work time away from the office. This same consortium hosted the nation's first "virtual" job fair, where students interviewed with organizations throughout the country using videoconferencing technology. At The Pennsylvania State University, students at branch campuses use videoconferencing to interview with employers at the flagship campus without needing to travel. Such innovations, with the proper marketing and staff support, should significantly broaden students' employment opportunities, especially opportunities with small businesses and international companies that have traditionally not utilized college career centers. Federal legislation has also initiated the development of state based "one-stop career centers," which would act as host sites for collection on the Internet of all job vacancies in particular regions. Schools with marketing centers in airports, public libraries, and city centers may also include kiosks with career information.

Practitioners such as Donald Casella of San Francisco State University claim that career services offices will serve more students, but see fewer of them because of remote technology (Casella, 1992). The new career center must constantly research, teach, and incorporate new strategies that fit into the information age, while not losing sight of the important components of teaching students how to research a career field, help themselves, and develop their own networks.

Collaborators to Engage Key Constituencies

Higher education institutions are becoming less and less ivory towers of insular learning. In many cases, the community demands educators' involvement; in others, it seeks out cooperation and consultation. Career centers are closely linked to the community and can be invaluable in building external relationships. Thus, as the development director feels greatly pressured to create special giving opportunities, as an academic dean tries to open a door to a new company, and as the admissions office has to market unique services, the career center should be responsive to the needs of these internal customers.

Students can be assisted more effectively by the new career center's closer involvement with external relations. Some institutions have developed sophisticated relational databases incorporating company information, including the number of alumni who work there, the nature of the business, the past hiring and college relations activity, experiential learning programs, site visits, and gift history. In preparing to approach and research organizations, students are given access to portions of these interconnected databases from the career center, development, alumni offices, and academic departments; such is the case at Indiana University's school of business. Career centers often take the lead in coordinating these programs with other administrative offices on campus. With advances in technology, such systems should become more viable on campuses across the nation.

The bridge the career center provides to the external community includes connections not only to employers but to alumni and parents as well. Alumni and parents are two external groups with demands for the career center that range from needing assurance and information about the job market to direct service delivery. Alumni are changing careers more often, and they may turn to their alma mater for assistance. Parents are key external customers; they are also an essential source of support. Parents are concerned about the value of their educational dollar, and they often fear that their son or daughter will become jobless and move back home. But parents and alumni can play valuable roles in assisting students with career and job information and choices. Students can make these important connections through alumni or parent career mentoring and networking programs. For example, Bucknell University has a separate Parents as Resources network to assist students informally with career and job information; also, parents of Bucknell students conduct mock interviews at career fairs. Similar programs connecting students with alumni and parents exist at many other institutions. For an alumnus, sharing one's career experience, advice, and expertise in these roles is often more rewarding than sending a single small check, and it can lead to longer-term connections and gifts. Villanova University received a $1 million donation to the career center to be used for career-related programs for students because the donor wanted his gift to have a direct effect on current student's lives; a similar opportunity was granted to Hood College by another donor. The career center of the future may find that services traditionally offered by professional staff can be delivered effectively by selected alumni and parents, thus freeing up valuable time for new roles.

Educators to the Campus Community Through Research

The campus career center has traditionally been the agency responsible for conducting graduate follow-up surveys to determine the rate and nature of graduates' employment and entry into graduate or professional school programs. Such placement reports remain critical to institutions, but new methods of gaining such information in more reliable ways through state employment wage databases have been adopted by some states (Joint Commission on Accountability Reporting, 1996). Career centers and institutional research offices need to collaborate more closely in the future to ensure that effective and reliable information is disseminated to governing bodies, the campus community, and other interested constituencies in a timely fashion. Career centers of the future, however, should assume a much broader research and education role on the campus community. In order for campuses to fully embrace the integration of career development in the undergraduate experience, career centers must become expert at disseminating information about student employment trends, student career choices and work values, and supply and demand for college graduates, for example. Such information requires centers to be equipped both to conduct original research and to distill and disseminate research conducted by others so as to educate the broader campus community. Michigan State University's Collegiate Employment Research Institute (with which chapter author Philip Gardner is associated) is a model program for such research and education.

Consultants for Outcomes Assessments

Standards for career centers require them to "regularly conduct systematic qualitative and quantitative evaluations of program quality to determine whether and to what degree the stated mission and goals are being met" (Council for the Advancement of Standards, 1997, p. 12). Yet too few career centers currently engage in such rigorous assessment activities, particularly in conjunction with learning outcomes assessments, nor do they have the necessary resources and institutional support to do so. The emerging career center can support the institution's outcomes assessment efforts if given the proper resources and support. Either as consultants to the institutional research office or through their own research, career centers can provide important assistance in designing research, collecting data, and interpreting results. Research relating to outcomes assessment might include alumni perceptions of the value of their education to their current professions; employer satisfaction with graduates' skills and abilities in the workplace; the impact of participation in experiential learning on development of critical thinking skills; and the impact of senior capstone classes on academic integration, career clarity, employment rates, and graduate and professional school admissions. Some of these topics have been researched by the Collegiate Employment Research Institute at Michigan State University.

These new roles for the emerging center require a paradigm shift in the way career centers conceptualize their mission and the nature of the programs and services they offer. However, the burden does not rest solely with the career center. Institutions must also embrace the leadership role of the career center working in partnership with the whole campus community to facilitate the accomplishment of student career development goals for undergraduate education and in particular for the senior year experience.

HOW SHOULD CAREER SERVICES BE ORGANIZED?

We have already attested to the advantages of current trends to merge the functions of student employment, experiential learning, postgraduation career and employment assistance, and career development services. Primarily, such mergers can provide cost containment, service delivery that has a visible career development focus, increased faculty involvement, and potentially greater customer (student, employer, faculty, and so on) involvement and satisfaction through one-stop shopping. We have also made strong arguments for career development in general and the senior year experience in particular as an institutional responsibility and priority. In doing so, we have emphasized the critical role of faculty involvement in the career development of students, particularly with regard to experiential learning programs. Such arguments are beginning to raise questions regarding the appropriate organizational reporting for career centers. Currently, the majority (70 percent) of career centers report through student affairs (National Association of Colleges and Employers, 1993). However, a recent trend is to move career centers organizationally into academic affairs or at least to more visibly align the centers with academic departments or colleges. Are career services better or differently administered if the unit reports to academic affairs versus student affairs, especially if credit for experiential learning is a key focus? What are the ramifications of multiple career centers versus one centralized unit?

The debate about the reporting line of career services to academic affairs or student affairs is not new, and there is not a universal solution. Within student affairs, a developmental approach (based on student development theory) to career services is more likely to be understood and supported. Within academic affairs, it is more likely that greater integration of career development into the curricula, and therefore faculty support and involvement, will occur. However, the reporting line of career services neither precludes nor ensures either of these statements. Whether career services report to academic affairs or student affairs, there are factors—in addition to adherence to the professional standards for career services discussed previously—that are the key to successful delivery of such services on any campus: (1) faculty support and involvement; (2) financial support and budget allocations to career services set in direct accordance with expected outcomes; (3) career service goals realized in institutional planning and budgeting cycles by the most influential leaders in the institution; (4) career services and student affairs professionals who collaborate using a student development philosophy; (5) career services staff who embrace the importance of public relations, alumni relations, and institutional fundraising needs (Shea, 1995); and (6) the presence of a clear and designated campus leader for student career development (National Association of Colleges and Employers, 1997).

Many institutions are so large that centralization may at first appear impractical, particularly if the institutional philosophy embraces attention to the individual student. Criticisms of centralized career services also include inadequate attention to job development, lack of sufficient staff to ensure in-depth knowledge of academic programs and faculty expertise, and the perception that services are geared only toward students whose academic majors are currently in high demand in the workplace. Arguments for decentralized career services (career services within specific academic units) include increased employer relations; job development and fundraising efforts; greater and more focused attention to individual student career needs; and higher levels of faculty involvement and support for student career development, including experiential learning.

However, decentralization of career services raises important questions about quality and consistency of service delivery across academic units. Overall, as academic units compete for funds that are allocated differentially, student career development may suffer duplication and inconsistency of services; policies, procedures, and systems that vary across academic units; and differential priority given to career services by deans or academic unit heads. Historically, decentralized career services units have overemphasized postgraduation employment or "placement" services, often without proper attention to or support for important pregraduation career development activities (discussed earlier in this chapter) and assistance to students applying to graduate and professional schools.

Additionally, a decentralized approach to career services may compromise customer service efforts, both for students and employing organizations. To illustrate, an employer seeking computer systems analysts might be faced with either contacting several different academic career services offices (computer science, math, computer engineering, and management information systems)— something that employers neither like nor have time for—or choosing only one discipline or academic unit, resulting in an incomplete candidate pool, robbing qualified students of employment opportunities, and ultimately decreasing institutional placement rates. Similarly, students in cross-disciplinary programs or with multiple academic majors might find themselves visiting more than one office in order to get their career needs met. In the current customer service environment, centralized services frequently mean better response to the majority of employers who have multidisciplinary needs, provide comprehensive and consistent services to students, and create one-stop shopping for all customers.

Some institutions have chosen a centralized-decentralized approach in an effort to capture the best of both organizational structures. The University of Virginia and Cornell University have had such arrangements in place for over a decade. Others, like the University of Maryland, are evolving into this arrangement. Although practices and funding sources differ by institution, the advantages to this hybrid approach are greater knowledge for career services staff of academic programs and how they prepare students, improved employer relations, expanded job and experiential learning opportunities, and increased faculty participation and support—all the while preserving a career development emphasis in programs and services for students and maintaining a coordinated, consistent approach to services.

Regardless of the approach taken by an institution toward developing and delivering career services for students, or toward placing its organizational home in student affairs or academic affairs, the NACE standards stress a "centralized coordinated approach" at a minimum: "There should be a designated leader who will be responsible for developing collaborative efforts and cooperative strategies" (National Association of Colleges and Employers, 1997).

Staffing

In today's career center, whether centralized or decentralized, most professionals need to possess strong career counseling competencies, gained through appropriate graduate study and practice, and preferably credentialing by the National Board of Certified Career Counselors. They also need skills in employer relations and job development, faculty relations and curriculum development, marketing, event planning, information technology, and making presentations or teaching. General worker traits such as ability in organization, teamwork, negotiation, problem solving, initiative, self-management, and creativity are also highly sought. The demands and pressures on career services staff are great, and staff must be equally comfortable with students, faculty, employers, parents, and administrators.

Legal and Ethical Considerations

In servicing various constituents—employers, faculty, and students—a career center in this day and age cannot operate in a vacuum, separated from a legalistic society. Laws on employment, selection, hiring, employment compensation, and discrimination can affect students even before they engage in full-time career positions. Career centers must increase students' awareness of their rights and responsibilities and actively educate all parties on their expected code of conduct when making use of career services on college campuses. NACE has developed such a code, entitled *Principles for Professional Conduct* (National Association of Colleges and Employers, 1995). For example, faculty who refer favorite students to an employer without informing others in their discipline about the opportunity could put the institution in danger of being sued; at the least they are acting in a discriminatory or exclusionary manner. The career center must connect students, faculty, and employers in a highly ethical environment that advocates equal rights, opportunity, and fair treatment for all students.

Services for Seniors Only

Several career centers across the country have been delivering special programs just for seniors, tailored to assist them in maximizing their chances for success after graduation. One of the most common is a series that might be entitled Transition to Work or Preparing for Life After College. Topics include practical advice about managing expenses, taxes, benefits, and investments; expectations for job performance; how to handle internal politics and assess organizational culture; how to use support staff and secretaries; dealing with ageism, sexism, racism, and harassment in the workplace; finding a mentor; ethics; and safety issues. Often panels of recent alumni share their advice on these and related topics. Another effective program is the one-day conference. At the University of North Carolina at Chapel Hill, seniors are invited early in the fall semester to a conference-style forum, held by the career office at a local hotel, to prepare them for the job search and transition to work. Similarly, Bowling Green State University has had a successful tradition of bringing seniors to campus on a Saturday prior to the start of the fall term for marathon sessions on topics such as résumé writing, interviewing, and the job search. Several faculty offer dedicated classes on career issues for seniors, and many career staff teach senior job-search seminars. Forming a job club or support effort can be effective; some colleges have explored the possibility of having job clubs officially recognized by the student governance system so that funding can be received. Brochures, manuals, and workshops teach seniors how to evaluate contract agencies, temporary agencies, résumé database services, and third-party recruiters. Seniors also need to be introduced to the reality of temporary employment agencies and contract work.

Lastly, parent, student, and alumni advisory boards may sponsor receptions or programs designed to help seniors network, make the most out of career fairs, maximize the interview process, learn proper etiquette for business meals, and encourage graduate study.

CONCLUSION

The success of today's college seniors in their future roles in society can be influenced significantly by the quality and comprehensiveness of student career development on college and university campuses. To graduate seniors who are focused and fully prepared to make the best use of their undergraduate education in their initial transitions to employment or graduate study demands a radically different vision from higher education—a vision that sees student career development as an integral part of the mission of higher education. Implementation of such a vision requires institutional commitment and leadership at the highest levels, appropriate and designated budget allocations, faculty support and support for faculty involvement, and properly credentialed and competent career services staff. We have argued in this chapter that the new vision must be based on the philosophy that career development is a lifelong dynamic process. Therefore, student career development services and interventions should occur throughout the undergraduate experience in a comprehensive approach, culminating in a visible senior year career program that is clearly articulated and understood by the entire campus community. Such a model must have both curricular and cocurricular components, emphasizing creative interventions such as experiential learning programs that assist students in integrating academic learning with practical experience in real-world settings. We have underscored the importance of cultivating partnerships between faculty, staff, alumni, parents, and the employment community in implementing and delivering comprehensive career services. This new comprehensive approach can contribute in important ways to issues of student academic advising and retention, student learning outcomes, institutional accountability and assessment, institutional advancement, and community relations. High-quality career development for students also requires curricula, programs, and services that respond to and embrace a diverse student population, in the broadest meaning of the word *diverse.* In the future, successful undergraduate education that fully integrates student career development will require higher education to be more responsive to the changing needs of a global society, as colleges and universities continue their long-held tradition of preparing critical thinkers, humane individuals, and independent citizens for tomorrow.

 CHAPTER THIRTEEN

College-to-Career Transition Programs
for Multiethnic Students

Linda Bates Parker
Katrina S. Jordan
Ann E. Keeling

The title of this book is *The Senior Year Experience,* but clearly not all seniors are the same or share the same experiences. Consider these comments from recent African American college graduates at the University of Cincinnati:

Making it to college is an accomplishment in itself for many African American students. Graduating from college and making the transition from college to career is yet another challenging task.

I have been working as a mail clerk for six years. Now with my bachelor's degree in human resources, I hope to get a better job. But I have experienced so much racism and sexism in my current job that I am not certain that my degree will really make a difference. After putting so much time and money into this degree, I sure hope it pays off.

I am happy to already have obtained a job, but I realize that I am one of a few black males selected, so my relations with my white coworkers is a big question mark for me.

These graduates demonstrate the added anxieties many students of color feel as they complete college and prepare for the uncertainties of the world of work. Their concerns reflect a certain cautiousness—for some a lack of confidence— not in their ability to be successful but in their ability to successfully overcome the racial barriers that they face as they transition from college to career. Their comments, coupled with the experiences of the writers of this chapter and those of colleagues across the United States, affirm the need for targeted programs that help retain and graduate African Americans and other students of color in far greater numbers. We believe institutions must go beyond the efforts already described in previous chapters to prepare and address the unique transition needs of seniors from diverse or multiethnic backgrounds.

In this chapter, we examine college-to-career transition issues facing multi-ethnic college students in light of current trends that question the appropriateness of race-conscious programs. We also identify what we believe are the best college and university practices in minority student transition efforts.

In 1989, we conducted an ambitious three-year longitudinal study of African American students from thirteen colleges across the country. The focus of the survey was to investigate success points and indicators for these students. In preparing this chapter, we asked twenty-four of our colleagues across the country who had participated in our previous research to identify current transitional programs on their campuses designed specifically for multiethnic students and to determine whether such programs are still viable. Three historically black and nine predominantly white institutions accepted our invitation. We also surveyed recent African American graduates to obtain information regarding college and work adjustment issues, career concerns, and obstacles anticipated as they transition from college to the world of work. The results of our reading and research provide a current and important perspective from the frontline on the continued need for, and relevancy of, special college to career transition programs for diverse student populations.

Our initial research focused specifically on African American students. There is a real need to encourage broader research and writing by a wide range of multiethnic writers on the subject of the senior year experience and its implications for diverse student populations, especially Asians, Latinos, Native Americans, and Pacific Islanders. Our experience and writing relates primarily to one subset of the multiethnic population; in no way should it be construed as a blanket portrayal of all of the issues facing these or any other multiethnic students as they transition from college to career or to the next educational phase of their lives.

THE CURRENT CLIMATE FOR HIRING GRADUATES OF COLOR

As employers across the United States seek multiethnic college graduates to fill their hiring needs, they are also grappling with the challenge of hiring for diversity amid the confusing and conflicting national debate over affirmative action. Recent U.S. Supreme Court rulings reflect the current mood of the nation, which has drastically shifted away from support for affirmative action, set-asides, and race-conscious educational scholarships and programs. The 1996 passage of California's Proposition 209, aimed to eliminate race and gender-based programs in state government and academic institutions, clearly demonstrates the rising tide of opposition to race- and gender-focused services. The controversy will continue far into the future, as opposing groups in California have already filed actions to halt or continue 209's implementation. As appeals are pursued, so far only a few programs have been targeted for dismantling. As Tirso del Junco, a Republican regent at the University of California, states, "just because 209 passed, it doesn't mean all of our outreach programs are going to stop" (Russell, 1996, p. 8). Del Junco asserts that he wants the school's outreach, recruiting, and mentoring programs to continue.

As the affirmative action debate continues, it is very clear that special programs for special populations in organizations and educational institutions will survive, even if they are revamped. In 1997, the promise of escalating discussions on affirmative action is high. As President Clinton stated, following a review of affirmation action, "Amend it, don't end it." The simple bottom line is that "as long as there are votes involved, we will probably continue to hear that equal employment opportunities are perverse and passé, but at the same time the pressures of the real world will carry more weight with corporations. Equal opportunity lawsuits facing such corporations as AT&T, GM, Dupont, and Exxon fly in the face of political rhetoric" (*Resource/Fact Book 1995*, 1995, p. 7). Thus, "most Fortune 500 companies say they are committed to affirmative action. Creating a diverse workforce, they say, is good business in an increasingly diverse world. Even if the feds go all the way and eliminate their requirements, some sort of affirmative action, however informal, is likely to remain" (Thomas, Cohn, and Smith, 1995, p. 21). It is predicted that the example of Texaco, with its recent multimillion dollar settlement with black employees, hangs in the air as a warning to other companies that they must promote minority managers fairly—or else (Beamon, 1997). One thing that the various program initiatives have been unable to eliminate is the persistence of racist employee attitudes. Because of these attitudes, African Americans, as well as other ethnic groups, still have great difficulty assimilating and advancing in the workplace. Programs that support multiethnic recruitment and retention will remain viable for the foreseeable future.

National surveys indicate that most whites believe that equality is a reality for African Americans and other ethnic groups both in education and in the workplace. But the data tell another story. In 1994, a study entitled Taking America's Pulse, commissioned by the National Conference of Christians and Jews, surveyed nearly three thousand people nationwide and identified the vast differences in perceptions of blacks and whites related to equal opportunity. Sixty-nine percent of whites believe that there are equal opportunities for African Americans in obtaining quality education, and 63 percent believe there are equal opportunities for African Americans in obtaining skilled jobs, but 80 percent of African Americans feel they lack opportunities equal to those of whites. Similarly, 60 percent of Latino Americans feel that they do not have opportunities equal to those of whites. Even among Asian Americans, whose responses in other parts of the survey are most consistently aligned with whites, 57 percent are convinced their opportunities are not equal to those enjoyed by whites. This survey confirms the divergence of opinion and perception among America's racial groups regarding equal opportunity (*Resource/Fact Book 1995,* 1995).

Although there has been much national discussion regarding the "angry white male" affirmative action backlash, a new report by the U.S. Labor Department's Glass Ceiling Commission demonstrates that, regardless of white males' beliefs, they still crowd the ladder at the top in corporate America. The continuing spiral of corporate buyouts, downsizing, and flattening of corporate hierarchies has caused whites in middle management to fear that minorities will gain unfair advantage in the competition for the best jobs. The *Glass Ceiling Report* exposes the painful disparities between belief and reality (Thompson, 1995).

In the 1993 Labor Department Survey of Consumer Expenditures, African Americans represented a $257 billion consumer market. This market size, along with the growing Hispanic consumer market and the need for U.S. companies to compete globally, is driving much of corporate America's push for diversity in hiring and promotions (Thompson, 1995).

In the twenty-first century, many of the changes that are now occurring in employing organizations and on college and university campuses will have a particularly adverse impact upon students of color. The more visible trends affecting this group disproportionately include reengineering, restructuring, layoffs, reorganizing, firings, and affirmative action setbacks (Brimmer, 1993). For many new hires, obtaining that first job and believing that it is something that can be counted on and feel secure about is the milestone. Multiethnic employees, and "African Americans in particular, must be uninhibited in their thinking, question the status quo, and devise novel ways to accomplish the organization's goals" (Vessel, 1991, p. 116). "Security lies in the skills that one can carry from job to job" (p. 114), and it is unrealistic to become comfortable in specific jobs because there are no guarantees. Survival in a demanding workplace requires graduates to be knowledgeable regarding current market trends, aware of requisite skills needed to be effective in the job market, competitive and creative, and willing to take the initiative.

As we fast-forward to a new decade, change is a constant in all organizations. Industry will look different; it must begin to address the needs of diverse workers, and managers will no longer give orders without explanations. In addition to looking different, organizations will look for a different type of worker. Those who learn how to become indispensable to the organization by working independently, functioning as part of a team, and showing leadership and initiative to assist the organization in realizing its goals have the greatest potential for success (Vessel, 1991). (Chapters Five and Seven, by Philip Gardner and Elwood Holton, respectively, further elaborate on organizational change, specifically the broader skill dimensions needed by students entering today's job market.)

In light of these new organizational imperatives, colleges and universities have to examine how prepared students are to meet the demands of the new marketplace. Colleges must be concerned whether graduates have realistic expectations of the job market, are effective in dealing with changing market trends, have the required skills and abilities to address the needs of the new workplace, and have the ability to adjust to new corporate and organizational structures. Most important for students of color, colleges must help assess their ability to negotiate in environments that continue to be plagued by discrimination and racism, and college must help design programs to manage these challenges. Today, younger, better educated African Americans work longer hours and make less money than whites (Roberts, 1995); "despite all the controversy surrounding preferential hiring of African Americans, fewer blacks now have steady jobs of any kind, and their unemployment rates have been growing progressively worse relative to those recorded for whites" (*Resource/Fact Book 1995*, 1995, p. 11).

Likewise, in a 1993–1994 study by the Hispanic Association on Corporate Responsibility (HACR), research revealed the existence of poor representation of Hispanics in U.S. corporations (Thomas, 1994). Hispanics continue to encounter barriers when facing growth opportunities and advancement. A 1990 General Accounting Office report found widespread employment discrimination against Hispanics by employers. The GAO also reported that 19 percent of employers admitted they had adopted discriminatory hiring policies against Hispanics (Fleming, 1994). According to Harry Pachon, president of the Tomas Rivera Center, in Claremont, California, darker foreign-sounding Hispanics are believed to experience much more discrimination than light-skinned acculturated English-fluent Latinos. However, there is a marked tendency among Latinos to deny or fail to acknowledge that they have experienced discrimination (Fleming, 1994). Such continuing discrimination substantiates the complex nature of today's job market and the accompanying challenge for most multiethnic new hires of combating the negative consequences of overt and covert racism. No wonder multiethnic college graduates are skeptical, or at the least cautiously optimistic, about their career futures.

Research supports the need for continuation of special college-to-career transition programs in order to give diverse students the same opportunities and the same chances to succeed as other students. Institutions are challenged to demonstrate how they can be more responsive to the needs of diverse student populations. Past practices and behaviors have shown a disregard or ignorance of multiethnic students' career transition needs. Many of these students have formulated negative reactions to current college efforts because of past negligence (Sherman, Giles, and Williams-Green, 1994).

REPORT CARD FROM CAMPUSES

As the cycle of American education reform has continued, many entering multiethnic college students still arrive on campus with poor academic preparation, having fought throughout grade school and high school the prejudices of society and various education systems. In other cases, multiethnic students arrive with strong academic skills, but limited financial resources, families knowing little about college life, and the lack of broader educational experiences create equally formidable challenges to succeeding in higher education.

How are our campuses faring in assisting diverse students in completing college and making college-to-career transitions? Often, programs and services that assist multiethnic students are themselves peripheral and marginal in terms of the mission of the college or university. Has the core of the institution been modified to respond to the changing student body? In the vast majority of instances, the response is no. There have been difficult dialogues, but the core has not changed. In practice, what has come about is half-hearted willingness to accept the challenges of increased multiethnic student enrollments with token programs that insulate the core of the institution from any meaningful change. Multiethnic staff and the few tenured multiethnic faculty in predominantly white institutions have been the major impetus for assisting students from diverse backgrounds (Roberts and others, 1994).

Despite all of the best efforts, there is much to be done if the educational pipeline and graduation rates of African Americans and other multiethnic students are to be improved. Educators must not be deceived by current trends that would equate some progress in the area of equal opportunity with a declining need for special programs for diverse student populations. Today, despite affirmative action and equal employment opportunity laws and numerous diversity initiatives, many of these graduates are still concentrated in positions that do not make full use of their talents (Brimmer, 1993) and are absent in the educational pipeline in fields where they are needed and underrepresented.

Therefore, when well-meaning educators and legislators question the relevance and need for continuing targeted outreach programs for various multiethnic populations, the answer is simple. Until there is real equality in the education of multiethnic students from elementary through high school levels, limited numbers of African Americans and other multiethnic students will successfully matriculate and graduate in higher education. For many of those who make it to college, it is necessary to offer targeted academic bridge programs, experiential education, group learning initiatives, and peer motivational experiences that help retain, influence higher graduation rates, and prepare them for the work challenges of the twenty-first century.

To address these complex issues, career counselors must be careful not to lump all African American, Native American, Latino, Hispanic, Asian, or other multiethnic populations into one category. There is great diversity between and among all ethnic groups. Individuals working with these populations must have a high degree of sensitivity and awareness of cultural and racial issues. These individuals must be able to show understanding and empathy and have the skills to help students overcome many of the challenges cited in this chapter.

Career counselors need to remember, however, that not every minority student is disadvantaged or underachieving. Just as for majority students, for students of color, succeeding in college and transitioning from college to career can be an exhilarating experience. "I refused to be a statistic," proudly stated a recent graduate who—pregnant at sixteen—might have been thought headed for welfare. Instead, she connected early with a high-school-to-college support program, Jobs for Cincinnati Graduates, designed to help motivate at-risk students toward greater achievement. She graduated from high school with good grades and enrolled at the University of Cincinnati in a rigorous business program. She became a leader in the ADVANCE student program, mentioned later in this chapter, and graduated in 1996 with a double major in accounting and information systems (DiFilippo, 1996).

Those multiethnic students who have strong academic records of performance, who are career focused, determined, and motivated to succeed, face fewer college-to-career transition problems. They are goal oriented and directed toward specific *careers* when entering college. They come from strong families where successful role models are present and where there is continuing emphasis on achievement. Because of their strong determination to succeed, most obstacles are easily overcome. Two of the main challenges facing these students on campus are networking with the right people and obtaining viable career information. They also benefit from exposure to professional role models of their race and culture, especially in nontraditional career fields, who might not have been seen previously as accessible to them. Through her networking and association with positive professional role models, the graduate just described, now twenty-four and single with an eight-year-old son, was able to realize her career goals by accepting a technical sales position with a major U.S. corporation, with a salary over $40,000.

There is another group of students of color for whom life has been a constant challenge, who face real economic hardships and lack positive experiences or role models and for whom skepticism about the future is absolutely understandable. Some of these students are economically and socially disadvantaged. There are also students of color living in better economic circumstances but feeling the negative impact of racism and other forms of discrimination and oppression. Fundamentally, they believe that the American dream is a myth and that goals of career success are unreachable. These students continue to face many obstacles. They have great difficulty staying focused and motivated, balancing college requirements, and making appropriate decisions regarding career choices. Transitioning to the senior year is equally overwhelming. Poussaint (1988) indicates that people of color and people who are poor and have faced racism and discrimination grow up with self-doubt. Not only do they face the challenge of being in a minority group, but they develop a minority personality. Instead of a take-charge attitude, vigor, and enthusiasm, they have a tendency to question their existence and wonder whether they will ever be accepted and able to succeed. These students must be helped to see the linkage of their hopes and dreams to a better life; they must be shown that their college degree is a passport to the future. Further, they need help in seeing that experiential learning through participation in cooperative education programs, internships, and college-to-career transition activities greatly aids in making abstract career aspirations more realistic and concrete. They are not likely to initiate contact with the placement office because their self-doubt leads them to question whether such services are relevant to them; for some, this uncertainty is well placed.

One African American senior, when questioned about her reactions after an employment interview, said she simply did not fit any of the molds into which her career counselor seemed to be trying to squeeze her. When asked about her career accomplishments, she cut off the question, saying, "My greatest accomplishment is that I am alive." The statement is understandable given her background as the daughter of an emotionally abusive mother and her health problems while in college. Despite this, she was bright and persistent enough to graduate from Stanford University, though two years behind schedule. She worked several low-paying jobs and survived an impulsive marriage to a man who turned out to be mentally ill. It is no surprise, under these circumstances, that her career has been so erratic. She candidly laments:

> My life has taken me to unforeseeable emotional and mental extremes, as well as physical life-and-death crisis. I have been forced to seek out opportunities to come to terms with estrangement from my birth family, complete loss of health, poverty, and many other less sudden and overwhelming changes. Working has had to fit in with other aspects of my life, into other circumstances that were much more compelling. So I worked as I was able, in whatever capacity I was able to do. But I have not yet experienced myself as being in a position of having much control over my work conditions and opportunities. I have never perceived myself as being a decision maker about my career. Today I feel lucky that I graduated Phi Beta Kappa from Stanford University and even more fortunate still to claim that I survived the years with my sanity relatively (I hope!) intact [Katchadourian and Boli, 1994, p. 117].

Educators must be trained and prepared to work with diverse and academically gifted students who come from complex backgrounds such as these. Extensive outreach efforts and comprehensive intake screening is needed to better identify the concerns and needs of these students while targeting them for twenty-first-century opportunities. Institutions must demonstrate how they can be responsive to the needs of special populations through the development of effective intervention activities: linking high school to college outreach programs, establishing precollege academic bridge programs, enhancing college survival courses and yearlong orientation programs, target marketing of internship and cooperative education programs, creating career mentoring networks with multiethnic alumni, monitoring student academic and leadership progress through degree audits and student leadership transcripts, and designing special career support groups and workshops that address the needs and concerns of these students (Sherman, Giles, and Williams-Green, 1994). African Americans and other ethnic students do not want special preferences or unearned opportunities any more than other students do; they want supportive programs that enable them to effectively address the real societal barriers they face so that they can successfully swim in the mainstream.

SURVEY FINDINGS

In 1989, the authors conducted an ambitious three-year longitudinal study of African American students. The survey participants were graduating seniors at thirteen colleges across the country. The purpose was to investigate the success potential and success indicators for these students. Then in spring 1995, two hundred students were asked to complete a survey at Tyehimba, an annual pre-graduation celebration for African American students and their families at the University of Cincinnati. Graduates were asked to respond to a variety of questions on how they financed their education, academic challenges, career choices, use of the career center, future career prospects, job opportunities, work challenges, and potential barriers to success. Of the two hundred surveys distributed, ninety-five, or 48 percent, were returned. Because of the nature of the sample and selection process, these findings have limited generalizability.

The average age of the respondents was twenty-five, and 75 percent were female; this reflects an older and more gender-weighted population in comparison to traditional students from the majority population. Several students indicated that they had dropped out sometime during their college careers and cited various reasons, reporting an average of five years to complete their degree. It was not uncommon for these students to have changed major at least once during their academic careers.

In both the 1989 and 1995 samples, graduates indicated feeling fairly confident about being successful in their careers. Paralleling the 1995 study, the 1989 graduates' career decisions, goals, and hopes for the future were heavily influenced by religious beliefs and families. Despite experiencing conflicting feelings of confidence and apprehension, these students remained optimistic about their futures. It is important to note that this phenomenon is not unusual with African American students. They have reached a pinnacle of success and beaten the odds to become college graduates. This enhances feelings of confidence while the recognition that they still face barriers of racism tempers their celebration. It is important for career counselors to encourage students to express their optimism concerning their future career success while also showing understanding and empathy for the apprehensions expressed as these graduates anticipate succeeding in hostile work environments.

As is typical of challenges faced by many college graduates today (majority or minority), the African American students in the study indicated that they had accumulated significant debt from college loans. Many of the students helped finance their education by working ten to forty hours per week while attending school. In addition to the financial challenges faced while trying to obtain an education, students also indicated other challenges of a personal nature. For example, several students were parents and single heads of household. Several reported that rearing children while working and attending classes was particularly stressful (Bates Parker and others, 1994).

The graduates also expressed their feelings about special career programs targeted to African American or other ethnic students. Through these programs, some graduates felt they could gain greater access and insight into their future work environment (Bates Parker and others, 1994). Said one member of the Class of 1995, "Black students often do not have the family or friends or the family ties in the corporate world as do many of their white counterparts." Untested confidence is admitted by another Class of 95 student, who said, "There are some people who are not ready for the transition, but they think they are." Others voiced concern regarding the job search. As one said: "Black students will have more difficulties finding employment, so any assistance is beneficial." The majority of graduates indicated that they felt a need for targeted efforts because they did not find other programs sensitive to their needs.

It is the opinion of the authors that the career transition issues voiced by African American graduates in this 1995 study mirror concerns of many of today's graduates. The responses show concerns around financial obligations, adjusting to the work environment, relationships with coworkers, job security, and proving themselves. However, African American students' concerns differed in terms of serious questions about unequal treatment in the workplace and their uncertainty about relationships with their white coworkers. This anticipation of potential discrimination or racism was reflected in the 1989 study results, where 83 percent of the graduates felt they would encounter racism in the future (Bates Parker and others, 1994). The 1995 graduates expressed similar concerns.

At a time when these students should be celebrating their unique achievements as African American college graduates, their comments exemplify conflicting emotions and some anxiety. As one more Class of 1995 student lamented,

"I feel confident that I will find employment, but where are all those employers that are supposed to be hiring black college graduates? I think it is a myth. Most of my friends, like me, are still searching, and we graduate tomorrow."

IMPLICATIONS FOR PRACTICE

How can concerned educators link their efforts with the concerns of African Americans and other ethnic students? One way is to be direct and ask students what their needs are and also collaborate with campus colleagues or other institutions to determine the best practices in reaching this population. Another compelling question asked by colleagues and individuals assigned to work with multiethnic students is how to motivate these students. There are no magic answers. The key to successful programming is utilization of creative marketing strategies and programming trial and error. What works today may not be effective tomorrow. What works for some may not work for others.

To learn more about existing successful programs, the authors sought out colleagues who had previously collaborated on the college-to-career transition issues of African American and other multiethnic students. Of the twenty-five institutions invited to participate in the original 1989 survey, twelve elected to participate in the follow-up study, representing a 48 percent response. The survey revealed a number of traditional career programs modified to reach students of color; duplicative, or at least similar, multiethnic outreach programs; and one-of-a-kind efforts or ideas. The participating institutions included nine predominantly white and three predominantly black schools: Arizona State University, University of Cincinnati, Cornell University, Georgia Institute of Technology, Howard University, Southern Illinois University at Carbondale, Miami University at Oxford, Ohio, Michigan State University, Morgan State University, University of Michigan at Flint, North Carolina A&T State University, and Temple University. These programs offered leadership, experiential learning, career shadowing, and specially designed programs addressing the career concerns of diverse students.

Based on the feedback from the institutions surveyed, the programs can be categorized in four clusters.

Experiential learning. Arizona State's S.O.L.I.D. Program (Student Opportunities for Leadership, Internship, and Development) is a career and leadership development program designed to teach multiethnic students the professional skills required to be the most marketable candidates in their chosen careers. The program's objective is to empower students to succeed academically and embrace their dreams by exploring and realizing their career aspirations. The program successfully places students in career related internships.

Minority career days and fairs. Minority career fairs such as those described by North Carolina A&T, Miami University, Howard, Georgia Institute of Technology, Michigan State, Morgan State, and the University of Cincinnati are extremely popular; they are designed to heighten career awareness and help students develop realistic career expectations. The career fairs are also designed to expose students, faculty, staff, and administrators to careers and to the many types of employers who recruit multiethnic students. Thousands of students attend these programs annually. They have successfully linked multiethnic students with internships, cooperative education positions, and full-time employment opportunities. Employers reported in the 1995 job outlook survey conducted by the National Association of Colleges and Employers that career fairs continue to be a valuable resource for meeting potential employee candidates and alerting them to employment opportunities in specific organizations ("Spotlight on Career Planning, Placement and Recruitment," 1995).

Career shadowing or spotlight programs. Miami University's Minority Career Services Network has as its objective to communicate to students about career opportunities and issues. Career information is distributed specifically to minority student organizations weekly through campus mailings to the career planning and placement office liaisons assigned to each organization and to minority faculty and staff. This program has significantly increased student awareness of career options and career search strategies. The success of this program is measured by qualitative information from surveys.

The University of Cincinnati's academic bridge program for incoming multiethnic engineering students is a model that has successfully improved retention of engineering students for the last five years. The program's objective is to make UC's College of Engineering nationally recognized not only for recruiting and educating but also for graduating targeted ethnic engineers. Over the past five years, the program has grown from a walk-in help office serving approximately sixty undergraduates to a long-range program that has ongoing involvement with more than four hundred graduates, undergraduates, and precollege ethnic students. One freshman in electrical engineering summarizes the importance of this program for him this way: "I have not only learned about academics through the cooperative learning *classes,* but I have become aware of whom I am, what my cultural background is, and what I want out of life. The program has given me confidence, encouragement, and direction."

Michigan State offers a comprehensive minority careers service and markets its programs to Michigan's diverse student populations. Its purpose is to provide focused assistance to minority, international, and physically challenged students with regard to career development and employment opportunities. Emphasis is placed on individual career advising, goal setting, and other related workshops. The program assists multiethnic students in developing contacts with employers for internships, co-op, and full-time employment opportunities.

Outreach and marketing strategies. A major task in promoting programs to prospective participants is to develop a variety of outreach activities and not take anything for granted. Programs are not viewed as intrinsically valuable by multiethnic students just because they exist. To ensure participation, more than one activity should be undertaken; student planning and marketing committees are essential.

Successful targeted marketing techniques used by survey participants include:

- Corporate-sponsored workshops, where employers invite specific multiethnic students or organizations

- Career fairs, where emphasis is placed on multiethnic student participation

- Displaying multiethnic publications in career centers

- Advertising multiethnic career programs in academic departments

- Involving diverse faculty members in program planning and implementation of multiethnic activities

- Visitation and program interaction and collaboration with students in African American or multicultural centers

- Hiring students of color in career services, to visibly convey welcome and inclusion

- Career services newsletters targeted to African Americans and other students of color

- Direct-mail and direct-telephone solicitations to multiethnic students

- Housing multiethnic peer advisers, peer ambassadors, or peer support groups in career centers

- Career center recognition of multiethnic student success stories such as "we got jobs" placement center advertisements in campus media

- Targeting specific multiethnic student organizations to host career activities

- Updating career services publications to portray multiethnic students using career services

- Inviting multiethnic alumni to career spotlight and career exploration programs

- Writing letters to multiethnic parents, informing them of career programs and services they should encourage their sons or daughters to attend

- Name dropping—effectively and sensitively using language, cultural icons, and other symbols to which multiethnic students can relate

In addition to these marketing strategies, one-third of the respondents indicated that they were currently conducting or considering developing a college-to-career transition program for African American students in the near future, and one-third were not. The remaining respondents were uncertain or did not respond.

ARE THESE EFFORTS REALLY NECESSARY?

When asked whether there was a need to continue offering these types of transition programs, the response was 75 percent positive and 25 percent uncertain, with no distinctly negative reply. A number of reasons were expressed for continuing such programs:

- To expose students to the variety of career opportunities available to them, and prepare them to understand and develop appropriate behaviors valued by the employer community

- To prepare students for the real work world and the challenges it brings

- To ensure that African Americans and other students of color are better informed of career issues and opportunities on campus

- To acknowledge the students' need for support and let them know there are professionals who care about their future

- To inform them that the right type of preparation leads to future success

With continual programming of college-to-career transition activities, some of the work adjustment issues experienced by African American graduates—tokenism, lack of positive role models, unrealistic expectations, isolation, being overly scrutinized, and lack of experience on the job—can be addressed earlier in the students' career development and some of the anxieties can be alleviated.

EXEMPLARY PROGRAMS

From personal experiences of the authors and review of the literature, three other programs are identified as worthy of special recognition. Rutgers University's South Jersey campus in Camden, New Jersey, reports that it holds the distinction of being the only one in the country with a leadership development program that targets minorities. The program's objective for the Center for Strategic Urban Community Leadership is to develop leadership qualities among the African American, Latino, Asian, Native American, and poor white communities. The goal of the center is to teach participants problem-solving skills that they can use in their communities. Ultimately, the idea is to train leaders currently in these communities by having good representation of what America looks like. Another goal of the center is to develop minority leadership and teach new values, skills, and tools to create bridges, as well as teach political savvy and organizational culture.

The center's program includes the Hispanic Women's Leadership Institute, Latino Fellows Public Policy Leadership Institute, Leadership Management for Project LEAP (Leadership Education and Partnership) and Math, Science, and Technology Academy for pre-K–8 teacher preparation. The Latino Fellows program is designed to expose college students to public careers and encourage them to participate in community projects. The program targets students in underrepresented fields, including pharmacy, banking, engineering, business, government, and human services (Rodrigues, 1995).

The ADVANCE program at the University of Cincinnati is a career education program under the auspices and leadership of the Department of Career Development and Placement. ADVANCE seeks to enhance the professional development of African American students through experiential activities that give ADVANCE members awareness of organizational dynamics. With the assistance of an African American corporate board of directors, important issues are addressed: managing the GPA, securing internships, understanding business protocol, managing a mentor, being black and corporate, and leadership strategies for African American students in environments where another culture dominates. For many ADVANCE seniors, the program represents a capstone experience where they are able to put their education and work experience to the test as they lead the program's extensive annual schedule of events.

ADVANCE introduces students to corporate life and professional mentors and encourages their growth beyond what is learned through their co-op and related work experiences. In spring 1995, ADVANCE organized the Spring Break Corporate Tour, visiting several black-owned and white-owned corporations in Tennessee, Indiana, and Chicago. ADVANCE has successfully located internships for its students, given them direct exposure to corporate experiences and human resources, and prepared them to compete effectively for high-level careers in corporations and other organizational entities. This award-winning program attracts undergraduate students campuswide, and it has served as a valuable retention tool for the university. The program greatly enhances the Career Development and Placement Department's relationships with African American students and employers wishing to recruit for diversity. The program also aids career development and placement efforts to market underserved populations and keeps the department intimately aware of the challenges still faced by African American students as they move into their careers. The UC ADVANCE program celebrated its tenth anniversary in 1996.

The Competitive Edge program at the University of North Carolina at Chapel Hill is designed to address three special needs of African American students:

dispelling African American misconceptions regarding job opportunities in specific career areas, handling issues of transition to the world of work, and addressing declining enrollment. The program comprises eight key elements. The first two are surveys, one mailed initially to freshmen to determine whether career counseling needs differ according to race and sex and the second mailed to African American alumni to identify their career backgrounds and willingness to offer advice to current students. Third is organization of career information, where recent graduates share their experiences with African American seniors. A user-friendly computer program, the Carolina Connection, tracks alumni willing to offer career advice and other related information to students. Fifth is a shadowing program with alumni. A career-planning orientation seminar has been established for sophomores and their parents during parents' weekend. The last two elements are sponsorship of the Capstone Career Seminar and organization of the Survival Skills Workshop for seniors.

The program is an overwhelming success. The university's African American students and staff view this initiative by career planning and placement services with renewed awareness and appreciation for the positive approach to serving the special needs of these students. Employer complaints about the lack of student participation have been greatly reduced, and student usage continues to remain strong (Jones, 1992).

In summary, as the national debate on affirmative action continues, one thing is clear: a significant number of college and university colleagues continue to believe in the importance of targeted outreach efforts for African American and other multiethnic students. Career directors and counselors who do not currently have programs anticipate creating them. They also have to help make systemic changes on campus, to rethink notions of the "nontraditional" student. In many cases, minority students are becoming the majority of new admissions; treating their interests and concerns as peripheral, marginal, or outside the norm is fast becoming organizationally obsolete. The question is not whether these programs should continue, but how and when they can be strengthened and expanded.

CONCLUSION

As affirmed by the authors and their colleagues across the nation, today more than ever there is a need for targeted programs to help retain and graduate multiethnic college students in greater numbers. In support of this effort, career counselors must provide relevant guidance to students of diverse backgrounds. These are not hollow thoughts; these beliefs are supported by student concerns that reflect the continuing need for college initiatives designed to assist differing student populations in preparing for today's competitive workplace.

Career counselors must understand that systemic economic and educational conditions still thwart the academic success and career development of certain students on campus. Career counselors are needed who are aware of and sensitive to the challenges these students face, and who want to assist them in strengthening their confidence while identifying strategies to reduce the barriers that prevent them from realistically pursuing their dreams. According to Murray and Mosidi (1993), for African Americans to gain access to careers and experience success it is imperative that those obstacles that have contributed to their lower economic attainment be overcome. Without development of relevant programs and interventions geared toward removing these obstacles, representation in careers reaping greater financial rewards and advancement will be nonexistent. To counteract or reverse these negative trends, career counselors must vigorously seek creative solutions to empower students to overcome the obstacles.

When one looks at the percentage of children of color born in poverty, attending segregated and disadvantaged school systems, and feeling disenfranchised by the ravages of racism, the challenges are exhausting for those who make it to college while fighting for their rights, compensating for continued inequities, and just fitting in. As racist stereotypes and prejudices are allowed to grow, they threaten the prospects for educational equality for all people of color (Marable, 1995). They also seriously affect career aspirations and success for college students. Well-developed and sincere programs targeted to ethnic students can provide psychic relief to those very real barriers.

The key to successful programming is to utilize creative marketing strategies and learn from trial and error. The model programs outlined in this chapter provide a wealth of ideas for reaching out to multiethnic students. The success of these programs lies in the sensitivity of career development staff, targeted marketing programs, and multiethnic student and faculty involvement, with ongoing, culturally sensitive advertising.

Educators and progressive employer organizations committed to workforce equity must not be deterred by the current political rhetoric. Well after the political debate subsides, the nation will still be forced to rectify the long history of benign neglect, educational inequity, and systemic exclusion of people of color from the workplace. Toward that end, special programs and services may be redefined and emerge as essential institutional mandates to help campuses meet the challenges of preparing students to be successful in a complex, diverse, and challenging world.

CHAPTER FOURTEEN

Preparing Seniors for Roles as Active Alumni

Jeffery W. Johnson

Peter D. Eckel

As earlier chapters define and describe it, the senior year experience involves many components. An additional element yet to be discussed is the supportive transition from students to alumni, which creates a challenge for colleges and universities. Developing active alumni begins prior to graduation and should be an important element of any senior year experience program.

An article in *Currents,* the magazine of the Council for the Advancement and Support of Education, argues that institutions should begin the process of developing active alumni during the students' traditional undergraduate years; the article offers suggestions for doing so in each of the four years (Jackson, 1994). We agree that development of active alumni and recognition of the connection between students and alumni should not begin in the final year on campus; however, specific activities can be introduced in the final year to help students "become dedicated, enthusiastic alumni who are willing to give back to their alma mater" (Larson, 1993, p. 93). This chapter examines the connections between the senior year experience and alumni development, describes elements important to enhancing the connection between the two, offers a brief institutional self-assessment guide, and describes initial results from two institutions' efforts.

DEVELOPING ALUMNI INVOLVEMENT WITH THEIR ALMA MATER

No college or university should believe that just because students enroll and graduate from their institution, these same graduates automatically become active alumni. Most students who graduate know very little about how or why alumni involvement is crucial or about their options for continuing their relationship with their alma maters after graduation. At the same time, many college and university administrators, staff, and faculty fail to clearly recognize that today's students are tomorrow's alumni—or to recognize the connection between seniors' experiences and future alumni involvement and support.

Why should colleges and universities develop an institutional advancement agenda in their senior year experience? The answer is straightforward: because colleges and universities increasingly depend upon prospective alumni, and the relationship of these future alumni to their alma mater is tightly linked to their experiences as today's seniors. To paraphrase one alumni development officer, students are just alumni on campus who haven't graduated yet (Jackson, 1994). This section describes the partnership between the senior year experience and development of invested alumni. As with any alliance, there are at least two parties. Here, the first party involved is the institution, and the second is the student.

Institutional Benefits from Alumni Involvement

Though not the only type of alumni involvement, the most recognized form is financial contribution. Alumni donations continue to play an increasing role in the well-being of most colleges and universities. In the public sector, legislatures are cutting budgets and allocating less to their state colleges and universities. According to an annual survey conducted by the American Council on Education, in 1995 one-half of public institutions had no funding increase and expected budget cuts the following year (El-Khawas, 1995). In the private sector, decreased enrollments and increased costs and financial aid expenditures are making budgets tighter and tighter. These trends make alumni contributions central to the financial health of the institution. Although this chapter focuses on alumni involvement, not just financial giving, the two are inextricably linked. For example, at the University of Kansas during its five-year capital campaign (1988 to 1992), more than 85 percent of the alumni contributions to the institution's capital campaign came from dues-paying members of the Kansas University Alumni Association.

In addition to financial gifts, alumni assist their institutions in other ways, notably through their time, energy, and effort. Many alumni are active ambassadors for their institutions, serving as alumni volunteers and lobbyists, acting as mentors to undergraduates, cheering on athletic teams, attending concerts and recitals, and sitting on institutional boards. Graduates who feel positive about their undergraduate experience are most likely to engage in institutional volunteer activities, thus enhancing many campus initiatives—some of which are central to the existence of the college or university. Carleton University in Ontario utilized alumni volunteers to provide academic counseling to incoming students who did not live near campus (Dessoff, 1994). At one point, the Carleton faculty required academic advising for all students, creating a burden on new students living far from campus. The institution solved its dilemma by enlisting alumni to serve as para-academic advisers for the students unable to travel to see an on-campus adviser. Other institutions involve alumni volunteers in admissions and recruitment activities such as making phone calls to prospective students, hosting summer send-off activities for new students and their families, and representing the institution at high school recruitment fairs and local college nights. For example, the University of Hartford involves three hundred volunteers in its Alumni in Admissions program (Jackson, 1996).

Barriers to Alumni Development

The experiences of students while enrolled are strongly coupled to their later feelings about the institution as alumni. Graduates who had a rewarding undergraduate experience may feel more connected to their alma mater, become more involved, and contribute financially when able. Conversely, students who had an unsatisfying experience may not stay connected, act as ambassadors, or assist their institutions when possible. Thus one large barrier to overcome in poor alumni relations is rooted in a past experience that cannot be easily changed.

In fundraising, for example, students who had a positive experience are more likely to contribute financially, whereas alumni who do not feel that their institutions were invested in them as students in turn are not financially invested in their institutions (Baade and Sundberg, 1993). Dissatisfied alumni are lost opportunities for institutional gain, similar to the dissatisfied customers who no longer patronize a store. Institutions fight an uphill battle cultivating future alumni gifts when former students associate negative experiences and dissatisfaction with their alma mater. As an editorial in a student newspaper put it, "What our campus is failing to realize, and what may keep the university from ever being an effective fund raiser, is that . . . the fouled up bureaucracy is destroying any connection a student might feel to this campus, and the people who are in charge of fund raising should sit up and take notice" (Cummings, 1993). Graduates who do not feel positive about their undergraduate experience are probably not going to be future spokespersons for the institution.

A survey of graduating seniors at the University of Maryland (Schmidt, 1993) lends empirical evidence to this argument. In a study of over one thousand graduating seniors, a statistically significant relationship was found between satisfaction with the quality of academic advising and future plans to participate in alumni fundraising activities at the institution. Survey respondents who indicated an intention to contribute financially to the institution as alumni also indicated they found academic advising helpful. However, those who expressed dissatisfaction with their academic advising were significantly less likely to report plans to contribute financially as alumni.

Today's difficult job market is also placing heavy burdens on campuses as it causes many recent graduates to feel animosity about their undergraduate experiences. Seniors are having difficulty finding optimal employment (the most expected outcome of college attendance), which is causing them as alumni to feel frustrated, bitter, and disillusioned toward their alma mater (Holton, 1993). As many as 20 percent of recent college graduates are employed in jobs that do not require a college diploma, and the unemployment rate for those twenty to twenty-four is 4 percent above the national unemployment rate for all age groups (Ellin, 1993; Sullivan, 1993). An illustration of the "closed door" for college graduates is the practice of some women college graduates' taking secretarial positions, hoping to land a more desirable position once within the company (Kleiman, 1994). When students graduate with feelings of animosity toward their alma mater, they are not likely to want to become involved alumni. As one senior said, "My future relation to this campus depends upon what happens to me this last semester—that is my whole experience."

There are clear institutional benefits to having large numbers of active alumni. Colleges and universities cannot take alumni development for granted, nor can they assume that once students are admitted they no longer need to be cultivated as alumni.

THE IMPORTANCE OF THE SENIOR YEAR TO ALUMNI DEVELOPMENT

Currently enrolled students (or "alumni-in-residence," as some would like to think of them) need to know that the path from undergraduate to alumnus or alumna is continuous. Ideally, as students enter an institution, they should realize that they will someday become their alma mater's alumni. Faculty and administrators, however, need to understand that in reality most seniors are unaware of what being alumni means, the importance of staying connected to their alma maters, and what alumni associations are all about. Furthermore, any beliefs they do have are mostly based upon myths and misperceptions of the roles of alumni and alumni associations.

Overcoming Lack of Awareness

The first step toward transforming seniors into active alumni is to increase student awareness of the institution's alumni and the role of its alumni association in advancing the institution. Students often hold misperceptions about alumni and alumni associations. They perceive that the only alumni valued by the institution are the "big ticket" donors or the gray-haired alumni celebrating special class reunions. They believe that the only type of assistance sought from alumni is financial. The alumni most often seen by students are those who receive special treatment by the institution and the advancement staffs or who are paraded around campus. Students see alumni as sitting in the best seats at athletic or cultural events and receiving preferential parking when they return to campus. Otherwise, students only encounter alumni when they invade campus for homecoming or other alumni activities in which they "take over" the campus. Beyond these mysterious and infrequent visits and limited contacts, the information students have about alumni and the alumni association is often inadequate and incomplete.

Students need to be educated about the reasons alumni return to their alma mater and why they are important to their institutions (which goes beyond cheering for athletic teams). Students need to learn that alumni come to events that hold significant meaning for them as former students. They have returned to honor the place that provided them with their education, to celebrate personal or professional accomplishments, to share successes with past faculty or other mentors, to root for their favorite teams, or to relive and attempt to recapture the exciting times of their undergraduate days. But they also come back to their alma mater to share the celebrations and milestones of the institution they hold dear. Finally, alumni return to give gifts that benefit their alma mater and—directly or indirectly—the students enrolled.

Additionally, students have to learn the roles of the campus units responsible for involving alumni. As new students, they were introduced to the campus offices of the bursar and the registrar. As seniors, they need information about the units that work with alumni and potential donors. Alumni associations are the formal link between the institution and its former students; they are the student government bodies for the institution's former students. They keep alumni informed about and involved with the institution and keep alumni connected with each other. Many alumni associations manage a database of alumni names and addresses so classmates are able to remain in contact with one another after graduation. Alumni offices and associations also coordinate and offer on- and off-campus programs and events for alumni. Examples of on-campus events are homecoming and founder's day activities, as well as *alumni colleges* in which alumni come back to school for a period of classroom learning. The Duke University Alumni Association works with several academic departments to coordinate a marine science alumni college that includes class lectures, field trips, and excursions on the school's marine lab research vessel (Jackson, 1996). Alumni associations also hold events off campus, including career development and professional networking activities and social events in cities across the country for local alumni. The University of Vermont Alumni Association, for example, works in conjunction with the institution's Center for Career Development to sponsor a network of approximately twenty-four hundred alumni volunteers across the nation who give career advice and promote job openings to current and former students (Jackson, 1996).

Debunking Myths About Recent Alumni Roles and Involvement

The lack of information and seniors' misperceptions lead many of them to develop myths about the roles and types of involvement of alumni, and they extend these to recent alumni as well. As we have suggested, students tend to be familiar with the alumni who are "big deals" to the institution. They read about alumni who give big donations in the campus newspaper; they listen to famous alumni give speeches at commencement or other campus events; and they are aware of alumni attending their twenty-fifth, fiftieth, or seventy-fifth reunions.

The biggest myth to be debunked is that as new graduates they will be asked immediately only to make financial contributions, when in fact institutions benefit from new alumni involvement in different ways. For many students, this myth can deter the desire to become involved with the alumni association. Like many current alumni, they read invitations to be involved as invitations to contribute financially, which is not always true (Ellis, 1996). Recent graduates are very conscious of the money they have just spent on tuition and their education, and many graduate with student loan debts. Students must learn that financial support is not the only type of postgraduation involvement. They must learn the difference, as one director of alumni affairs described it, between "fund raising and friend raising" (Dessoff, 1994, p. 26). Institutions and advancement staffs realize that not all alumni can donate financially, and seniors must believe that institutions understand this as well.

The second myth to be debunked is that most alumni are heavily involved and donate substantial time or undertake large projects. Students are unaware of alumni volunteering their time to the institution or to the alumni association in diverse ways. They may read about an alumnus who coordinates a large fundraising project or chairs homecoming activities—projects that take a tremendous amount of time and energy—or an alumna who lobbies with the state legislature on behalf of the institution. But alumni are also involved in more discreet roles (Ellis, 1996). Seniors are not exposed to, and thus are frequently unaware of, alumni who spend a few hours to represent their institutions at local high schools once a month or who staff information booths annually at homecoming. They do not see alumni working in graphic design who lend their expertise to a local alumni club to develop new recruitment brochures or produce quarterly newsletters.

Staying Connected

Finally, it is essential for students to understand the importance of staying connected to their alma mater. As recent graduates, they are very busy. Many are beginning their careers or embarking on new ones. They may be relocating and facing a series of challenges and transitions. New graduates may not have the time, energy, or money to be involved with their alma mater, but at least they should stay connected. Recent graduates who keep in touch do not need to go through an uncomfortable period of becoming "reacquainted" after several years (or decades) and are likely to be aware of multiple future opportunities for involvement when they do decide to get involved. Some institutions are beginning to rely on technology to keep alumni connected (pun intended) to their institutions. For example, Princeton, Stanford, Yale, and Massachusetts Institute of Technology are preparing to offer E-mail addresses (Young, 1996), and other institutions have developed home pages on the World Wide Web or put their alumni magazines online. Staying involved may be as simple as putting a decal in a car window or hanging institutional memorabilia in a new office. It is these simple acts that help build strong connections over time.

ENHANCING THE SENIOR YEAR EXPERIENCE: ALUMNI CONNECTION

Many institutions hastily send correspondence about alumni matters to seniors or newly minted graduates during the weeks surrounding commencement. If an institution has not intentionally developed an advancement or alumni development agenda for the students during their senior year, the only thing graduates may take with them from commencement is their diplomas. Institutions—faculty, student affairs professionals, advancement staffs, and senior administrators—should work diligently to ensure that students are connected to the institution before graduation as the basis for their future relationship with the campus once they become alumni. To cultivate involved and dedicated alumni, institutions must start with their largest concentration of potential alumni located in any single area: the students currently enrolled on campus, especially the seniors. Colleges and universities must systematically work with their students to ensure that as many as possible can make informed decisions on how they might stay involved with their alma mater in the future.

This section presents ideas that can be incorporated into senior year experience efforts to enhance the transition from students to active alumni. The ideas and examples below are not exhaustive; many of them overlap, illustrating more than one element. We hope that this list helps institutions start or continue to develop a senior year experience program that leads to developing involved, dedicated alumni. To enhance the senior year experience–alumni connection, institutions should (1) begin early, (2) use familiar avenues of involvement, (3) make expectations explicit about alumni involvement, (4) involve the whole campus, (5) focus on issues important to seniors, (6) mark the transition to alumni, and (7) create a new alumni development strategy.

Begin Early

As George Kuh argues in Chapter Ten, institutions should not wait until the senior year to begin cultivating alumni. Some campuses have developed programs that begin this process as early as the first year. For example, Bowie State University (Maryland) holds a prealumni induction ceremony for freshmen. The event includes a student processional and speeches by alumni and the president, and it ends with a student pledge to support the university (Jackson, 1994). The University of Alabama at Birmingham does not go to this extent but rather focuses on increasing student awareness of the alumni society. Each year, the alumni society recognizes outstanding Greek intramural athletic teams, gives homecoming scholarships of $1,000, and provides water bottles to band members and leather portfolios to student leadership conference participants, each with the society's logo (Jackson, 1996).

Other institutions have created specific opportunities for their students during their senior year to learn about potential alumni involvement opportunities. The Senior Class Cabinet at UCLA sponsors a series of events for seniors throughout their final year, many in conjunction with alumni and one that specifically includes an alumni club fair.

Use Familiar Avenues of Involvement

Institutions need to help students understand that their activities and involvement as students can continue as alumni, thus developing opportunities for their involvement. Many students serve their campuses in a variety of roles. They sit on important institutional or academic committees; undertake leadership roles in homecoming, Greek week, commencement, and other campuswide events; help recruit prospective students; and act as institutional ambassadors working with alumni, legislatures, board members, and the media. Many of these activities parallel those of alumni. Alumni associations and other institutional units sponsor events that need alumni volunteers who have worked with cross-institutional committees, planned programs with campus staffs, communicated with the media, or worked with legislatures and boards of trustees. Institutions must actively recruit seniors to take on alumni responsibilities with which they are familiar following graduation, helping these soon-to-be alumni use their skills and knowledge in accustomed ways to make the connections between collegiate activities and those of active alumni.

Finally, institutions must recognize that "the alumni body will first and foremost be a collection of individuals varied in their attitudes, interests, philosophies, social standings, and perceptions of their institution" (Reichley, 1977, p. 286). Because students are involved with their institutions in different ways, alumni activities must reflect the types and diversity of activities in which students are engaged. For some students, attendance or participation in intercollegiate or intramural athletics is important. For others, Greek life, student government, or residence life are important activities; and for still others, involvement with their academic departments, discipline-based student organizations, and honor societies are important. Finally, students—especially those of color—are involved with their institutions through multicultural and ethnic student groups, such as the Black Student Union, the Asian-Pacific Student Association, or the Hispanic Student Union. Institutions should provide avenues for new alumni to stay involved through programs, services, and clubs that mirror those activities students participate in as undergraduates, such as black alumni groups, alumni athletic organizations, professional societies, or Greek alumni chapters.

The effort and energy required to participate in alumni opportunities must also reflect varying degrees of student involvement. Some students are highly involved and spend a significant amount of time and energy in campus life. Other students, because of family responsibilities or employment commitments or by choice, spend less time on campus. Opportunities for involvement must allow alumni who are able and have the desire to be highly involved, while allowing others who do not have the time or desire to be less involved.

Make Expectations Explicit

Graduating seniors must receive information on the reasons alumni involvement is needed by the institution, different ways they can become active, and why the alumni association exists (to foster the relationship between former students and their alma mater). Messages to students about future involvement need to be stated clearly and explicitly. All too often, alumni associations and institutions assume students receive this message. But many institutions sponsor events that make explicit the "stay involved" message. For example, the University of Kansas sponsors a commencement breakfast on the morning of graduation for new graduates and their families. At this event, speakers send messages of class unity and espouse the virtues of active alumni involvement to new alumni. The University of Maryland sponsors senior receptions for all graduating students at the president's house. Seniors hear the president talk about alumni involvement, meet with alumni staff, and receive information from the alumni association. They are also able to subscribe to the Young Alumni Club's mailing list at the door of the reception.

As was mentioned, undergraduate activities contribute to making good alumni, but institutions must ensure that seniors get this message. Administrators, staff, and faculty must help students make the connection between their activities as undergraduates and possible future ways to become involved and dedicated alumni. Without intentional conversations about the relationship of their student activities to future alumni involvement, seniors may not make these connections at all.

Involve the Whole Campus

The entire campus must embrace the senior experience and assist with the transition of students from undergraduates to alumni. The alumni association and development offices are the official institutional units responsible for connecting alumni to campus. They sponsor events for alumni, facilitate alumni groups and clubs, and help connect alumni with one another. But the responsibility can no longer fall only within their domain. Just as the recruitment of new students is not the function of only the admissions staff but depends upon faculty, staff, student affairs professionals, and others, so does the development of dedicated alumni. From the faculty who teach students their final classes to the professionals in the career development center who help with interviews and résumés, and from the campus activities staff who plan senior week to the physical plant staff who literally set up the stage for commencement, multiple units on campus play salient roles in alumni development. Faculty, administrators, student affairs professionals, and development staff must realize that students' undergraduate experiences end fairly quickly but their alumni experiences never do. The paths that lie ahead in early alumni development can no longer be paved only with good intentions or left solely to alumni development staffs. The campus as a whole must work together to cultivate future alumni.

Alumni and development staffs should begin to build coalitions across institutional units and departments. One way is to collect information and anecdotes about seniors, their experiences, and their intentions to be involved as alumni. For example, Boston College conducts focus groups with cohorts of seniors about their senior year experiences, and Carnegie Mellon University conducts an annual senior survey. The results can be shared with others who may be able to effect change, help students make the transition to alumni, and remove barriers hindering that transition. Another strategy is to encourage units across the campus to sponsor joint programming directed at seniors.

Finally, some institutions involve the campus community in alumni development via student alumni associations or senior class councils. These two types of student organization can be helpful in bringing together diverse areas of an institution through their programming efforts, activities sponsorship, and student-faculty networks. Student alumni associations are undergraduate organizations working primarily with alumni associations to assist with the transition from students to alumni (Todd, 1994). Senior class councils are organizations that focus predominantly on students during their final year. The purposes of these two groups overlap; thus at some institutions only one or the other exists (though it is not uncommon to find both thriving). Michigan State University, University of California-Los Angeles, Iowa State University, and the University of North Carolina at Chapel Hill all have senior class councils or student alumni associations, involved in class gift selection and fundraising, sponsoring programs on career services, presenting outstanding student and faculty awards, and coordinating senior weeks. These student organizations bring together seniors, alumni, faculty, and administrators to execute successfully their events. For example, the University of Illinois holds a Zero-Year Reunion, coordinated by its alumni office and the student alumni association.

Focus on Issues Important to Seniors

The senior year can be the focal point from which to bring undergraduates into the alumni fold. But to be successful, programs must be important to seniors and must meet their special needs (Todd, 1994). They are saying good-bye to friends and to a place that many call home. They are concerned about career development issues, relocating, starting new jobs, or resuming old ones. Some are juggling family demands or are concerned with responsibilities off campus. Successful alumni development programs should focus on those issues of importance, ones that can facilitate the transition to alumni and strengthen the connections between seniors and their institutions.

For example, many institutions have developed alumni mentor programs in which seniors and alumni in similar fields are paired together or work-shadow programs in which students shadow alumni in their place of employment. Other programs use alumni to conduct mock interviews, giving students an opportunity to polish their interviewing skills prior to real interviews. All of these introduce students to alumni networks, allow them to interact with alumni on a personal basis, and center on a topic important to graduating students: finding a job and making a smooth transition to the world of work or graduate or professional school. At Texas A&M University, the Association of Former Students and the offices of student activities and career planning and placement sponsor a one-day program called Real World: Life after Aggieland, which includes a range of activities for students to learn about and discuss concerns and issues related to leaving the university.

Mark the Transition to Alumni

Commencement is the largest and most public ceremony (or series of ceremonies on some large campuses) denoting the transition to alumni. It is usually the final collective face-to-face opportunity for an institution to share the stay-involved message with its seniors. Some institutions formally mark the transition to alumni by incorporating alumni induction ceremonies into commencement activities; others include speeches by famous alumni or a welcome by the president of the alumni association.

At times institutions also mark the alumni transition distinctly from the commencement ceremony. Some sponsor events and receptions on commencement day in which to honor new graduates. For example, James Madison University (Virginia) holds a candlelight ceremony for all seniors on the lawn prior to graduation, Florida State University and the University of North Carolina at Chapel Hill sponsor campuswide receptions immediately following a centralized commencement ceremony, and schools at Stanford University host separate receptions following their commencements. Other institutions hold specific events for their new graduates on different days. For example, the Former Student Association at Texas A&M holds an annual alumni induction banquet in which seniors are formally welcomed into the association, and The Pennsylvania State University sponsors the Zero-Year Reunion on the last day of classes, a campuswide celebration for graduating seniors.

In addition to specific events, another way to mark the transition is to give graduates keepsakes and mementos (Kleppinger, 1993) or to practice such senior traditions as class gifts. For example, The University of Southern Mississippi has an open house at its alumni center for new graduates and provides graduates with photos taken at the event of them with their friends or family. The University of Maryland gives all of its graduates key chains that say "Terp for Life" ("terp" is short for terrapin, the institution's mascot). Many institutions also have senior class gift programs in which seniors, during their final year or semester, make financial pledges to the gift. The gift is usually made to the president on behalf of the graduates at commencement. Michigan State University, Albright College (Pennsylvania), and the University of Virginia are examples of institutions that have class gift programs.

Create a New Alumni Development Strategy

Finally, institutions should create a strategy for intentional recruitment, retention, and development of new alumni. This strategy provides a foundation to which the institution might link senior year activities and provides something they can refer to and "market" to seniors and recent graduates. A new alumni strategy might include social activities, events that bring recent graduates back to campus, programs that assist them with their transition from student to employee or graduate student, networking opportunities to meet other alumni, or any combination of these. Each institution should develop a strategy to best fit the profile and desires of its recent alumni. For example, North Carolina State University has developed a Young Alumni Program that includes social events geared toward younger alumni, including trips and reunions. One way to better understand recent alumni and their needs is through surveys and focus groups (Todd, 1994). Institutions or alumni associations may want to know if most alumni live in the immediate area, what the best time of day or year is to hold events, or what types of events alumni would be willing to pay for and if so how much they would pay.

As part of their plan, institutions should consider making immediate contact with new alumni soon after commencement (Bolar, 1993). North Carolina State University and Florida State University have both developed special new-member packages sent to recent graduates, which include the alumni magazine, travel information, and alumni memorabilia.

A SENIOR YEAR EXPERIENCE
ALUMNI SELF-ASSESSMENT GUIDE

Having presented an argument for developing alumni as part of the senior year experience and offered suggestions to enhance alumni development efforts throughout the senior year, this chapter now shifts to initial implementation strategies. The initial step of any strategy is to understand the point of departure, or where you are currently. The following series of questions may be helpful for institutions concerned with creating an alumni development agenda as part of their senior year experience efforts. It includes two sets of questions; the first four focus on students, and five through seven focus on the institution.

Understanding Student Experiences

Most new graduates do not automatically seek membership in their alma mater's alumni association or become involved with their institution immediately after graduation. The following questions may help institutions begin to better understand students' levels of awareness or interest in alumni activities.

1. What three things are seniors most satisfied with at your institution? To what extent do these vary by subgroups of seniors (that is, by race or ethnicity, major or academic department, age, residential status)? How might these areas of satisfaction be incorporated in the development of dedicated alumni?

2. What are the three most important complaints of students as they graduate? What has been done to alleviate those problems? How might those problems affect future alumni development and recruitment efforts?

3. What do students know about alumni and the alumni association? From what sources do seniors receive their information? To what extent is this information accurate? What avenues can be used to provide them with additional and accurate information?

4. What are the two biggest benefits or incentives for recent graduates to become involved as alumni? To what extent do these match the needs of recent graduates?

Understanding Institutional Efforts

Most institutions do not intentionally engage in activities or sponsor events that help to cultivate involved new alumni from the ranks of their undergraduate students as part of their senior year experience. The following questions may help readers assess their own institution's efforts.

5. What activities occur on campus that intentionally link the senior experience to alumni development? Who sponsors those activities? Who attends them?

6. Which areas or units of the institution directly benefit from alumni involvement? Which benefit indirectly? In what ways do they benefit? How might these units become more involved in enhancing the senior year experience effort?

7. To what extent is the institution committed to its alumni? What yardsticks are used to measure this commitment? To what extent is the institution committed to its recent graduates? What steps can be taken to enhance these commitments?

EARLY RETURNS FROM INSTITUTIONAL EFFORTS

Do the efforts to link the senior year experience and alumni development really make a difference? On most campuses engaged in these projects, only anecdotal evidence exists. But some results are beginning to appear. The University of Kansas Alumni Association has received a positive return from its investment in early alumni outreach programs for seniors and new graduates. Its greatest measure is seen in the number of new graduate memberships in the association. The class of 1994 enlisted 18 percent of its first-time degree-holders as dues-paying members. This is up considerably from the 10 percent who joined the association from the class of 1990.

The University of Maryland has also seen a rise in some potential indicators of recent alumni involvement and senior satisfaction as the institution continues to develop its senior year experience program. For example, both the number of participants and the amount of money pledged to senior class gifts rose steadily over the first five years of Maryland's senior year experience efforts, attendance has increased at commencement as well as at receptions for graduating seniors at the president's home, and interest and membership has grown in an alumni association club for young alumni.

CONCLUSION

Students—especially seniors—need to be encouraged to stay involved with their institutions after graduation. The more these soon-to-be-alumni understand this message and their future alumni roles, the more apt they are to open mail received, become volunteers, serve on institutional committees, and contribute financially to their alma mater. Helping seniors identify with the message to stay involved should be very important to campus officials, faculty, and staff. Each year, the roster of potentially active alumni grows, and faculty, student affairs professionals, and development and advancement staff are in a better position to assist their seniors to understand more completely the roles of alumni and the many ways in which they, as graduates, can stay connected to their alma mater. The final test of this agenda should be to determine whether or not students now know, understand, and appreciate the specific ways they can continue to be involved in the life of their alma mater after graduation and, of course, the degree to which they ultimately become active participants.

PART FOUR

IMPLICATIONS FOR CAMPUS SERVICES AND PRACTICES

Now that the case for the senior year experience has been established, exemplary programs presented, and the need for academic affairs, student affairs, development, and alumni offices to work together, how would you go about making such efforts happen on your campus? Part Four provides practical suggestions for institutionalizing a senior year experience through the vehicles of assessment, incorporation of change theory strategies, and recommendations of the authors for policymaking and program development.

In this part, we examine the status of the assessment movement in higher education, identify the benefits of assessment for both the institution and the student, and provide models particularly appropriate for use in the senior year. Our authors assert that a comprehensive campus assessment program can serve dual purposes, being a means for enhancing student learning and reflection as well as serving the more traditional notion of data collection and measurement.

For those wondering where to begin to address the needs of seniors and how to introduce new programs in times of scarce resources, a case study of one institution's attempt to implement a senior year experience in the context of organizational change theory is also presented.

Finally, this book concludes with observations, findings, and recommendations for improved campus practices, based on the editors' synthesis of the preceding chapters, their learnings from The Senior Year Experience conferences, and their own campus experiences addressing senior year issues.

CHAPTER FIFTEEN

Looking Back, Moving Ahead

Assessment in the Senior Year

Karl L. Schilling
Karen Maitland Schilling

Benjamin is a very bright, highly philosophical, senior English major, graduating with a 3.97 GPA. He is disappointed that he has not been admitted to the competitive graduate programs in literature to which he applied. His description of late night conversations with friends about what they have done and what they will do next demonstrates a level of uncertainty, anxiety, and anticipation about the future: "I've been trying to look beyond, to reevaluate things. . . . I'm baffled. . . . Conversation after conversation, just like up 'til the wee hours of the morning, trying to get some focus and evaluate what we've done here. . . . Too many people glide through without considering these things . . . no obvious next step. . . . I'm struggling with that thought/action dichotomy."

Cherise is a very scattered, disorganized theater major with a 2.85 GPA. She characterizes her four years of college as involving "drastic changes." Having struggled in her first years as an accountancy major, she eventually concluded that "I am not that kind of thinker. . . . I can only look, see, and do. . . . I can't take information in and hold it." Cherise has a summer apprenticeship with a theater company, hoping eventually to assume a career in acting or directing: "I'm happy, scared, relieved, I have to pay back all of my bills. . . . I got a very

---

All students names, except Amy, are pseudonyms.

rounded education. . . . I wouldn't have changed it. . . . I got what I needed. . . . I've realized where my talent lies, not in the analytical, but in the creative. . . . I expect to be at the bottom of the pile again and have to work my way up, make new contacts and new friends, and that's gonna be hard."

Commenting on her major, Joan, a subdued young woman with a 3.0 GPA, says, "I really don't know if my heart is in zoology. It really wasn't something that fit all of my interests." She did complete the AFROTC program and faces officer candidate school just a few weeks after graduation. But she is still uncertain about her future plans, describing her Air Force experience as "something that will buy me some time and still allow me to make some money doing it." She says of her course-taking pattern, "I spread myself way too thin . . . the majority of classes within my major I didn't like. . . ." Joan anticipates the time to come: "long hours . . . a lot of uncertainty . . . I have to be ready for anything . . . lots of anxiety in not knowing what's going to happen."

Although these three students seem different in that they have experienced varying degrees of academic success, pursued different majors, and are headed in separate directions, nevertheless they share the experience of uncertainty that accompanies a clear shift in personal circumstances. Similar to their transition from high school to college, as these students move from college to postgraduate activity (graduate school, jobs, and so on) they again experience anxiety, fear, and expectancy.

Victor Turner, an anthropologist, labels these periods of transition as liminal states. He defines *liminality* as literally "being on a threshold," as "a state or process which is betwixt-and-between the normal, day-to-day cultural and social states or processes of getting and spending, preserving law and order, and registering structural status . . . it is a time of enchantment when anything might, even should, happen" (Benamou and Caramello, 1977, p. 33).

Alternating between reflection and anticipation, these seniors are positioned to offer compelling perspectives on their experience of the campus. Turner compares liminal experiences to standing in a doorway: one can either move forward into a new room or retreat back into the room from which one came. For the moment in the doorway, there is a state of "roomlessness," a time of not being a part of either room. The seniors have the ability to ponder the significance of the room from which they have come and, at the same time, anticipate the room they are about to enter. The quotes from the students all reflect their liminal state, as they ponder the experiences they are about to leave behind and anticipate the world of work or graduate school they are about to enter. The heightened reflective sense that arises from this liminal state provides an ideal moment in which to capture students' observations about their college experience, free from the coloration of immediate immersion, yet still fresh and strong in their minds.

TRANSITIONS AND ASSESSMENT IN HIGHER EDUCATION

For well over a decade, John Gardner and his colleagues at the University of South Carolina have brought important emphases to points of transition in college years. Initially focusing attention on the first-year experience, Gardner, along with an increasing number of colleagues nationally and internationally, has identified both the vulnerabilities and potentialities inherent in students' transition to college that match Turner's description of a liminal state. These higher education advocates have championed and envisioned special programs to ensure more successful transitions for incoming students. A host of new programs, beginning with University 101 at the University of South Carolina, have been effective in fostering greater retention and in enhancing the satisfaction of students making this important transition.

More recently, Gardner and his colleagues have directed their attention to the senior year, yet another critical time of transition for college students and the topic of this volume. However, the foci for indexing success are different in the latter case, and thus rather than retention or satisfaction, the loci of intervention may be bridging or facilitating connections. A national movement of concerted efforts to support students through this transitional phase appears to be building.

Paralleling the growth of focus on important transition points in the first and senior years and the concomitant growth of developmental perspectives on college has been the growth in assessment of student outcomes. In assessment, focus on the learner and the learning processes has supplanted earlier "black box" conceptions of college outcomes. Consequently, in describing the impact of college on students through assessment activities, attention is much more likely to be focused on the changes within students in their experiences over time rather than on simple before-and-after snapshots. Also, rather than assumptions of uniformity of experience. there is likely to be a much clearer recognition of differences among students and the need for approaches and methods to capture those differences. Exhortations to "get behind" outcomes have yielded a variety of creative approaches to understanding the rich texture of students' experiences over time within our institutions. Thus the lens has moved away from a rather exclusive focus on inputs (resources initially invested) to broader consideration of the value added by educational programs.

Traditionally, a great deal of assessment has focused on first-year students and seniors. However, this work has not concerned itself with the fact that the first and senior years are important transition periods. Instead, it has conceptualized the first and senior years as static end points: the before and after, the pretest and posttest drawn from social science methods. In contrast to such a static approach, this chapter focuses on assessment in the senior year, recognizing the very dynamic character of this transition period and highlighting the benefits liminal status provides for understanding both individual development and institutional impact.

By virtue of their transitional status—being still *of* the institution but almost *beyond*—seniors have perspectives on their experiences within an institution and on the institution itself that offer the potential for bringing new dimensionality to our understandings—providing a more complex picture than can be gained from students at other points during their college or postcollege years. In this chapter, we briefly review the status of assessment in American higher education, noting the benefits of assessment throughout the college years. We focus particularly on assessment during the senior year, identifying advantages to the institution and the student. Finally, we describe a number of assessment strategies and share the kinds of information generated by each strategy. Student voices are scattered throughout the presentation to facilitate the grounding of theory and practice in students' lived experiences.

A BRIEF HISTORY OF ASSESSMENT
IN RELATION TO THE SENIOR YEAR

Since the 1984 National Institute of Education (NIE) Study Group Report *Involvement in Learning* and the first American Association for Higher Education conference on assessment in 1985 gave impetus to the current assessment movement, a number of different approaches to assessment have emerged, almost all of which have made use of senior-level assessment, albeit for differing purposes. In the years immediately following the report, the accountability agenda predominated. Most institutions focused on assessment with the goal of convincingly demonstrating the positive impact of their educational programs on students. Only later did the idea of using assessment to improve educational programs and the experience of students come to the forefront.

From 1984 to 1990, what is commonly termed *value-added* assessment played a prominent role. The conceptual model upon which the value-added framework drew was experimental psychology, with its focus on documenting differences by comparing carefully matched samples of first-year and senior students or contrasting the performance of the same students at the beginning and end of their college experience. This approach used primarily standardized nationally normed tests. These tests yielded quantitative data, and the analyses focused on increases in scores as demonstrating the value that the college experience had contributed. Although this approach showed some utility for fields in which a nationally standardized curriculum existed (nursing, engineering, accounting, and several other technical fields), it proved less useful in most liberal arts fields and of very little benefit in assessing general education programs. On almost no campus did available tests actually match the general education curriculum.

Furthermore, this approach was not particularly useful to the individual student. Graduate schools were not interested in such tests (except for the GRE), nor were employers; tests failed to invite senior students into the kind of reflective experience that might be most useful as they made the transition from college to work. Indeed, aside from a few places like Alverno and King's Colleges, assessment was primarily aimed at program evaluation rather than individual student feedback. Many colleges gave students their scores, although few made the effort to make the testing valuable for the students as well as the institution. (Notable exceptions are William and Mary and Rhode Island Colleges.) At Miami University, more than 120 students were involved in a four-year FIPSE-funded assessment project that employed a number of different nationally standardized tests of liberal arts skills (see Banta and Associates, 1993, for details). Students were sent copies of their scores on these tests. Follow-up advising and opportunity for reflection and discussion were offered, yet only 4 of the 120 students availed themselves of such interaction. The students saw the testing as something they were doing for the institution. They understood that it had little or no consequence or meaning for them. Indeed, motivating students to perform at their highest level on these tests became a major problem, because the students quickly figured out that there was little if any benefit for them. Although first-year students were generally compliant with the entry-level testing, performing to the best of their abilities, seniors were not similarly inclined.

Beginning in the late 1980s, more colleges began experimenting with alternative approaches to assessment. These alternatives drew on a different conceptual model, anthropological rather than experimental. This anthropological approach often resulted in qualitative, not quantitative, findings. These activities focused less on trying to demonstrate the value of college and more on attempting to understand the college experience. Indeed, one of the primary reasons that the standardized testing approach did not prove useful was that it could not be directly connected to the curriculum. As a result, many institutions began to discover that they knew very little about the *lived curriculum,* that is, the one the students actually experienced. Their knowledge was instead limited to the *paper curriculum,* which existed solely in their catalogues. It became clear that it was the lived curriculum that mattered if an institution wanted to improve the educational experience of its students.

Also, a number of institutions decided that assessment activity should be more embedded within the daily functioning of the institution, rather than existing outside the normal activity on campus. This decision involved not only developing assessment approaches that made use of existing materials and information but also generating assessment results that would be meaningful for students. Through leadership provided by the American Association for Higher Education's Assessment Forum (most notably the contributions of Ted Marchese and Pat Hutchings) as well as Peter Ewell of the National Center for Higher Education Management Systems, a rich variety of new methods has emerged, from locally developed tests of various competencies to a broad range of portfolio-based approaches, interviews, focus groups, alumni surveys, and so on. These methods offer context-sensitive information that is more useful in improving curricula and programs on a campus than were data from previous approaches (Banta and Associates, 1993).

VARIED METHODS FOR CAPTURING STUDENT EXPERIENCE

The range of assessment approaches available today is limited only by the stretch of one's imagination and the focus of one's interest in the experience of students. We describe some of the most commonly used methods, sketching only the briefest outlines of each strategy, in order to suggest the possibilities for understanding the senior experience.

Standardized Tests

When there is widespread agreement within a discipline about knowledge expectations for graduates, nationally normed standardized measures may provide a ready assessment. In chemistry, nursing, and engineering programs, such measures are commonly employed. Field examinations are available through the Educational Testing Service in a variety of disciplines. Area tests on the GRE are very similar, though standardization samples for this test are students planning on graduate school enrollment rather than the less selective group of students completing the undergraduate degree program in the designated area.

When all students perform on these tests at or above the expected level, this result may reflect positively on both the students and the program. Similarly, when students who have performed poorly in the coursework of the program also perform poorly on such tests, confidence in both the program and the test may be enhanced. However, when students have performed well in the coursework of the program but poorly on these exams or have performed poorly in the program's coursework but well on these exams, an uncomfortable set of questions surfaces. Should students who cannot pass the test but who have done well in their courses not graduate? What are the problems with their curriculum? What are the problems with this test? Is the relatively high cost worth it?

Locally Developed Tests

Within many disciplines, the agreement about a standard curriculum may not be nearly so widespread as is necessary to make a nationally normed standardized test a reasonably valid indicator of student learning. When departments or programs are clear about their particular learning objectives and design their curriculum around them, a locally developed instrument that assesses student performance in the major program may be a more attractive alternative than one of the standardized measures that do not closely match objectives of the local curriculum. The State University of New York at Fredonia, under the leadership of Minda Rae Amiran, created a set of assessment instruments designed to assess the complex, abstract goals of their newly developed liberal education program (Banta and Associates, 1993). These instruments were imaginative, owned by the faculty, and designed so that they would provide immediately useful insights into the effectiveness of the new program. It is the case, however, that most departments or programs have a great deal of difficulty agreeing upon and specifying learning objectives with the clarity necessary to develop such instruments. Additionally, changes in the curriculum or in faculty course assignments may require costly and labor-intensive modifications of such measures so frequently as to make the substantial investment of faculty energies in developing quality instruments impractical.

Senior Declamation, Comprehensive Exams, and External Examiners

Approaches based upon the model of the senior declamation, common in universities in the nineteenth century, are employed at other institutions as ways of gauging student mastery of materials. (Senior declamation provided the students a chance to demonstrate what they had learned by responding to a series of questions from a jury made up of faculty who had instructed them.) To enhance the validity or credibility of these assessment approaches, other institutions have relied upon external examiners. Bobbie Fong prepared an interesting overview of this assessment approach in his work with the Association of American Colleges and Universities (Fong, 1987). Typically, external examiners are faculty at other institutions who examine senior graduates of a program in a manner that allows certification of particular students' abilities and also commentary on a department's courses and curricula. Swarthmore has used external examiners (faculty members or other professionals from outside the institution) for honors candidates for the college since 1923, with very positive review of the approach by students, faculty, and examiners. Alverno College's approach to external examiners is a bit different (Mentkowski and Doherty, 1983). Rather than faculty from other institutions, it employs local professionals and employers in the process, which provides extensive orientation to all prospective examiners.

Capstone Experiences

Increasingly, departments and programs are using senior capstone experiences as a central component of their assessment activities. The capstone is intended to provide an opportunity for students to integrate their experiences in the full range of courses in the major (or entire curriculum). Thus the work done in the capstone—the products generated, or the process engaged—should provide a reasonable reflection on the adequacy of students' preparation in their program. The capstone provides a work sample that can be the basis for commentary on the adequacy of an individual student's preparation or that across several students, may allow inferences about the quality of a program that leads to generation of such products by a group of students. At the Hutchins School, an interdisciplinary college within Sonoma State University, entering students are presented with a set of competencies they are expected to develop through their college experiences. Working with an adviser, the students select pieces of work done in class that they believe demonstrate achievement of these competencies. The senior capstone engages the students in a series of exercises designed to assist them in reflection and evaluation of their achievements in relation to these competencies.

Performance Assessments

Similar in many ways to the capstone, performance assessments may be used to determine a student's learning as well as a program's effectiveness. Whether assigned a case to analyze in business, a lesson plan to develop and execute in education, a senior recital in the performing arts, or a design project in engineering, the emphasis in performance assessment is on application of knowledge acquired in a more "authentic" context, one that more closely approximates the real demands that a student is likely to face in practice in the chosen field. At DePaul University, several of the fine arts departments have taken the lead in teaching the rest of the university how to use performance assessments effectively to index progress of individual students and evaluate the program. Outside critics (or the collective faculty serving as a jury) provide feedback to each student on individual performance. This feedback is followed by a discussion with the faculty about the strengths and weaknesses that seem to transcend the students. Such cross-cutting patterns, it is believed, are probably a reflection on the program rather than on individual students.

Surveys

Reports on self may yield valuable and different information about program effectiveness than that generated through testing or performance assessments. For example, for many years institutions across this country have learned a great deal about the characteristics of their entering classes through participation in Alexander Astin's Cooperative Institutional Research Profile. The CIRP, a simple self-report instrument, inquires about a number of different activities, attitudes, and demographic characteristics, providing information on variables as diverse as parental income and education, participation in various extracurricular activities during high school, average number of hours spent studying in high school, political attitudes, and professional aspirations. Recently, Astin and his colleagues have begun marketing a senior year version of the CIRP, the College Student Survey (CSS). The CSS provides information on the student experience in college closely paralleling the CIRP questions (values and attitudes held, activities engaged in, demographic information, and goals and expectations), thereby enabling valuable comparisons to be made between entry and exit characteristics of the students.

Locally developed surveys may index students' perceptions of the effectiveness of various components of the curriculum, provide estimates of frequency of library use or concert attendance, or provide information on the contributions of student life to curricular goals. Many institutions have put in place senior exit surveys to inquire about issues of particular interest to the campus. Pairing these with graduation checks or other senior contacts required by their programs or the institution ensures higher rates of participation and return of surveys.

Most institutions across the country survey alumni on some regular basis, if only as a means of cultivating prospects for future fundraising activities. Alumni and alumnae are able to reflect on their college experiences in light of their current activities and involvements. For example, questions focused on the adequacy of institutional supports for handling the senior year transitions into the world of work or graduate study and former students suggestions for improving such supports would yield useful information for any institution. Working with the Consortium on Financing Higher Education (thirty-one highly selective private colleges), Joseph Pettit of Georgetown University has developed some of the more interesting alumni surveys in use today. These surveys, for example, have examined issues of civic engagement that support institutional claims to develop citizenship. The surveys also take a complex approach to examining the quality of the educational programs by asking not only how well various areas were taught but also how important they are in the work lives and personal lives of the alumni. Several alumni surveys, available for purchase from ETS and ACT among others, provide nationally normed information to which institutions can compare results from their own alumni. When students have become accustomed to participating in assessment activities during their college years and have witnessed productive use of assessment results by their institutions, they are much more inclined to continue this practice as alumni.

Surveys of employers or internship supervisors very often provide valuable insights into an institution's programs and curricula. Any survey may be tailored to answer the questions that are most important for a campus at the time. The less generic such surveys are, the more useful they are likely to be in provoking campus discussions. For example, recently on one campus with an engineering program a faculty member reported that in a survey of employers conducted one year after students' graduation the reports were glowingly laudatory. Surveys of these same employers on these same employees five years after graduation, however, revealed far less satisfaction. Employers reported that the institution's curriculum did a fine job of preparing students for their first job but failed to provide the background that facilitated students' dealing with transition, change, and the demands of a second or third job. These data initiated some important discussions of curricular revision on this campus.

Although surveys that use numerical rating scales may be easier to summarize, those that are open-ended may invite more thoughtful reflection and yield the kinds of detailed understandings that are often difficult to extract from a mean score on a rating scale. Freewriting, which has its origins in the teaching of English composition (Elbow, 1973), is an uncomplicated approach to assessment that can yield useful information without a great investment of time and energy in survey design. Respondents are simply given a small number of questions or a single one and asked to write their response for a prescribed time period (three to five minutes) without lifting pen from paper.

Portfolios of Student Work

It is possible to learn a great deal about student experiences in our institutions by reviewing the actual work that students complete for their courses. Portfolios are collections of a student's work. This work can either be comprehensive (everything that students turn into instructors) or best work (pieces selected by the students as their best piece of work in a particular class) or chosen to demonstrate that a student has achieved a certain educational competency or goal. Some institutions have also begun using course portfolios of student work collected by instructors to demonstrate the range of performance on the assignments they have made in a course.

At some institutions, clear criteria are specified for inclusion of types of work in a portfolio. At Alverno College, for example, portfolios are tied to particular curricular goals. Students may be instructed to include their best work from a specified list of courses or to include a research paper, an informal essay, one critical review paper, and so on. Some portfolios focus only on work in the major; others focus on the general or liberal education. At Miami University of Ohio, a randomly selected sample of students in each entering class are asked to keep comprehensive portfolios of all of the work that they submit for all of their classes. Over four years' time, the curriculum is made visible in the collections of student work. (The products of the curriculum provide a clear focus for examining the effectiveness of courses and assignments in facilitating achievement of identified curricular goals.) Portfolios provide a ready vehicle for comparing the work of seniors to that of first-year or second-year students. They can provide a focus for faculty discussion of demands placed on students at various points in their progress through the institution. For example, are seniors asked to engage in more analytic and synthetic work than are beginning students? Do they customarily rely more on the use of original sources? Do they write more?

As an illustration, drawing upon the Miami portfolio project and looking at data from the sample of students keeping portfolios in the graduating class of 1995, we see the following pattern of work (percentages are based on the number of assignments appearing in the senior year portfolios):

33 percent exams (of which 45 percent included multiple choice,
43 percent short answers, 9 percent calculation, 38 percent essay)

26 percent papers (of which 54 percent were reaction papers, 17 percent research, 13 percent rough drafts, 11 percent process, 4 percent rewrites, and 1 percent creative)

17 percent quizzes

11 percent computer projects

5 percent projects

4 percent group projects

3 percent labs

1 percent in-class work

Because these percentages reveal a picture of what is happening in the curriculum, we must question whether the observed pattern of work is suitable for senior students. What pattern of work do we think is most desirable? Is the observed pattern due to seniors' scheduling practices? Are they taking mostly lower-level work in the senior year? As noted earlier, the goal is to use these materials to engage faculty in conversation about their collective work with students.

Collecting work for portfolios also benefits students directly. Concrete prompts encourage thoughtful reflection on their work across four years. Students often are able to identify development in their own thinking through review of papers and projects from across their years at the institution. Discussion of these changes with a faculty member can be particularly useful in reflecting and making sense of progress and in charting future directions.

Interviews

Joseph Katz was for many years prior to his death a distinguished leader in higher education and an articulate spokesperson for the importance of attention to students and learning. He suggested that if he could institute one assessment strategy on any campus, he would recommend that every faculty member interview one graduating senior each year. Face-to-face interaction with a student around a predetermined set of topics or questions related to the student's learning affords many faculty members an informative interaction that they rarely have with students. For example, as students talk about the relative effectiveness of various teaching strategies for them or share views on their interaction with other faculty and reflect on what worked and what did not, interviewers are able to reflect on their own pedagogical choices with an openness and nondefensiveness that would be unlikely were the focus directly on their own teaching. As students are asked for overall reflections, faculty can play an important role in facilitating students' understanding and synthesis of their experiences at the institution. Faculty also have a rare opportunity in this context to hear how the pieces fit together for students. Too often, the focus of faculty attention is on "my own course" or occasionally on the courses in "my area or program," but rarely are faculty afforded opportunities to understand how their small piece fits into the student's overall experience of the institution. Interviews can facilitate a campuswide focus on student learning and experience in the institution and a more in-depth understanding of the impact of college on students. A report on assessment activities at the University of Virginia aptly summarizes the typical student response to interviews: "Most especially, students' enthusiasm for the interview itself seemed to substantiate our findings that students not only welcome, but crave opportunities for personal conversations with faculty members and administrators. Interviewers found that students looked forward to the interviews each year and participated actively in them. Students told interviewers that they appreciated having the opportunity to reflect on their experiences and gain some perspective about the past year. For many students, the interviews represented the most time any of them spent with a faculty member discussing their university experience" (*Undergraduate Education at the University of Virginia,* 1994, p. 44).

The quotations from students that appear in this chapter are in fact drawn from interviews of Miami University of Ohio students by faculty. Numerous stories have emerged from faculty interviews about how the practice sharpened their understanding of Miami students' learning styles and in many cases caused them to change their teaching strategies.

Focus Groups

At several institutions, focus groups—a method commonly used in marketing research in the corporate sector—have provided important information about student experiences. Like interviews, focus groups usually center on an outline of questions or issues to be explored in open-ended fashion. Six to ten participants meet with a leader. The level of detail on the experience of any individual participant is likely to be less than that obtained in an individual interview, but the group process itself facilitates movement toward summary impressions from more than one respondent. At the University of Hartford, Temple University, and American University, focus groups have been used to gather information from students about the effectiveness of various components of their general education programs. After a brief orientation to the process, advanced students, particularly those in social science disciplines, are usually quite capable of conducting focus groups involving their peers.

Diaries, Behavioral and Field Observations, Unobtrusive Measures

Many of the questions of greatest interest to faculty and administrators relate to the actual day-to-day experience of students at our institutions of higher education. How much time are they spending on academic pursuits? How often do they visit the library or make use of new information technologies? How much drinking or drug use is occurring? What kinds of social interactions are occurring in residence halls? How great a commitment do students have to paid employment or family responsibilities? Although surveys may provide some information on these issues, self-report of the frequency of daily behaviors is often not very accurate. Richard Light (1990) at Harvard has used diaries to study student use of time. Similar methods have been used at Indiana University to try to understand the amount of time students devote to academic pursuits. At Miami University, Hope College, and the University of Scranton, experience-sampling methods popularized by psychologists Csikszentmihalyi and Larson (1987) have been used to study student time use. During a typical week in a semester, a sample of students wears programmable watches. These watches signal the students about one hundred times during the week on a predetermined random schedule. When signaled, students record briefly the activity they are involved in at that moment. A composite picture of student time investments is developed from the coded student entries. For example, during the senior year in their waking hours, the students in the sample of the Miami University Class of 1995 spent 38 percent of their time in academics; of the remaining time, 1 percent was athletic, 9 percent social, 17 percent leisure, 16 percent personal, 10 percent eating, 6 percent working, 3 percent extracurricular. This information can be compared with their patterns of time use during the previous three years to see consistency and change in patterns. Moreover, it can be used by individual students to reflect upon their time use in comparison to that of the larger group, and it can be used by the faculty to assess whether the students appear to be spending the desired amount of time on academic work.

Ethnographic Methods

Michael Moffatt's *Coming of Age in New Jersey* (1989) represents yet another approach to understanding student experiences. Anthropologist Moffatt lived in residence with students at Rutgers University for over a year and chronicled their day-to-day interactions in this now-classic study of college life. These rich "think descriptions" (a term coined by anthropologist Clifford Geertz to refer to detailed descriptive accounts of experiences of individuals within a particular culture or setting) of campus life defy simple categorization and hardly suggest simple responses for practitioners interested in program design, but they compellingly capture the complexity of campus life. For example, they offer rich insights into the variety of ways that students deal with transitions in their last weeks or months at an institution.

PRINCIPLES UNDERLYING EFFECTIVE ASSESSMENT

The availability of an almost unlimited range of methods unfortunately leaves many assessment programs far too consumed by methodology and not appropriately concerned about the utility of assessment practice within the broader institutional context. In trying to link ongoing data collection activities with the agenda of program improvement within colleges and universities, we have formulated a set of ten principles that we believe are embodied in some of the current best practices in assessment. We offer these principles as suggestions for consideration in developing any program of assessment for the senior year.

- In recognizing the enormity of the task, good assessment *proceeds by identifying manageable chunks.* We might think of our assessment agenda as working toward a CAT scan of our educational process: a three-dimensional picture composed by assembling thousands of slices taken at varying angles. Each slice adds a bit more clarity and acuity to our view of the overall process. We should not be daunted by the total number of slices we need "at the end" to make the definitive diagnosis. Rather we should recognize that each slice contributes to our total understanding.

- We need to commit ourselves to cumulative and *ongoing process.* Assessment is not something we "get over"; it is something we "get on with."

- We need to commit ourselves to cumulative and *incremental* models of understanding, recognizing that understanding the whole picture of any dynamic system is always going to be an elusive goal.

- We need to abandon the fallacy of the perfect measure, recognizing that assessment is necessarily *imperfect,* and avoid the unproductive "paralysis of analysis."

- Assessment that has an impact *begins with questions of greatest interest to the faculty about the curriculum.* Reams and reams of reports already exist on most of our campuses that "should" inform curriculum and instruction but have not and never will do so because the data have not been related to the day-to-day concerns of faculty in their interaction with subject matter and students. Adding fuel to an existing fire is likely to have more positive results than trying to ignite a new flicker.

- We must model the processes that we would like rooted within our institutions. We must demonstrate the value of data in decision making by *making optimal use of existing data* before we engage in new data collection activities. It is far easier to build momentum for assessment by including numerous previous data collection activities as valid assessment endeavors than by imposing some new definition and standard and trying to cultivate new efforts. Similarly, compelling demonstrations of the utility of data in decision making leave people far more inclined to commit to new data collection. We all know of far too many examples of data collected and never analyzed. The skepticism faced by assessment has developed based upon real experiences within our institutions.

- Meaningful assessment *raises as many questions as it answers.* Given the complexity of the issues within the curriculum that will be our focus, we are unlikely to reach definitive and unquestionable conclusions about effectiveness.

- Assessment involves judgment, not just measurement. Values permeate considerations of data on effectiveness. This is *an interpretive enterprise.*

- Many faculty reject reductionist approaches to assessment that capture only one perspective, one way of knowing, one kind of evidence. Valid assessment approaches must try to recognize and accommodate the nature of the university's *multiperspectival* enterprise. Physicists and poets do not process in the same way and do not reach the same conclusions even when presented with identical evidence.

- Assessment practices cannot be divorced from their context and institutional history. They are necessarily *tied to local culture and meaning making.* Practices or evidence from one campus cannot simply be transported to another without translation that is sensitive to local meanings and traditions.

VARIED PURPOSES FOR ASSESSMENT

Assessment may serve several purposes for and within an institution. Most commonly, assessment helps answer questions about program effectiveness and points to directions for improvement. For example, differences between entry-level writing abilities and those demonstrated in a senior exit examination may provide evidence of the effectiveness of writing instruction at an institution. Or such an assessment might suggest the need for program modification, such as more writing in the major, more attention to writing for different and real-world audiences, or more formal research paper writing. Surveys of employers of former students might suggest overall satisfaction with the preparation of students but dissatisfaction with the level of their analytic capacities. Or differences may be revealed among those completing different major programs, suggesting the need for focus on the development of quantitative abilities among students in the arts and humanities.

Assessment can play a critical role in faculty development. Assessment data can be used to open the classroom door—making the curriculum visible to the faculty (and broader public) and bringing teaching and learning into the public discourse of an institution. *Descriptive assessment* (Schilling and Schilling, 1993; Musil, 1992) seeks to paint a picture of what is happening in the curriculum without offering evaluative conclusions. Faculty are then able to reflect on the implications of the work that students are completing—its match with the expectations and curricular goals they have—for their own individual work with students as well as their responsibility as part of a collectivity.

Assessment may also be used to cultivate important intellectual dispositions of personal reflection and evaluation on the part of students. When students are enlisted to comment on the adequacy of their preparation in various areas— their strengths and weaknesses and the areas where they would benefit from additional preparation—or when they are called upon to collect and review portfolios of their work, assessment may be seen as playing a direct educational role. Although at many institutions data are currently collected that would support assessment as a direct educational intervention, such uses of assessment are still rare.

Collection of information on students' performance is useful throughout their experience at educational institutions. Entry-level assessments provide valuable information about who students are and what abilities and expectations they bring to their classes. Students' reflections on their experiences in the first year are likely to bear the mark of their transitional status. Doubts, concerns, or dissatisfactions are likely to be attributed to the self and the choices one has made rather than to the institution and its programs. Follow-up assessments each year or each semester allow tracking of the development of abilities and competencies to understand better the impact of various components of the curriculum on students. Reflections of students during these middle years at the institution are much more likely tainted by an individual agenda for a particular institutional change; dissatisfactions are often attributed to features of the institution, its programs, or curricula. In contrast, assessment in the senior year based upon student reflections most often provides a balancing act—retrospection balanced against the prospective gaze, weighing the perceived strengths of the institution against perceived limits in one's experiences as a student.

ASSESSMENT IN THE SENIOR YEAR

The liminality associated with the senior year makes it an ideal time for students to assess both their own experience and the institution's programs and offerings. Much can be gained from asking seniors to share the benefits of alternating their focus between self and institution. Our experience has been that students are quite willing to tell their stories.

Self-Assessment

Self-assessment is particularly important in helping students bring closure to their college experience and assist them in making the transition to another stage in life. Integration and reflection are included among the curricular goals at many institutions, yet it is rare to have in place structures or opportunities to ensure that reflection occurs. Well-chosen assessment activities may provide powerful stimuli to such integration, as well as fertile ground for cultivating reflective and integrative habits of mind. Students are much more likely to draw connections among diverse fields when the connections are experienced as meaningful in their own lives.

Jennifer majored in sociology and spent her junior year abroad. In an interview with a faculty member, she reflects on major changes in her thinking:

> I would have to say that, my first two years here, it was very much, sort of, not perpetuating but reaffirming everything that I learned as a child growing up in a very religious and conservative type family. . . . I would have to say that Luxembourg definitely was what was the pivotal time, when I think I started to question my values, what it was I believed, what was important. . . . And then after coming back, this year has definitely been a huge change. I have just questioned why I do what I do, why I believe what I believe, what is it that has caused me to believe the things that I do, whether that be social factors or family, professors or what you've learned, and I think more than anything sociology, and even some other classes that I have taken outside of the department, have just taught me not to revoke what I have learned in the past but to question why I have learned it and why I continue to perpetuate, like, stereotypes and ways of thinking. More than anything I just think it's the questioning, not always, I guess, um, say, revoking what I've learned, but just asking why it is that I've learned it and looking beyond it. . . . I guess I have begun to question what is truth.

Students often use interviews with faculty members as opportunities to reflect on the views of their work at the university that others have shared with them. Expectations of parents are experienced by many students as a source of considerable pressure. Airing these expectations in conversations with other adults can be a liberating experience for students. Cynthia majored in graphic arts and struggled a lot with the program. She began her interview with a question: "Is it really worth it? I'm graduating, but yet I feel like I'm not ready to. . . . I paid for my college and my family says, 'That'll get you a good job,' but the jobs that are out there for me right away aren't going to be the high-paying jobs, and it's almost like factory work is offering better wages for me now, and it's like, 'Is college work worth it then?' cuz it won't pay anything right now. The satisfaction is there, but they don't see it like that."

Continuing her interview with a faculty member, Cynthia gives voice to the worth she seemed to be seeking in her questioning, by commenting on changes she has experienced:

> People I talk to . . . they are so much more into what is going on in the world. They are so intelligent. I mean, it's really weird. . . . I mean, you can talk and you have these really deep conversations and people know what is going on in the world, they know business and they really take things to heart. . . . I mean, and really know what is going on, more so than what [is the case] at home or anything like that. I guess it makes me even want to know more, cuz I never used to watch the news or anything like that and now I find myself picking up and reading more . . . and just . . . I want to know what's going on more, just from, being around these people has just kinda rubbed off on me now.

Institutional Assessment

The transitional status of the senior year supports thoughtful reflection. Students are inclined to offer well-considered suggestions for improvement of curricula and programs. In balancing what role the institution, program, or curriculum has played in their development with their own accomplishments and limitations, seniors most often provide candid observations of the strengths and weaknesses of programs. We have heard surprisingly few examples of students trying to advance a particular agenda or grind a personal ax in comments about the institution. Rather, most often comments are offered in a spirit of helpfulness. Here again, senior status accords valuable insights, for their status leaves seniors feeling somewhat detached from the immediacy of their experience, yet close enough to provide specific information and elegant examples that are powerfully persuasive. For examples, several students commented on their appreciation of the attempts of faculty members to integrate group work into their instruction and their genuine enthusiasm for this innovation, yet they shared the feelings of being overwhelmed in trying to schedule four or five extra project group meetings in already busy schedules.

Asked to freewrite about her advice for the institution, Jane listed several suggestions:

- Require professors to take a seminar on teaching methods and communication skills every two years. . . .
- Incorporate computers as a teaching tool for the professors. . . .

- Make it policy that a student who is a nonmajor/not needing the credit for graduation be able to take a class outside their major curriculum credit/no credit.
- Implement more classes that teach practical stuff which the students can actually take with them and use. I do not feel that I have learned a whole lot since I have been here.
- Offer more integrated classes which use a holistic approach to studying a certain area. . . .

Linda majored in interdisciplinary studies. She shared the powerfully positive impact of an internship experience in an inner city school on both her personal and intellectual development. This experience also led her to more critical and pointed observations about the institution. Asked to freewrite about advice she would give to the institution, Linda offered: "Incorporate more co-op, field work, volunteer requirements. I don't feel that courses included a hands-on component. The criticism that Miami is sheltered and privileged is fairly accurate in the aggregate. I would like to see a stronger service philosophy. Accounting classes could organize to offer tax-form advice to the poor or senior citizens. Stuff like that."

CONCLUSION: ASSESSMENT, LIMINALITY, AND THE SENIOR TRANSITION

Each of the assessment approaches we describe makes particular use of the senior year. Those which seem most valuable to us serve both the student and the institution. Assessment approaches can be combined to present a complex picture of the experiences a student has had during the undergraduate years. Both students and faculty can use these materials for reflection and evaluation. Most important, because the materials are descriptive rather than evaluative in character they invite conversation rather than defensiveness. Faculty and seniors can explore the results in a contemplative manner and bring their own values to the information presented, allowing the project to reach its goal of generating discussions that lead to improvement. For seniors, these are summations of what they have done in college, both inside and outside the classroom. As the student voices scattered throughout the chapter demonstrate, the materials have prompted thoughtful assessments by Miami students of their lives inside the institution—reflections that are balanced and constructive and lead them into lives outside the academy. The desired outcome is that assessment is so embedded in the institution and its curriculum that it actually contributes to the educational experience of students. This is particularly important in relation to assessment in the senior year. Because of their unique liminal status, seniors have much to tell us if we provide the appropriate mechanisms for them to do so. More important, the act of telling can serve as part of the transition process for the seniors themselves. Thoughtful assessment approaches that provide materials for reflection offer one of the most important bridges between undergraduate college and the world that follows. They afford seniors the opportunity to move forward and to look back.

The following excerpt is from a speech given by Amy early in the spring semester of her senior year to her classmates in Miami's Western Program at a senior luncheon. She was introduced to the literature on liminality in her first semester of college in a course focusing on the transition into college. She demonstrates her ability to translate that experience to fit the challenges she is now facing. She ends the talk by expressing her appreciation for having been given the opportunity to reflect on the past four years in relation to the future and acknowledging the power of such reflection as she looks forward, while gazing back:

So many ideas seem appropriate to reflect on our years in the Western Program. But one idea seems particularly fitting considering what will happen in May. Remember the doorway? Remember "liminality"—that "in between" period? That reintegration period we learned about when we were in the reintegration period. Almost four years ago we were conscious of this changing stage in our lives, maybe for the first time. We discussed how the liminal stage could make us feel stressed, anxious, tense. Sound familiar? Once I got more familiar with Western, more comfortable in my new college surroundings, I felt as if I had moved through the doorway of liminality, which meant the most confusing and difficult phase of my rite of passage was complete.

But that doorway we passed through almost four years ago is not the same doorway which we are so quickly approaching. Now, I'm not saying all this to make you feel tense, or stressed, or anxious about entering the liminal stage again. I am reminding you of this rite of passage phenomena so that you might be more prepared to enter it and more assured since you have survived liminality before, you will do it again. I know everyone is asking you do you have a job lined up, or have you been accepted into graduate school. I do not deny that this semester, as I near that next doorway, I feel very anxious. But I think we have all found the benefits of lingering in the doorway of liminality and then finding the courage or strength or whatever it took for each of us to move out of that "in between" place, into the hallway which led us to this next door when we leave Western.

I am glad I was asked to speak today because it caused me to consider my future changes in a positive way, whereas before I was dwelling on all the negative issues of change—the biggest of which for many of us is uncertainty. I don't know if I'll be working after graduation. I don't know if I'll be going to graduate school next year. But I do know that I will soon be standing again in the door of liminality.

Assessment in the senior year reinforces the kinds of habits of mind or intellectual and personal dispositions articulated in the mission statements of most of our colleges and universities. How do all of these ideas fit together? What is important about what I've done? Where is this leading me? Do these ideas have any value? What are the implications of what I've studied for how I'll live my life? How do I resolve these contradictions? Rather than simply reflecting on the end point, or the "after" in the before-and-after comparison, and enclosing the college years in a neat package, in attempting to understand and support the dynamic processes of meaning making that occur during the senior year through our assessment activities, we welcome graduates into the kind of questioning and reflecting, doubting and reconsidering needed for active citizenship. Victor Turner noted, "Liminality is full of potency and potentiality. It may also be full of experiment and play" (Benamou and Caramello, 1977, p. 33). We miss wonderful opportunities if we do not invite our seniors into this experimentation and play, and join them in this process through our assessment activities. In addressing her peers, Amy gives clear evidence that she has heard this invitation.

CHAPTER SIXTEEN

Mobilizing Campus Support for Senior Year Programs

William L. Thomas, Jr.

The Senior Year Experience has been defined in previous chapters as a structured set of experiences designed to enhance the successful transition of college students from undergraduate life to the succeeding one. For institutions, it is an opportunity to intentionally nurture a semester-long or yearlong set of experiences focused on preparing the primary products of their labor for entry into the workforce for advanced or different career paths, or for additional schooling. It is also richly fertile soil for alumni offices wanting to grow a long-term commitment to the institution. A senior experience allows colleges and universities to nurture, support, and cultivate a lasting bond with the students who were admitted, taught, learned, and billed; who paid and, in significant ways, trusted the college with their lives, present and future.

But few do! The tenure of a student in far too many of today's institutions passes with only a modest measure of truly meaningful education. More regrettably, the extraordinary discoveries and insight that do occur among students are not usually shared beyond a few moments with the professor or mentor of the moment and perhaps a few close friends.

Institutions are undeniably responsible for their learning environments. But they do not organize and manage them sufficiently. Do we effectively engrave in the minds of the great majority of our students that the revelations, discoveries, and change they experience are *wonderful,* and that the *rest of their lives* will be energized and filled by such things? Do we engage our students enough to transmit not only knowledge but the benefits of knowing, and significantly link to them the experiences, values, and wisdom of those of us who were charged to teach and to lead? Do we collaborate with our students and among ourselves to make some overall sense out of all they are exposed to? When they leave us, will they be able to construct a cohesive and unique mosaic out of their many experiences, one they will proudly reveal to others, one that will serve them well the rest of their lives? Do they share enough time and talk with friends, family, faculty, and classmates to understand what happens to others while college is happening to them?

Many such questions can be posed; unfortunately, few generate a comforting response from thoughtful observers of today's colleges and universities. To the contrary, it seems that far too many of our graduates leave us with only a superficial sense of what the institution has meant and will mean to them. We are often saddened to learn we have been in charge of a grand adventure that is seen afterwards as less than grand. We are unsettled when students admit they suspect that their classmates—but somehow not they themselves—really got a good college education.

Such deficiencies, of course, resist simple solution. But they can be addressed. For graduating seniors and for their institutions, positive outcomes can dominate the collective psyche and push away the specter of unfulfilled promise. But such thinking involves institutional change that charges programs to address the legitimate needs and expectations of students who are near the completion of their academic degrees, and then to dedicate energy and resources to address those needs.

Change comes slowly to institutions of higher education. In his book *Academic Strategy,* George Keller proposes tongue in cheek that colleges and universities are resistant to change because "there is no time for change, it is unnatural, God prohibits it, and there is no money" (1983, p. 57). Historically, change in American education has been viewed largely as a process of natural diffusion: new ideas arise in some fashion and spread unplanned from department to department or from campus to campus (Owens, 1987). In the 1970s, however, scholars began to document specific strategies and tactics for planning, managing, and controlling organizational change (Katz and Kahn, 1978; Havelock, 1969). More recently, business-sector organizational initiatives such as total quality management and reengineering have become commonplace in educational settings.

This chapter provides readers with a blueprint for introducing and adopting a comprehensive senior year experience on a college campus, based upon lessons learned at the University of Maryland. First, in a context of managing *change* in a complex institution—more precisely, to introduce a significant new initiative—I identify the key individuals on campus who can contribute to such an effort and their stake in the outcome. This is followed by a list of specific steps to consider in designing an institutional change process. I maintain that the change process employed at one campus has many generic elements that can be replicated at other colleges and universities on behalf of enhancing the senior experience. Finally, the Senior Experience at Maryland is described to give the reader a concrete illustration of a change process and its ultimate outcomes in enhancing the senior year experience.

STAKEHOLDERS IN THE CHANGE PROCESS

Chin (1982) identifies three major approaches to planned organizational change: (1) empirical-rational strategies, based on the concept that change can be fostered through researching new ideas and their subsequent development and dissemination; 2) power-coercive models, which involve the use of sanctions and rewards to obtain compliance from adopters; and 3) normative-reeducative approaches such as organizational development, where the organization evolves an internal capacity for continuous problem solving. One of the most talked about topics in business circles today is reengineering, defined by Hammer and Champy (1993) as "the fundamental rethinking and radical redesign of business processes to achieve dramatic improvements in contemporary measures of performance, such as cost, quality, service, and speed" (p. 32). Although each of these approaches involves a different set of actions or steps to accomplish the objective of change, a common element for all is the necessary commitment and involvement of leaders.

Campus Leaders

Schein (1992) proposes that all organizations have definable cultures involving a shared history and set of assumptions. The primary role of leaders in the culture, according to Schein, is to create, manage, and change the culture as needed. A successful senior year experience must claim the open and strong support of the leadership of the institution. This is evidenced by appropriate references in the publicly stated priorities of the president, vice presidents, and deans as well as the general governance of the campus, from the board of trustees to the student government association. The senior experience and many of its events should be fashioned to become a significant part of the quilt of traditions that define and distinguish institutional life. Such stature would have resource implications. Campus calendars would reflect the priority given. Leaders would be visibly involved.

Campus leadership can be identified easily by formal positions (president, vice president, deans), faculty leaders through departmental leadership and campuswide visibility, and student leaders through governance or individual performance. Key informal leaders, however, can also play significant roles. These include visible or popular faculty within colleges and departments, influential advisers to student leaders, middle managers who have the reputation of making things work on campus, people with access to budgeting priorities and allocation decisions, opinion makers who speak or write in the campus media, and individuals located almost anywhere on campus whom students seem to trust.

In seeking to introduce and implement any process to change the delivery system of services for seniors, appropriate representatives of these groups need to be involved. A successful senior experience has the support of a broad array of leaders on the campus. An effort that does not is unlikely to succeed.

Faculty Involvement and Investment

Given the role of faculty in determining curriculum and as the student's primary point of contact with the institution, a successful senior experience effort must have faculty support and involvement. When the typical college experience is dissected and examined closely, it becomes clear that contact with faculty, mostly in classes and labs, is the primary investment of resources that an institution makes with its students while they are enrolled. Unfortunately, this contact is commonly characterized by fragmentation and unconnectedness. Nonetheless, this is where the greatest opportunity for an improved experience lies.

Graduates are testimony to the effectiveness of their academic curricula. At any point in time, it is fair to assume that a faculty has under its collective management the content of its curricula, providing to enrolled students knowledge for a competitive world as well as timeless principles. Yet a sense of cogency may well escape the graduate who has not been instructed by the same professors for several classes and who has not been instructed or conditioned to view his or her curriculum as part of a bigger picture, fitting reasonably into the nonacademic world the graduate is about to enter. Certainly, in large universities this deficiency is commonplace.

Faculty should be invested in correcting such a condition for three sound reasons. Some closure on the curriculum, albeit conditional and tentative (properly so, given the inevitable expansion of knowledge and perspective), would assist each student to conceptualize the academic class and lab work as recognizable increments of knowledge, experience, and understanding. Second, significant numbers of students pursue advanced formal education, and faculty and institutional reputations are at stake when graduates are exposed to faculty at other institutions. Finally, the current climate is one of accountability to "customers," supporters, and society.

A successful senior experience effort is characterized by faculty who:

- Recognize their centrality to broad institutional missions and embrace learning outcomes as more important than teaching processes
- Initiate creative and timely opportunities to enhance student-faculty interactions

- Determine and embrace the advantages to be accrued by an effective senior experience focus
- Collaborate with institutional efforts to support a senior experience via college and departmental practices, the academic calendar, administrative processes, and the setting of unit priorities
- Know individually a substantial percentage of each graduating class
- View the senior experience as a special interest in which they personally participate

In order for faculty to embrace these ideas, they must be involved in all aspects of exploring and introducing interventions to address the senior experience.

Staff Leadership and Involvement

In American higher education, a plethora of staff positions evolved over several decades because of the specialized nature of work tasks that responded to changing expectations of students, families, and society—and the faculty of growing institutions. "Staff" members (administrators, counselors, advisers) have become important and often vital performers in the operation of institutions. They have developed considerable skills in organizational management. They have attempted to establish and maintain legitimate, helpful relationships with students. Their role as professional educators is dearly held and stoutly defended. The skills attained, along with the continuing motivation to be an effective contributor to students' direct learning experiences and their educational environments, make staff members extremely valuable to institutions.

These characteristics assembled in the bodies of administrative staff make an effort like the senior experience conceptually and logistically possible, as well as efficient.

Within a complex institution, in seeking a broadly embraced program, *position power* is a relevant ingredient as well. Staff who need to be committed to the success of the senior experience include:

- A designated head or coordinator who is a team builder
- Persons representing significant institutional officers and facilities
- Representatives of student affairs
- Representatives of academic deans or major departments
- Representatives of institutional advancement and alumni offices
- Marketing talent
- A data person (surveys, research, records)
- Clerical and logistical support

Student Involvement, Investment, and Leadership

Even the best and most logical idea on a college campus cannot survive the disinterest of students. Nor will it survive noninvolvement of significant members and numbers of students.

As they approach graduation, students are *the* targeted constituency, the prime benefactors of the senior experience. They must be strong supporters of the program. The demonstrated interest and involvement of students is also likely to be most consistently persuasive with leaders of academic institutions. The lessons of the late 1960s and early 1970s have not been lost on higher education. Current concerns for "customer" satisfaction are the latest development on that continuum of response to student needs that began in response to chanting mobs of students three decades ago.

A successful senior experience demonstrates student involvement that has:

- A program inspired and actively assessed by students who, generally, have campus identities that are positively regarded among the student body at large

- A student leadership team that trusts, likes, and listens to the staff

- A student leadership team that views membership as an honor on the campus and whose members view themselves as worthily chosen for reasons they can identify and feel good about

- A graduation ceremony viewed as an important experience in their collegiate life

- A student leadership team that is enthusiastic, creative, involved in the life of the campus, representative of the student body, and of good intent and humor

- Other highly visible student leaders and performers supportive of the program and participating as appropriate

STRATEGIES TO GAIN INVESTMENT

It is no simple task to gain adequate investment of support for a new initiative among the many forces that compete for attention on a college campus. As previously mentioned, it requires the involvement and commitment of a variety of players. A successful planned change process takes into account the campus environment, the stakeholders, the competing issues, the histories of similar efforts, and the aspirations of a broad range of potential supporters and opponents.

Principles of Change in Higher Education

Colleges and universities, like other formal organizations, are complex bureaucracies with varying degrees of hierarchy and centralization. According to Hage and Aiken (1976), numerous characteristics affect the rate of change in bureaucratic organizations and need to be taken into consideration: formalization of decision-making processes, size, structure of the organization, and so on.

There is no substitute for understanding how things work and who causes them to work in a complex organization. Assessing institutional characteristics is one of the first steps to consider in undertaking planned change. Formal decision-making processes are usually not difficult to ascertain, but discovering and understanding informal ones may require considerable effort. Effectiveness is usually highly correlated with positional power. In spite of the exceptions that almost everyone can cite, there is in corporate organizational structures—and most institutions of higher education are organized along a corporate model—a clear relationship between assigned responsibility and authority. Since authority equals power to make things proceed, attention to who has access to authority is a critical aspect of finding effective people.

Early attention should identify the longer-term sources of support and energy for a successful new initiative. It is initially important to find seed money and meet enthusiastic founding fathers and mothers, but a long-term human infrastructure and recurring budget allocations are even greater challenges—particularly in times of fiscal difficulty. Matching and "marrying" (securing some vow of commitment) any new initiative with the various constituencies who have a stake in the potential outcome is an important task. With a successful initiative, there are a core set of notions about it that are understood by almost everyone. But it is likely that some aspects of the program may be received very differently from one group to another. These differences must be anticipated and exploited (rather than necessarily avoided). There are many legitimate benefits to be marketed; matching the appropriate approach to the audience must be thoughtfully performed.

There are certain intentional approaches to gaining knowledge about organizational dynamics that may accelerate understanding the power culture of a particular campus:

- *Network with established and productive veterans.* Select and nurture a manageable number of ably performing colleagues whose experience and wisdom can be shared.

- *Backtrack recent initiatives.* Select currently successful new programs or efforts and trace the processes, approvals, and origins involved in establishment.

- *Identify successful campus change agent entrepreneurs.* Study the styles, positions, networks, and agendas of those who have been successful with recent projects.

- *Experiment.* Take an obviously good, innovative idea (but not one you want to live or die by) and try to get it accomplished. Move ahead persistently and keep detailed notes of the bumps, bruises, and blocks.

Strategies for Change

How do you get a new idea introduced and accepted on a college or university campus? Change usually occurs in organizations in response to a need. The need can be driven by external forces perceived as threatening or by internal recognition of organizational maladaptation or misfunction.

After defining a need for change, it is important to identify goals and a strategy for achieving them. According to Owens (1987), scientific production of new knowledge and the need to spread new ideas and practices resulted in the promotion of a number of planned change approaches, known collectively as knowledge production utilization. These approaches involve a sequence of steps leading in an orderly process from theory to practice. They are often grouped into four distinct phases: (1) *research,* the invention or discovery of a new idea; (2) *development,* the developing, producing, and packaging of the innovation; (3) *dissemination,* the marketing activities to sell the innovation; and (4) *adoption,* the limited testing of the product prior to final institutionalization.

Organization-development approaches to change emphasize the need to identify target populations, establish a timetable, commit resources necessary to fulfill the strategy, and tailor it to the particular circumstances of the organization. To be successful, planned change must involve all parties who are affected by the change and requires the participation and commitment of a change agent or sponsor to guide the organization through the process (Owens, 1987).

The Change Agent (or Agency)

On college campuses, change can usually be traced back to one individual or small group of individuals with a new idea and a commitment to the change process. A new program like the senior experience requires a vision, an idea, which must include, first, enough of a currently perceived deficiency in the quality of campus life to justify the effort and, second, sufficiently attractive outcomes to move the institution forward. The vision must include the ongoing involvement (during much of the program design stage as well as later) of a healthy portion of the body politic of the campus. The most obvious way to do this is to establish a team, committee, or task force that studies an environment, its programs, and its people to determine the nature and scope of the problem.

The task force must have validity, with membership including individuals whose work involves regular and knowledgeable contact with significant elements of the problem. If alumni relations are known to be problematic and attraction of new graduates into active involvement as alumni is perceived to be in need of enhancement, then a staff member familiar with this issue would be important to the group. Advising, graduation issues, career issues, traditions, and other related institutional activities have experts at work in a variety of settings who might be a part of the group.

A simple truth is that certain individuals have more credibility than others in their work settings. Credibility is won by performance, enthusiasm, integrity, courage, and many other individual characteristics. One useful perception is that if a credible person lends involvement to a task, it is likely to be done honestly and thoroughly, thus making any subsequent report or recommendations more powerful. Further, issues of gender and race—and to a lesser degree, certain other individual characteristics that have attained a strong political identity locally—must be considered. A task force effort may be derailed because of insufficient attention to diversity issues.

Access to the President

If the change agent or sponsor is not the chief executive officer (as is frequently the case), the change agent and committee or task force must have access to this position. The power of any individual or authority on a campus to influence support, display noninterest, or resist an initiative is very much a function of the relationships held by an individual or agency with the chief decision maker of the campus. Every organization is headed by individuals in key positions who are the *most* significant decision makers. American higher education rarely invests that role in anyone other than the chief executive officer. Intermediate and lower-order decision making is normally decentralized. An intelligent strategy to win support for a new initiative brings each significant level of decision making into a position of support if at all possible. But the one level of support that must not be ignorant of or opposed to an initiative is the person with the ultimate, campus-governing power. Thus, securing the attention of the president is essential. Whether the response is favorable or benign, it can be made to work; but if the president has no knowledge of the project, critical decisions are likely to be made by others and as a result any subsequent appeal to the president becomes complex and uncertain. If the president initially responds negatively, he or she could still be convinced otherwise or encouraged to withhold final judgment until the team charged with designing an effort completes its task and is permitted to make its case more persuasively.

Phase One: Research

First, we must *establish the need*. Claiming the attention of colleagues, students, administrators, or faculty in a modern collegiate setting requires a very determined effort. From accumulated incidents, credible noninstitutional sources, opinion surveys, or other relevant sources, there has to be some accountable evidence that there is a problem, that important segments from among our various constituencies are upset about it, that our problem is worse than the problems of others, and that a possible solution gives us an advantage over our competitors.

It is impossible to overemphasize the importance of credible data in the task of getting attention in a collegiate setting. We may be emotionally moved by stories and events, but we are intellectually persuaded by data. No initiative that requires resources of any significance in today's world is likely to progress without persuasive data both to support the effort being made and to predict better outcomes if the issue is addressed. A focus group of seniors who register concerns about being unprepared to enter a search for employment after graduation but who have not made reasonable use of an existing career center does not alone move the hearts of a modern campus to intervene in the students' behalf. Legitimate student concerns, however, that have not been adequately recognized nor addressed by campus actions do claim attention.

Moreover, issues that are substantive in the life of an institution are rarely issues that exist on that campus alone. National media stimulate our society with stories and problems that range over many institutions. Similarly, national, regional, or statewide reports continually cite deficiencies or concerns that most likely address issues each campus can recognize. Connecting in some realistic ways to a hot education reform issue makes attention getting easier. Proposed solutions are more readily acceptable and can actually help persuade the undecided that the problem is serious if data exist to confirm that similar solutions have worked elsewhere.

Phase Two: Developing the Product

The process of developing the product or idea may require several distinct stages.

Draft a report. A formal report that results from a credible task force study of an issue is a critical requirement for new initiatives. Such a report effectively communicates the issue or problem to be addressed, offers persuasive data and reasoning to reach conclusions that appear appropriate to an informed reader and are consistent with experiences that can be documented from other settings. The report is well constructed, intelligently yet succinctly written; it transmits a sense of urgency and of confidence that the new initiative will produce positive outcomes.

The needs of students or the environmental problems identified should instinctively appeal to important constituencies. Here are examples relevant to the senior year:

- Concern for better employment and graduate school placement opportunities for graduating seniors
- A desire that alumni who are recent graduates be enlisted early in their adult life in order to enhance long-term support for the institution
- A more connected feeling among graduating seniors with respect to their fellow classmates and their class as a group
- A capstone academic experience that better defines and integrates their undergraduate studies for graduating seniors

These needs have instinctive appeal for almost everyone. Starting here and then systematically applying relevant data to reach reasonable conclusions can make a powerful formula for acceptance and support.

The report must be essentially error free; it must persuade; and it should have a useful life of at least three or four years into a general implementation of its recommendations. Finally, the report needs champions who position and maintain it high on their agenda until implementing action is agreed upon. The champions might be best placed if they have differing paths or access to more than one of the critical administrators influencing the fate of the new initiative.

Formulate recommendations. Most recommendations for action that are proposed must be viewed at first glance as attainable. But there are some that are not so viewed, and debate ensues. The debate is often limited to the more idealistic or costly ones. A likely outcome of such a circumstance is that a major portion of the recommendations wins general support, even if certain other parts do not.

Involve students. Along the way, either by deliberate involvement of representative students or through collection of data from students, it is essential to win enthusiastic support from students for the initiative. This can occur any number of ways: (1) original concerns come from students, (2) student organizations address a particular aspect of the problem, (3) students contribute data and the data are used powerfully, (4) student leaders are consulted throughout the study and construction of the report, and (5) students serve on the task force.

Prepare a budget. It is always important to envision realistic ways to provide needed resources to fund the recommendations. If seed money is used for the beginning year, early attention to replacing that source is advisable. If there is room to negotiate for the continuance of early funding, then organizing the time, place, and manner to make such an argument should be a high priority. This problem is even more difficult because it is likely to occur as we are trying to get the initiative underway in its first year.

If new funding sources are to be counted on, the detailed planning and follow-through related to securing such funds is ongoing and requires close attention.

Phase Three: Disseminating the New Idea

It is critical to disseminate the new idea and to use multiple methods of communicating it to various groups.

Plan communication strategies. It is not an unwise investment to plan for a significant attention-getting moment. If the sponsor or change agent were a politician or a highly visible athletic director, he or she would call a press conference and reporters with cameras would appear. More likely but less dramatic means have to suffice for us. The release of the report may be the occasion. Appearance on the agenda of a critical governance meeting might work. Media coverage—particularly in the campus press—is essential, even if you have to purchase space. The problems to be confronted, some of the proposed solutions, and the morale of the task force usually benefit from a high-profile public announcement to the campus.

Use credible forums for discussion. It is productive to be ever-responsive to opportunities for taking the issues to various groups within or associated with the campus. Asking for agenda time in the faculty senate, the student government association, the alumni board of directors, relevant campus committees, the dean's council, the president's cabinet—all these and others are important forums for gaining support and expanding discussion. Ongoing coverage in the relevant campus media helps; it can be somewhat influenced by a series of columns or letters to the editor.

Avoid purgatory. In the process of getting attention, care must be taken to avoid dead-end streets. It is probably not wise to seek premature approval or excessive support from important offices too early. A projected price tag for the project that is on its face too high makes it easy for decision makers to simply shelve the matter at first reading because there is (of course) no money to spare. If there are personnel commitments that compete with other tasks, opponents from those ranks may emerge to resist changes. The better approach is to anticipate the dead ends and wherever possible offer optional paths—even if they are yet to be determined—and thus enable the initiative to be fully presented and debated later.

Begin with incremental steps. In most complex organizations, where authority and accountability are widely distributed, phases of programs are continually being altered "at the margin." Applying that organizational behavior here means that a single recommendation included in the report (yet to be adopted in its entirety) may be implemented in the meantime by a unit within the institution, solely on its own merits. This is not unusual and should be both encouraged where appropriate and applauded when successful. It is a challenge for the sponsors of new initiatives to record and relate the changes occurring to the integrity and usefulness of the report, at the same time being careful to give full credit to the creative managerial talent of those who implemented the new action and those who supported it.

Seek out allies. Allies can frequently be found among those who complain, who have unmet needs, or who are openly frustrated about certain issues on the campus. It may be possible to relate recommendations of this initiative to the issues about which others have concerns. For example, a professor in the school of business and management may complain about the level of career assistance available to the recent graduates of that school, but his or her efforts to get additional support from existing resources may have been fruitless. Tying this concern and energy to the broader, but larger, concerns for senior career advising would probably strengthen the effort overall—as well as possibly reducing the squeak heard from that particular wheel.

Another example: the chief development officer is preparing for a new capital campaign. His alumni rolls are incomplete, with high "no address" rates among graduates within the past decade. Relating a more inclusive, friendlier, identity-building set of experiences for seniors to this concern for keeping up with graduates is a natural linkage. Mutual support for these efforts would be most likely.

Allies may well be found in other "new" programs or efforts:

- *Faculty research grants,* where graduating students might work with accomplished senior faculty in research activities that are related to the students' career or graduate education goals.

- *Service learning programs,* tied in with federal, state, and local governmental agencies, where senior students could fulfill a public service obligation, earn money, build a résumé, and learn under supervision a range of skills and understandings that will serve them throughout life.

- *New living and learning centers,* where the academic path is integrative with major themes that challenge our society and our institutions. Senior students can serve as facilitators and team advisers for both on-campus and off-campus activities.

Any such new ally can help the initiative if creative relationships can be imagined and constructed. Old allies also exist. Established and ongoing organizations and agencies can be partners in a senior experience effort. If the question were posed to every administrative office, What can you do to help implement a set of broad senior-enhancement experiences? the range of answers would probably excite any advocate. The same is likely true for most internal campus organizations, from a social sorority to the student concert board to the Asian American Student Association—to any and all.

All these allies and relationships can serve implementation of a senior year experience. Choosing, engaging, and nurturing the ones most likely to move the initiative forward is the challenge.

Link to other campus initiatives. Institutions are usually subject to some new management effort, vision statement, or set of priorities. The implementation strategy for a new initiative must take into account all such efforts or pronouncements and seek supportive compatibility where appropriate. If total quality management or business process reengineering is in vogue, find a way to be a part of that effort. If a new vision statement is guiding institutional priorities, find language in it that accommodates your initiative and embrace it purposefully. Of course, such actions result in commitment to the embraced principles or means and should not be entered into frivolously, but new campuswide strategies can be a powerful engine to help move an initiative along.

The implementing of strategies should include periodic opportunities to reassert the major objectives of the initiative through campuswide visibility of some type. Essentially, an ongoing marketing plan for the first two or three years of a new initiative would make deliberate use of campus information systems and local media to reinforce and build upon the initial momentum of the effort.

Phase Four: Adoption of the New Idea

The final phase of bringing about a change is working for the adoption of the new idea.

Implement. The goal of most innovations is to become the norm. If such a goal is worthy, then there are a set of ways and conditions that serve to move toward that end.

Attach to traditions and ceremonies. For a senior year experience, obvious attachments would be graduation ceremonies and homecoming activities. But other ceremonies and traditions are ripe for embracing. Such predictable occasions as sporting events, parents' weekend, minority focus weeks, spring breaks, career days, and others can be used (usually with the sponsor's delight and possible support) to bring seniors together. A banquet or dance for new seniors can quickly become a part of the traditions of the campus. A senior week might combine special career activities and social gatherings, as well as opportunities to recognize outstanding contributions to the campus made by graduating seniors. But traditions and ceremonies do not just happen. They are carefully conceived, planned, supervised, evaluated, and kept in touch with changing people and times. When achieved, they are powerful magnets for the attention of all campus citizens and worth the effort to build.

Nurture an effective senior class organization. Student organizations have great difficulty surviving the passing of current leadership and enthusiasm. Knowledgeable advisers plan for and nurture the necessary human resources that ensure a viable student group. A successful student group is often characterized by (1) a place in the institutional fabric that is more or less accepted by the campus community at face value; (2) a clear set of purposes that require doing something as a group or as a participating member (to just "be" is not enough to sustain interest or validity); (3) a recognizable set of common interests; (4) a highly effective and determined adviser; and (5) recognition for accomplishment by the campus community.

Organize and nurture a standing oversight committee. Making use of the campus governance system or creating a new committee to provide continuing oversight is a strong move toward permanence. Such a committee should have face validity and should have ongoing tasks built into its charge in order to ensure involvement of participating members.

Continue to collect data. As data established the need to begin an initiative, continuing data from graduating seniors confirm the benefits of the program, provide stimulus for the changes needed, and serve as an effective vehicle for staying in touch with graduates after they leave the institution.

Establish physical evidence of leadership and senior council activities. Class gifts properly labeled, a senior council hall of fame, class pictures, citation of senior contributions to campus activities, and other such memorabilia located in a visible space on the campus affirm the value and permanence of a senior experience.

Maintain a list of supporters. A well-catalogued list of supporters among faculty and staff provides access to supporters over time for a variety of purposes.

Award annual or regular recognition for service. Finding ways to systematically recognize the leaders and major contributors to the success of a senior experience adds to a long-term campus presence. Graduation ceremonies are a natural opportunity for recognition. Letters of appreciation, use of the local media, invitations to special campus events, and evenings with the president are similarly reenforcing.

Make effective use of regularized marketing within the campus culture. Programs need exposure in order to maintain interest, support, and participation. A deliberate and continuous marketing plan adds to the place of the senior experience within the campus culture.

Stay in touch with alumni programs. The imminent alumni status of graduating seniors is a natural attraction to alumni leaders and thus is likely to be a long-term source of support for a senior experience. In turn, senior experience activities must be cognizant of and supportive as appropriate to campus alumni efforts.

THE UNIVERSITY OF MARYLAND: A CASE STUDY

I was first introduced to The Senior Year Experience concept at a regional NASPA (National Association of Student Personnel Administration) conference for chief student affairs officers in the summer of 1990, at which John Gardner, of the University of South Carolina, spoke of a new initiative out of the National Resource Center for The Freshman Year Experience and Students in Transition that would focus on seniors. The idea both excited and intrigued me. Over the previous several years, I had been working with a group of seniors on a senior class giving effort. Based upon interactions with these students and other seniors, I knew of the anxieties many—indeed most—were feeling with their impending graduation transition.

In 1991, the University of Maryland surveyed several institutions regarding the success of their senior giving or senior gift activities. We confirmed the suspicion that our seniors gave substantially less money, and less enthusiastically, than seniors at peer institutions; but we also discovered that those other institutions were benefiting from a range of specific programs and services for seniors beyond the opportunity to contribute to a class giving effort. Assessing that our campus had little specific programming for seniors beyond a few, low-profile academic departmental activities, and stimulated by our survey, I appointed a task force "to examine the needs and expectations of University of Maryland College Park (UMCP) seniors, relevant current campus programs/service offerings, and ideas from other campuses." I also asked that the task force make recommendations to the campus community.

The Task Force

Under very effective leadership, the task force performed extremely well. Thirty-two citizens of our campus community made up the group: eight undergraduate students, two graduate students, five staff with academic rank, and seventeen staff without academic rank. Their report, *The Collegiate Senior Experience: The Successful Completion of All Requirements* (Van der Veer and others, 1994), is a broadly conceived and expertly presented document that put forward the case for a senior year experience effort at Maryland.

In retrospect, four phases of the effort that established the Senior Experience at Maryland can be discerned.

Phase One: Research

The task force organized into subcommittees and conceived several different research projects to identify and establish the problem. A survey was conducted to assess the current needs and expectations of graduating students on campus.

Over one thousand responses were collected from students in their final semester on campus. Another survey was distributed to all deans, directors, and department heads to document current programs and services offered specifically for seniors and to identify potential gaps. Phone interviews were conducted and listserv requests made to create a list of other campuses' programmatic efforts for seniors. Although the list of individual programs at different campuses was impressive, few if any had an overall, comprehensive strategy for addressing the needs of this particular population of students. Finally, focus groups with seniors representing different colleges within the university resulted in anecdotal data used to strengthen the case made in the report.

Phase Two: Developing the Product

Two issues were of importance in this phase: the report and resources.

The Report. The primary purposes of the report were to establish the problem through documented research and to offer recommendations for change. The body of the report was organized to communicate the origins and philosophy of the senior experience, the charge to the task force, research methodology and findings, a statement of the problem, recommended courses for action, and estimated costs of implementation. The appendices included a timeline of the task force's activities, the survey data, and references.

Another cadre of faculty, staff, and student leaders were involved in reviewing drafts of the report and providing comments. Some forty-eight individuals attended a half-day retreat to help formulate the recommendations contained in the report. In retrospect, the effort stands as one of the most thoughtful, inclusive, and productive of its type that we have experienced at University of Maryland.

The Resource Issue. The initial financial and participatory support for the task force in identifying the various aspects of the problem was forthcoming and essentially trouble-free. We enjoy a collaborative spirit among institutional agencies at UMCP, as well as an extraordinary set of talented faculty-staff colleagues throughout the campus. My office was available to manage operational costs and staffing assignments without the necessity of seeking dollars from other sources. Many of the initiatives were conceived and implemented by a student leadership team created early in the process and called "the senior council." The mission of this group is to provide important and valued services, information, and opportunities for students about to graduate. Phase Four below details the activities of the senior council. But one effort addressed in part was the resource issue. The senior council joined forces with the alumni office and helped market a University of Maryland credit card. Successive senior councils now organize the marketing of the card to their classmates and other students and share in the negotiated profits from the sponsoring bank. These funds are used essentially to support the activities of the senior council.

Phase Three: Disseminating the Product

At the time of the report, we strategically chose to link our concept to the campus continuous quality improvement (CQI) initiative. Launched in 1990 by the president and a campuswide council including cabinet members, the CQI effort was established to enhance institutional practices based upon customer feedback. The decision to link the Senior Experience at Maryland initiative to CQI was based on several factors:

- The CQI effort was much in favor and had spawned several campuswide efforts.
- Resources for new initiatives were not readily visible through normal channels. To the contrary, anticipated cutbacks appeared likely.
- The recommendations of the report spanned dramatically over academic affairs, institutional advancement, and student affairs. This reality fit comfortably with CQI since the model of *cross-unit teams* was a hallmark of the CQI effort.
- The Senior Experience at Maryland was viewed by a small core of critical observers as a potentially useful vehicle for bringing about profound changes in the entire undergraduate culture. That goal was interwoven (at the time somewhat ambiguously) with the broad CQI goal, generally embraced, to serve student needs better campuswide.

A Senior Year Experience CQI team was formed and did its work, culminating in a team report (Wolvin and others, 1995) that essentially confirmed the work of the earlier task force. Its major recommendation was formation of a separate office, under the supervision of the vice president for student affairs but, importantly, headed by a senior faculty member. That report was received by the CQI Council; the two principal vice presidents involved (academic and student affairs) continue to consider alternatives for implementing the recommendations. A long-term institutional commitment is still being pursued and a faculty-staff advisory team is being considered for long-term collaboration throughout the academic, student affairs, and other administrative departments.

Phase Four: Adoption of the New Initiative

The recommendation to create a separate and enhanced office for the Senior Experience at Maryland is still under study, but many of the individual recommendations outlined in the task force report have been and continue to be implemented as agencies and offices are encouraged to deliberately address reported deficiencies:

The Alumni Office

- Vacated a marginally successfully "student alumni" organization in favor of active involvement and collaboration with the senior council
- Added a senior council representative to the alumni board of governors
- Initiated an alumni mentoring effort
- Organized a Young Alumni Club

The Senior Council

- Constructs and regularly updates and distributes a graduation handbook.
- Maintains a senior telephone "hotline" (314-GRAD) that provides schedules of events, timely reminders of deadlines and graduation requirements, opportunities for student feedback, and response to questions.
- Sponsors "Senior Nights" at local establishments.
- Sponsors a series of senior receptions (hosted by academic units, given the size of each graduating class) at the president's home each semester. Faculty and graduating seniors are invited.
- Cosponsors with the alumni office the sale of UM credit cards and shares the commissions earned.
- Sponsors or cosponsors special career-related programs with the career center.
- Determines a senior gift to the institution annually and raises funds via graduating senior pledges and contributions. Gifts have included a welcome-to-the-university sign and plantings (1993), a garden adjacent to McKeldin Library (1994), a large bronze University of Maryland seal properly installed on the North Gate House (1995), and a fountain at the new Maryland Center for the Performing Arts (1996).
- Selects senior marshals each semester who have gained significant roles and a distinctive presence in institutional graduation ceremonies.
- Sponsors senior week prior to each semester's graduation ceremonies.

It should be noted that the total senior class gift amount pledged over the past three years (1994, 1995, and 1996) was $126,905. Representatives of the senior council present the money at graduation ceremonies.

Academic Unit Initiatives

- Opportunities for seniors to work on research projects with faculty members, including paid employment, have been increased.
- Student internships have increased.
- Student participation in regional professional conferences is encouraged.

- Informal seminars are held on professional activities in chemistry.
- Deans' receptions for graduating seniors are now held in most colleges.
- The criminology department sponsors alumni mentoring programs.
- A six-hour senior thesis is presented to the entire geology department.
- Capstone courses are given in aerospace engineering and in government and politics.
- Faculty invite seniors to lunch with food science professionals in the nutrition and food service department.
- A senior seminar is given in American studies.

Career Center Initiatives
- Expanded significant résumé referral, placement assistance, interviewing information, and career advising for seniors
- Expanded use of computer-assisted career activities
- Created a student employment center, with enhanced assistance for internship, co-op, and workshop opportunities

These measures are consistent with our aspirations. We have yet to determine the course and effect of the senior experience effort, as well as that of many of the events, but we are immensely encouraged by the changed level of activity.

LONG-TERM PROSPECTS

An immediate outcome of a good program is the notion that if it is good now, it will be good forever. An immediate counternotion is that since we have now done it, we need not do it again and again. Both notions are simplistic, but both are relevant to the phenomenon of a significant change to a campus culture. We continue to pursue change, yet we realize that the institutionalization of a program or priority requires careful understanding of how the culture allows itself to change. Change is often seen only in relation to its creator or stimulus, as typically happens with a new chief academic officer's plan for program review or a new president's set of initiatives. Change is often measured in degrees of permanence, that is, if it survives long enough, it is now part of campus life. Change can come crashing in with a new mandate, such as a landmark Supreme Court decision. Or change can be slowly, deliberately, and only incrementally achieved one step, one brick, or one program at a time. After our initial successes, I believe it is the latter gradual approach that is now happening for the Senior Experience at Maryland.

A broadly conceived initiative like the Senior Experience at Maryland is going to make a significant difference in the lives of succeeding classes and the campus undergraduate culture only if it is woven into the fabric of campus life. Knowing when and which threads to introduce, knowing that each one requires artistry at the loom, that the tapestry changes in appearance each time a new thread is added, that the change is noticed, and that many pass judgment on the new look—all these understandings are essential.

Altering graduation exercises in order to include more senior participation, reestablishment of senior class "officers" via a senior council, senior capstone seminars in all academic majors, and we hope other initiatives all will be tried, tested, altered, and tried again. If they persist through a few graduating classes of students (perhaps six to eight years), they will have won a firm place in the Maryland culture—at least for a while.

CONCLUSION

Change in an institutional setting is complex. It requires leadership, understanding of the culture, intentional and strategic planning, and systematic implementation. The change procedures employed at Maryland have many generic elements that can be employed at other institutions.

The introduction and implementation of the Senior Experience at the University of Maryland is evolving and making positive contributions to the culture of the campus and to its students.

The Maryland experience reveals generally that stakeholders in a senior experience initiative can be identified and enlisted for support, that the organizational culture can be receptive to change, and that the support of campus leadership is essential. The Maryland effort also suggests that four phases of activity are required to generate institutional action: research, development of a new product or idea, effective dissemination of the idea, and adoption and implementation.

CHAPTER SEVENTEEN

A Summary Agenda for Enriching the Senior Year

John N. Gardner
Gretchen Van der Veer

This book has addressed the final period of the undergraduate experience, a year or series of final terms we define as *the senior experience*. There are really two most critical transitions during the college years: the one in (the freshman year experience) and the one out. Both deserve an equal amount of attention, support, campuswide participation, and intentional curricular and cocurricular linkages and response.

The preceding chapters have presented and discussed the characteristics and needs of seniors and the importance of bringing closure, connectedness, integration, and reflection to the diverse set of experiences students have as undergraduates. Several chapters have provided practical suggestions for addressing this need through curricular approaches such as senior projects, seminars, internships, and capstone courses. Other chapters have emphasized such cocurricular strategies as intentionally planned and executed senior year rituals and traditions and use of various assessment techniques to enhance student learning. An additional theme of this book is the opportunity in the senior year for institutions to help students graduate with the kinds of skills they need to be successful in the workforce, in graduate school, or as citizens in local communities. Practical suggestions for developing special support services for seniors and the roles that certain offices and campus units can play in organizing to address issues related to the senior year have also been presented.

In its entirety, *The Senior Year Experience: Facilitating Integration, Reflection, Closure, and Transition* provides readers with a comprehensive overview of the issue, what is happening in the field, and a historical and theoretical context for a focus on seniors. The many exemplary programs highlighted and initiatives proposed in this book cut across institutional types and divisions and involve multiple departments, services, and organizations. Although the primary goal of institutional attention to this issue is to benefit graduating seniors, the authors point out the potential for realizing larger organizational goals as well.

In this chapter, we certainly do not need to replow ground already covered well by our contributors. The key questions to be examined in this concluding chapter are the implications and recommendations for practitioners, for those who have responsibility for or simply care about seniors. As a result of our own involvement with The Senior Year Experience conferences, experiences at our own institutions, and work with the authors contributing to this book, we have had the opportunity to gain knowledge and insight about various campus approaches to evaluating and strengthening the senior year and the principles that need to guide practice. In this final chapter, we provide a synthesis of our observations and learnings, followed by some final recommendations, thoughts, and conclusions.

KEY OBSERVATIONS AND LEARNINGS

We derive three primary observations and learnings from the chapters in this volume.

Seniors are a special population. In spite of the many personal characteristics that differentiate seniors from each other, as a group of students in transition they also have special needs in common—needs that may or may not be adequately addressed intentionally by the campus. As mentioned in the first chapter, a striking consensus has developed among the various chapter contributors, without any intentional plan to direct and achieve it, that the most basic needs of seniors are for (1) integration and closure, (2) opportunities for reflection on the meaning of the college experience, and (3) campus-provided holistic support for their transition to postcollege life.

This need for colleges and universities to prepare students better for practical success beyond graduation was found by our authors to be a universal issue for institutions regardless of type, size, history, and mission. However, it is also apparent that faculty and administrators need to do their own evaluation and formulate their own conclusions about what the senior experience means or should mean for the students on their campus. Support services should then be designed accordingly, bearing in mind that some seniors need more attention and support in transition than others—for example, those less likely to have certain opportunities after graduation and more likely to be discriminated against in employment and promotion situations.

The unique needs of seniors require special campus support services. As we have learned from enhancing freshman students' success, creating and maintaining intentional support services can be valuable to fostering a successful transition for seniors. Through its appropriate disciplinary specialists and its student affairs administrators, the academic community has accumulated an extensive amount of knowledge about life stage theory and how to effect and support successful transitions.

The practice of providing special programs and services for seniors is not new. Most campuses have career planning and placement centers. Senior seminars, thesis projects, and internships are not uncommon across the higher education spectrum. Likewise, almost every institution hosts a commencement or graduation celebration to mark the end of the undergraduate experience. What is new, however, is emphasis on evaluating and coordinating these programs and services more intentionally to improve the overall quality and nature of the final quarter of the student's baccalaureate experience.

For example, given the enormous changes in the world of work caused by globalization, downsizing, outsourcing, restructuring, and so on, it would seem a given that the senior year's critical venue of support, the career center, would be a special area for focusing and strengthening. Transitional support could also be designed as an intentional aspect of capstone seminars, special counseling and advising groups, residence hall programming, career-planning workshops, and alumni mentoring and work-shadowing efforts. Assessment activities could be designed not only to collect important campus information but to provide seniors with important opportunities for reflection and closure as well.

Meeting the needs of seniors requires campus coordination and partnerships. The senior year experience involves a set of newly defined initiatives designed to promote and enhance greater learning, satisfaction, and more successful transition for college students during the final quarter of their baccalaureate degree. These initiatives must be emergent from, dependent on, and connected to the curriculum and the teachings of faculty, but they must also reflect that student learning occurs both inside and outside the classroom. This requires marshaling institutional resources and rethinking how campus policies are designed and services delivered.

The emphasis on approaching the senior year from a comprehensive perspective is based on the same underlying principle that has guided the freshman year experience: that a focus on seniors needs to be holistic, on the total developmental needs of departing students (academic, personal, social, professional, financial, employment, physical, and spiritual). They came to us as complex, potentially whole persons, and we want them to leave even more whole.

The campus must accept responsibility for this holistic educational goal and reflect this in the institutional mission statement, by which the effort to reach that goal must ultimately be assessed. Meeting this need requires expanded partnerships and collaboration between various units of the campus: faculty, academic affairs, student affairs, and alumni and development offices.

FINAL THOUGHTS AND RECOMMENDATIONS

The principles contained in these learnings have guided us in formulating our final thoughts and recommendations for further consideration and action by campus practitioners. We hope readers find these prescriptive suggestions helpful for planning a more deliberate and thoughtful conclusion to the undergraduate experience on their campuses.

Create a high-profile campus task force. We recommend creation of a permanent high-profile campus committee or task force to assess the current status of the senior year experience, make recommendations for improvement, and monitor this process. Change does not occur on a college or university campus without compelling reasons for its initiation and adoption. The value of data collection to document deficiencies in meeting seniors' needs and expectations on a campus cannot be overestimated in establishing a senior experience effort. The task force should ideally represent all stakeholder groups and have representation from the president, the chief academic officer, the chief student affairs officer, the faculty senate, faculty curricular bodies, career center, alumni, and representatives of key student organizations. An outstanding model for such assessment, change agent, and oversight group has been developed at the University of Maryland. Further information on this can be obtained by contacting the author of Chapter Sixteen, William Thomas.

Secure the commitment and support of campus leaders. We recommend that the senior year experience—its current status and future improvement—be a top priority of campus leaders, including the chief executive officer, whose primary role, according to Peters and Waterman (1982), is to manage the values and culture of the organization. His or her visible involvement in providing encouragement and direction for new types of senior support is essential.

We recommend, in similar fashion, that the role of the chief academic officer be critical. He or she must exercise leadership for guiding and encouraging the faculty in reexamining and strengthening curriculum and other faculty initiatives to enhance seniors' learning about transitions, assessment initiatives, and the linking of the curriculum and the cocurriculum (as in service learning, internships, and other connections with the career center).

Develop partnerships among key campus leaders. We recommend development of a strong working partnership between the chief academic officer and her or his counterpart chief student affairs officer, to ensure effective coordination and integration of their respective areas of responsibility in support of senior students.

Include the senior year experience in overall assessment efforts. We recommend special focus for the senior year experience in the overall assessment efforts on campus. To take maximum advantage of this, as argued so cogently by the Schillings in Chapter Fifteen, particular attention needs to be paid to linking the initial assessment during the freshman year with senior outcomes, assessing the lived curriculum, and developing qualitative as well as standardized measures. This assessment process must be owned by the faculty and be primarily faculty driven. Assessment must have a manageable focus and be gradually incremental and dynamic. It must be remembered that, at best, assessment is an imperfect process, but one that can yield rich insights to enhance teaching and learning. The first step for special assessment of seniors is to start with the existing data and build from there. We recommend that practitioners pay particular attention to the Schillings's "principles underlying effective assessment" in Chapter Fifteen. It must be realized that the senior year is an ideal time to do assessment, for seniors are very willing to tell their stories—and stories they do have! Continuing in that vein, if we give them more opportunities to tell us their stories, there is less likelihood some of those stories may be told in a venue or manner less favorable to the campus. It must be understood and remembered that assessment can be a powerful focus of integration, reflection, and closure for departing students. It may be also be one further form of learning as we help them, in departure, to make sense of the meaning of this experience.

To increase the likelihood of achieving the potential of assessment, we recommend creation of a special campus task force on assessment of seniors. It should have representatives from institutional research, the chief academic officer, the faculty, student affairs, the student body (especially seniors), recent alumni, and, if possible, employers of our students.

As appropriate starting points for the work of such a task force, first of all, determine what kind of data already exist. Second, it would be in order to review the plethora of practices already under way on other American college and university campuses, such as those outlined in Chapter Fifteen. Third, it is absolutely critical to be able ultimately to connect your assessment efforts with measurement of whether or not and to what extent the goals set forth in the institutional mission statement are being achieved among your graduating seniors. In other words, assessment measures and outcomes ultimately have to be tied to that most fundamental institutional goal statement. Inevitably, assessment is a catalyst to reexamine the mission statement and whether or not it has remained appropriate for the dynamic circumstances of the changing characteristics of colleges, students, the demands of employers and graduate schools, and the larger society's need for better leaders.

Institute mandatory capstone experiences. We recommend further that the appropriate faculty curriculum bodies of your institution consider a mandatory academic capstone experience for all graduating students, as in senior seminars, senior projects, theses, and examinations. Based on the voluminous testimonials received and qualitative data presented at The Senior Year Experience conferences on the power of senior capstone courses, we particularly recommend these for incorporation into every academic major. One of this chapter's authors (Gardner) has had recent experiences in developing a pilot capstone senior transition seminar at the University of South Carolina, Psychology 589 (Psychology and the Transition to the World of Work). Based on that experience, we suggest possible goals for capstone transition seminars:

- To study transition in the senior year experience.

- To prepare students for transition during and after the senior year.

- To have students engage in self-assessment, reflection, and analysis on the meaning of their undergraduate experience in its totality.

- To have students demonstrate what they have learned from their liberal arts and general education courses, and to demonstrate the interrelationship between at least two disciplines.

- To demonstrate what they have learned in a career planning process provided in this course.

- To prepare a portfolio that documents and portrays what they have learned and how they have developed in college, academically and personally.

- To participate in an academic support group of fellow students, in which they receive instruction, support, and feedback from their instructors and classmates and provide the same to them.

- To consider holistically a variety of issues to be faced in the process of leaving college and in life immediately after college. The issues are in these possible dimensions: personal, social, vocational, spiritual, political, civic, financial, practical, philosophical, psychological, and physical.

See Resource A of this work for expanded delineation of the characteristics of capstone experiences and courses.

Create intentional support groups. We also recommend, as we have learned in enhancing freshman students' success, that intentional support groups be created. We believe an especially productive and useful type of group support may be the special senior seminars designed to be analogous to freshman seminars in addressing holistic student transition needs.

Pay attention to rituals, ceremonies, and celebrations. We recommend that special attention be paid to the institution's currently existing, officially sponsored rituals, ceremonies, and celebrations to mark seniors' completion of their undergraduate experience. It may also be necessary to pay even more attention to those unofficial, nonsponsored senior rituals that may bring harm to the students or unfavorable publicity to the institution. At the very least, there needs to be a standing committee responsible for commencement(s) and other rituals for departing students. Such a group must have representation from the faculty, student affairs, student governance organizations, and appropriate administrative offices such as facilities, the registrar, and so on. Such rituals as commencement represent a unique opportunity to make students feel special and help them leave the campus feeling positive about the institution and the time and the money they have spent there. Senior rituals also present a marvelous opportunity for reflection, integration, and closure.

Departing ceremonies, rituals, and customs also provide an outstanding opportunity for intentionally linking the new graduates with alumni and beginning a sense of ownership and responsibility for the future of the campus. Practitioners wishing to improve senior rituals and celebrations need to pay careful attention to Kuh's excellent presentation of this subject in Chapter Ten and in particular make sure that campus practices intentionally relate to Kuh's five potentially important outcomes for such senior rituals:

1. Unifying the senior class
2. Recognizing achievement
3. Cultivating loyal grads
4. Encouraging students to reflect on the meaning of their experience
5. Easing the transition to life after college

Evaluate exiting practices and policies. In order to maximize the chances of having seniors depart from campus with an attitude engendered of goodwill toward the alma mater, we strongly recommend a review of those practices and policies that could strike seniors as particularly offensive and thus engender ill will. At the top of this list is the fairly ubiquitous practice of charging students an add-on fee for a diploma. Would the reader of this book, as a successful college graduate about to purchase a luxury car with virtually all the customary conveniences and functions included in the base price, be willing to pay $35 extra for a radio antenna? Or even more analogously, the keys?

The analogy here is accurately stretched when we consider that many of our graduates, their families, and their governments have already invested more than $100,000 in earning a baccalaureate degree for which there is now a measly surcharge added for final verification that the student's work has indeed been completed. As a further measure of goodwill, why don't you throw in the cap and gown and announce this new policy in your first letter to seniors prior to graduation in which you also ask them to join the alumni association at a special pregraduation rate? We also recommend that you even allow them to be members free for the first year if they simply take the time to enroll. That enrollment could also be enhanced by an appropriate ceremony of initiation into the ranks of alumni as part of the larger commencement process. Imagine the reaction when students are asked to join the alumni association, make their first contribution, pay $45 for the diploma, incur rental fees for the cap and gown, and attend the commencement ceremony in which students play no active role in speaking and have no input on selecting the speaker!

Finally, for residential students, how student-friendly are the policies regarding graduating students' mandatory checkouts? May they stay on campus through commencement in the halls in which they have been living for the entire year or longer? May they remain in their rooms for a reasonable time after the ceremony to permit a less harried, lingering, even poignant final departure?

Cultivate alumni before they leave the campus. We recommend that a much more careful and intentional eye be cast upon developing seniors into alumni before they leave campus. Students need to be aware that their alma mater needs alumni for many kinds of support, counsel, and assistance far more than simply for giving money. Here is another opportunity for positive contributions and new initiatives from an appropriate task force. Senior capstone courses can be an ideal curricular vehicle for consideration of the roles, responsibilities, and possibilities of alumni status.

Another useful vehicle is to create a student alumni association or group, that is, a group of currently enrolled students who can work with alumni on joint projects for the improvement of the institution. The University of South Carolina, for example, has a long history with a highly successful, active, energetic, student alumni association. The University of Maryland has a highly visible senior council whose purpose is to provide important and valued services, information, and opportunities for students about to graduate—including information about the responsibilities and benefits of being an alumnus. We commend these models for your further consideration.

Creation and maintenance of "young alumni" groups and chapters can provide a bridge for anxious new graduates entering new communities and situations of work. The connection between young alumni and recent grads can produce additional institutional benefits. This group needs to be listened to and solicited for feedback, as they are one of the richest sources of qualitative data and information on the usefulness of the undergraduate education they have just received on your campus.

Evaluate the services provided by your career center. Because of the absolute necessity of having a dynamic, effective, successful, supportive career center, we recommend a special focus on and assessment of the current status of the campus career center. This unit must receive top priority not only from the chief student affairs officer to whom it typically reports but from the chief academic officer, chief executive officer, chief development officer, and the faculty. The reader is directed to the numerous excellent recommendations of Smith and Gast in Chapter Twelve. What are the current linkages of the career center to students, faculty, employers, alumni and advancement, parents, opportunities for internships, co-ops, technology use, and assessment strategies? These centers must be high priorities for resource allocation, and they must be comprehensive. Special consideration should go to enhancing the involvement of faculty in expanded career center initiatives. We can no longer—if we ever could—tolerate academic detachment from practical postcollege employment realities.

Evaluate transition support services for multiethnic and disabled students. We recommend further that the career center, academic units, and campus officials responsible for equal opportunity and affirmative action pay special attention to the need for support for students in transition who are likely to face discrimination in the hiring process. As Bates Parker, Jordan, and Keeling argue so persuasively in their chapter, there is abundant evidence both that discrimination in the workforce still exists and that there are many proactive strategies colleges can pursue to assist underrepresented students in gaining appropriate employment and being successful once they are employed. Simply getting in the door is desirable but not sufficient. If the larger society continues to back away from affirmative action, there is a particularly important moral vacuum here for campuses to attempt to fill in order to realize the potential and promise of higher education for all graduates.

Evaluate campus efforts to support students who aspire to graduate or professional school. More and more students are opting for graduate and professional school over full-time employment after graduation. Yet what we hear from our authors and others we have talked to at The Senior Year Experience conferences is that students are often confused about where to go for help in navigating the graduate and professional school application process. At the very minimum, campuses should have central advising centers or an adviser responsible for assisting students in applying to graduate school within each academic department. In addition, institutions should think about special programs to encourage students—particularly those from underrepresented populations—to consider continuing their education and prepare them for the rigors of graduate and professional school. Undergraduate research and teaching fellowships or internships are among the vehicles for addressing this challenge.

Create campus linkages with potential employers. We recommend that the senior year experience be enhanced by creating more linkages with employers, particularly to provide faculty and student affairs professionals with feedback about the competencies students need for success in the workforce and how an institution measures up compared with others. This is inextricably related to the institutional assessment efforts addressed above. This is so important, as Elwood Holton and Philip Gardner argue persuasively in their respective chapters, that we wish to highlight here the ample evidence that colleges are successful in providing employers with employees who possess the requisite cognitive skills but not in endowing those future employees with a variety of other skills that are equally critical or more so. These include the complex work skills of interpersonal communications, teamwork, applied problem solving, self-management, a work ethic, self-responsibility, and self-motivation. The historical separation of faculty—especially in the liberal arts—from responsibility for many of these outcomes is no longer acceptable and leaves us vulnerable to continuing criticism from our various publics about the unrealistic isolation of the ivory tower. This is an area where senior campus leaders, including the president, advancement and alumni officers, and faculty, must take the initiative to bring more employers into the feedback loop.

Identify and institute strategies to address the leadership and citizenship development of students. We recommend that campuses concerned with the ideals argued for by Sax and Astin (Chapter Nine) and Schwartz and Lucas (Chapter Eight), that is, the need for citizenship and leadership education as necessary goals for the college experience, pay more attention to the growing academic field of leadership studies. No longer an isolated fringe nonacademic and cocurricular movement, the academic study of leadership is moving to the core on many campuses, as Schwartz and Lucas argue. We recommend that the chief academic officer create a special faculty group to study these new curricular initiatives for further consideration on your campus. One of the authors of this chapter (Gardner) may also be of assistance by providing access to the findings and proceedings of the special conferences on Leadership and the Liberal Arts organized by his center.

Likewise, the movement to combine classroom learning with community service opportunities continues to gain strength and momentum within the higher education community. Through such vehicles as Campus Compact (a confederation of U.S. colleges and universities dedicated to promoting student involvement in volunteer service), Learn and Serve America (a federally funded program providing grants to U.S. campuses to integrate service into the curriculum), and the International Partnership for Service Learning (which places students in eleven countries (the United States and India and also countries in Central and South America and Europe) for academic term–length courses combined with related service learning), more campuses are requiring student involvement in service than ever before. A federally funded study of these programs by Sax and Astin has produced preliminary data indicating a positive relationship between service involvement and civic responsibility, academic achievement, and life skills development. According to Astin (1996), it appears there may even be a relationship between service participation and the likelihood that graduates donate money to the college in the future.

Find ways to link the curriculum and the cocurriculum to enhance student learning. One of the best ways to promote student success beyond the campus is to promote students' independent thinking and make students aware of the variety of learning styles, ways of communicating, and importance of a critical mind and eye. Opportunities to participate in out-of-classroom experiences that complement in-classroom teaching have been found to reinforce these kinds of learning goals.

We believe that faculty, academic administrators, and student affairs officers should collaborate in designing and delivering seamless curricula that actually reflect the interrelated ways that students learn. The attributes of leadership and citizenship development may be best approached by these kinds of intentional efforts to link the curriculum and cocurriculum as well.

Involve faculty in leadership capacities. We have already recommended a number of initiatives that bear directly upon the curriculum. Here we briefly reiterate the desirability of exploring the merits of courses in leadership studies; capstone courses, projects, examinations, and theses; expanded assessment initiatives; examination of faculty roles in commencements and other senior rituals and celebrations; increasing faculty linkages to employers; requiring faculty to devote more attention to the noncognitive skills necessary for success in the workplace; increasing faculty connections with the career center; faculty participation on a campus task force to study the current status and possible enhancement of the senior year experience; and more faculty and student affairs partnerships to forge greater connections between the curriculum and the cocurriculum (as in service learning, internships, and so on). Clearly, faculty must be involved in meaningful leadership roles in virtually every initiative to enhance the learning and success of departing students. We wish to suggest here once again the three guiding principles for enhancing the senior year experience that bear special relevance to the work of the faculty—that it is desirable to make faculty cognizant of, and incorporate into their teaching pedagogies, the overriding needs of seniors for (1) integration and closure, (2) reflection, and (3) support for transition to life after college.

Given the vast knowledge accumulated through scholarship on transition, life stage development, the aging process, and the specifics of myriad transition issues, there is a wealth of legitimate academic subject matter for incorporation into courses—if the faculty are aware of and act upon the desirability of doing so. If students are to have sufficient—let alone ideal—opportunities to engage in self-assessment, summative self-evaluation, reflection, and introspection, it is largely due to the stimuli and catalysts provided by their faculty. We recommend that appropriate faculty bodies take additional steps, such as those suggested by Smith in Chapter Six, to link more intentionally general education to their majors. The senior year is the ideal academic and intellectual context to make sure these connections have been made explicit, are understood, and have been put into practice. The senior year is also the institution's last opportunity to provide for undergraduates those basic competencies sought by virtually all employers (and, sadly, most neglected at some larger institutions): speaking, writing, analytical, critical-thinking, problem-solving, interpersonal communications, values clarification, and decision-making skills. John Gardner has particularly found, in teaching university seniors in capstone transition courses, the need for more opportunities for seniors to practice writing, public speaking, self-assessment, reflective analysis, and group teamwork skills.

Include the senior year experience in campus marketing literature. We recommend that the senior year experience initiatives and the character and formats of this experience, be given explicit attention in institutional marketing literature such as the viewbook and individual department and college brochures and also in verbal presentations by college admissions officers. Prospective college students and their families want to know: What are you going to do for me when I arrive (that is, the freshman year experience), and what will the institution do for me when I leave (the senior year experience)? What kind of help will it offer me in securing satisfactory employment? How successful is the campus in preparing its graduates for graduate school? What kinds of opportunities will the college offer me along the way (for example, internships) to be successful after I have secured employment? Are there any special culminating rites, ceremonies, and occasions to look forward to that will make attending the institution truly worth the time, effort, and expense?

Affirm the high priority of the senior year transition. Finally, we recommend that the senior year experience be a priority equal to the freshman year experience in terms of institutional commitment from the leadership; leaders must perceive its value to the institution's short-term and long-term future, educational and financial. This is to say that the way in which the institution regards its seniors as important and responds accordingly should be as intentional, important, focused, and supported as those initiatives directed at entering students, even though initiatives toward seniors do not yield immediate financial gains as is the case with increased revenues from efforts to retain first-year students. The long-term financial consequences (from supportive alumni) in addition to a host of other important benefits for the institution, however, are equally as great—and in fact vastly exceed the initial short-term revenues generated by first-year retention efforts.

CONCLUSION

Now, in the spirit of closure, we bring these thoughts and recommendations to a conclusion with an optimistic prediction for the outcomes of this developing and gathering national conversation on the needs of college seniors for more attention and support in all areas of campus life.

We have seen the great successes in the first critical transition—the freshman year experience—when presidents, provosts, and senior faculty make this transition a priority; when academic and student affairs partnerships are developed; when the needs of students in transition are addressed holistically; and when special courses and seminars are developed to explicitly teach the knowledge needed for successful transition.

We are mindful of the many differences of the senior year experience, but the similarities are also compelling. We are not asking for campuses to start expensive new initiatives in a vacuum. Many of these initiatives are already under way but may be scattered, unfocused, understaffed, uncoordinated, and not enjoying sufficient support or attention from campus leaders. As in the freshman year experience, it is not that faculty and administrators do not know what needs to be done; there is abundant knowledge and an experiential base on which they can draw for model programs and inspiration. What is needed now is will and encouragement.

As the excellent contributors, our colleagues, have shown in this book, the senior year experience is a worthy academic and scholarly endeavor about which much is already known and accomplished. We now need a higher level of national dialogue and action to legitimize the many works in progress described in this book. Foreseeable protestations of insufficient funds are not persuasive. Most of the recommendations we make herein do not have significant resource implications or may cost virtually nothing at all. Many are a matter of doing differently what colleges and universities are already doing, not doing something new. For that matter, we believe—naïvely, some readers may say—that institutions always find a way to do what they most value. It is not a case of resources. It is a case of priorities. Here, the issue is how much all of us value our graduating students, our seniors, our future alumni.

We thank you for joining us in this growing national conversation of great importance for the improvement of American higher education. And we invite you to join this growing national network for further research, scholarship, sharing of information, assessment, inspiration, and action. We especially encourage you to adapt as many as possible of the recommendations given herein for the enhancement of the senior year experience on your campus.

RESOURCE A.
CAPSTONE EXPERIENCES: A PRIMER

John N. Gardner

BASIC THEMES, OBJECTIVES, AND CHARACTERISTICS

Capstone is a term used to describe a variety of experiences, including:

- Freestanding courses
- Components of existing advanced courses in the major
- Out-of-class programs, events, or activities

Whatever their particular form, capstone courses or experiences are generally designed to address the following needs or issues:

- Connecting the major to the institution's general education or core curriculum.
- Addressing such basic questions as, What have I learned in the major? and, How can this be demonstrated?
- Determining and assessing the relationship of the major and its outcomes to the institution's mission statement.
- Relating the major and its outcomes to the world of work.
- Addressing the needs of students who will either continue to graduate school or transfer to another four- or two-year institution.
- Linking students in undergraduate majors to alumni in related fields.
- Linking undergraduate majors to employers.

301

- Offering students a seminar experience. The seminar is a small, interactive, shared class in which all students are potential teachers.
- Linking the major with at least one other discipline.
- Enabling students to explore the personal, social, emotional, and practical issues of transition from college to life beyond.
- Preparing students to become active alumni, both immediately and in the long run.

CAPSTONE EXPERIENCE PEDAGOGIES AND METHODS

- Internships and co-op learning experiences
- Travel study learning opportunities
- Team-teaching by faculty
- Team-teaching by students
- Group or individual projects, which may be research projects or demonstrations
- Senior theses
- Comprehensive examinations, written and oral
- Exhibition of mastery, whereby seniors are required to demonstrate publicly that they have achieved mastery of some subject or skill of their choosing
- Portfolios (a portfolio can be started in the very first term of college, added to regularly, and completed in the last term)
- Use of alumni as guest speakers
- Use of employers as guest speakers
- Linkage with other courses, for example, linking a capstone course with an internship or taking a theoretical course with a practical course
- Linkage with the career center
- Work-shadowing (may be a subset of career center linkage)
- Exploration of character and values development, the ethical implications and aspects of the student's discipline and career choice
- Work in small groups and teams
- Use of the case method
- Teaching and demonstrating mastery of discipline- or profession-specific communication skills
- Development of self-presentation skills
- Analysis of the college culture versus the corporate culture: examination of similarities and differences and the implications thereof for the success of college graduates

RESOURCE B.
SYLLABUS FOR A SENIOR
CAPSTONE TRANSITION COURSE

John N. Gardner

OFFICIAL COURSE DESCRIPTION

University of South Carolina
College of Liberal Arts
PSYC 589, Section 2

PSYC 589: *Psychology and the Transition to the World of Work*

This senior capstone interdisciplinary course focuses on multiple issues of adult life transition, especially those from undergraduate school to multiple roles in American society post-baccalaureate-degree attainment. The central focus of the course is on the psychology of the transition from undergraduate student life to the world of employment after graduation. Students will be engaged in a process of self-assessment, reflection, and analysis of the meaning of their undergraduate experience and its applicability to successful employment and living after college. Students will be able to demonstrate what they have learned from their liberal arts and general education courses and to demonstrate the interrelationship between several disciplines. Students will also participate in an intensive career-planning process. In addition, students will prepare a portfolio that documents and portrays what they have learned and how they have developed in college. Special attention will be paid to the insights of the discipline of psychology in helping students understand and prepare for the postgraduation transition. The course considers holistically a variety of issues to be faced in the process of leaving college, in the following dimensions: personal, social, vocational, political, civic, financial, practical, and philosophical. This is a writing- and speaking-intensive course. Team projects—individual and group, written and oral, reports and presentations—will be used; there will be a midterm exam.

INTRODUCTION

This is the second offering by the University of South Carolina of a special topics senior transition course. For more than two decades, the university has been a pioneer in developing ways to successfully assimilate and support the transition of students who enter the university in what we have come to call The Freshman Year Experience. We believe that there are really two critical transitions during the undergraduate experience, the transition in and the transition out. The latter is now being called The Senior Year Experience, and many colleges and universities are taking increased steps to provide seniors with more support to make a successful transition into what students have long called "the real world." In fact, the University of South Carolina, through its Division of Continuing Education, and the National Resource Center for The Freshman Year Experience and Students in Transition have hosted four The Senior Year Experience national conferences. From these, we have learned a great deal about the kinds of activities, courses, and information that might help our own seniors become more successful. The professor in this course also recently completed a three-year-long process of collaborating on a book for college seniors with three professors at his alma mater, Marietta College. This book, *Ready for the Real World,* will be used as the primary text in this course. This is, in effect, an experimental course in which student feedback about the usefulness and appropriateness of the class activities will be constantly sought to determine whether it would be helpful to continue offering such a course for students.

GOALS OF THE COURSE

1. To study transition in the senior year experience.
2. To prepare you for transition during and after the senior year.
3. To have you engage in self-assessment, reflection, and analysis on the meaning of your undergraduate experience, in its totality.
4. To have you demonstrate what you have learned from your liberal arts and general education courses, and to demonstrate the interrelationship between at least two disciplines.
5. To demonstrate what you have learned in a career planning process that is provided in this course.

6. To prepare a portfolio documenting and portraying what you have learned and how you have developed in college, academically and personally.

7. To participate in an academic support group of fellow students in which you receive instruction, support, and feedback from your instructors and classmates and in which you provide the same to them.

8. To consider holistically a variety of issues to be faced in the process of leaving college and in life immediately after college. These issues are in the following possible dimensions: personal, social, vocational, spiritual, political, civic, financial, practical, philosophical, psychological, and physical.

REQUIRED TEXT

Ready for the Real World (1st ed.), William C. Hartel, Stephen W. Schwartz, Steven D. Blume, and John N. Gardner (Belmont, Calif.: Wadsworth, 1994). Readings as assigned. You must purchase the textbook in one of the bookstores. Bring it to each class period.

REQUIRED ACTIVITIES

Class Team Project

Because much of your life after college will be spent working in groups, it is appropriate that you have at least one class team project. Specifically, you will be asked to make an assessment of the adequacy of the university's present resources, procedures, rituals, and ceremonies to assist students such as yourself in the senior transition. What services, programs, resources, rituals, and ceremonies should the university provide, at a minimum, for all graduating seniors? What kinds of specialized support might be needed for students in particular majors and schools? Of even greater specificity, what kinds of assistance do the members of your class need? Now, compare and contrast your findings in these respects to what you believe the university is actually providing to support your senior year transition. You are to determine the adequacy of what we offer to you, based on your perception of what is needed. You will present your findings in two fashions. First, you will do an oral presentation (on November 15) to a select group made up from the university's faculty administration and student affairs staff. Second, you will provide a written report (also on November 15). All members of the class will receive the same evaluation on this project, for 75 percent of the project grade. The balance (25 percent) of the project grade will be computed based on an averaging of ratings of your participation in the project provided by your peers. You will work out your own division of labor in all phases of the team project. It is expected that all members will make appropriate contributions. The public presentation will be videotaped, and each student will be provided a copy (at the university's expense).

Portfolio

One of the main themes of this course is self-assessment, for its intrinsic value and also to help you be more successful as you leave college and enter the workforce or graduate school. Toward that end, you will be required to assemble what has become known in a number of fields, including college teaching, as a portfolio. A portfolio is a collection or compendium of documents, objects, works, and products that represent you, in this case as a graduating senior. This portfolio is to be a tangible record of your growth process, change, learning, progress, and accomplishments over the entire spectrum of your undergraduate career. The objective of the portfolio is for you to demonstrate in a graphic way where you have come from developmentally in *both* academic and personal dimensions, what you have learned, where you are now, and perhaps suggest some direction of where you would like to go from here. The portfolio is not a résumé. It is a much more creative, tangible, hands-on product than that. It is something that we envision that you could use for a presentation to potential employers; at the very least, it's something you could save to show your children and grandchildren. One basis, of course, for your portfolio will be your academic transcript. In addition, you could base your portfolio in part on the construction and presentation of a cocurricular transcript, a concept we shall explain in class.

You will present your portfolio to the class (on November 29, December 6, or December 15), at which time you will explain and clarify its highlights. You will also submit your portfolio to your instructors for their review and feedback. This is one of the most important aspects of the course.

Career-Planning Process

Similar to the portfolio, but quite distinct from it, the career-planning process is another very important aspect of our course that you will work on both during and outside of class. The goal of this process is not to show you what you should or must do after college. Instead, it is to teach you a process of self-analysis, information retrieval, decision making, and self-presentation that you could use at varying points in your life during and after college. This process includes the following mandatory steps:

1. Completion and submission of the exercises in the chapter on career planning from *Your College Experience,* copies of which we will provide for you, and in the chapter by Dr. Larry Salters in the course textbook.

2. Completion of the Myers-Briggs Type Indicator (MBTI), the most widely used personality inventory in the United States.

3. Visiting the Career Center on September 6 for a tour and interpretation of the MBTI.

4. Use of the Career Library, in which you will research and report in writing on at least one career, the current job market, the requirements of entering this profession, its initial and potential incomes, and other relevant considerations. Items 5 and 6 below will assist you in this process.

5. Complete a profile analysis of a potential employer. See separate handouts entitled "Company Investigation Assignment," "Company or Organization Information," and "The Information-Gathering Interview."

6. Work-shadowing. You will shadow a member of a profession or occupation in which you could conceivably imagine yourself at some point in the future for a total amount of time equivalent to at least one full professional day's work (eight to twelve hours—whatever it takes). *Note:* Items 4, 5, and 6 can be combined and fulfilled simultaneously.

7. Résumé preparation. You will submit your résumé along with the following item.

8. A paper in which you lay out what you have learned about yourself from completing the above process.

Characteristics Most Sought by Employers: Self-Assessment Exercise

In this course, you will participate in class in two separate panel presentations to help you think clearly about what personal and professional qualities you will be able to present to future employers. First, you will hear (on September 13) a panel of relatively recent graduates, that is, former college seniors, who will talk about their own transition experiences to the world of work or graduate school.

Second, you will participate (on September 27) in a panel discussion of Columbia-area employers from both the for-profit and nonprofit sectors. They will talk to you about what kinds of specific qualities they seek in college graduates whom they hire in their organizations. You will then be expected to take the information learned from both these presentations to develop a checklist of qualities sought in college graduates. As a final step, you will apply this checklist to yourself in a self-assessment process (due on October 4). I want you to be able to conclude which of these qualities you already possess and which ones you may still be lacking. You will need to suggest what kind of a game plan you have in mind for developing the ones that you lack and that you therefore conclude you may need in order to be successful in employment after college.

Liberal Arts Exercise

As you know, the university has a core curriculum and a set of general education requirements for each major. The rationale is that these courses help you become a liberally educated person.* You will have also read (for class on September 20) a chapter in *Ready for the Real World* by William Hartel and others on the meaning and significance of the liberal arts. In addition, complete the reserve reading, in *College Is Only the Beginning*, of chapter 9, "The Liberal Arts and Critical Thinking: Building Blocks of the Educated Person," by H. Thorne Compton. This particular course activity asks you to reflect upon and, in an essay, assess the impact of the liberal arts on your intellectual and personal development during the college years. This paper is due on September 27 and should demonstrate your awareness of the connection between at least two different subjects or disciplines you have studied in college. How do they fit together in some coherent and meaningful way to make you a more liberally educated person?

EXAMINATION

There will be a midterm exam, administered in class on October 11.

GUIDELINES FOR SUBMISSION OF WRITTEN REPORTS

Each of your written reports is to be submitted in word processed format and in three copies. One copy is for our files, one copy will be to returned to you with Professor Gardner's comments, and the third copy will be returned to you with the graduate student assistant's comments. Each written submission must be carefully proofed beforehand for accuracy, correct spelling, grammar, and so on. Also, each submission must have a clearly identifiable introduction, body, and conclusion. All work used in the preparation of written assignments that is not your original idea as author must be appropriately footnoted, with citations and bibliography.

OPTIONAL ACTIVITY

Attend a class supper at Professor Gardner's home. A complementary meal will be provided for you and your classmates. This will be an excellent opportunity for all of us to get to know each other better. Date to be determined later.

---

*If you are a transfer student, your previous institution should have offered you something on the order of a core curriculum or general education courses too. If in doubt, discuss this with me.

OFFICE HOURS

Professor Gardner

Call my office to request an appointment. Messages always can be left and phone calls will be returned. If you can't reach me in the office and you need me after hours, call me at home or leave me a voice-mail message. This is the fastest and easiest way to reach me directly.

Graduate Student Assistant

I will be assisted in this course by a graduate assistant. Please understand that she speaks for me, and therefore your cooperation is expected. She will be involved in all aspects of planning our course and the reading and evaluation of your written work.

ABSENCES

You will be allowed one unexcused absence at the maximum. Cuts in excess of this are grounds for not receiving credit for this course. Excused absences are those for such reasons as bona fide illness, death of an immediate family member, official religious holiday, and so forth.

GRADING POLICY

Assignments will be returned to you with written comments and both a letter and a numerical grade. You will receive evaluative feedback from both Professor Gardner and the graduate assistant. Each required course activity will have both a number (percentage) grade, and its letter-grade translation. The grading scale we will use for assignments is as follows:

A+ = 98–100
A = 93–97
A– = 90–92
B+ = 88–89
B = 83–87
B– = 80–82
C+ = 78–79
C = 73–77
C– = 70–72
D+ = 68–69
D = 63–67
D– = 60–62
F = 59 and below

Your final grade for the course will be computed by using the following weighting system:

Midterm Examination	10 percent
Class Team Project	25 percent
Portfolio	20 percent
Career-Planning Project	25 percent
Liberal Arts Self-Assessment Exercise	10 percent
Characteristics Sought by Employers (Self-Assessment Exercise)	10 percent
	100 percent

Your percentage grade on the above formula will be translated into a final course grade, submitted to the university as follows:

90–100 percent	=	A
88–89 percent	=	B+
80–87 percent	=	B
78–79 percent	=	C+
70–77 percent	=	C
68–69 percent	=	D+
60–67 percent	=	D
59 percent and below	=	F

PSYC 589: CLASS OUTLINE

(*Note:* reading assignments will be announced at each class and are due for the following class. Assignments listed below are due on the date indicated.)

August 30	Introduction and overview of the syllabus. Collect MBTI.
September 6	Meet in University Career Center, room [ ]; interpretation of MBTI and tour of Career Center. Complete exercises in Salters's chapter in *Ready for the Real World* (*RFTRW*) and exercises from *Your College Experience*.
September 13	Recent graduates panel. Meet in Visitors' Center. Read chapters 2 and 4 in *RFTRW*.
September 20	Examination of the meaning of liberal arts. **Class will meet in Long Street Theatre.** Presentation by Dr. Thorne Compton, chair, Department of Theatre and Speech. Room location TBA.

	Read essay on reserve by Compton on "The Liberal Arts and Critical Thinking: Building Blocks of the Educated Person." Read chapter 4 in *RFTRW.*
September 26	Class supper at home of John Gardner, 6:00 P.M.
September 27	Panel of employers on topic: What Are the Characteristics of Graduates Sought by Employers? Meet in Visitors' Center Conference Room. Paper due on meaning of concept of liberal arts.
October 4	Exercise due on Characteristics Sought by Employers. Readings to be discussed, including chapter on reserve by Ed Holton.
October 11	Dr. Richard Lawhon, director of admissions, USC Graduate School. Topic: Graduate School vs. Undergraduate School. Read chapter 10 in *RFTRW.* Readings to be discussed: chapters 1, 6, 7.
October 18	Career project due. Readings to be discussed: chapters 5, 11, 12, 13.
October 25	Readings to be discussed: chapters 15, 16, 17.
November 1	Readings to be discussed. Prof. Keith Davis, chair, Department of Psychology, on topic of careers in "helping people" and alternatives to graduate school for liberal arts degree recipients.
November 8	Readings to be discussed: chapters 18, 19, 21. Midterm examination.
November 15	Class project with public oral presentation. Written group project due.
November [ ]	No class (Thanksgiving holiday).
November 29	Individual presentation of portfolios.
December 6	Individual presentation of portfolios.
December 15	Individual presentation of portfolios during final examination period. Discuss chapter 22.

REFERENCES

Adkins, C. L. "Previous Work Experience and Organizational Socialization: A Longitudinal Examination." *Academy of Management Journal,* 1995, *38*(3), 839–862.

Alliger, G. M., and Janak, E. A. "Kirkpatrick's Levels of Training Criteria: Thirty Years Later." *Personal Psychology,* 1989, *42,* 331–340.

Alverno College. *Assessment at Alverno.* Milwaukee, Wis.: Alverno College, 1979.

Alverno College. *Liberal Learning at Alverno College.* (5th ed.) Milwaukee, Wis.: Alverno College, 1992.

Alverno College. *Ability-Based Learning Program.* Milwaukee, Wis.: Alverno College, 1994a.

Alverno College. *Student Assessment-as-Learning at Alverno College.* Milwaukee, Wis.: Alverno College, 1994b.

American Association of Higher Education. Bulletin. 1993.

American College Personnel Association. *The Student Learning Imperative: Implications for Student Affairs.* Washington, D.C.: American College Personnel Association, 1994.

Applebome, P. "More Schooling, Workplace Efficiency Linked." Reprint from the *New York Times. Charlotte Observer,* May 14, 1995, p. 49.

Arnold, J. "Tales of the Unexpected: Surprises Experienced by Graduates in the Early Months of Employment." *British Journal of Guidance and Counseling,* 1985, *13*(3), 308–319.

Arthur, M. B., and Rousseau, D. M. *The Boundaryless Career.* New York: Oxford University Press, 1996.

Ashford, S. J. "Individual Strategies for Coping with Stress During Organizational Transitions." *Journal of Applied Behavioral Science,* 1988, *24,* 19–36.

Ashford, S. J., and Taylor, M. S. "Adaptation to Work Transition: An Integrative Approach." In G. R. Ferris and K. M. Rowland (eds.), *Research in Personnel and Human Resources Management.* Greenwich, Conn.: JAI Press, 1990.

Association of American Colleges. *Integrity in the College Curriculum.* Washington, D.C.: Association of American Colleges, 1985.

Association of American Colleges and Universities. *The Challenge of Connecting Learning.* Vol. 1: *Liberal Learning and the Arts and Sciences Major.* Washington, D.C.: Association of American Colleges and Universities, 1990.

Association of American Colleges and Universities. *The Challenge of Connecting Learning.* Vol. 2: *Reports from the Fields.* Washington, D.C.: Association of American Colleges and Universities, 1991.

Association of American Colleges and Universities. *Changing the Major: Innovation Priorities in the Fields.* Washington, D.C.: Association of American Colleges and Universities, n.d.

Astin. A. W. *Four Critical Years.* San Francisco: Jossey-Bass, 1977.

Astin, A. W. *Achieving Educational Excellence: A Critical Assessment of Priorities and Practices in Higher Education.* San Francisco: Jossey-Bass, 1985.

Astin, A. W. *Assessment for Excellence: The Philosophy and Practice of Assessment and Evaluation in Higher Education.* New York: Macmillan, 1991.

Astin, A. W. "Diversity and Multiculturalism on the Campus: How Are Students Affected?" *Change,* Apr. 1993a, pp. 44–49.

Astin, A. W. *What Matters in College? Four Critical Years Revisited.* San Francisco: Jossey-Bass, 1993b.

Astin, A. W. "The Role of Service in Higher Education." *About Campus,* 1996, *1*(1), 14–19.

Astin, A. W., and Sax, L. J. *How Service Benefits College Students.* Los Angeles: Higher Education Research Institute, University of California-Los Angeles, 1996.

Astmann, S. K. "Saving and Reinvesting the Senior Class." *NASPA* (National Association of Student Personnel Administrators) *Journal,* 1969, *2*(1), 47–48.

Baade, R. A., and Sundberg, J. O. "Identifying the Factors That Stimulate Alumni Giving." *Chronicle of Higher Education,* Sept. 1993, pp. B1–B3.

Banta, T., and Associates. *Making a Difference: Outcomes of a Decade of Assessment in Higher Education.* San Francisco: Jossey-Bass, 1993.

Barr, R. B., and Tagg, J. "From Teaching to Learning: A New Paradigm for Undergraduate Education." *Change,* Nov./Dec. 1995, pp. 13–25.

Bates Parker, L., and others. "Black College Graduates Transition Project: A Longitudinal Study." *Journal of Cooperative Education, Special Thematic Issue: Diversity and Cooperative Education,* 1994, *29*(2), 60–76.

Bateson, M. C. *Composing a Life.* New York: Atlantic Monthly Press, 1989.

Baxter-Magolda, M. *Knowing and Reasoning in College: Gender-Related Patterns in Students' Intellectual Development.* San Francisco: Jossey-Bass, 1992.

Beagle, R., and Johnson, C. M. "Minority Exposure to Corporate America (MECA): Enhancing Business and Organizational Career Success." Paper presented at the Second National Conference on The Senior Year Experience, San Antonio, Mar. 1991.

Beamon, K. "How Texaco's Hard Lessons Can Fuel Your Career." *Minority MBA*, Spring 1997, pp. 6–9.

Beitz, C. A. "What Is Your Transition Style and What Impact Does It Have on How You Deal with Transitions?" Paper presented at the Third National Conference on The Senior Year Experience, Arlington, Va., Mar. 1993.

Benamou, M., and Caramello, C. *Performance in Postmodern Culture.* Madison, Wis.: Coda Press, 1977.

Bennis, W. *On Becoming a Leader.* Reading, Mass.: Addison-Wesley, 1989.

Betz, N. E., and Fitzgerald, L. F. *The Career Psychology of Women.* Orlando: Academic Press, 1987.

Bikson, T. K., and Law, S. A. *Global Preparedness and Human Resources: College and Corporate Perspectives.* Santa Monica, Calif.: RAND Institute on Education and Training, 1994.

Bird, A. "Careers as Repositories of Knowledge: A New Perspective on Boundaryless Careers." *Journal of Organizational Behavior*, 1994, *15*(4), 325–344.

Bloom, A. *The Closing of the American Mind.* New York: Simon & Schuster, 1987.

Bloom, B. S. *Taxonomy of Educational Objectives: The Clarification of Educational Goals.* New York: McKay, 1956.

Bok, D. *Universities and the Future of America.* Durham, N.C.: Duke University Press, 1990.

Bolar, D. W. "Fond Farewells: Keeping the Student Spirit Alive After Graduation." In B. T. Todd (ed.), *Student Advancement Programs: Shaping Tomorrow's Alumni Leaders Today.* Washington, D.C.: Council for the Advancement and Support of Education, 1993.

Boswell, S. K., Fraites, T., and Poonawala, A. "Disorientation." Paper presented at the First National Conference on Students in Transition, Dallas, Nov. 1995.

Bowen, H. R. *Investment in Learning: The Individual and Social Value of American Higher Education.* San Francisco: Jossey-Bass, 1977.

Bowen, W. G., and Rudenstine, N. L. *In Pursuit of the Ph.D.* Princeton, N.J.: Princeton University Press, 1992.

Boyer, E. L. *College: The Undergraduate Experience in America.* New York: Harper-Collins, 1987.

Boyer, E. L., and Hechinger, F. M. *Higher Learning in the Nation's Service.* New York: Carnegie Foundation for the Advancement of Teaching, 1981.

Boyett, J. H., and Conn, H. P. *Workplace 2000: The Revolution Reshaping American Business.* New York: Dutton, 1991.

Brammer, L. M., and Abrego, P. J. "Intervention Strategies for Coping with Transitions." *Counseling Psychologist,* 1981, *9*(2), 19–36.

Brand, M. "The Challenge to Change: Reforming Higher Education." *Educational Record,* Fall 1993, pp. 7–13.

Bray, D. W., Campbell, R. J., and Grant, D. L. *Formative Years in Business.* New York: Wiley, 1974.

Breitling, W. J. "The Capstone Course in Management: The Evolution of Strategic Management." Paper presented at the Second National Conference on The Senior Year Experience, San Antonio, Mar. 1991.

Bridges, W. *Job Shift: How to Prosper in a Workplace Without Jobs.* Reading, Mass.: Addison-Wesley, 1994.

Brimmer, A. F. "The Economic Cost of Discrimination." *Black Enterprise,* 1993, *24*(4), 27.

Brinkman, M. "Integration by Departments: Outer Limits of an Art." Paper presented at the Second National Conference on The Senior Year Experience, San Antonio, Mar. 1991.

Buffalo, J., McLaughlin, T., Majorey, L., and Olin-Ammentorp, W. "Senior Project/ Senior Seminar: The Six-Credit Integrated 'Grande Finale.'" Paper presented at the Third National Conference on The Senior Year Experience, Arlington, Va., Mar. 1993.

Burdick, T., and Mitchell, C. "Real World Changing for Class of 1993." *Washington Times,* May 4, 1993, p. 1.

Burns, J. M. *Leadership.* New York: HarperCollins, 1978.

Burns, T., and Laughlin, C. "Ritual and Social Power." In E. d'Aquili, C. Laughlin, and J. McManus (eds.), *The Spectrum of Ritual.* New York: Columbia University Press, 1979.

Busby, J. B., and Nichols, K. W. "Utilizing Alumni Programs for Student Orientation to Life After Graduation: Unexpected Benefits for Students in Transition and Alumni." Paper presented at the Second National Conference on Students in Transition, San Antonio, Oct. 1996.

Campbell, K., and Turk, J. V. "The Senior Semester Experience in Journalism." Paper presented at the Third National Conference on The Senior Year Experience, Arlington, Va., Mar. 1993.

Cannon, D. "Generation X: The Way They Do the Things They Do." *Journal of Career Planning & Employment,* 1992, *52*(2), pp. 34–38.

Carnegie Foundation for the Advancement of Teaching. *Campus Life: In Search of Community.* Lawrenceville, N.J.: Princeton University Press, 1990.

Casella, D. "Phone Power: The Use of Voice Technology in Connecting Employers and Candidates." College Placement Council (now National Association of Colleges and Employers) Conference, San Antonio, May 1992.

Casson, J. J. "The Career Management Course at Kean College of New Jersey: Helping Seniors Launch Their Careers." Paper presented at the Third National Conference on The Senior Year Experience, Arlington, Va., Mar. 1993.

Chao, G. T., and others. "Organizational Socialization: Its Content and Consequences." *Journal of Applied Psychology,* 1994, *79,* 450–463.

Chickering, A. W. *Education and Identity.* San Francisco: Jossey-Bass, 1969.

Chickering, A. W., and Schlossberg, N. K. *Getting the Most out of College.* Needham Heights, Mass.: Allyn & Bacon, 1995.

Chin, R. "Basic Strategies and Procedures in Effecting Change." In E. L. Morphet and others (eds.), *Educational Organization and Administration Concepts, Practice, and Issues.* Upper Saddle River, N.J.: Prentice Hall, 1982.

Clark, B. R. "The Organizational Saga in Higher Education." *Administrative Science Quarterly,* 1972, *17,* 178–184.

Clark, M. B., and Freeman, F. H. (eds.). *Leadership Education '90: Source Book.* Greensboro, N.C.: Center for Creative Leadership, 1990.

"The College Park Experience: Quality Education Right from the Start." Report on undergraduate education, prepared by the [University of Maryland] College Park Campus Senate Ad Hoc Committee on Undergraduate Education, Aug. 19, 1987.

Collins, M. "Who Are They and What Do They Want?" *Journal of Career Planning and Employment,* 1996, *56*(4), 41.

Commission on National and Community Services. *Service America.* March 1993, *1*(2).

"Companies Seek Same Qualities in Job Applicants." *The Collegian,* Jan. 30, 1995, p. 2.

Copeland, S. T., and Wiswell, A. K. "New Employee Adaptation to the Workplace: A Learning Perspective." *Academy of Human Resource Development 1994 Proceedings,* 1994, 35–40.

Council for the Advancement of Standards. *Standards and Guidelines for Student Development Programs.* College Park: Office of the Vice President for Student Affairs, University of Maryland, 1997.

Cronin, T. E. "Reflections on Leadership." In W. E. Rosenbach and R. L. Taylor (eds.), *Contemporary Issues in Leadership.* Boulder, Colo.: Westview Press, 1983.

Cross, K. P. "Enhancing the Productivity of Learning: Reaction." *AAHE Bulletin,* 1993, *46*(4), 7–8.

Csikszentmihalyi, M., and Larson, R. "Validity and Reliability of the Experience-Sampling Method." *Journal of Nervous and Mental Disease,* 1987, *175,* 526–536.

Cummings, E. "The Misadventures of a Typically Frustrated Student." *The Diamondback* (University of Maryland student newspaper), 1993, n.p.

Cuseo, J. B. "The Senior Year Experience: Goals, Objectives and Practices." Paper presented at the Third National Conference on The Senior Year Experience, Arlington, Va., Mar. 1993.

Cuseo, J. B. "The Senior Year Experience in Higher Education: Purpose, Practice, and Promise." Paper presented at the Fourth National Conference on The Senior Year Experience, Orlando, Mar. 1994.

Daggett, W. R. *Preparing Students for the 1990's and Beyond.* Schenectady, N.Y.: International Center for Leadership in Education, 1992.

Deal, T. E., and Kennedy, A. A. *Corporate Cultures: The Rites and Rituals of Corporate Life.* Reading, Mass.: Addison-Wesley, 1982.

DeMott, B. "On Leadership Education." Unpublished report, Worthington, Mass., 1994.

Dessoff, A. L. "Programming Partners." *Currents,* 1994, *20*(9), 26–28.

Dey, E. L., Astin, A. W., and Korn, W. S. *The American Freshman: Twenty-Five-Year Trends.* Los Angeles: Higher Education Research Institute, University of California–Los Angeles, 1991.

DiFilippo, D. "'I Refused to Be a Statistic.'" *Cincinnati Enquirer,* June 27, 1996, p. B1.

Dill, D. D. "The Management of Academic Culture: Notes on the Management of Meaning and Social Integration." *Higher Education,* 1982, *11,* 303–320.

Division of Continuing Education. University of South Carolina. "Call for Papers" for the First National Conference on The Senior Year Experience. Columbia: Division of Continuing Education, University of South Carolina, 1989.

Dixon, N. M. "The Relationship Between Trainee Responses on Participation Reaction Forms and Post-Test Scores." *Human Resource Development Quarterly,* 1990, *1,* 129–137.

Doyle, D., and Galloway, R. "Decision in an Ethical Court." Paper presented at the Second National Conference on The Senior Year Experience, San Antonio, Mar. 1991.

Dressel, P. L. *College and University Curriculum.* Berkeley, Calif.: McCutchan, 1968. (See chapter entitled "Competencies and Their Attainment.")

Drucker, P. "The Age of Social Transformation." *Atlantic Monthly,* 1994, *247*(5), 52–80.

Dupuy, G. M. "Launching Your Career: A Transition Module for Seniors." Paper presented at the Second National Conference on Students in Transition, San Antonio, Oct. 1996.

Ehrlich, T. "Taking Service Seriously." *AAHE* (American Association for Higher Education) *Bulletin,* 1995, *47*(7), 8–10.

El-Khawas, E. *Campus Trends.* Washington, D.C.: American Council on Education, 1995.

Elbow, P. *Writing Without Teachers.* New York: Oxford University Press, 1973.

Ellin, A. "Post-Parchment Depression." *Boston Phoenix,* Sept. 1993.

Ellis, P. M. "The Required Capstone Course: A Double-Edged . . . Tool?" Paper presented at the Third National Conference on The Senior Year Experience, Arlington, Va., Mar. 1993.

Ellis, S. J. "Take It from the Top." *Currents,* 1996, *22*(3), 29–32.

Ewell, P. T. "Total Quality & Academic Practice: The Idea We've Been Waiting For?" *Change,* May/June 1993, pp. 49–55.

Falk, R. J. "Darland Center Internships Corps: 'Senior to Senior' Connection." Paper presented at the Second National Conference on The Senior Year Experience, San Antonio, Mar. 1991.

Feitler-Karchin, B., and Wallace-Schutzman, F. "Campus to Career: Bridging the Gap." *Journal of College Placement,* 1982, *43,* 59–61.

Feldman, D. C. "Socialization, Resocialization, and Training: Reframing the Research Agenda." In I. L. Goldstein and Associates, *Training and Development in Organizations*. San Francisco: Jossey Bass, 1989.

Findley, C. "Senior Capstone Course: Responsibility for the Future." Paper presented at the Fourth National Conference on The Senior Year Experience, Orlando, Mar. 1994.

Finkelstein, B. "Rescuing Civic Learning: Some Prescriptions for the 1990s." *Theory into Practice*, 1988, *27*(4), 251–256.

Fisher, C. D. "Organizational Socialization: An Integrative Review." In G. R. Ferris (ed.), *Research in Personnel and Human Resources Management*. Greenwich, Conn.: JAI Press, 1986.

Fitzgerald, L. F., and Crites, J. O. "Toward a Career Psychology of Women: What Do We Know? What Do We Need to Know?" *Journal of Counseling Psychology*, 1980, *27*, 44–62.

Fleming, M. "The Faces of Discrimination." *Hispanic*, 1994, *7*(6), 22–28.

Fong, B. "The External Examiner Approach to Assessment." Paper commissioned by the American Association for Higher Education Assessment Forum for the Second National Conference on Assessment in Higher Education, Denver, June 1987.

Freeman, F. H., Knott, K. B., and Schwartz, M. K. *Leadership Education: A Source Book*. Vols. 1 and 2. Greensboro, N.C.: Center for Creative Leadership, 1996–1997.

Gabelnick, F., MacGregor, J., Matthews, R. S., and Smith, B. L. *Learning Communities: Creating Connections Among Students, Faculty, and Disciplines*. New Directions for Teaching and Learning, no. 41. San Francisco: Jossey-Bass, 1990.

Gaff, J. G. *New Life for the College Curriculum: Assessing Achievements and Furthering Progress in the Reform of General Education*. San Francisco: Jossey-Bass, 1991.

Gardner, J. W. *On Leadership*. New York: Free Press, 1990.

Gardner, P. D. "Learning the Ropes: Socialization and Assimilation into the Workplace." Paper presented at the Second National Conference on The Senior Year Experience, San Antonio, Mar. 1991.

Gardner, P. D., and Lambert, S. E. "It's a Hard, Hard, Hard, Hard, Hard, Hard World." *Journal of Career Planning and Employment*, 1993, *53*(2), 41–49.

Gardner, P. D., and Motschenbacher, G. *More Alike Than Different: Early Work Experiences of Co-Op and Non Co-Op Engineers*. East Lansing: Collegiate Employment Research Institute, Michigan State University, 1993.

Garvin, D. A. "Building a Learning Organization." *Harvard Business Review*, 1993, *71*(4), 78–92.

Ginzberg, E. "Toward a Theory of Occupational Choice: A Restatement." *Vocational Guidance Quarterly*, 1972, *20*(3), 169–176.

Ginzberg, E. "Career Development." In D. Brown, L. Brooks, and Associates, *Career Choice and Development: Applying Contemporary Theories to Practice*. San Francisco: Jossey-Bass, 1984.

Ginzberg, E., Ginsburg, S. W., Axelrad, S., and Herma, J. L. *Occupational Choice: An Approach to a General Theory*. New York: Columbia University Press, 1951.

Goldberg, H., Golden, D., and McGillin, V. "Developing Reflective Leaders: Serendipity and Synergy." *NSEE* (National Society for Experiential Education) *Quarterly*, 1996, *22*(2), 29.

Goodsell, A., and others. *Collaborative Learning: A Sourcebook for Higher Education*. University Park, Pa.: National Center on Postsecondary Teaching, Learning, and Assessment, 1992.

Hage, J., and Aiken, M. *Social Change in Complex Organizations*. New York: Random House, 1976.

Hammer, M., and Champy, J. *Reengineering the Corporation*. New York: HarperCollins, 1993.

Handy, C. *The Age of Unreason*. Boston: Harvard Business School Press, 1989.

Hartel, W. C. "Model for Humanities Senior Capstone/Transition Experience." Paper presented at the Third National Conference on The Senior Year Experience, Arlington, Va., Mar. 1993.

Hartel, W. C., Schwartz, S. W., Blume, S. D., and Gardner, J. N. *Ready for the Real World*. Belmont, Calif.: Wadsworth, 1994.

Havelock, R. G. *Planning for Innovation Through Dissemination and Utilization of Knowledge*. Ann Arbor: University of Michigan, 1969.

Hedges, J. L. "It's Time for a Change: The Commencement Ceremony Has Lost Much of Its Historical Value and Power." *Chronicle of Higher Education*, June 28, 1989, p. A32.

Heid, W. H. "Leadership and the Ideal Male: Sources in the Old-Time Colleges." In *Conference Proceedings, Leadership and the Liberal Arts*. Marietta, Ohio, Apr. 1993.

Heilbrun, C. *Writing a Woman's Life*. New York: Norton, 1988.

Hengesbach, T. W. "Student Responsibility for Learning." Paper presented at the Second National Conference on Students in Transition, San Antonio, Oct. 1996.

Hirsch, E. D. *Cultural Literacy: What Every American Needs to Know*. Boston: Houghton Mifflin, 1987.

Hobaugh, R., and McCormick, T. "The Senior Ethics Course: The Pilot Year." Paper presented at the First National Conference on The Senior Year Experience, Atlanta, Mar. 1990.

Holland, J. L. *Making Vocational Choices: A Theory of Careers*. Upper Saddle River, N.J.: Prentice Hall, 1973.

Holton, E. F., III. "The New Professional: Everything You Need to Know for a Great First Year on the Job." Princeton, N.J.: Peterson's Guides, 1991.

Holton, E. F., III. "Teaching Going-to-Work Skills: A Missing Link in Career Development." *Journal of Career Planning and Employment*, Spring 1992, 46–51.

Holton, E. F., III. "Managing the Transition to Work: Twelve Essential Steps for a Fast Start to Your Career." Bethlehem, Pa.: College Placement Council, 1993.

Holton, E. F., III. "College Graduates' Experiences and Attitudes During Organizational Entry." *Human Resource Development Quarterly*, 1995, *6*, 59–78.

Holton, E. F., III. "The Flawed Four-Level Evaluation Model." *Human Resource Development Quarterly*, 1996a, *7*(1), 5–29.

Holton, E. F., III. "New Employee Development: A Review and Reconceptualization." *Human Resource Development Quarterly,* 1996b, 7(3), 233–252.

Holton, E. F., III, and Russell, C. J. "Enhancing New Employee Development: A Longitudinal Examination of Socialization Processes and Turnover." In H. Preskill and L. Dilworth (eds.), *HRD in Transition: The Cutting Edge in HRD: 1996.* Washington, D.C.: International Society for Performance Improvement, 1997.

Hornak, R. T., and Shiflett, R. B. "Capstone Course: Transition Tactics for New Horizons." Paper presented at the First National Conference on The Senior Year Experience, Atlanta, Mar. 1990.

Horowitz, H. L. "Alma Mater: Design and Experience in the Women's Colleges from Their Nineteenth-Century Beginning to the 1930s." Amherst: University of Massachusetts Press, 1993.

Huston, A. C., and others. *Big World, Small Screen: The Role of Television in American Society.* Lincoln: University of Nebraska Press, 1992.

Hyman, H. H., and Wright, C. R. *Education's Lasting Influence on Values.* Chicago: University of Chicago Press, 1979.

Jackson, L. C. "On the Road to Alumni." *Currents,* 1994, *20*(9), 20–25.

Jackson, L. C. "On the Road to Alumni." *Currents,* 1996, *22*(6), 35–38.

Jacob, P. E. *Changing Values in College.* New York: HarperCollins, 1957.

Johnson, C. W., and Edgerly, J. "Leadership Style Changes and Transitions." Paper presented at the Third National Conference on The Senior Year Experience, Arlington, Va., Mar. 1993.

Johnson, K. "In the Changed Landscape of Recruiting, Academic and Corporate Worlds Merge." *New York Times,* Dec. 4, 1996, p. 28.

Johnstone, D. B. *Learning Productivity: A New Imperative for American Higher Education.* Studies in Public Higher Education, Vol. 3. Albany: State University of New York, 1993.

Joint Commission on Accountability Reporting (JCAR) (American Association of State Colleges and Universities, American Association of Community Colleges, and National Association of State Universities and Land-Grant Universities). *A Need Answered: An Executive Summary of Recommended Accountability Formats* and *JCAR Technical Conventions Manual.* Washington, D.C.:American Association of State Colleges and Universities Publications, 1996.

Jones, E. A. "Defining Essential Critical Thinking Skills for College Graduates." Paper presented at the American Educational Research Association Annual Meeting, San Francisco, Apr. 1995.

Jones, S. L. "Providing Minority Students with the Competitive Edge." *Journal of Career Planning & Employment,* 1992, *52*(3), 36–40.

Josselson, R. *Finding Herself: Pathways to Identity Development in Women.* San Francisco: Jossey-Bass, 1987.

Jutras, P. "A Leadership Development Program for Management Seniors." Paper presented at the First National Conference on The Senior Year Experience, Atlanta, Mar. 1990.

Kapferer, B. "The Ritual Process and the Problem of Reflexivity in Sinhalese Demon Exorcisms." In J. MacAloon (ed.), *Rite, Drama, Festival, Spectacle: Rehearsals Toward a Theory of Cultural Performance.* Philadelphia: Institute for the Study of Human Issues, 1984.

Karr, S. D., and Mahrer, A. R. "Transitional Problems Accompanying Vocational Development and College Graduation." *Journal of Vocational Behavior,* 1972, *2,* 283–289.

Katchadourian, H., and Boli, J. *Cream of the Crop.* New York: Basic Books, 1994.

Katz, D., and Kahn, R. L. *The Social Psychology of Organizations.* (2nd ed.) New York: Wiley, 1978.

Katz, R. "Organizational Stress and Early Socialization Experiences." In T. A. Beehr and R. S. Bhagat (eds.), *Human Stress and Cognition in Organizations.* New York: Wiley, 1985.

Keenan, A., and Newton, T. J. "Work Aspirations and Experiences of Young Graduate Engineers." *Journal of Management Studies,* 1986, *23,* 224–237.

Keller, G. *Academic Strategy: The Management Revolution in American Higher Education.* Baltimore: Johns Hopkins University Press, 1983.

Kelley, R., and Caplan, J. "How Bell Labs Creates Star Performers." *Harvard Business Review,* 1993, *71*(4), 128–139.

Kendall, J. C., and Associates. *Combining Service and Learning: A Resource Book for Community and Public Service.* 3 vols. Raleigh, N.C.: National Society for Internships and Experiential Education, 1990.

Kendall, J. C., and others. *Strengthening Experiential Education Within Your Institution.* National Society for Experiential Education, 1986.

Ketcham, R. "In the Nation's Service: A Rationale for Civic Education." *Educational Record,* 1992, *73*(2), 19–22.

King, P. M., and Kitchener, K. S. *Developing Reflective Judgment: Understanding and Promoting Intellectual Growth and Critical Thinking in Adolescents and Adults.* San Francisco: Jossey-Bass, 1994.

Kirby, D. "Owning Your Own Career." Keynote address, Employment Management Association Conference, Phoenix, Apr. 1996.

Kleiman, C. "Secretarial Work Becomes a First Step for More Women Fresh out of College." *Washington Post,* Mar. 27, 1994, p. H4.

Klenke, K. "Leadership Education at the Great Divide: Crossing into the Twenty-First Century." *Journal of Leadership Studies,* 1993, *1*(1), 112–127.

Kleppinger, T. L. "Student Programs: Creating Ties for Future Alumni." In B. T. Todd (ed.), *Student Advancement Programs: Shaping Tomorrow's Alumni Leaders Today.* Washington, D.C.: Council for the Advancement and Support of Education, 1993.

Kluge, P. F. *Alma Mater: A College Homecoming.* Reading, Mass.: Addison-Wesley, 1993.

Kreppel, M. C., and Arthur, A. "Graduating Reflective Practitioners in Engineering Design." Paper presented at the Fourth National Conference on The Senior Year Experience, Orlando, Mar. 1994.

Kuh, G. D. "Appraising the Character of a College." *Journal of Counseling and Development,* 1993, *71,* 661–668.

Kuh, G. D. "Creating Campus Climates That Foster Student Learning." In C. C. Schroeder, P. Mable, and Associates, *Realizing the Educational Potential of Residence Halls.* San Francisco: Jossey-Bass, 1994.

Kuh, G. D. "Guiding Principles for Creating Seamless Learning Environments for Undergraduates." *Journal of College Student Development,* 1996, *37,* 135–148.

Kuh, G. D., and Hall, J. "Using Cultural Perspectives in Student Affairs." In G. D. Kuh (ed.), *Using Cultural Perspectives in Student Affairs Work.* Washington, D.C.: American College Personnel Association, 1993.

Kuh, G. D., and Whitt, E. J. "The Invisible Tapestry: Culture in American Colleges and Universities." AAHE-ERIC/Higher Education Research Report, no. 1. Washington, D.C.: American Association for Higher Education, 1988.

Kuh, G. D., and others. *Involving Colleges: Successful Approaches to Fostering Student Learning and Development Outside the Classroom.* San Francisco: Jossey-Bass, 1991.

Kutakoff, L. S. "The Senior Internship: Linking Academics to the World of Work." Paper presented at the Second National Conference on The Senior Year Experience, San Antonio, Mar. 1991.

Lambert, S. E. "Goodbye Yellow Brick Road: Denial as Part of the Senior Year Experience." Paper presented at the Second National Conference on The Senior Year Experience, San Antonio, Mar. 1991.

Lane, R. "Computers Are Our Friends." *Forbes,* May 8, 1995, pp. 102–108.

Larson, J. "Graduating with Honors: Planning Special Events for Seniors." In B. T. Todd (ed.), *Student Advancement Programs: Shaping Tomorrow's Alumni Leaders Today.* Washington, D.C.: Council for the Advancement and Support of Education, 1993.

Lasher, H., and Brush, C. "Enhancing 'Success Behavior Skills' Perceived as Relevant and Necessary for Effectiveness in the Business Environment: An Innovative Capstone Learning Approach." Paper presented at the First National Conference on The Senior Year Experience, Atlanta, Mar. 1990.

Leibowitz, Z. B., Schlossberg, N. K., and Shore, J. E. "Stopping the Revolving Door." *Training and Development Journal,* 1991, *45*(2), 43–50.

Levinson, D. J. *The Seasons of a Man's Life.* New York: Knopf, 1978.

Levinson, N. S., and Skillings, S. "Critical Success Factors for the Senior Year Experience." Paper presented at the Third National Conference on The Senior Year Experience, Arlington, Va., Mar. 1993.

Levitz, R., and Noel, L. "Connecting Students to Institutions: Keys to Retention and Success." In M. L. Upcraft, J. N. Gardner, and Associates, *The Freshman Year Experience: Helping Students Survive and Succeed in College.* San Francisco: Jossey-Bass, 1989.

Light, R. *The Harvard Assessment Seminars: Explorations with Students and Faculty About Teaching, Learning, and Student Life.* Cambridge, Mass.: Harvard University, 1990.

Loacker, G., Cromwell, L., and O'Brien, K. "Assessment in Higher Education: To Serve the Learner." Paper presented to the Assessment in Higher Education Conference, Columbia, S.C., Mar. 1985.

Louis, M. R. "Surprise and Sense Making: What Newcomers Experience in Entering Unfamiliar Organizational Settings." *Administrative Science Quarterly,* 1980, *25,* 226–251.

Louis, M. R. "Acculturation in the Workplace: Newcomers as Lay Ethnographers." In B. Schneider (ed.), *Organizational Climate and Culture.* San Francisco: Jossey-Bass, 1990.

Luebke, B. F., and D'Lugin, V. "Celebrating Diversity." Paper presented at the First National Conference on The Senior Year Experience, Atlanta, Mar. 1990.

Lundberg, C. C. "Surfacing Organizational Culture." *Journal of Managerial Psychology,* 1990, *5*(4), 19–26.

Lunney, C., Gardner, P., and Williams, A. *Transitions to the Workplace: Expectations and Reality for Liberal Arts Graduates.* Technical Report. East Lansing: Collegiate Employment Research Institute, Michigan State University, 1996.

Lybrook, D. "Transition Two Ways: A Mentoring and Leadership Program." Paper presented at the First National Conference on Students in Transition, Dallas, Nov. 1995.

MacGregor, J. (ed.). *Student Self-Evaluation: Fostering Reflective Learning.* New Directions for Teaching and Learning, no. 56. San Francisco: Jossey-Bass, 1993.

Maestas, L. "From College Student to Professional Self: A Career/Life Planning Model to Ease the Transition and Last a Lifetime." Paper presented at the Second National Conference on The Senior Year Experience, San Antonio, Mar. 1991.

Magner, D. K. "Many Colleges Design Courses and Programs to Prepare Seniors to Live in the Real World." *Chronicle of Higher Education,* Mar. 21, 1990, pp. A33–A34.

Manning, K. "Campus Rituals and Cultural Meaning." Unpublished doctoral dissertation, Indiana University, 1989.

Manning, K. "Properties of Institutional Culture." In G. D. Kuh (ed.), *Using Cultural Perspectives in Student Affairs Work.* Washington, D.C.: American College Personnel Association, 1993.

Marable, M. "Racism on College Campuses." *Cincinnati Herald,* Apr. 22, 1995.

Marchese, T. "TQM: A Time for Ideas." *Change,* May/June 1993, pp. 10–13.

Martin, G. R., and Rosselli, M. A. "Professional Practice Seminar." Paper presented at the Second National Conference on Students in Transition, San Antonio, Oct. 1996.

Martinez, J. M. "The Pregraduate Mentorship Program: Preparation for an Academic Career." Paper presented at the Third National Conference on The Senior Year Experience, Arlington, Va., Mar. 1993.

Maryland Longitudinal Study Steering Committee. *Maryland Longitudinal Student Research Highlights.* College Park: Office of the Vice Chancellor for Student Affairs, University of Maryland, 1986.

Masland, A. T. "Organizational Culture in the Study of Higher Education." *Review of Higher Education,* 1985, *8,* 157–168.

McCoy, B. T., and Barnard, C. A. "The Last Six Weeks: A Programming Model." Paper presented at the First National Conference on The Senior Year Experience, Atlanta, Mar. 1990.

McKenzie, R. "Experiential Education and Civic Learning." *NSEE* (National Society for Experiential Education) *Quarterly*, 1996, *22*(2), 21–28.

McWilliams, G. "Coming off the Drawing Board: Better Engineers?" *Business Week*, Aug. 2, 1993, pp. 70–71.

Mechling, J., and Wilson, D. S. "Organizational Festivals and the Uses of Ambiguity: The Case of Picnic Day at Davis." In M. Jones, M. Moore, and R. Snyder (eds.), *Inside Organizations: Understanding the Human Dimension.* Thousand Oaks, Calif.: Sage, 1988.

Mentkowski, M., and Doherty, A. "Careering After College: Establishing the Validity of Abilities Learned in College for Later Careering and Professional Performance." Final report to the National Institute for Education. Milwaukee, Wis.: Alverno Productions, 1983.

Meyer, J. P., and Allen, N. J. "Links Between Work Experiences and Organizational Commitment During the First Year of Employment: A Longitudinal Analysis." *Journal of Occupational Psychology*, 1988, *61*, 195–209.

Meyer, J. P., Paunonen, S. V., Gellatly, I. R., Goffin, R. D., and Jackson, D. N. "Organizational Commitment and Job Performance: It's the Nature of the Commitment That Counts." *Journal of Applied Psychology*, 1989, *74*, 152–156.

Mitzman, B. "Reed College: The Intellectual Maverick." *Change*, 1979, *11*(6), 38–43.

Mobley, W. H., Griffeth, R. W., Hand, H. H., and Meglino, B. M. "Review and Conceptual Analysis of Employee Turnover Process." *Psychological Bulletin*, 1979, *86*, 493–522.

Moffatt, M. *Coming of Age in New Jersey: College and American Culture.* New Brunswick, N.J.: Rutgers University Press, 1989.

Mooney, C. J. "As Wave of Curricular Reform Continues, Its Scope and Effectiveness Is Questioned." *Chronicle of Higher Education*, Jan. 8, 1992, pp. 17–18.

Moore, S., and Myerhoff, B. (eds.). *Secular Ritual.* Netherlands: Van Gorcum, 1977.

Morgan, A., and Armstrong, K. "How Qualitative Research Provided Insights for New Student Development Programming with Seniors." Paper presented at the Third National Conference on The Senior Year Experience, Arlington, Va., Mar. 1993.

Morrill, R. L. *Teaching Values in College.* San Francisco: Jossey-Bass, 1980.

Morrison, E. W. "Newcomer Information Seeking: Exploring Types, Modes, Sources, and Outcomes." *Academy of Management Journal*, 1993, *36*, 557–589.

Morrow, P. C., and McElroy, J. C. "Work Commitment and Job Satisfaction over Three Career Stages." *Journal of Vocational Behavior*, 1987, *30*, 330–346.

Morse, S. W. *Renewing Civic Capacity: Preparing College Students for Service and Citizenship.* ASHE-ERIC Higher Education Report no. 8. Washington, D.C.: School of Education and Human Development, George Washington University, 1989.

Morton, S. T. "Socialization-Related Learning, Job Satisfaction and Commitment for New Employees in a Federal Agency." Unpublished doctoral dissertation, Virginia Polytechnic Institute and State University, 1993.

Murphy, M. W. "An Interdisciplinary Capstone Requirement: The General Education Senior Seminar at UW-Green Bay." Paper presented at the Second National Conference on The Senior Year Experience, San Antonio, Mar. 1991.

Murray, E., and Mosidi, R. "Career Development Counseling for African Americans: An Appraisal of the Obstacles and Intervention Strategies." *Journal of Negro Education*, 1993, *62*(4), 442.

Murray, N. "Bridge for the Xs: A New Career Services Model." *Journal of Career Planning & Employment*, 1993, *52*(3), 28–35.

Musil, C. *Students at the Center: Feminist Assessment.* Washington, D.C.: Association of American Colleges, 1992.

Myerhoff, B. "We Don't Wrap Herring in a Printed Page: Fusion, Fictions, and Continuity in Secular Ritual." In S. Moore and B. Myerhoff (eds.), *Secular Ritual.* Netherlands: Van Gorcum, 1977.

Myerhoff, B. "A Death in Due Time: Construction of Self and Culture in Ritual Drama." In J. MacAloon (ed.), *Rite, Drama, Festival, Spectacle: Rehearsals Toward a Theory of Cultural Performance.* Philadelphia: Institute for the Study of Human Issues, 1984.

National Association of Colleges and Employers. *Career Services Survey.* Bethlehem, Pa.: National Association of Colleges and Employers (formerly College Placement Council), 1993.

National Association of Colleges and Employers. "1994 Graduating Student and Alumni Survey." Bethlehem, Pa.: National Association of Colleges and Employers, 1994.

National Association of Colleges and Employers. *Principles for Professional Conduct.* Bethlehem, Pa.: National Association of Colleges and Employers, 1995.

National Association of Colleges and Employers. "Professional Standards for College and University Career Services." Working draft 3. Bethlehem, Pa.: National Association of Colleges and Employers, Jan. 1997.

National Institute of Education Study Group. *Involvement in Learning: Realizing the Potential of American Higher Education.* Washington, D.C.: National Institute of Education, 1984.

National Research Council. *Summary Report 1993. Doctorate Recipients from U.S. Universities.* Washington, D.C.: National Research Council, National Academy Press, 1995.

National Research Council. *The Path to the Ph.D.* Washington, D.C.: National Academy Press, 1996.

Newell, W. H., and Davis, A. J. "Education for Citizenship: The Role of Progressive Education and Interdisciplinary Studies." *Innovative Higher Education*, 1988, *13*(1), 27–37.

Newman, F. *Higher Education and the American Resurgence.* Princeton, N.J.: Carnegie Foundation for the Advancement of Teaching, 1985.

Nichols, J.A.L. "Capstone Courses in the Major Versus General Education Capstone Courses: An Examination of the Relative Advantages and Challenges." Paper presented at the Fourth National Conference on The Senior Year Experience, Orlando, Mar. 1994.

Nichols, K. W., and Hood, S. A. "Using Assessment to Build a Bridge over Troubled Waters." Paper presented at the Third National Conference on The Senior Year Experience, Arlington, Va., Mar. 1993.

Nicholson, N., and Arnold, J. "Graduates' Early Experience in a Multinational Corporation." *Personnel Review,* 1989, *18,* 3–14.

Nicholson, N., and Arnold, J. "From Expectation to Experience: Graduates Entering a Large Corporation." *Journal of Organizational Behavior,* 1991, *12,* 413–429.

Nicklin, J. L. *Chronicle of Higher Education,* Nov. 3, 1995, p. A56.

O'Hara, C. "Connecting the Major and Liberal Learning: A Senior Integrated Assessment." Paper presented at the Fourth National Conference on The Senior Year Experience, Orlando, Mar. 1994.

Ostroff, C., and Kozlowski, S.W.J. "Organizational Socialization as a Learning Process: The Role of Information Acquisition." *Personnel Psychology,* 1992, *45,* 849–874.

Owens, H. F. "The College Experience: An Investment in Your Future." In J. N. Gardner and A. J. Jewler (eds.), *College Is Only the Beginning.* Belmont, Calif.: Wadsworth, 1989.

Owens, R. G. *Organizational Behavior in Education.* Upper Saddle River, N.J.: Prentice Hall, 1987.

Parsons, F. *Choosing a Vocation.* Boston: Houghton Mifflin, 1909.

Pascarella, E. T., Ethington, C. A., and Smart, J. C. "The Influence of College on Humanitarian/Civic Involvement Values." *Journal of Higher Education,* 1988, *59,* 412–437.

Pascarella, E. T., Smart, J. C., and Braxton, J. "Postsecondary Educational Attainment and Humanitarian and Civic Values." *Journal of College Student Personnel,* 1986, *27*(5), 418–425.

Pascarella, E. T., and Terenzini, P. T. *How College Affects Students: Findings and Insights from Twenty Years of Research.* San Francisco: Jossey-Bass, 1991.

Peters, T. J., and Waterman, R. H., Jr. *In Search of Excellence: Lessons from America's Best-Run Companies.* New York: HarperCollins, 1982.

Petty, M. M., McGee, G. W., and Cavender, J. W. "A Meta-Analysis of the Relationships Between Individual Job Satisfaction and Individual Performance." *Academy of Management Review,* 1984, *9,* 712–721.

Plater, W. M. "Future Work: Faculty Time in the Twenty-First Century." *Change,* 1995, *27*(3), 22–33.

Poussaint, A. "Black Collegians and the Future." *Black Collegian,* 1988, *19*(2), 50.

Prince, J. G. "An Assessment Model for Exiting Elementary Education Majors." Paper presented at the Second National Conference on The Senior Year Experience, San Antonio, Mar. 1991.

Reich, R. B. *The Work of Nations: Preparing Ourselves for Twenty-First Century Capitalism.* New York: Knopf, 1991.

Reichers, A. E. "An Interactionist Perspective on Newcomer Socialization Rates." *Academy of Management Review,* 1987, *12*(2), 278–287.

Reichley, R. A. "Volunteers: Who Are They?" In A. W. Rowland (ed.), *Handbook of Institutional Advancement.* San Francisco: Jossey-Bass, 1977.

Resource/Fact Book 1995. Hands-on Multi-Ethnic Recruitment & Retention: An Employer Training Institute. Career Development and Placement Publication. Cincinnati, Ohio: Division of Student Affairs and Human Resources, University of Cincinnati, 1995.

Richards, E. W. "Early Employment Situations and Work Role Satisfaction Among Recent College Graduates." *Journal of Vocational Behavior,* 1984a, *24,* 305–318.

Richards, E. W. "Undergraduate Preparation and Early Career Outcomes: A Study of Recent Career Graduates." *Journal of Vocational Behavior,* 1984b, *24,* 279–304

Roberts, H., and others. *Teaching from a Multicultural Perspective.* Thousand Oaks, Calif.: Sage, 1994.

Roberts, S. "The Greening of America's Black Middle Class." *New York Times,* June 18, 1995, pp. 1–4.

Rodrigues, R. "Leadership Program at Rutgers Tackles Urban Problems." *Black Issues in Higher Education,* 1995, *12*(5), 20–21.

Rost, J. C. *Leadership in the Twenty-First Century.* Westport, Conn.: Greenwood Press, 1991.

Rost, J. C. "Leadership in the Future." In W. E. Rosenbach and R. L. Taylor (eds.), *Contemporary Issues in Leadership.* Boulder, Colo.: Westview Press, 1993.

Rudolph, F. *The American College and University: A History.* New York: Vintage Books, 1962.

Russell, J. "209 Passes. What's Next?" *Hispanic Business,* 1996, *18*(12), p. 8.

St. Norbert College. Citizen Leadership Development Center brochure. De Pere, Wis.: St. Norbert College, 1996.

Sanders, B. "Whither American Democracy." *Los Angeles Times,* Jan. 16, 1994, p. M5.

Sanford, N. *Where Colleges Fail.* San Francisco: Jossey-Bass, 1967.

Sax, L. J., Astin, A. W., Korn, W. S., and Mahoney, K. *The American Freshman: National Norms for Fall 1995.* Los Angeles: Higher Education Research Institute, University of California-Los Angeles, 1995.

Scheetz, L. P. *Recruiting Trends 1993–94.* East Lansing: Career Services and Placement, Michigan State University, 1993.

Scheetz, L. P. *Recruiting Trends 1994–95.* East Lansing: Career Services and Placement, Michigan State University, 1994.

Schein, E. H. *Organizational Culture and Leadership.* (2nd ed.) San Francisco: Jossey-Bass, 1992.

Schilling, K. L., and Schilling, K. M. "Descriptive Approaches to Assessment: Moving Beyond Meeting Requirements to Making a Difference." In North Central Association of Colleges and Schools, Commission on Institutions of Higher Education (ed.), *A Collection of Papers on Self-Study and Institutional Improvement.* Chicago: North Central Association of Colleges and Schools, 1993.

Schlossberg, N. K. "Major Contributions." *Counseling Psychologist,* 1981, *9*(2), 2–15.

Schmidt, J. *The Senior Year Experience at UMCP. In/sights: Research and Information About UMCP Students.* College Park: Division of Student Affairs, University of Maryland, 1993.

Schroeder, C. C. "New Students: New Learning Styles." *Change,* Sept./Oct. 1993, pp. 21–26.

Sefchik, J. *Lifelong Skills, Lifelong Success!* Longwood, Fla.: Wilson Learning, 1995.

Senior Transition Survey. College Park: Office of the Vice President for Student Affairs, University of Maryland, 1993.

Shea, D. D. "Merging Careers and Ex Ed Center: A Perspective." *Journal of Career Planning and Employment,* 1995, *51*(2), 29–35.

Shea, D. D., and others. *Experiential Learning Council Report and Recommendations.* Charlotte: University of North Carolina, 1995.

Shelley, K. "More Job Openings—Even More New Entrants: The Outlook for College Graduates, 1992–2005." *Occupational Outlook Quarterly,* 1994, *38*(2), 5–9.

Sherman, T., Giles, M. B., and Williams-Green, J. "Assessment and Retention of Black Students in Higher Education." *Journal of Negro Education,* 1994, *63*(2), 168.

Shipton, J., and Steltenpohl, E. "Educational Advising and Career Planning: A Life-Cycle Perspective." In A. W. Chickering and Associates, *The Modern American College: Responding to the New Realities of Diverse Students and a Changing Society.* San Francisco: Jossey-Bass, 1981.

Simpson, G. "Providing Corporate Outplacement Career Counseling Services to Graduating Seniors." Paper presented at the Fourth National Conference on The Senior Year Experience, Orlando, Mar. 1994.

Smith, B. L. "Taking Structure Seriously." *Liberal Education,* 1991, *77*(2), 42–48.

Smith, B. L. "Creating Learning Communities." *Liberal Education,* 1993, *70*(4), 32–39.

Smith, W. "The Last Lecture: Applying Capstone Principles to Life After Graduation." Paper presented at the Second National Conference on The Senior Year Experience, San Antonio, Mar. 1991.

Spitzberg, I. J. "Paths of Inquiry into Leadership." *Liberal Education,* Mar./Apr. 1987, pp. 24–29.

"Spotlight on Career Planning, Placement and Recruitment." *Biweekly Newsletter of the National Association of Colleges and Employers,* 1995, *18*(8), 3–10.

Steinberg, N. *If at All Possible Involve a Cow: The Book of College Pranks.* New York: St. Martin's Press, 1992.

Stitts, D. K. "Curricular Approach to the Senior Year Experience: The Seminar in Marketing." Paper presented at the Fourth National Conference on The Senior Year Experience, Orlando, Mar. 1994.

Strike, K. A. "Democracy, Civic Education, and the Problem of Neutrality." *Theory into Practice,* 1988, *27*(4), 256–261.

Stumpf, S. A., and Hartman, K. "Individual Exploration to Organizational Commitment or Withdrawal." *Academy of Management Journal,* 1984, *27,* 308–329.

Sullivan, R. E. "Greatly Reduced Expectations." *Rolling Stone,* Mar. 18, 1993, pp. 2–4.

Super, D. E. "Vocational Development Theory." *Counseling Psychologist,* 1969, *1,* 2–30.

Taylor, M. S. "Effects of College Internships on Individual Participants." *Journal of Applied Psychology,* 1988, *73,* 393–401.

Terenzini, P. T., and Pascarella, E. T. "Living with Myths: Undergraduate Education in America." *Change,* Jan./Feb. 1994, pp. 28–32.

Thomas, E., Cohn, B., and Smith, V. "Rethinking the Dream." *Newsweek,* June 1995, *125*(26), p. 21.

Thomas, I. M. "Hispanics on Corporate Boards." *Hispanic,* 1994, *7*(6), 30.

Thompson, C. L. "Reverse Discrimination?" *Black Issues in Higher Education,* 1995, *12*(5), 32–34.

Thompson, K. "Learning at Evergreen: An Assessment of Cognitive Development." Monograph no. 1. Olympia, Wash.: Washington Center for Undergraduate Education, Evergreen State College, 1991.

Thompson, K. "Learning at Evergreen II: Writing and Thinking." Monograph no. 2. Olympia, Wash.: Washington Center for Undergraduate Education, Evergreen State College, 1992.

Thompson, K., Highsmith, R., and Brumbaugh, P. "Beyond Elon: Transition Tactics." Paper presented at the Third National Conference on The Senior Year Experience, Arlington, Va., Mar. 1993.

Tiedeman, D. V., and O'Hara, R. P. *Career Development: Choice and Adjustment.* New York: College Entrance Examination Board, 1963.

Tierney, W. G. "Organizational Culture in Higher Education." *Journal of Higher Education,* 1988, *59,* 2–21.

Tinto, V. *Leaving College: Rethinking the Causes and Cures of Student Attrition.* Chicago: University of Chicago Press, 1987.

Tinto, V., Goodsell Love, A., and Russo, P. "Building Community." *Liberal Education,* 1993, *79*(4), 16–21.

Todd, J. S. "Something for Everyone." *Currents,* 1994, *20*(2), 28–33.

Tommerup, P. "Teaching and Learning at Evergreen: An Ethnographic Study." Unpublished monograph, Evergreen State College, Oympia, Wash., 1993.

Toomey, J. T. "From Campus to Corporation: The University of Idaho Business Enterprise Program." Paper presented at the Third National Conference on The Senior Year Experience, Arlington, Va., Mar. 1993.

Tyree, L. W. "Leadership Across the Curriculum." *About Campus*, 1996, *1*(3), 32.

Undergraduate Education at the University of Virginia: Final Report of a Longitudinal Study. Charlottesville: Institutional Assessment and Studies, University of Virginia, 1994.

U.S. Bureau of the Census. Voting and Registration in the Election of November 1992. *Current Population Reports*, P20–466. Washington, D.C.: Government Printing Office, 1993.

U.S. Department of Education, National Center for Education Statistics. *The Condition of Education, 1995.* Washington, D.C.: Government Printing Office, 1995a.

U.S. Department of Education, National Center for Education Statistics. *Digest of Education Statistics, 1995.* Washington, D.C.: National Center for Education Statistics, 1995b.

U.S. Department of Education, National Center for Education Statistics. *The Condition of Education, 1996.* Washington, D.C.: Government Printing Office, 1996.

Van der Veer, G., Gast, L., Schmidt, J., and Lucas, N. "The Senior Experience: Are America's Future Leaders Prepared?" Paper presented at the Third National Conference on The Senior Year Experience, Arlington, Va., Mar. 1993.

Van der Veer, G., and others. *The Collegiate Senior Experience: The Successful Completion of All Requirements.* A Report from the Senior Experience Task Force, University of Maryland. College Park: University of Maryland, May 5, 1994.

van Gennep, A. *The Rites of Passage.* (M. B. Vizedom and G. L. Caffe, trans.). Chicago: University of Chicago Press, 1960. (Original work published 1908.)

Van Maanen, J., and Schein, E. H. "Toward a Theory of Organizational Socialization." In B. M. Staw and L. L. Cummings (eds.), *Research in Organizational Behavior.* Greenwich, Conn.: JAI Press, 1979.

Vessel, H., "Excelling in Workplace 2000." *The Black Collegian*, 1991, *22*(2), 114–119.

Vickio, C. J. "The Good-bye Brochure: Helping Students to Cope with Transition and Loss." *Journal of Counseling and Development*, 1990, *68*, 575–577.

Walters, T., and Hart, C. "Senior Seminar: A Semester-Long, One-Credit Required Course for Communication Majors at Slippery Rock University." Paper presented at the Second National Conference on The Senior Year Experience, San Antonio, Mar. 1991.

Wanous, J. P. *Organizational Entry: Recruitment, Selection and Socialization of Newcomers,* Reading, Mass.: Addison-Wesley, 1980.

Warr, P., and Bunce, D. "Trainee Characteristics and the Outcomes of Open Learning." *Personnel Psychology*, 1995, *48*, 347–375.

Weinberg, C. "College Women in Transition: A Course for Graduating Seniors." *Journal of College Student Development*, 1988, *29*, 472–473.

Weinstein, C. E., and Meyer, D. K. "Cognitive Learning Strategies and College Teaching." In R. J. Menges and M. C. Svinicki (eds.), *College Teaching: From Theory to Practice*. New Directions for Teaching and Learning, no. 45. San Francisco: Jossey-Bass, 1991.

White, C. "A Model for Comprehensive Reform in General Education: Portland State University." *Journal of General Education*, 1994, *43*(3), 167–229.

Whitley, L. S. "The Senior Seminar as a General Education Capstone Course: A Working System in a Regional University." Paper presented at the First National Conference on The Senior Year Experience, Atlanta, Mar. 1990.

Wilkins, A. L. *Developing Corporate Character: How to Successfully Change an Organization Without Destroying It*. San Francisco: Jossey-Bass, 1989.

Williams, M. *The Velveteen Rabbit*. New York: Henry Holt, 1983.

Williamson, E. G. *How to Counsel Students*. New York: McGraw-Hill, 1939.

Wilson Learning. *Success Skills 2000: Benchmarks for High Performance*. Longwood, Fla.: Wilson Learning, 1992.

Wingspread Group on Higher Education. *An American Imperative: Higher Expectations for Higher Education. An Open Letter to Those Concerned About the American Future*. Racine, Wis.: Johnson Foundation, 1993.

Wolf, N. "A Woman's Place." *New York Times*, May 31, 1992, Op-Ed. p. 19.

Wolvin, A., and others. *Proposal for the Creation of "The Senior Experience Office."* College Park: CQI/Senior Experience Implementation Team, University of Maryland, June 30, 1995.

Wren, J. T. "Teaching Leadership: the Art of the Possible." *The Journal of Leadership Studies*, 1994, 1,(2), 73–93.

Wren, J. T. "The Problem of Cultural Leadership: The Lessons of the Dead Leaders Society and a New Definition of Leadership." *The Journal of Leadership Studies*, 1995, 2(4), 122–139.

Wright, R. H., and McMahn, R. G. "Travel-Study: Combining Experience and Formal Learning for the Senior Adult Student." Paper presented at the First National Conference on The Senior Year Experience, Atlanta, Mar. 1990.

Young, G. "Students Found Befuddled by Credit." *The Diamondback* (University of Maryland student newspaper), Nov. 29, 1993, p. 1.

Young, J. R. "Colleges Offer Alumni Campus E-Mail Addresses." *Chronicle of Higher Education*, June 14, 1996, p. A31.

NAME INDEX

SUBJECT INDEX

A

Ability-based education, 87–90

Absolute learning, 73

Academic advising, and alumni support, 229–230

Academic affairs: career center reporting to, 205–207; student affairs partnership with, 33–34, 291

Academic major: connecting with workplace, 22, 24, 96–115; and employability, 65, 67; integrating with general education, 15, 22, 23–24, 83–84, 90; integration within, 22, 24, 83–84, 90–91. *See also* Cumulative curriculum; Curriculum; Domain skills; Seamless curriculum; Transition to work

Academic Strategy (Keller), 267

Academy of Leadership, University of Maryland, 120–121, 125–126, 131

Accountability: and assessment, 35–36, 248; and the assessment movement, 9–10; and senior year experience movement, 3–4, 9–10; for transition to work, 113. *See also* Workplace accountability skills

Achievement recognition, 155, 156

ACT, 253

Adult life span, 45, 48–50; for women versus men, 49–50. *See also* Life-span perspective

Affirmative action, 211–213, 226, 295

African Americans, 210–211; career development programs for, 220–225; and citizenship, 141; college-to-career transition of, 210–226; financial challenges of, 219; longitudinal study of, 211, 218–225; status of, in job market, 211–214. *See also* Cultural awareness; Diversity; Multiethnic students; Racial understanding

Albertson's, 30

Albright College, 238

Alma Mater (Kluge), 155

Alumni: career center collaboration with, 203; contributions of, 228–229, 232; maintaining connection with, 232–233; myths about, 232; outcomes assessment of, 35–36; for senior life-planning support, 31; seniors as future, 6, 11, 22, 31–32, 294; student awareness of, 230–232, 294; support of, for senior year program, 280, 284; surveys, 253; transition to, 237–238, 293. *See also* Graduates

Alumni associations, 236–237; fees for membership in, 294; increasing students' awareness of, 230–232, 294; student, 294

Alumni colleges, 231

Alumni development, 16, 22, 31–32, 227–241, 294; barriers to, 229–230; campuswide involvement in, 236–237; cultural events for, 157–158, 168; explicit expectations in, 235;